ALSO BY EDWARD J. LARSON

An Empire of Ice: Scott, Shackleton, and the Heroic Age of Antarctic Science

A Magnificent Catastrophe: The Tumultuous Election of 1800, America's First Presidential Campaign

The Constitutional Convention: A Narrative History from the Notes of James Madison (with Michael P. Winship)

Summer for the Gods: The Scopes Trial and America's Continuing Debate over Science and Religion

Evolution: The Remarkable History of a Scientific Theory

Trial and Error: The American Controversy over Creation and Evolution

Evolution's Workshop: God and Science on the Galapagos Islands

Sex, Race, and Science: Eugenics in the Deep South

Praise for *The Return of George Washington*

"Larson is a sure guide through the complexities of writing and ratifying the Constitution, [with an] almost Washingtonian sense of gravity and balance. . . . Dramatic. . . . Restoring the politics to Washington's rise adds motive and depth to the nationalist who rose north to the rescue."   —*New York Times Book Review*

"A fascinating account of the years in George Washington's life between the end of the Revolutionary War and the beginning of his Presidency. . . . This is an important book, elegantly written, which adds greatly to our understanding of the way in which one man's personality and popularity helped create a strong new country out of the fragments of the old colonial system."
       —Lawrence M. Friedman, Marion Rice Kirkwood Professor of Law
               at Stanford University and author of *A History of American Law*

"Fine and engrossing. . . . Larson engagingly argues that the stretch between 1783 and 1789 was as important to Washington—and to America—as all that preceded and followed it. . . . [A] splendid account. Larson brings an invigorating immediacy to the wranglings that went on among the delegates charged with inventing a wholly new form of government. . . . [A] valuable, lively account."   —*Wall Street Journal*

"A fresh and elegant portrait of the hero we thought we knew, but didn't, quite—a man who was not merely an irresistible force, an immovable object, and a hands-on manager in the Revolution and the Presidency but also in the years in between, as he actively influenced the Constitution's framing and ratification in ways not previously understood. . . . An indispensable book about America's 'indispensable man.'"
       —Akhil Reed Amar, Sterling Professor of Law and Political Science
               at Yale University and author of *America's Constitution: A Biography*

"Rare among historical figures, Washington becomes more admirable, and likable, the closer up you get. . . . Larson's account is rich in detail and telling anecdotes. . . . An exceptionally fine and engaging writer. . . . Clear, precise, graceful prose. . . . Larson has taken up what might seem to be a niche in this great man's life and career, and found there the core of his personality and greatness."   —*Dallas Morning News*

"Fantastic. . . . The Washington who emerges in these pages is always human, flaws and all, and yet he still manages to be a figure worth revering for his unwavering sense of duty." —Daily Beast

"In this very readable account of the critical but little-known interlude in Washington's career between the Revolutionary War and his election as first President of the United States, Edward J. Larson reveals how Washington was indeed first in peace as much as he was first in war by both his resigning from the army, which helped preclude the possibility of a military coup, and by the key role he played in winning support for the adoption of the Constitution. Indeed, this book is one of the best illustrations of the ability of individuals to change the course of history. Washington's commitment to a strong national government is relevant to the debate about the limits of government today. He knew all too well that the revolutionary cause almost foundered because of its anti-government rhetoric, which undermined the ability of the new nation to pay the army and to coordination a national war effort."
—Andrew O'Shaughnessy, professor of history at the University of Virginia; vice president of the Thomas Jefferson Foundation; Saunders Director of the Robert H. Smith International Center for Jefferson Studies; author of *The Men Who Lost America*, winner of the George Washington Book Prize

"Illuminating. . . . Profound, even affectionate, scholarship infuses every graceful sentence." —*Kirkus Reviews* (starred review)

"Larson's compulsively readable history shines new light on a little-discussed period of Washington's life, illustrating his role as the indispensable American. —*Publishers Weekly*

"Deeply researched and certainly persuasive. . . . A powerful corrective to the notion of Washington as a mere figurehead, Ed Larson—with his signature wit and light touch—delivers a living, breathing man, who is revealed to be a true visionary leader, but who also possesses the political savvy and ability to get things done that is as rare as it is compelling. An important addition to the literature on the Founding of the United States."
—Douglas Bradburn, PhD, founding director of the Fred W. Smith National Library for the Study of George Washington at Mount Vernon

"While mountains of books have been written about George Washington most have covered his wartime or presidential careers. Few have discussed in any depth the period between his remarkable resignation as commander in chief through his inauguration of President. That is precisely the scope of this utterly fascinating book. . . . Very readable and highly recommended." —*Journal of the American Revolution*

"Larson's understanding of Washington's motives and mental and emotional processes allows him to engage the man almost as a friend, a colleague. . . . *The Return of George Washington: 1783–1789* is a brilliant snapshot of six years in the life of a man and a country, and well worth the read." —*Washington Independent Review of Books*

"Edward J. Larson's highly readable book brings to the front a little-studied period of George Washington's life. It's a well-balanced account of a man conflicted by his desire for life at Mount Vernon and his keen awareness of his centrality to the constitutional revolution that dominated the Confederation Period. Larson judiciously clears away the naive myths that have so long obscured Washington's ideas and role during the 1780s."
—Kenneth R. Bowling, coeditor of *Documentary History of the First Federal Congress* and adjunct professor of history at George Washington University

"Larson has left us with a richer portrait of the vital role Washington played before, during, and after the Constitutional Convention. . . . Now we can appreciate even more fully why Washington is the indispensable figure in the history of America's founding." —*Weekly Standard*

"Eloquently written. . . . Larson synthesizes a vast amount of primary source material with great aplomb. . . . Serious scholarship presented in an engaging and concise manner." —*Washington Times*

"As well-researched and well-told a work of popular history as anything published this year. . . . Intensely good." —*The National* (UAE)

"Larson's impeccable research and impressive storytelling acumen may be just the thing readers need to restore appreciation for the system of government we inherited, and still strive to perfect." —*BookPage*

"This fine book, well researched and engagingly written, is one more example of why George Washington undoubtedly deserves to be viewed as America's greatest leader and premier statesman. Edward Larson ably reveals that he was 'the indispensable man' not only in the winning of America's independence and in securing the union as its first president but also in his role in the writing and ratifying of the U.S. Constitution. . . . A first-rate book."

—*Virginia Magazine of History and Biography*, the quarterly journal of the Virginia Historical Society

"Larson is a skilled storyteller combining scholarly research with a flair for relating historical events and personages to general readers. Recommended for those who enjoyed Ron Chernow's *Washington: A Life* as well as biography hounds and history buffs."   —*Library Journal*

"Engaging. . . . With a discerning eye for detail and nuance, Edward Larson has written a book that will be of interest to students of George Washington and the early national period."   —*Providence Journal*

"Well researched and readable."   —*Valdosta Daily Times*

"Drawing from letters, diaries and other sources, Larson brings a welcome personal dimension to the story of the [Constitutional] Convention. He gives us a sense of what these men thought about themselves and each other, their role in history, and the future of the country."   —*American Spirit* magazine

THE RETURN OF
GEORGE WASHINGTON

Uniting the States, 1783–1789

EDWARD J. LARSON

WILLIAM MORROW
An Imprint of HarperCollins*Publishers*

IN MEMORY OF

Pauline Maier & Edmund Morgan

Two Extraordinary Historians of the Revolutionary Era

Who Passed During the Writing of This Book.

To Paraphrase Isaac Newton and Bernard of Chartres:

We See Further by Standing on the Shoulders of Giants.

HarperCollins books may be purchased for educational, business, or sales promotional use. For information please e-mail the Special Markets Department at SPsales@harpercollins.com.

A hardcover edition of this book was published in 2014 by William Morrow, an imprint of HarperCollins Publishers.

FIRST WILLIAM MORROW PAPERBACK EDITION PUBLISHED 2015.

Designed by Lisa Stokes

Title page illustration: Reception of President Washington at New York, *by John Rogers, 1857, courtesy of Library of Congress.*

Library of Congress Cataloging-in-Publication Data has been applied for.

ISBN 978-0-06-224868-8

15 16 17 18 19 ov/rrd 10 9 8 7 6 5 4 3 2

Contents

Preface   xi

BOOK I
From New York to Mount Vernon, 1782–1786

CHAPTER 1
Retiring Becomes Him   3

CHAPTER 2
Reeling in the West   33

CHAPTER 3
To Go or Not to Go   67

BOOK II
To, From, and In Philadelphia, 1787

CHAPTER 4
The Center Holds   101

CHAPTER 5
In His Image   135

CHAPTER 6
"Little Short of a Miracle"   167

BOOK III
From Mount Vernon to New York, 1788–1789

CHAPTER 7
Ratifying Washington   201

CHAPTER 8
The First Federal Elections   235

CHAPTER 9
The Inaugural Parade   267

EPILOGUE   297

Notes   305
Illustration Credits   355
Index   359

Preface

ON A CHILLY SPRING morning in April 2014, I sat on Mount Vernon's broad front piazza watching the sun rise slowly over the Potomac River. The window off George Washington's upstairs bedroom was over my right shoulder, and the east-facing door to his first-floor office stood directly behind me. Washington would have seen much this same view 225 years earlier, knowing it might be a long time before he observed it again. The American people had called him to the presidency, and he was preparing to leave his beloved Mount Vernon plantation for the seat of government in New York on April 16, 1789. Due to private preservation efforts and public land-use restrictions, this vista over the Potomac, the one that Washington most loved and built his piazza to frame, survives virtually unchanged in the midst of Northern Virginia's urban sprawl.

As an inaugural fellow at the Fred W. Smith National Library for the Study of George Washington, with a residency on the grounds of Mount Vernon, I was able to enjoy this and other scenes on Washington's plantation many times over the course of a year. The view from the piazza became my favorite, too, especially at sunrise in the spring, when flowering trees and soft green leaves give off a warm glow in the early-morning light. It was obvious why Washington was reluctant to leave Mount Vernon for public service in a job that he neither sought nor wanted.

The words that Washington sent six months earlier to fellow Virginian James Madison urging him to serve in the new federal government applied equally to himself, however. Supporters of the new Constitution and the union it created, he had implored Madison, *forgetting personal considerations,* must combine their collective efforts through service in the new government to avert the "great national calamities that impended" without it.[1] By 1787, four years since the United States secured its independence, Washington had come to believe that the country faced as grave a threat from internal forces of disunion in the mid-1780s as it had from external ones of tyranny in the mid-1770s, when he accepted leadership of the patriot army at the outset of the Revolutionary War. Now his country again called on his service, this time as the elected leader of the world's first extended republic.

Countless books tell the story of Washington as commander in chief of the Continental Army during the American Revolution, and nearly as many relate the history of his role as the first President of the United States. Indeed, books about Washington could fill a library. They fill a bookcase in mine. Few of them focus on the six years between his wartime and presidential service, which is the subject of this one. Even the finest full biographies of Washington—from Douglas Southall Freeman's six-volume classic of the late 1940s and early 1950s through James Thomas Flexner's masterful four-volume series of the late 1960s and early 1970s, to Ron Chernow's superb 2010 *Washington: A Life,* all Pulitzer Prize winners—devote the interlude between his military tenure and presidential terms mostly to presenting his life as a Virginia planter. Moreover, when biographers reach the Constitutional Convention, over which Washington presided, they typically present him as a stiff, silent figure who mainly contributed his prestige and dignity to the proceedings. The standard narrative then has him retiring to Mount Vernon through the ratification debates and first federal election until called to the presidency.

With this book, I retell the story from Washington's resignation as commander in chief through his inauguration as President. Not meaning to diminish the importance of his domestic life during this period, I stress his crucial role as a public figure and political leader during these critical years between the end of the Revolutionary War in 1783 and the start of the federal government in 1789. Many accounts, such as David Hackett Fischer's riveting *Washington's Crossing*, present Washington as *The Indispensable Man* (as Flexner famously called him) during the Revolutionary War. Others show his similar centrality as President, perhaps most notably Forrest McDonald's *The Presidency of George Washington*. I argue that Washington was equally important— equally indispensable—during the interval between these two better-known stages of his life. Often working behind the scenes but still very much in the public imagination, he helped to bind the states into a single federal republic. This period in Washington's public life merits as much attention as those that preceded and followed it. It built on what came before and laid the foundation for what followed. From 1775 until his death, Washington was the indispensable American.

As Washington understood matters, the immediate threat to America during the 1780s flowed from the weakness of the central government. More than anyone, he led the effort to reform it. "The honor, power, and true Interest of this Country must be measured by a Continental scale," Washington wrote in 1783. "Every departure therefrom weakens the Union, and may ultimately break the band, which holds us together."[2] Supplementing his efforts to strengthen the central government, he worked to link the country's economy, particularly by joining the emerging regions west of the Appalachian Mountains to the settled ones on the coast by a navigable waterway. "Unless we can connect the New States, which are rising to our view in the Regions back of us, with those on the Atlantic by interest," Washington warned in 1785, "they will be quite a distinct People; and ultimately may be very troublesome neighbours to us."[3] He worried that America, far from serving as a beacon of enlightened liberty and republican rule, was becoming "contemptable in the eyes of Europe."[4] By 1786, Washington privately vowed to do all that he could "to avert the humiliating, & contemptible figure we are about to make, in the Annals of Mankind."[5] Washington's vision and continuing service led the way toward the new American union that endures to this day.

I CAN ONLY BEGIN to identify the many institutions and individuals that have helped me to conceive, research, and write this book, and can never adequately thank them all. The idea for it began while I was teaching American constitutional law and history to Australian students as a visiting professor at Melbourne Law School. Retelling the story to non-American students helped me to reconceive it in my own mind. Research for this book began in earnest while I was teaching as a visiting professor at Stanford Law School, where I benefited from the chance to discuss the topic with such extraordinary colleagues as Dean Larry Kramer, Jack Rakove, Michael McConnell, and Lawrence Friedman. In my final stages of writing, I enjoyed the privilege of working as a Fellow at the Fred W. Smith National Library for the Study of George Washington, where I could call on the likes of Douglas Bradburn, Mary Thompson, Stephen McLeod, Mark Santangelo, Dawn Bonner, James Martin, Susan Schoelwer, and Adam Shprintzen for assistance. Throughout, I have enjoyed the ongoing support of Pepperdine University, where I teach history and law. My special thanks go to Pepperdine's president Andy Benton, Law School dean Deanell Tacha, Seaver College dean Rick Marrs, and Research Librarian Jodi Kruger.

Friends and family made major contributions to this book. First of all, I am deeply indebted to historian of the Revolutionary Era

Ray Raphael, First Federal Congress Project co-director Kenneth R. Bowling, and constitutional scholar Dan Coenen for reviewing vast swaths of my manuscript. When it comes to this period in American political history, Ray and Ken know the forest and every tree. Among the many other scholars who suffered my questions and gave wise counsel, Akhil Amar, William Baude, Richard Beeman, Michael Coenen, Susan Dunn, Paul Finkelman, and Pauline Maier merit special mention, as do my editor, Peter Hubbard, and my book agent, B. G. Dilworth. For starting me on this course, my belated thanks go to my teachers James MacGregor Burns, Norman K. Risjord, Robert M. O'Neil, Laurence Tribe, and John Hart Ely. Most of all, my gratitude goes to my wife, Lucy, and our children, Sarah and Luke. Research and writing take so much time away from every other part of life.

My thoughts turn to those people who have helped me so much as I write these words with dusk settling over the fields behind Mount Vernon on this, the 225th anniversary of the day that Washington took the presidential oath in New York. His wife, Martha, had remained behind until housing was arranged and perhaps, seeing a similar sunset on this date in 1789, thought about her spouse and the life that lay ahead for them in New York. He would rather have been here with her and, being here, I can understand why.

Edward J. Larson
Mount Vernon, Virginia
April 30, 2014

BOOK I

From New York to Mount Vernon

1782–1786

1782 print of General George Washington during the Revolutionary War.

CHAPTER 1

Retiring Becomes Him

IT WAS AND REMAINS one of the most remarkable events in the history of war, revolution, and politics. General George Washington retired. Although a spoken act, like so much that set him apart, it was less what he said than what he did.

On Tuesday, December 23, 1783, the commander in chief of American forces during the just-concluded Revolutionary War, accompanied only by two trusted aides, David Humphreys and Tench Tilghman, strode into the Assembly Chamber of the Maryland State House in Annapolis. Congress had been meeting there ever since fleeing from its own mutinous troops in Philadelphia, the United States' customary seat of government. Self-describedly gray at age fifty-one following nearly nine years of wartime service, Washington stood erect—still a towering figure on a solid frame. Only twenty members representing but seven states remained in attendance at the little respected and largely ineffectual Confederation Congress. Washington had arrived in Annapolis the previous Friday to a cannon salute that brought a throng of well-dressed citizens into the streets to hail him as the country's liberator. On Saturday, in accord with his oft-stated intent, he inquired of Congress about the manner of resigning his commission and returning to private life now that the war had ended. Congress requested a formal audience.

Following a script prepared over the weekend by a congressional committee chaired by Thomas Jefferson, Washington entered the Assembly Chamber at noon on the twenty-third and took a seat opposite the seated president of Congress, his former aide-de-camp, Thomas Mifflin. The other members of Congress also sat, all wearing hats. The French ambassador, Maryland state officials, and leading citizens of Annapolis then entered the hall—men standing at the rear; women in the gallery above. Once the spectators settled in their places, the president of Congress addressed the General: "Sir, The U.S. in Congress Assembled are prepared to receive your Communications."[1] Washington rose and bowed to Congress. On this cue, the members doffed their hats but did not stand. This stiff protocol maintained that the members of Congress were respectfully superior to the commander in chief. Drawing a paper written in his own hand from a coat pocket, Washington then read his final address as a military commander. Scarcely three hundred words long, it made history.

"The great events on which my resignation depended, having at length taken place," Washington began, his hand visibly trembling as it held the speech, "I have now the honor of offering my sincere Congratulations to Congress, and of presenting myself before them, to surrender into their hands the trust committed to me." Soon he needed both hands to steady the page. After noting the "diffidence" with which he initially accepted the post, acknowledging the "obligations" he owed to the army in general and his closest aides in particular, and "commending the interests of our dearest country to the protection of Almighty God," Washington concluded, "I retire from the great theatre of action, and bidding an affectionate farewell to this august body, under whose orders I have so long acted, I here offer my commission, and take my leave of all the employments of public life."[2] By this point all the spectators were weeping, one observer noted, "and there was hardly a member of Congress who did not drop tears."[3] Drawing his commission from his coat pocket, Washington then stepped forward and handed it to the president.

A future American government chose to memorialize precisely this moment in one of eight historical paintings decorating the rotunda of the United States Capitol. Turned slightly to the right toward Congress, Washington dominates the image at center framed by a broad pilaster, added to the background by the artist John Trumbull to convey stability. His left hand on a riding whip to suggest the haste with which he rode to Congress to relinquish power, Washington extends his right hand—holding the commission—toward Mifflin, who stands on a raised platform, slightly higher than the General to show civilian authority but still smaller than him and painted in flat profile within a formal group portrait of all twenty congressmen. To depict the four future Virginia presidents as united for this foundational episode, Jefferson, James Madison, and James Monroe are identifiable in this stylized grouping even though Madison had not rejoined Congress following its remove to Annapolis. Behind Washington on his left stand an equal number of spectators, with his wife, Martha, who was not actually there, gazing down from the gallery in domestic garb.

At this point in the real proceedings, President Mifflin stiffly read the elegant response that Jefferson's committee had drafted for the occasion, on behalf of the entire country. "The U.S. in congress assembled receive with emotions too affecting for utterance this solemn Resignation of the authorities under which you have led their troops with Success through a perilous and doubtful war," it began in soaring words that surely came from Jefferson, who had penned the lofty Declaration of Independence eight long years before. "Having defended the standard of liberty in this new world . . . you retire from the great theatre of action with the blessings of your fellow citizens, but the glory of your virtues will not terminate with your military command, it will continue to animate remotest ages."[4]

Having turned on Washington during the war's darkest days by trying to replace him as commander in chief with Horatio Gates, Mifflin played an awkward but necessary part in this pageant. As Congress's chief officer before the creation of an executive branch, he personified civilian rule in America. Observing in his prepared response that Washington had accepted his post when the lack of both foreign alliances and a central—or "general"—government made the war's outcome doubtful, Mifflin now hailed the commander in chief's military leadership and deference to civilian authority. Concluding his recitation, Mifflin prayed to God for Washington that "a life so beloved may be fostered with all his care; that your days may be happy as they have been illustrious; and that he will finally give you that reward which this world cannot give."[5]

His resignation duly accepted, Washington bowed again to Congress and was free to go. He stayed only long enough to greet the members following their adjournment and was riding toward his beloved Mount Vernon plantation by two o'clock. He had promised Martha that he would be home for Christmas. He kept his word.

EXTOLLED BY LATER HISTORIANS as a signal event that set the country's political course—Thomas Fleming called it "the most important moment in American history"[6]—Washington's retirement was similarly praised at the time. Citing examples from Julius Caesar to Oliver Cromwell, British leaders during the war had scoffed at Americans for rebelling against one King George only to gain another in George Washington. Successful rebel leaders inevitably become tyrants, they charged. Indeed, in England, when expatriate American painter Benjamin West predicted that Washington would retire upon the cessation of hostilities, a skeptical King George III reportedly replied, "If he does that, he will be the greatest man in the world."[7] Writing from London after word of Washington's resignation reached that city, West's American student, John Trumbull, wrote to his brother in Connecticut that the act "excites the astonishment and admiration of this part of the world. 'Tis a Conduct so novel, so inconceivable to People, who, far from giving up powers they possess, are willing to convulse the Empire to acquire more."[8] No wonder Trumbull later painted the scene with such feeling.

In America, Washington at once became a second "Cincinnatus," the legendary ancient leader twice called from his farm and given supreme power to rescue republican Rome from its enemies only to relinquish power and return to his farm once the dangers had passed. A firsthand account from Annapolis, printed in countless American newspapers during January 1784, described the event as "extraordinary, and to the General more honourable than any that is recorded in history."[9] A member of Congress from Maryland and future secretary of war, James McHenry, writing to his fiancée on the twenty-third, spoke of it as "a solemn and affecting spectacle; such an one as history does not present."[10] An editorial in a New York newspaper soon proposed new coins for the country with Washington's image stamped on the front and a shepherd reclining under a pine on the back. "Peace, the fruit of Glorious War," read the proposed inscription.[11]

After three months' reflection on what had transpired, Jefferson commented, "The moderation and virtue of a single character probably prevented this revolution from being closed, as most others have been by a subversion of that liberty it was intended to establish."[12] Even more than the commander in chief's distinguished and disinterested service during the Revolutionary War, which was performed without salary or leave for more than eight and a half years, voluntarily surrendering the trappings of power for private life on a Virginia plantation made Washington a venerated American hero and world-renowned personification of republican virtue.

AT LEAST IN THE UNITED STATES, Washington's act did not surprise. Looking back, this becomes clear. Since accepting command of American forces in 1775, Washington frequently professed his intent to resign when the war ended. Indeed, just ten days after his appointment, he famously declared that, by becoming a soldier, he "did not lay aside the Citizen."[13] It was his way of affirming civilian rule and renouncing military pretensions. As the war wound down following the victory of combined American and French forces under Washington over British troops at Yorktown in 1781, the commander in chief spoke more openly and often about resuming a pastoral lifestyle after independence. Of course, the British could have fought on after Yorktown—they still occupied New York City and possessed deep reserves—but Parliament in London seemed increasingly inclined to cut the empire's losses and accept an English-speaking trading partner in place of embittered and unruly colonies. Peace negotiations gained momentum in Paris.

For Washington, retirement made sense. He treasured reputation over power and always was happiest at Mount Vernon. Further, the country lacked any position that could tempt him even if he had been so inclined. With peace, the army would melt away. Leading it could not satisfy Washington. The general government had little authority and no chief executive. The states were mired in debt from the Revolutionary War and most struggled with weak economies due to wartime restrictions on overseas trade and high postwar foreign tariffs. Any government office would further delay Washington's return home without enhancing his fame or fortune. He hoped to rebuild his finances by restoring Mount Vernon to profitability and speculating in land on the frontier. To his cherished former lieutenant, Marquis de Lafayette, Washington wrote shortly after resigning his commission, "I am not only retired from all public employments, but I am retiring within myself; and shall be able to view the solitary walk, and tread the paths of private life with heartfelt satisfaction."[14]

Moreover, as a practical matter, it is hard to see how anyone—even Washington—could have used a military position to consolidate political power in the United States of the early 1780s. The army itself was largely a state-based body of citizen-soldiers united by a shared desire for independence from Britain. Most of its members actually served in the various state militias rather than in the national or "continental" force. Once the external threat disappeared, nothing could keep those militias together as a combined army. And with thirteen coequal states and no single center of political authority, a mutinous army or power-hungry general would face the same dilemma that bedeviled British military strategists throughout the American Revolution. Troops could occupy cities and capture individuals, but they could not impose their will beyond the reach of their arms. If people doubted this, they need only look nine months prior to Washington's retirement, when, in the waning days of the war, a small group of prominent Americans close to the General conspired to stage, or at least threaten, a military coup d'état as a means to secure political and personal ends. Washington's suppression of this conspiracy in March 1783 had further enhanced his reputation for republican virtue and set the stage for his voluntary retirement nine months later.

At the time of the conspiracy—which occurred after the Battle of Yorktown but before the British evacuated New York—a peace treaty with the United Kingdom appeared likely but not certain. Active warfare had virtually ceased. The main American army camped quietly under Washington's immediate command in the lower Hudson River valley around Newburgh, New York. There it kept watch on the larger but similarly dormant enemy force that still occupied Manhattan Island.

The United States then operated under the Articles of Confederation, which created a league of thirteen sovereign states. Without an executive or judicial branch, a single-chamber Confederation Congress directly handled the country's business. Although each state could send as many delegates as it wanted to Congress, every state had just one vote; at least nine votes were needed for important decisions. Further, the state legislatures—not the people—chose the member of Congress and could recall them at will. The Articles gave Congress authority over foreign affairs and the war effort without giving it the power to levy taxes or raise troops. To pay soldiers, purchase supplies, and perform other functions, Congress relied on voluntary requisitions from the states, coupled with foreign and domestic loans. Neither source, nor both together, brought in enough hard cash to cover expenses. Any enforceable national tax required ratification by all thirteen state legislatures.

Without taxing authority, Congress defaulted on some of its debts and all but stopped paying the troops. Fearing they would never be repaid, an increasing number of domestic lenders sold their government bonds to speculators—sometimes for pennies on the dollar—creating a new class of government creditors whom many citizens did not feel morally obliged to compensate. Further, in 1779, as the war wore on with no end in sight, the Continental Congress promised army officers who remained in service a postwar pension of half pay for seven years—and extended it to half pay for life a year later—creating another unfunded government obligation that many Americans opposed. These elite officer-pensioners would form a privileged class at taxpayer expense, critics complained.

These unpopular debts provided excuses for cash-strapped states to cut their payments to Congress, which was on the verge of bankruptcy by the end of 1782. With war having bound the states together in cooperation, its impending end threatened to further undermine their support for Congress. Soldiers and creditors alike worried that, once peace came, they would never be paid. Although many details of the conspiracy that brewed in the Newburgh encampment remain murky, this desperate fiscal situation served as its necessary backdrop.

BY THIS POINT, Washington stood out as the most famous person in America, if not the world, but that fame had not come easily. Possessed with striking stature and immense personal dignity, he had leaped to the forefront of the patriot cause at age forty-two in June 1775, when the Second Continental Congress tapped him to lead the ragtag army of volunteers and New England militia troops besieging the British army in Boston. Prior to this appointment as commander in chief, Washington had a largely local reputation as leader of the Virginia regiment during the colonial French and Indian War. The Massachusetts cousins Samuel and John Adams, Pennsylvania's incomparable Benjamin Franklin, and Virginia orator Patrick Henry certainly had wider reputations as revolutionary leaders than Washington in 1775, but they lacked military experience. When the patriot cause became an armed struggle following the Battles of Lexington and Concord, Congress turned to Washington for leadership in part because of his war record and in part because his presence as a respected Virginia planter commanding a mostly New England force would serve to nationalize the conflict and solidify southern support. Washington had much to learn about leading a large but poorly trained force against a disciplined and well-equipped army, however.

Taking full advantage of a strong position, troops under Washington's command forced the British to evacuate Boston in March 1776, only to face near disaster five months later in New York. The British had returned with overwhelming force and, beginning with the Battle of Long Island on August 27, 1776, routed Washington's army in a series of clashes that drove the Americans across the Delaware River into Pennsylvania by the end of November. Seeking to consolidate their gains in New York and New Jersey, the British then settled in for the winter with the expectation of finishing off the rebels in the spring. Leading his beleaguered army back across the Delaware during Christmas Night, however, Washington captured advance British outposts at Trenton and Princeton in surprise attacks. The British viewed these defeats as minor but patriot propagandists made the most of them and morale rebounded. Despite a disastrous summer, Washington became a national hero.

The summer of 1777 went much like the summer of 1776 for Washington, with the British pushing his army back through New Jersey and into Pennsylvania. Philadelphia fell in September, but not before patriot troops staged a respectable defense of the city at the Battle of Brandywine. In October, before settling into winter quarters at Valley Forge, Washington added a credible (though failed) counterattack in the Battle of Germantown that helped keep the British from pushing beyond Philadelphia. Meanwhile, in the Battles of Saratoga, a separate American force under Horatio Gates captured a British army invading from Canada, leading France to join the war on the patriot side and some to call for Gates to replace Washington as commander in chief.

The British responded to these setbacks by withdrawing from Philadelphia to New York in 1778 and shifting the main theater of war to the southern colonies, which they viewed as more valuable and loyal than the northern ones. Shadowing this movement to New York, Washington's army engaged the British army at the Battle of Monmouth and then effectively bottled it up in New York for the remainder of the war in the North. Initially at least, the British had more success in the South. After Savannah and Charleston fell in 1778 and 1780, a British army under Lord Cornwallis routed a counterattack led by Gates in South Carolina at the Battle of Camden and pushed north into Virginia by 1781 even as a reconstructed American army under Nathanael Greene liberated much of the Carolinas and Georgia. Washington then boldly shifted his main army from New York to Virginia and, working with the French, captured Cornwallis's army at Yorktown, which all but compelled Britain to accept America's independence. By defeating the world's leading power, Washington became a living legend by age fifty. Returning with his troops to the lower Hudson, he watched over the remaining British forces in Manhattan for nearly two years while Franklin, John Adams, and other American peace negotiators in Paris struggled to resolve the war on favorable terms.

IT WAS THEN THAT the Newburgh Conspiracy hatched. During the closing days of 1782, a delegation of officers from the encampment carried a petition to Congress in Philadelphia appealing for back pay and expenses. It also contained an offer to accept lump-sum payments in lieu of the officers' unpopular half-pay pensions. "The uneasiness of the soldiers, for want of pay, is great and dangerous," the petition warned. "Any further experiment on their patience may have fatal effects."[15]

Upon its arrival, the delegation was embraced by Congress's superintendent of finance Robert Morris, who managed the government's business operations with a firm hand. A cunning and wealthy Philadelphia merchant, Morris had championed the cause of a strong general government for so long and with such ardor that he had split Congress into pro-Morris and anti-Morris camps. During the mid-1780s, these would evolve into recognizable nationalist and anti-nationalist factions, with the former favoring centralized control over interstate and international economic, military, and diplomatic matters and the latter preferring a weak confederation of sovereign states.

The delegation reached Philadelphia only days after Morris learned that the states had failed to ratify his proposal for a national tax or "impost" on all goods coming from overseas, which he had pushed through Congress as the means to pay past debts and finance ongoing operations. Nationalists in Congress saw the officers' petition as a timely tool to revive the impost. All they needed to gain its ratification, some overly optimistic nationalists believed, was for the army to link its worthy cause and veiled threats with the creditors' political clout and Congress's proposed solution.[16] More cynical nationalists privately conceded that it might take an actual show of force by the unpaid troops to secure taxing authority for Congress from the states. And there were no greater cynics among the nationalists than Washington's former aide Alexander Hamilton and Robert Morris's wise and worldly assistant, Gouverneur Morris (no relation). After conferring with them, members of the delegation began warning Congress that the troops might mutiny without pay. Here lay the conspiracy with the army at its heart.

DESPITE THESE PROVOCATIONS, Newburgh remained quiet until mid-February 1783, when word reached the United States that the British government had agreed in principle to American independence. Then, on March 8, an officer with ties to General Gates arrived in the encampment from Philadelphia with promises of aid from other government creditors and support from nationalists in Congress should the army rise up and demand payment.[17] The cabal may have included Gates and the Morrises.[18] Hamilton almost certainly knew about it. Some historians surmise that he orchestrated it.[19]

On March 10, the conspirators at Newburgh distributed an anonymous call for a general meeting of field officers and company representatives on the following day, coupled with an unsigned address outlining their demands. Congress has promised to pay the troops, the address began, "but faith has its limits." The meek language of the officers' earlier petition had produced nothing, the writer noted. "If this, then, be your treatment while the swords you wear are necessary for the defense of America, what have you to expect from peace?" To avoid "poverty, wretchedness, and contempt" in old age, the address called on officers to "suspect the man who would advise to more moderation"—presumably Washington—and tell Congress that the army would not disband without payment.[20]

Washington reacted swiftly. He issued general orders disallowing the anonymously called meeting. Perhaps fearing that it might proceed anyway without an orderly alternative, he authorized a similar gathering for March 15 and directed Gates to preside.[21] The orders suggested that Washington would not attend. In a second unsigned address, the conspirators accepted the later meeting date.[22] Their mutinous demands remained the sole item on the meeting's agenda. The camp buzzed in anticipation.

Officers from every unit in the Newburgh encampment attended the meeting. As soon as Gates called the session to order, Washington dramatically entered the hall and asked to speak first. It was the Ides of March—the anniversary of the day that Brutus and his fellow conspirators had murdered Julius Caesar.

As was his custom on formal occasions, Washington read a prepared statement. Less than two thousand words long, it spoke of his sacrifice, a soldier's duty, and the impracticability of the conspirators' scheme. To secure the officers' back pay and future pensions, he vowed to do as much "as may be done consistently with the great duty I own to my country." He admonished the officers, however, that "as you value your own sacred honor," you should "express your utmost horror and detestation of the Man who wishes, under any specious pretenses, to overturn the liberties of our Country, and who wickedly attempts to open the flood Gates of Civil discord."[23]

After concluding his short but stern speech, Washington reached into his coat pocket for a letter from a supportive member of Congress. It reiterated the extreme gravity of the government's financial situation and summarized the ongoing efforts of Congress to address it. Struggling with the handwriting as he quoted from the letter, Washington drew reading glasses from his waistcoat and asked, "Gentlemen, you will permit me to put on my spectacles, for I have not only grown gray but almost blind in the service of my country."[24] Few of the officers had seen Washington wear glasses. Coming on the heels of his hard address, this soft show of familiarity in their presence moved many. It both humanized and elevated him. Whether from his lofty words or his lowly gesture, some officers wept openly. With this finely timed performance that some historians suspect was rehearsed, Washington carried the day. After he left, the officers approved resolutions asking Washington to represent their interests before Congress and repudiating both the "infamous propositions" contained in the two unsigned addresses and the conspirators behind them.[25]

AS WORD OF THE ENCOUNTER reached Congress and then spread across the land in newspaper accounts, Washington gained yet another laurel. Already first in war, he was now first in peace and clearly first in the hearts of his countrymen. He had no rivals. As their own financial situation went from bad to worse, however, many of the unpaid officers soon regretted their decision to trust Congress. Even Washington began to doubt the course that he had recommended for them, at least to the extent that it relied on the goodwill of Congress. By this time, though, the twig was bent and so it grew.

Taking his vow to champion the officers' cause to heart, Washington began using his platform as America's leading citizen to call for quickly and fairly compensating the troops, and ultimately for building a strong union that could support those payments and some form of permanent military establishment. He argued his case in a series of letters to members of Congress. It took days for mail to pass between Newburgh and Philadelphia, however, and circumstances could change dramatically in the meantime. In response to Washington's initial report of the anonymous addresses circulating in Newburgh but before hearing about the outcome, for example, a panicked Congress approved the officers' request to commute the half-pay pensions into lump-sum payments. By the time Congress got around to voting on a new import-tax measure to fund those payments and other government debts and expenses, members had learned both that Washington had defused the situation in Newburgh and that peace negotiators in Paris had agreed to a preliminary treaty. Nationalists lost the upper hand. As passed by Congress, the impost was limited to twenty-five years, could only be used to pay debts, and would be collected by the states. Hamilton was so disgusted that he joined a few extreme anti-nationalists in opposing the compromise. The states failed to ratify it anyway.

Confronted with fading prospects, Washington cut his demands on behalf of the officers. Immediately after the affair at Newburgh, he had asked Congress to ascertain the amount owed to each officer and establish a fund for its future payment. This at least would allow departing officers to obtain credit on the full amount due. By early April, with peace near and no new fund established, Washington sought only an accounting and partial payment—as little as three months' back pay—so that officers would not depart destitute. "To be disbanded at last without this little pittance," he wrote to one member of Congress, "will drive every Man of Honor and Sensibility to the extremest Horrors of Despair."[26]

By this point, Washington became so worried about unrest within the ranks that he privately counseled Congress to disband the army as soon as possible, with or without the ascertainment of accounts.[27] Following the official cessation of hostilities between the United States and Britain on April 19, 1783, and with Congress still lacking resources to pay the army, Washington endorsed a plan simply to release the troops that had signed on for the war's duration with orders that their states pay them. Although British forces still occupied New York pending a final peace treaty, Congress responded by furloughing most of the army in June. Departing officers were so resentful that they canceled a farewell banquet in Washington's honor.

IN A SERIES OF PRIVATE LETTERS to members of Congress, Washington lashed out at nationalists for betraying the army. They had used the officers "as mere puppets" to secure national tax revenues to repay all government creditors—including bond speculators.[28] "The Army was a dangerous Engine to Work with," he wrote in a letter to Hamilton that blamed the near mutiny at Newburgh on Robert and Gouverneur Morris.[29] "I have taken much pains to support Mr. [Robert] Morris's Administration in the Army," Washington added in another letter to Hamilton, "but if he will neither adopt the mode which has been suggested [for paying officers], point out any other, nor show cause why the first is either impracticable or impolitic, they will certainly attribute their disappointment to a luke warmness in him, or some design incompatible with their Interests." Further, the commander in chief objected to the nationalists' policy of putting unpaid troops on an equal footing with other government creditors. "I know that Distinctions are commonly odious," he wrote in April, "yet upon a candid Comparison, every Man, even the most interested, will be forced to yield the superior Merit and Sufferings of the Soldier."[30]

Hamilton responded in two remarkable letters that conceded most of Washington's charges but turned them on their head. "I do not wonder at the suspicions that have been infused" in your letters, he wrote in early April, "nor should I be surprised to hear that I have been pointed out as one of the persons concerned in playing the game described. But facts must speak for themselves." There are two parties in Congress, Hamilton explained: "one is attached to state, the other to Continental [or national] politics." Only the nationalists support the Continental Army, he suggested, but they do so as a means to create one nation from a confederation of states. The nationalists "have blended the interests of the army with other Creditors from a conviction," he stressed. "It is essential to our cause that vigorous efforts should be made to restore public credit." This required national taxes to supply "public necessities." An impost, Hamilton believed, would encourage domestic industry and bolster the national economy. "The necessity and discontents of the army presented themselves as a powerful engine," he wrote, and never denied seeking to use it for political ends.[31] What Washington had shunned as "dangerous"—using the military as a political tool in a republic—Hamilton embraced as "powerful": Cincinnatus versus Caesar.[32]

If he had not seen him as such before, Washington surely now saw Hamilton as a devious schemer ready to risk much to win all.[33] He had shown those traits before. Born out of wedlock to a socially scorned Frenchwoman in the West Indies and orphaned at age ten, but gifted with words and adroit at winning patrons, Hamilton relied on the charity of island planters and merchants to obtain an education at New York's Loyalist King's College, later Columbia, during the run-up to the Revolutionary War. Turning on his West Indian sponsors and Tory teachers, Hamilton found his voice in college penning philosophically and economically conservative essays denouncing

British rule, and he soon volunteered as a field officer in the Continental Army. By 1777, Washington had invited Hamilton to join his personal staff, on which he served until March 1781. Bathed in glory from his military service and newly married into a well-connected family of Hudson River valley patroons, Hamilton left the army in October 1781 to become a commercial lawyer and soon entered Congress as the sole nationalist in New York's state-minded delegation. Remarkably, until he was knee-deep in the so-called Newburgh Conspiracy, Hamilton had not written to Washington since leaving the army. By then, Hamilton needed him.

At this point, Washington could have turned his back on his former aide, who Washington now realized was willing to "make a sacrifice of the Army and all its interests" for partisan ends.[34] He didn't. Quite to the contrary, his responses to Hamilton sound almost apologetic for having squelched the Newburgh Conspiracy. "No Man can be more opposed to State funds and local prejudice than myself," he assured Hamilton in one of his letters on the nationalists' plot, and "I endeavor (I hope not altogether ineffectually) to inculcate [those sentiments] upon the Officers in the Army."[35] Expanding beyond simply expressing support for national taxing authority, Washington affirmed, "No Man in the United States is, or can be more deeply impressed with the necessity of a reform in our present Confederation than myself. No Man perhaps has felt the bad effects of it more sensibly; for to the defects thereof, and want of Powers in Congress, may justly be ascribed the prolongation of the War." His further assurance that "all my private letters have teemed with these Sentiments"—itself a bald overstatement—spoke only of private letters, not public statements.[36] Instinctively nonpartisan, Washington had largely avoided the intensely partisan debate over national powers—but that soon changed. Given his stature, taking a public stance on reforming the confederation instantly made him the country's leading nationalist.

• • • •

HAMILTON AND THE NEWBURGH CONSPIRACY may have helped to force the cautious Virginian's hand on the thorny issues of national sovereignty and constitutional reform, but Washington played it with conviction. Due to the formal cessation of hostilities in April 1783, and the pending furlough of most soldiers and officers over the following summer, the commander in chief had time to focus on the country's future as he waited with a skeleton force for the final peace treaty and the last British troops to leave New York. The process dragged on until nearly December. Early in that prolonged period of enforced inactivity, Washington issued the two most significant documents of his military career. Though both took years to bear fruit, they helped to lay a foundation for the new constitutional order that Washington would eventually lead.

The first, "Sentiments on a Peace Establishment," drew on the work of various staff and field officers but carried Washington's personal and official stamp. It ran counter to conventional wisdom. During the conflict, few Americans had thought realistically about the postwar military. Oppressed by professional British and paid Hessian soldiers before and during the Revolutionary War, and hesitant to assume the cost of a peacetime military, most Americans instinctively opposed a standing army. State and local militias had risen to the defense of individual liberty against imperial troops, and presumably would melt away with peace.

Monarchies needed a professional army to gain and retain power, many Americans thought, but not republics. These commentators lacked reference points, however. In the popular mind, the only successful republican governments were ancient Greek city-states and modern Swiss cantons. These tiny islands of democracy, so far as Americans knew, had been or were defended by citizen-soldiers. Republican Rome, once it gained size, had fallen to its own power-hungry military leaders. In his "Sentiments," Washington began changing the conversation at least insofar as it related to the needs of a continental republic with international commercial interests and imperial ambitions of its own on the western frontier.

"Altho' a *large* standing Army in time of Peace hath ever been considered dangerous to the liberties of a Country, yet a few Troops, under certain circumstances, are not only safe, but indispensably necessary," Washington began. These would be "Continental Troops" of the general government, he stressed, organized into four regiments of infantry and one of artillery to secure the western frontier and guard the border with British Canada. Existing state militias would be restructured on a Swiss model as a uniform force of citizen-soldiers ready for call-up in times of need. Washington also recommended that the general government establish coastal fortifications and a navy to protect commerce in wartime, maintain a base at West Point to block invasion from Canada, and open an academy to train army officers. But his main concern was the West—notably the old Northwest, where Virginians were settling and he had invested. States were in the process of ceding their western land claims to the general government and many people saw the West as key to the country's future. Washington called for creating a series of military posts up the Potomac Valley, along the Ohio River, north to the Great Lakes, and west to the Mississippi. "The Tribes of Indians within our Territory are numerous, soured and jealous," he warned.[37] If accepted, Washington's proposal would go a long way toward forging a continental union and giving it national purpose.

Of far greater import, Washington followed this proposal, which he submitted to Congress, with a circular letter to the thirteen state governments. An appeal for unity at a time when peace with Britain had removed the common enemy that had drawn the states together, the letter built to its main point: national supremacy. "It is indispensable to the happiness of the individual States, that there should be lodged somewhere, a Supreme Power to regulate and govern the general concerns of the Confederated Republic." Long on theme but short on specifics, the letter called for "an indissoluble Union of the States under one Federal Head," a continental army supported by uniform state militias, taxing power for Congress, and "complete justice to all the Public Creditors," particularly the unpaid troops. Its pounding theme throughout, however—from Washington's opening appeal to "citizens of America" through his depiction of "the glorious Fabrick of our . . . National Character" to his closing prayer for "a happy Nation"—was American nationhood. "It is only our united Character as an Empire, that our Independence is acknowledged," Washington reminded state leaders. If the nation split apart, Britain would reabsorb the states one by one, he warned.[38]

In opening and closing the letter, Washington played his trump card. His words on this matter could be trusted, he said, because he was relinquishing power soon and "not taking any share in public business hereafter." For the first time in a public statement, he declared his firm intent to retire. Not seeking power for himself, Washington observed, he could have no "sinister views" in promoting a strong national government. At the time, Washington viewed the circular letter as something of a farewell to the American people and asked that they accept it as "the Legacy of One, who has ardently wished, on all occasions, to be useful to his Country."[39] Certainly Americans received it as such. Hailed as "Washington's Legacy," the letter appeared in newspapers from New England to the Deep South and became one of the most celebrated documents of the day.[40] Though none of its nation-building recommendations were realized for over five years, they immediately became associated with Washington. Indeed, in the public imagination, that Virginian had become the first American.

WITH HIS LEGACY PUBLISHED in June 1783, Washington entered an interlude of relative quiet insofar as the commander in chief of a rapidly disbanding army can experience quietude. It lasted until the last British troops left New York five months later. Martha joined him in Newburgh for this period of quasi-peace that he once depicted in theatrical terms. "Nothing now remains," Washington wrote in general orders to the troops, "but for the actors of this mighty Scene to preserve a perfect, unvarying, consistency of character throughout the last act; to close the Drama with applause; and to retire from the Military Theatre."[41] In this closing act, he played his role with constancy through to his carefully scripted final exit before Congress on December 23.

Several tasks engaged Washington during this period. He furloughed four-fifths of the army in June, spent late July touring upstate New York with Hamilton and Governor George Clinton, and endured ten weeks of unsuccessfully negotiating with Congress over the peacetime military. These negotiations took place at cramped college quarters in tiny Princeton, New Jersey, where Congress convened for five miserable months during mid-1783. It had moved to Princeton in June to escape protests from local soldiers in Philadelphia demanding back pay and remained there until November, when it moved to Annapolis and later to Trenton before settling in New York. Congress's abrupt move to Princeton, where the well-born Madison complained of having to share a bed with another Virginia congressman, added to Washington's despair over the country's prospects. First the Newburgh Conspiracy, then mass furloughs without back pay, and now riotous troops in Philadelphia driving Congress to meet in a college lecture hall and dormitory. Meanwhile, the states were pressing ahead with plans for peace heedless of Congress. Washington saw no future in such designs—no chance for the states ever to open the West or remain independent in a hostile world. Small confederations might form, he thought, but no grand nation capable of taking its rightful place on the world's stage. Sharing Washington's disgust, both Hamilton and Madison left Congress during its exile in Princeton and never returned.

During this period, Washington's private letters capture his concerns more fully than his public pronouncement. To survive, Washington wrote to Lafayette, the United States must "form a Constitution that will give consistency, stability and dignity to the Union; and sufficient powers to the great Council of the Nation for general purposes."[42] He advised the commander of American forces in the South, Nathanael Greene, "It remains only for the States . . . to establish their Independence on that Basis of inviolable efficacious Union . . . which may prevent their being made the Sport of European Policy."[43] To his brother John, Washington wrote, "Competent Powers for all *general* purposes should be vested in the Sovereignty of the United States, or Anarchy and Confusion will soon succeed."[44] While he spoke in public only of strengthening the Articles of Confederation, in private Washington was already calling for a "Convention of the People" to draft a new "Federal Constitution."[45]

Effective November 3, after learning that the British were finally beginning to leave New York, Congress discharged the furloughed troops and disbanded most of the remaining army. No one received more than a pittance in back pay. This second round of contractions left the army with eight hundred men—split between bases at Fort Pitt on the frontier and West Point, near Newburgh—which was scarcely one-third of the number that Washington had proposed for the peacetime force.

One day before the discharges took effect, Washington beat the drum for nationhood again in his Farewell Orders. He used the army itself as an exemplar. Who could have imagined, he asked, "that Men who came from the different parts of the Continent, strongly disposed, by the habits of education, to despise and quarrel with each other, would instantly become but one patriotic band of Brothers?" After thanking the officers and soldiers for their service, he warned them that unless "the powers of the union increased, the honour, dignity, and justice of the nation would be lost forever." And by "justice," he meant their back pay. He challenged all of them to return home as champions of a continental republic, reminded them of his pleas to Congress and prayers to the "God of Armies" on their behalf, and assured them that they "must and will most inevitably be paid."[46]

Then they left, including most of the officers who had served longest with Washington. While the people sang his praises and Congress voted to erect an equestrian statute of him at its permanent seat—which might require putting the monument on wheels, some joked—his officers and soldiers departed Newburgh with decidedly mixed feelings about their commander. The remaining officers captured those feelings in a written response to Washington's Farewell Orders. Grudgingly conceding Washington had done everything he could do for them, it excoriated Congress and the states for failing to provide the just and promised compensation for the officers' long and dangerous service.[47] The public mostly sided with the states and Congress, particularly regarding officers' pensions, which many denounced as a ploy to create an aristocratic class. Word that the retired officers had organized a fraternal association for themselves and their male descendants, called the Society of the Cincinnati, fed popular fears that a homegrown nobility might emerge from the American Revolution. For some ardent republicans, these fears only intensified after the wealthy and well-born Washington consented to serve as the society's first president.

WHEN THE BRITISH FINALLY evacuated New York on November 25, Washington's rump force in and around Newburgh played the role of a liberating army with all the pomp and circumstance that it could muster. As they crossed the rural portions of northern Manhattan Island to the defended entrance of the inner city at the Bowery, the soldiers saw land stripped bare and houses in disrepair. There they paused until receiving word at about one o'clock that the last British troops had embarked and the Royal Navy had moved out to sea. After an advance guard, its flags taut in a stiff breeze, took possession of the city to the sound of fife and drum, General Washington and Governor Clinton, riding side by side on magnificent horses, led a triumphant procession of army officers and state officials down Broadway to the Battery.

Seven years of occupation by a hostile army that viewed even Loyalists with suspicion and contempt had left the city badly scarred. No tree stood anywhere and even the fences had been dismantled for kindling. Many of the city's finest homes were ruined. Damage from a massive fire that ravaged the city less than a week after the British captured it in 1776 remained starkly visible on the lower west side. Yet the remaining citizens turned out en masse to cheer the procession. Except for the empire's continued presence in frontier forts, the United States were at long last free of British troops.

Washington stood at the center of weeklong victory celebrations in lower Manhattan that far exceeded those occurring elsewhere in the country. They began on the first day with a banquet in the city hosted by Clinton, an ardent patriot who had served in Poughkeepsie as the state's governor since 1777 even as the British occupied Manhattan and the lower Hudson River valley. Despite his warm friendship with Washington, his notable war record, and his future service as Vice President under Jefferson and Madison, Clinton had emerged as a champion of state sovereignty. His banquet concluded without toasting Congress or the nation. "May a close Union of the States guard the Temple *they* have erected to liberty" was as near as these revelers came to acknowledging a general government in their thirteen toasts—a total chosen to correspond with the number of states.[48]

Ensuing days brought speeches, dinners, and balls. Celebrations culminated on December 2 with a fireworks display touted as the largest of its kind ever seen in America. Opening with a band playing popular tunes and interrupted by loud huzzahs for spectacular blasts, it lit up New York Harbor for over an hour with illuminated spirals, fire trees, exploding serpents, Chinese fountains, and repeated flights of thirteen rockets. Washington declared it "splendid."[49] He left after one more day, following a final farewell to his few remaining officers. Washington scheduled this good-bye for noon on the fourth in an upper room at Fraunces Tavern, which stood at the corner of Broad and Pearl Streets near the docks in lower Manhattan.

Deprived of the opportunity for a final dinner with officers after the mass furloughs in June or general discharge in November due to bitterness over back pay, Washington clearly wanted to get it right with this small remnant. The tavern was widely regarded as New York's finest public house and had acted as a meeting place for patriots prior to British occupation of New York, and for Loyalists during it. Constructed out of imported Dutch bricks as the town home for the wealthy DeLancey family in 1719, the handsome, five-story building became a tavern in 1762 when purchased by Samuel Fraunces, a popular cook and innkeeper believed to have come from the West Indies and possibly of mixed French and African ancestry. He served American officers before the fall of New York, British officers after it, and as steward of the presidential household during Washington's first term. He claimed to have passed critical information on British troop movement to Washington during the war and smuggled food to American prisoners. For Washington's farewell dinner, he laid an elaborate banquet, though little was consumed.

After everyone had a full glass of wine, Washington raised his in a shaking hand to toast the officers. "With an heart full of love and gratitude, I now take leave of you: I must devoutly wish that your latter days may be as prosperous and happy, as your former ones have been glorious and honourable."[50] Choked with emotion, he could not say more; nor could the others. Historians have debated whether it was simply sentiment about his retirement or also regret over his failure to get any officers their due. Whatever the cause, the result was the same. Washington wept. Then, after embracing each man, he left.

Governor Clinton, other officials, and leading citizens of New York were assembled outside the tavern to escort Washington to the nearby Whitehall wharf. They passed through lines of light infantry drawn from the First and Second New York Regiments, which had seen duty with Washington at the battles of Monmouth and Yorktown. A ceremonial barge with twenty-two oarsmen waited at the wharf to ferry the General across the Hudson River to New Jersey on the first leg of an emotional journey to deliver his commission to the Congress in Annapolis. What one newspaper described as "a great concourse of people" crowded every available viewpoint around the wharf to witness the departure.[51] Hamilton, who had moved back into the city upon its liberation, was noticeably absent. Biographer Ron Chernow blamed Hamilton's absence on "some secret wound" dividing him from Washington.[52] Certainly Hamilton should not have felt welcome among the officers at Fraunces Tavern if they knew how he had used them during the Newburgh Conspiracy.

FROM NEW YORK TO ANNAPOLIS, it was a triumphant two-week journey by the General and a few of his closest aides across New Jersey, Pennsylvania, Delaware, and Maryland. Something of a victory lap, it took them through the region where Washington's army had spent most of the war, suffered most of its casualties, and at one time or other lost and then liberated most of the towns. They passed through battle sites, such as Trenton, and near others, including Brandywine and Germantown. Citizens turned out everywhere to cheer them on their way. Official delegations welcomed them to each town. Bonfires lit the night. Baltimore hosted a ball lasting past 2 A.M. The legislatures of four states received them.

Many people thought this would be their final chance to see Washington; certainly he suggested as much. "Altho I now am returning to a much wished for retirement, yet I cannot bid adieu . . . without experiencing a certain pleasing, melancholly sensation," he said to the citizens of New Brunswick, New Jersey, "pleasing because I leave my Country in full possession of Liberty and Independence; Melancholly because I bid my friends a long, perhaps a last farewell."[53] To the Common Council of Wilmington, Delaware, he added, "Tho' I shall no more appear on the great Theatre of Action, the Wellfare of our infant States can never be indifferent to me."[54] Simply put, his message was similar at each stop: America was free, now make the most of it.

Aside from New York, Philadelphia offered the warmest and most extended welcome to Washington. He was escorted into the city by a delegation that included state officials, several generals, Robert Morris, and a cavalry unit. A cannon salute announced his arrival at the city gates. People flooded the streets to cheer him. The State House bell that had rung for liberty upon the first public reading of the Declaration of Independence now rang for him.

Washington was the toast of the town for a week. He thanked the University of Pennsylvania for awarding him an honorary degree and the American Philosophical Society for making him a member. "To you," a committee of local merchants declared, "your country turns her admiring eyes, and hails you her Favourite Son."[55] John Adams later complained to a Philadelphian that people would remember the Revolutionary War as simply "that Dr. Franklin's electric rod smote the earth and out sprang George Washington. Then Franklin electrified him . . . and thence forward those two conducted all the Policy, Negotiations, Legislations, and War."[56] If so, then the deification of America's two preeminent leaders was happening already as Washington entered Franklin's city.

Washington at last reached Annapolis—Congress's moving seat—on December 19, less than a week before his promised return to Mount Vernon for Christmas, and stayed there for four nights.

"His Excellency's arrival was announced by the discharge of cannon," newspapers reported.[57] Horatio Gates, of all people, escorted him into town. Formal dinners occurred nightly hosted by the city, the state, or Congress, and Maryland's governor invited some two hundred "persons of distinction"—as one observer depicted them—to a grand ball in Washington's honor for the night before his departure.[58] Hamilton and Madison had already resigned from Congress and gone home, but Jefferson and James Monroe were still present from Virginia. As a fellow member of Virginia's House of Burgesses, Washington had known Jefferson since 1768, and, at age nineteen, James Monroe had crossed the Delaware River with Washington on that already legendary Christmas night in 1776 for the battles that revived the patriot cause. A favorite aide, James McHenry, also now served in Congress. Washington was among friends even if a certain coldness frosted his relationship with another former aide, Congress president Thomas Mifflin.

Washington clearly enjoyed himself in Annapolis. He danced every dance at the governor's ball, accommodating all the ladies who lined up for the privilege of getting a touch of him. After the thirteen formal toasts at Congress's banquet, he added a concluding one of his own: "Competent Powers to Congress for general purposes."[59] It had become his mantra. As much as he wished to get home to Virginia, he was also at home here in the swirl of continental politics.

Precisely at noon on December 23, playing his role in the grand pageant of American history, Washington walked into the tableau that would become frozen in Trumbull's painting for the United States Capitol Rotunda. Declaring that he had "now finished the work assigned to me," Washington returned his commission to Congress and, accompanied only by his aide-de-camp David Humphreys on fast riding horses, reached Mount Vernon late on the following afternoon.[60] He was no longer the Virginian who had left that plantation more than eight years earlier, however. The war had made him an American—one of a new breed forged in revolution, dedicated to liberty, and actuated by republican virtue. In the months after the victory at Yorktown, as the powers of Congress eroded before the claims of state sovereignty, first Hamilton and later other officers suggested that Washington assume the reins of power. He rebuked them then and now retired. But he remained an American.

1780 map of the northern and central United States, including the western lands visited by George Washington in 1784.

CHAPTER 2

Reeling in the West

～～

WASHINGTON FACED AN UNSETTLING TRANSITION. One day, he was the most powerful person in the American government, commander in chief of its armed forces, and intensely involved in all its affairs. The next day, he was a private citizen operating an extended tidewater plantation that was in some disarray due to the war and his nine-year absence. Overnight, he changed from leading a public effort to win freedom for Americans to managing a private enterprise based on slave labor. Adding to the shock, soon after Washington arrived home, an unusually severe spell of cold weather froze the rivers, closed the roads, and isolated Mount Vernon from outside contact for more than a month. Due to ice and snow, he could not even travel freely about his estate during much of January. The general had trouble adjusting. By early March, he begged Jefferson for news—"any News that you are at liberty to impart"—from Congress.[1]

From the first, Washington referred to Mount Vernon as his "seat of retirement from the bustle of the busy world."[2] Yet he had plenty to do there. Washington wrote in mid-January 1784, "An almost entire suspension of every thing which related to my own Estate, for near nine years, has accumulated an abundance of work for me."[3] He did not trust his slaves and regularly complained that they shirked work, stole supplies, and broke tools.[4] He felt a need to watch them daily to keep them on task. Sometimes he would measure their output in his presence and then demand similar productivity during the entire workday, which lasted from sunrise to sunset with two hours for lunch, or up to fifteen hours per day, six days a week, in summer.[5] Washington often distrusted his hired overseers and paid workers as well, and closely monitored their efforts. He was a hands-on manager by nature, but conditions at Mount Vernon accented this trait. "I made no money from my Estate during the nine years I was absent from it, and brought none home with me," Washington explained, and wanted to right this unsustainable situation.[6]

After having the weight of a country and its people on his shoulders for nearly a decade, however, this work was retirement of a sort for Washington. "I am just beginning to experience that ease, and freedom from public cares which, however desirable, takes some time to realize," he wrote in late February to his successor as army chief, Henry Knox. "It was not 'till lately that I could get the better of my usual custom of ruminating as soon as I waked in the Morning, on the business of the ensuing day; and of my surprise, after having revolved many things in my mind, to find that I was no longer a public Man, or had anything to do with public transactions."[7]

Still, despite his talk of retirement, Washington was only fifty-one years old when he resigned his commission and returned to Mount Vernon. Although life expectancy in the United States at the time was a mere thirty-five years, that number was significantly brought down by infant mortality. Fifty-one was not old for senior statesmen of the Revolutionary Era. More than a quarter century Washington's senior, Benjamin Franklin gave no thought to retirement. Two years later, he began the first of three one-year terms as president of Pennsylvania. In 1784, Samuel Adams, ten years older than Washington, was the senate president in Massachusetts and later became its governor. George Clinton, John Hancock, and John Adams were only slightly younger than Washington but still burned with ambition. Clinton would be elected to four more three-year terms as New York's governor and two as Vice President of the United States. Governor Hancock of Massachusetts held his post for another seven years. Adams lived to see the fiftieth anniversary of the Declaration of Independence. The list could go on, including Roger Sherman, John Witherspoon, and George Wythe—all older than Washington but still fully engaged in civic affairs. Yet Washington intended to exit the public stage just as his country was born.

Or so it sounded in the letters he wrote during his first months at home. "I am at length become a private citizen of America, on the banks of the Potowmac; where under my own Vine and my own Fig tree—free from the bustle of a camp & intrigues of a Court, I shall view the busy world, 'in the calm lights of mild philosophy,'" he commented in a reflective note to the Chevalier de Chastellux, a French essayist and general who had served in the American Revolution. "I am not only retired from all public employments; but I am retireing within myself."[8]

In a similar letter to Lafayette, Washington expanded on what he meant by court intrigue. He described the statesman—a role he boasted of avoiding—as someone "whose watchful days & sleepless Nights are spent in devising schemes to promote the welfare of his own—perhaps the ruin of other countries, as if the Globe was insufficient for us all." With Mount Vernon at its hub, Washington's globe was sufficient for him. He wrote of treading the paths of private life "with heartfelt satisfaction" to the end of his days. "Envious of none," he added, "I am determined to be pleased with all."[9]

Yet Washington was far from pleased with all. With the country still very much on his mind, Washington's early postretirement letters from Mount Vernon railed about the Congress's lack of authority, failure to pay public creditors, and inattention to business. During the first months of 1784, he sent scores of missives to governors, former military colleagues, and members of Congress dispensing advice and all but issuing orders. In a message to the wartime governor of Connecticut, who had also just stepped down, Washington no sooner mentioned "the serenity of retirement" than he began grousing about the "deranged state of public Affairs."[10] To Virginia's states' rights governor, Benjamin Harrison V, Washington wrote about his hope for expanded national powers, "I have no fears arising from this source; in my mind, but I have many, & powerful ones indeed which predict the worst consequences from a half starved, limping Government."[11] In such letters, Washington showed little sign of actually settling into an obscure private retirement.

MOUNT VERNON ALONE would keep him busy. Washington had spent only ten out of the past three thousand days of war at his eight-thousand-acre working plantation, and its finances were confused. Ledgers and records were topsy-turvy from having been hastily packed and unpacked every time British forces passed near enough to threaten the estate. Intent on securing his fortune in land, prior to the war Washington had purchased farms adjoining Mount Vernon whenever they came on the market as well as undeveloped tracts on the frontier in western Virginia and Pennsylvania. He also had begun the process of expanding his residence into a proper manor house, with an eloquent banqueting hall, distinctive cupola, and grand piazza overlooking the Potomac River.

Attentive to even minor details, upon his return from war Washington assumed personal responsibility for restoring Mount Vernon to profitability, capitalizing on his western land holdings and completing renovations on his residence. Each weekday morning, he rode a circuit of the five farms comprising his plantation and assigned tasks for his nearly two hundred workers, most of whom were black slaves and many of the rest indentured servants. Washington always expected 100 percent effort from able-bodied individuals whatever their station in life, and by the 1780s came to recognize the inefficiency of a slave economy even though he felt powerless to change it. He often vowed to acquire no new slaves beyond those born of his current ones but invariably broke this promise.[12] Washington did free his own slaves after his death by his will, but these were only 123 of the 316 slaves then living at Mount Vernon. Most of the rest were the dower property of his wife, Martha, and they passed directly to her heirs upon her death in 1802.[13]

Following his morning ride, Washington typically hosted a formal midafternoon meal with visitors who had made the trek to his country seat. Some of these were neighbors, former colleagues, or friends; many were travelers wanting to meet the man who had freed America. Washington often worked in his library or garden following dinner. He developed a passion for improving his livestock and soil productivity by applying new methods of scientific farming. Supper was less formal than dinner, with Washington only eating with visitors and overnight guests if they included close friends or persons with important news or business. With them, he might talk into the evening. Washington's prewar hobbies of cards and foxhunting gave way to more serious pursuits. "His correspondence," biographer John Ferling notes, "not only turned especially sober, but was restricted almost solely to business concerns or matters of state."[14] In short, he acted the part of a self-employed citizen-statesman with a national perspective and international reputation.

Washington was conflicted about retiring from public service almost from the outset. "How far upon more mature consideration I may depart from the resolution I had formed of living perfectly at ease—exempt from all kinds of responsibility, is more than I can, at present, absolutely determine," he conceded to Jefferson scarcely three months after returning to Mount Vernon.[15] In some letters from 1784, Washington wrote about his family being "short-lived"—his father and two half brothers died before reaching age fifty—and his own expectation of soon being "entombed in the dreary mansions of my fathers."[16]

Given such "gloomy apprehensions," as Jefferson called them, and a lack of descendants to provide for, early retirement made sense.[17]

Another letter from the same year leaves a different impression of Washington's sense of survival and fecundity, however. In it, he asked Congress to return his military commission as a keepsake for his grandchildren. Although Martha had grandchildren, two of whom lived at Mount Vernon, they came from her son by a prior marriage. Washington never regarded them as his. Devoted to his wife, he knew that he would only have descendants if he outlived her and married a younger woman. Although he wrote about that possibility in confidence to friends, it seems too remote to account for his preoccupation with business and statecraft after the Revolutionary War.[18] He could have retired at ease.

Perhaps in the end, Washington's postwar activities simply reflected his desire to leave a legacy, make a difference, and exemplify republican virtue. He suggested as much in two 1784 letters that wax philosophic about cultivating tender plants and tending tall trees on his plantation. Even in retirement, he counseled a recently retired patriot leader, we should cultivate young plants toward their perfection.[19] And the tall trees that he planted as seedlings in his youth, Washington observed to Chastellux, trees whose very height now measured his own decline, show him gratitude by providing shade. "Before I go hence to return no more," he vowed, "for this, their gratitude, I will nurture them while I stay."[20] Whether writing metaphorically about nurturing the nation that he had planted or simply justifying his ongoing agricultural pursuits at Mount Vernon, Washington clearly intended to continue working in retirement. He might die soon, he confessed to Lafayette late in 1784, "but I will not repine—I have had my day."[21] He would have many more.

AFTER SPENDING THE FIRST NINE MONTHS of his so-called retirement trying to restore order to his Mount Vernon estate, Washington headed west to inspect his frontier properties in western Virginia and Pennsylvania. Having become accustomed to deference, if not adoration, the chilly reception that the former commander in chief received in the West, especially from squatters on his land, heightened his already considerable fears for the country's future. Despite its inclusion into the United States by the peace treaty with Britain, the trans-Appalachian West—so central to nationalists' hope for America's future—was not yet integrated into the new republic. Washington's desire to link East to West, motivated by mixed personal and public concerns, inevitably pulled him back into the nation's service. In a sense, his long journey back from retirement to the Constitutional Convention and the presidency began with his trip to the frontier in 1784. Expecting an adventure worthy of record, Washington resumed an earlier practice of keeping a daily diary.

The trip began well enough. Washington set out by horseback on September 1 with three slaves or servants and his longtime friend and physician James Craik for a planned six-week overland trek. Craik's son and Washington's nephew soon joined them. More had asked to go along but, as Washington explained to his brother, he did not want to take anyone "who would soon get tired & embarrass my movements."[22] Washington knew roughly what to expect. He had crisscrossed the territory several times as a young surveyor in the 1740s and as a colonial militia officer fighting the French and their Native American allies in the 1750s. On those trips, he sometimes traveled light and often slept under only a blanket.

Not this time. Although the party planned to stay in public houses or private homes whenever possible, for nights without lodging they carried an officer's marquee or grand tent for the four gentlemen and a horseman's tent for the attendants. Other baggage included bedding, sheets, silver cups and spoons, Madeira and port wine (again for the gentlemen), two kegs of rum for the frontier folk they would encounter, all manner of cooking equipment, assorted spices, extra horseshoes, and Washington's fishing lines. The differentiation of supplies for gentlemen, frontier folk, and slaves or servants, plus Washington's failure to name the accompanying attendants in any letter or diary entry, reflected an aristocratic sense of class that survived the American Revolution. On an earlier trip to the region, Washington described some settlers "as Ignorant a Set of People as the Indians," and always retained that view of frontiersmen.[23] He might respect their knowledge of the region and their ability to survive in it, but he never saw them as his equals and always remained aloof from them. And they recognized it.

The party's outbound route followed the Potomac River in a westerly direction from Mount Vernon to Cumberland, Maryland, and then, leaving the river, took a more northerly tack across the Allegheny Mountains on Braddock's Road toward Pittsburgh. The Potomac, which literally cuts through a parallel series of low ridges before turning south at Cumberland, marks the boundary between Virginia and Maryland. On this trip, Washington favored the Virginia side, where he owned scattered tracts that he leased to farmers. The river was navigable only to a few miles above Mount Vernon, where Alexandria, Virginia, and Georgetown, in what was then Maryland, stood at the terminus of shipping. Above these towns, the Potomac's Little and Great Falls, with a combined drop of over 110 feet, blocked river traffic. Between them and Cumberland—a distance of 170 miles—the river, though sometimes shallow and rapid, was rarely obstructed by more than an occasional rapids or low falls. In 1754, a twenty-two-year-old Washington ran it in a canoe with only modest difficulty at a few points. Now fifty-two and trotting on his great horse at a gait of about five miles per hour with frequent stops, he reached Cumberland on the trip's tenth day.

Opened for settlement by Virginia and Maryland prior to the Revolutionary War, the Potomac Valley below Cumberland had become an integral part of the eastern states by 1784. Many of its settlers had cast their lot with the patriot cause in 1776 and now gave Washington a hero's welcome. His tenants, strained by a decade of war and recession, paid what they could toward their long-past-due rents and cheered him on his way. Impressed by commercial development around the warm mineral springs at Bath, where he had taken the waters in earlier years, Washington contracted to build a house there. He already owned land in the area—some of his most valuable inland property. James Rumsey, a local builder, showed him a model for a mechanical boat allegedly capable of propelling itself upstream against the Potomac's strong current. Long interested in opening the river for traffic to his western properties, Washington gave Rumsey a certificate attesting to the boat's "usefulness in our inland navigation" and wrote to Virginia's governor about its potential value for securing "a large portion of the trade of the Western Country" for the state.[24] Capitalizing on Washington's name, Rumsey used the certificate to obtain patents and patrons for his innovative but ultimately inoperable invention. To this point, the trip could hardly have gone better.

FOR WASHINGTON, the troubles began after he left the settled lands east of the Alleghenys and began ascending Braddock's Road into southwest Pennsylvania. As a colonial militia officer serving under British general Edward Braddock during the French and Indian War in 1755, Washington had helped cut this pathway through the wilderness to support and supply a massive British assault on French positions in the Ohio Valley, and had retreated in terror across it after Braddock's crushing defeat. Now, twelve days after leaving Mount Vernon, the road took him by Great Meadows, the former site of Fort Necessity, which Washington had surrendered to the French in 1754 and later privately acquired as investment property.

The autumn rains had begun by this time, turning Braddock's Road into a muddy trough. His tenement here, Washington noted, was "little improved, tho' capable of being turned to great advantage."[25] In reality, it was as much a sodden fen in 1784 as when he surrendered it to the French thirty years earlier. Washington had posted it for lease, but so far had no takers. He did not linger. Great Meadows surely brought back bitter memories because here, in an unmarked grave to protect it from being mutilated by pursuing Native Americans, he had buried Braddock's body.

With his baggage bogged down by rain and mud, Washington rushed ahead with a single attendant to reach his much larger tract at a place called Washington's Bottom in time for the scheduled auction of a gristmill that he owned with Gilbert Simpson. Since 1772, Simpson had been Washington's agent in managing this 1,644-acre track and his partner in developing a farm and mill on part of it. Washington advanced the capital; Simpson provided the labor; they would share the profits. But there were no profits, or at least none that Simpson reported. Only promises.

Rarely charitable when it came to business, by 1775 Washington dismissed Simpson as a man of "extreme stupidity," but he was too preoccupied by war to wind down the partnership.[26] By the war's end, Washington suspected Simpson of something much worse: fraud. "How profitable our partnership has been, *you best can tell*," Washington wrote to Simpson in a February 1784 letter demanding a full accounting and payment, "& how advantageous my Mill has been, none can tell so well as *yourself*."[27] When a reply came back in April offering nothing but excuses, Washington exploded. More than anything, resolving this long-festering dispute with Simpson prompted Washington's trip west. In July, Washington advertised the farm for lease, its stock and slaves for sale, and the mill for auction. He went west to see these matters through.

Washington was accustomed to having his way with subordinates, and so his frustrations only mounted when he encountered his weaselly "partner" on Simpson's home turf. On inspection, the watermill, built by Simpson with Washington's money without Washington having seen it, lacked sufficient waterpower to operate. And the plots leased by Simpson as Washington's agent to individual settlers while Washington was at war offered little promise. "I do not find the land in *general* equal to my expectation of it," Washington wrote. "The Tenements with respect to the buildings, are but indifferently improved."[28] The tenants struck him "as people of a lower order."[29] He collected what he could from them in rent and arranged some new leases but when he tried to auction the mill, no one bid. It was worthless. To the suggestion that he invest more to improve it, Washington replied that he'd rather "let her return to dust" than lose another cent.[30] As for the house and farm occupied by Simpson, only Simpson bid. He renewed his lease for nothing down and five hundred bushels of wheat per year, but absconded before the first harvest, taking the farm's six slaves with him.

Washington wanted to get out of this place as soon as possible after the auction but a settled rain forced him to stay on with Simpson for three more nights. If this seemed like Washington's purgatory, then hell awaited at the next stop.

A FORETASTE OF THE COMING TORMENT arrived while Washington was still with Simpson. It came in the form of Seceders from his 2,813-acre track about thirty miles farther west at Miller's Run. The American frontier always attracted more than its share of religious groups seeking their Zion in the howling wilderness. Members of one such band, the Seceders—a poor but earnest sect of Scotch-Irish Calvinists—had the misfortune of staking their claim to a frontier haven on land already claimed by the father of their country. Since they freely submitted themselves only to God, and Washington always insisted on controlling his land, a clash of wills ensued.

Having known for a decade that Washington claimed the land where they squatted, upon learning that he was on his way to assert his rights they sent out a delegation to deter and dissuade him. The Seceders "came here to set forth their *pretensions*," Washington wrote in his diary about this initial meeting, "and to enquire into my rights." But he saw through their pretext of reasonableness. They really only wanted "to discover all the flaws they could in my Deed."[31] They saw themselves as called by Christ to Miller's Run and would not submit to a landlord who did not share their religious beliefs.

Named Seceders for good reason, they had seceded from ungodly society. While Washington typically said little in public about his personal religious faith beyond expressing a profound sense of divine providence, close friends variously characterized it as anything from Episcopalian to deist. Nothing in that range would satisfy a Seceder. Still battling Simpson when the Seceders showed up, Washington was in no mood to extend Christian charity to a band of self-righteous freeloaders. They had caught him on a bad day and, with the matter unresolved, would have to continue the conversation at Miller's Run.

Washington reached Miller's Run by week's end, but he put off meeting with the Seceders. "Being Sunday," he wrote in a diary entry that questioned the religiosity of anyone who disregarded property rights, "and the People living on my land, *apparently* very religious, it was thought best to postpone going among them till tomorrow." He later characterized them as "willful and obstinate Sinners" for "persevering . . . in a design to injure" him.[32] Inventorying the tract prior to the meeting, Washington identified fourteen separate Seceder households and listed the buildings, fencing, and acreage under cultivation of each. He found these farms in better condition than those on his other tracts, which impressed him.

When the two sides finally met on Monday, both asserted their right to the land. Such conflicts were common on the frontier. At the time, claimants to undeveloped land could base their rights either on a government grant, survey, and some improvement, or on occupancy, whichever happened first. Washington and most speculators used the former method; the Seceders and many other frontiersmen used the latter. For the Miller's Run tract, Washington had purchased a warrant issued to a soldier in payment for service in the French and Indian War, then hired a local agent, William Crawford, to survey the land in 1771 and to build a small cabin on it in 1772. The tract being otherwise empty, the Seceders moved onto it in 1773 and claimed the land by occupancy. Crawford told Washington about them but, at least once the war began, he could do little about it.

At a raucous confrontation on Monday, Washington insisted that the Seceders lease the land from him. They refused but offered to pay a modest price for it "to avoid contention."[33] Washington favored renting over selling his frontier property because he wanted to oversee its development. In this, he acted the part of a traditional English country gentleman tending his estate. Some Virginians still followed this model, but it was giving way to the practice of buying, dividing, and selling frontier tracts. Washington dismissed the new approach as rank speculation and always denied being a speculator. "It cannot be laid to my charge that I have been either a monopolizer, or land-jobber, for I never sold a foot of Land in the Country," he wrote in 1786 about his transactions west of the Alleghenys.[34] Washington styled himself a landlord and improver of property.

As the Seceders recounted their hardships in clearing the land and explained their religious convictions against leasing it, Washington softened somewhat. He offered to sell, but the sides could not agree on a fair price. Rather than pay much, the Seceders would fight the validity of Washington's warrant and survey in court. Barely able to control his temper, Washington called each one out and demanded that they individually declare whether they would accept his offer or see him at trial. If he thought that some might yield, then he underestimated the collective mind-set of this sect. "They severally answered that they meant to stand suit," Washington noted.[35] Local legend has him emitting an oath, for which he was fined. One of the Seceders' children later recalled him dangling a silk cloth by its corner and taunting, "Gentlemen, I will have this land just as surely as I now have this handkerchief."[36] Washington devoted considerable time over the next two years to assembling evidence to substantiate his warrant and survey for the tract. Both were shaky. In the end, thanks to a good lawyer, Washington won the case and the Seceders moved on with the frontier. (It did not hurt that the judge hearing the case, Thomas McKean, was a signer of the Declaration of Independence and old friend of Washington's.)

From Miller's Run, Washington planned to proceed southwest to his largest frontier holdings: nearly thirty thousand acres in various tracts near the confluence of the Ohio and Great Kanawha Rivers in what is now West Virginia. This property, which Washington described in 1784 as "rich bottom land, beautifully situated on these rivers & abounding plenteously in Fish, wild fowl, and Game of all kind," was undeveloped.[37] Washington had advertised it for rent earlier in the year and hoped to attract settlement groups, such as religious societies or bands of European immigrants, who would enter into long-term leases to develop entire tracts. Cooperative Seceders might do.

Word had spread of danger ahead, however. "The Indians, it is said, were in too discontented a mood, for me to expose myself to their insults," Washington wrote.[38] They were provoked by incursions onto land northwest of the Ohio River, "which they claim as their territory," and by the failure of Congress to negotiate a peace treaty with them following the Revolutionary War.[39]

Two years earlier, while leading an attack on an Indian village northwest of the Ohio, Washington's local agent, William Crawford, was captured, beaten, scalped alive, and slowly roasted to death. "No other than the extremest Tortures which could be inflicted by Savages could, I think, have been expected, by those who were unhappy eno' to fall into their Hands," Washington wrote about Crawford's capture by the Indians.[40] He obviously did not want to suffer a similar fate or risk a possible kidnapping for ransom. Having fought both with and against native tribes during the French and Indian War, Washington always regarded them as barbaric.

At first Washington asked for a military escort from Fort Pitt to his property, which was entirely southeast of the Ohio River. But then he decided to turn back. "I thought it better to return, than to make a bad matter worse by hazarding abuse from the Savages," he explained to General Knox.[41] As it turned out, Washington's new local agent wrote to him afterward, "The Indians by what means I can't say had Intelligence of your Journey and Laid wait for you."[42]

THE TRIP DISORIENTED and disconcerted Washington. It was as if the frontier and its people were conspiring to frustrate his plans. Even before turning back, the cascading setbacks forced him to confront issues in his personal finances and the country's future that he might have put off had he stayed at home.

On a personal level, his plans for a comfortable retirement relied on income from his large land holdings at Washington's Bottom, Miller's Run, and the Great Kanawha. With America supposedly at peace, Washington had gone west to make these three assets profitable in the postwar economy. He found no present potential for revenue from the first, obstinate squatters occupying the second, and hostile native tribes restricting access to the third. Any investor seeking profit on the frontier would face similar obstacles. Removing them, Washington decided, would require government action.

A lack of national power and resources lay at the heart of the matter. Scarcely a year had passed since Britain signed the treaty recognizing American sovereignty over the entire region east of the Mississippi River, south of the Great Lakes, and north of Florida. The British continued to occupy forts in the remote corner of this region northwest of the Ohio River, however, where they traded with the native peoples for furs. Set aside by Britain for those natives under the Proclamation of 1763, this district, later known as the Northwest Territory, remained largely undisturbed by colonists and mostly under the control of pro-British tribes.

With virtually no funds or forces, the United States government was powerless to secure the frontier. Moreover, Virginia ceded its claims over the old Northwest to Congress in 1784, making its defense entirely a national problem. If Congress could open, sell, and settle these lands, it could gain authority and revenue. If not, it risked losing them to a foreign power, and with them America's future. This became Washington's fear.

As he saw it, the danger was not limited to territory northwest of the Ohio River but encompassed the entire frontier. "The Western settlers, (I speak now from my own observation) stand as it were upon a pivot," Washington wrote upon his return from the West; "the touch of a feather, would turn them any way."[43] Spain controlled the mouth of the Mississippi and the trans-Mississippi West, he noted, and settlers could turn toward it for access to trade. Britain controlled the Great Lakes and the St. Lawrence River, offering another option for settlers. Native tribes still occupied most of the territory claimed by the United States west of the Appalachian Mountains.

He detected little loyalty to the United States or any eastern state in the people he encountered on the frontier. "The ties of consanguinity which are weakening every day will soon be no bond," he warned.[44] "If then the trade of that Country should flow through the Mississipi or St Lawrence," Washington cautioned a member of Congress, "if the Inhabitants thereof should form commercial connexions, which lead, we know, to intercourse of other kinds—they would in a few years be as unconnected with us, indeed more so, than we are with South America; and would soon be alienated from us."[45] For the good of the country and his personal financial well-being, Washington concluded, America should secure the frontier. It offered another urgent argument for enhanced national power.

Washington returned from his western journey advocating a policy of staged western development he called "Progressive Seating."[46] In letters to friends in Congress, he warned that, to the "great discontent of the Indians," land speculators were roaming across "the Indian side of the Ohio" marking out and sometimes surveying vast tracts: "fifty, a hundred, and even 500,000 Acres." They, like the frontiersmen whom Washington met, have "no particular predilection for us."[47] Without firm limits, the entire territory could be lost.

Congress should declare all individual claims of settlers northwest of the Ohio "to be null & void," Washington advised, then negotiate with the tribes to open the territory for settlement in stages, leading to the creation of one compact new state at time. "Any person thereafter, who shall presume to mark—Survey—or settle Lands beyond the limits of the New States," he wrote with grim firmness, "shall not only be considered as outlaws, but fit subjects for Indian vengeance." As for the land opened by Congress for settlement, he added, the government should sell it at prices "as would not be too exorbitant & burthensome for real occupiers, but high enough to discourage monopolizers."[48] By keeping these settlements dense, he explained, "Compact and progressive Seating will give strength to the Union; admit law & good government; & federal aides at an early period."[49] In concept if not in detail, Congress incorporated Washington's basic ideas into the Northwest Ordinance of 1785.

Washington's approach to western development aroused opposition. It echoed Britain's notorious Proclamation of 1763, which closed the Ohio Country to settlement in part to keep colonists from spreading beyond the king's reach. That proclamation helped to sow the seed of rebellion, and now the Revolutionary War's leader proposed adopting a modified form of it for similar reasons. He wanted to keep the country together. Even worse, some complained, Washington endorsed a controversial 1785 treaty with Spain closing the Mississippi River to American traffic. The United States should not "push our claim to this navigation," he advised Congressman Richard Henry Lee of Virginia, because trade would link the trans-Appalachian West to Spain. "It is in our interest to let it sleep."

Washington could not fathom why Spain wanted to block the traffic. So long as it did, however, and until the West became strong enough to force a change in policy, he saw an opportunity to unite the country through internal inland trade. In particular, he wrote to the states'-rights-minded Lee, efforts should be made to "open *all* the communications which nature has afforded, between the Atlantic States and the Western Territory, and to encourage the use of them to the utmost."[50] Washington had one such means of communication in mind: Potomac River navigation.

CANALING BECAME THE RAGE in the newly industrializing regions of Great Britain and Western Europe during the 1700s. The economic results were dramatic. Inland market towns located near the source of waterpower or with access to coal, like Manchester and Birmingham in England, exploded into teeming industrial cities producing goods for national and international markets. These expanding centers required a steady flow of raw materials, food, and supplies. In turn, they needed to deliver their products to consumers. During an age before motorized trains and trucks, water transport offered the only realistic option.

Connecting cites situated beyond the reach of navigable water with markets and suppliers necessitated deepening rivers, digging canals, or both. Typically such projects ran along the routes of nonnavigable rivers, using bypass canals with lift locks, dams and gates, or sluices to circumvent rapids and waterfalls or make them passable. Sometimes, builders would dig an entirely new channel next to an existing stream. Quickly becoming a primary means of internal communication and commerce, these overland waterways bound their countries into economic units much tighter than the feudal alliances of counties and shires that marked an earlier era—and made fortunes in the process. Entrepreneurs in the newly independent United States looked on with awe and sought to imitate.

Washington had dreamed of Potomac River navigation long before independence made it a patriotic cause. Not only could such a waterway improve access to his frontier holdings, it would channel western trade through the mouth of the Potomac near his Mount Vernon plantation. Both would increase his wealth. Following independence, he promoted this scheme on public as well as private grounds. But little had actually changed in Washington's thinking about the project since 1754, when he first suggested using the Potomac River to carry supplies for General Braddock's planned assault on French forces in the Ohio Valley. After Braddock opted for land transport, one of Washington's fellow officers in the Virginia militia, George Mercer, began a subscription drive to raise private funds for improving navigation on the river below Cumberland.

This effort made little headway until around 1770, when competing plans surfaced for tackling the river's toughest stretches with sluices, dams, lift locks, and bypass canals. Because the river ran between them, both Virginia and Maryland needed to authorize such developments. And due to the cost, developers asked both colonies to support the effort with funds. As members of its colonial legislature, Washington and Lee sponsored legislation for the project in Virginia; former Maryland governor Thomas Johnson promoted it in his state. With Washington serving as a trustee for the enterprise, construction began on a bypass canal around Little Falls by 1775, before the Revolutionary War intervened to put the entire project on hold. Now he wanted to revive and expand it.

In postwar Virginia, Washington was not alone in dreaming about a waterway connecting East and West by way of the Potomac. Even if they lacked Washington's broad prospective on national unity, many farsighted Virginians hoped to capitalize on the western trade by linking the eastern and western parts of their state, which then reached from the Atlantic Ocean to the Mississippi River. Because of his status as a war hero, Washington clearly would be the project's most effective spokesman and leader.

After consulting with Madison, Jefferson raised the issue in a letter to Washington less than three months after the General's retirement. Jefferson began by making the case for linking the Potomac and Ohio river systems by reiterating what Washington knew: it offered the shortest route from the upper Midwest to the Atlantic of any possible waterway. The most logical alternatives—either down the existing Mississippi River and around the Gulf of Mexico or across New York State on the course later followed by the Erie Canal—were much longer.

"We must," Jefferson wrote to Washington on behalf of all Virginians, "in our own defense endeavor to share as large a portion of this modern source of wealth & power that [is] offered to us from the Western country." He then asked the key question. "You have retired from public life," Jefferson wrote, "but would the superintendence of this work break too much on the sweets of retirement & repose?" Stressing the project's significance for Virginia and the West, Jefferson exclaimed, "What a monument of your retirement would it be!"[51]

Washington needed little encouragement. He wrote back with the next post, "My opinion coincides perfectly with yours respecting the practicability of an easy & short communication between the waters of the Ohio & Potomack, of the advantages of that communication & the preference it has over *all* others." Further, he added the patriotic argument for the effort by noting "the immense advantages which this Country would derive from the measure." If the "undertaking could be made to comport with those ideas," Washington stated, and "not interfere with" either his "other plans" or his retirement from public life, he would accept a leadership role in the project.[52] He viewed it as a major, and perhaps the final, public endeavor of his career.

At the time, no one knew if navigation could be extended beyond Cumberland along one of the Potomac River's upland tributaries to a practical overland portage for reaching a navigable branch of the Ohio River. Accurate maps of the upper Potomac and Ohio river systems did not exist. Accordingly, on the outbound leg of his western journey in September 1784, Washington asked people along the way about the headwaters of the Potomac and the Ohio, and where the two river systems came closest together. Although their answers often conflicted, he carefully recorded them in the hope of later determining the best transit route.

To reach his frontier holdings, however, Washington's party left the Potomac River at Cumberland and followed Bradford's overland road into the Ohio Valley. His travels cut short before reaching his property on the Great Kanawha, Washington decided to salvage what he could of the trip by leaving the known roads and working his way back home through uncharted wilderness in search of waterways. On a journey undertaken with the levelheaded purpose of inspecting his frontier land holdings, Washington abruptly transformed the return leg into a starry-eyed hunt for possible water routes.

A gray-haired retired general, America's leading citizen set off on September 22 from his land at Washington's Bottom for a ten-day cross-country trek across an unknown and unmarked route. He traveled light. Sending back most of his supplies and attendants with James Craik over the conventional route, Washington headed on horseback into the wilds with only his nephew, perhaps an attendant or two, and at times a local guide. Stands of white oak mainly covered the rocky hillsides. Washington noted, "In places there are Walnut and Crab tree bottoms, which are very rich."[53] At some points the travelers followed broad trails cut by wandering herds of buffalo that still populated the region; at others, they simply bushwhacked. For directions, the small party turned to the local wisdom of settlers living in isolated cabins scattered along the way, who often offered conflicting advice about the best way to go. It was a final wilderness expedition by a man who had spent much of his youth surveying the frontier.

The rain continued off and on throughout the trip, making the way miserable. Over six feet tall, broad in the hips, and riding high on his great horse, Washington continually pushed through wet branches that soaked him to the bone. The route went over ridges, through glades, and across rivers, with the party covering roughly thirty-five miles per day in a southerly direction. Even though Washington rarely complained about physical hardships in his diary, he did observe at one point that the aptly named "Briery Mountains" were "intolerable" to cross.[54] Traveling without a tent in a region lacking taverns or public houses, the party ate and slept in private homes if possible, or outside if not.

Imagine the surprise of isolated settlers when the legendary general appeared unannounced at their door in the backwoods. They could never have expected, nor would ever forget, the encounter. At one remote cabin, Washington noted, "we could get nothing for our horses, and only boiled Corn for ourselves." Still, it was better than the previous night, when he reported that he slept in a damp meadow "with no other shelter or cover than my cloak and was unlucky enough to have a heavy shower of Rain."[55]

On September 29, having reached the South Branch of the Potomac, which he had planned to follow north to rejoin Craik and the rest of his party on the main road, Washington again made a sudden decision to go his own way. Sending his nephew north to tell Craik to proceed without him, Washington continued south over the next ridge to the Shenandoah Valley and then turned east across the Blue Ridge at Swift Run Gap to the Piedmont and home. Following this course enabled Washington to inquire about a rival route, favored by some Virginians, for a western navigation along the James River. That waterway rises in the central Appalachians, cuts through the Blue Ridge above Lynchburg, and winds through Richmond and Williamsburg before reaching the sea at Norfolk. Already committed to the Potomac route, Washington found that the James River offered inferior passage to the Ohio.

For much of this final portion of his trip, Washington traveled alone or perhaps with a single attendant. Parts of the route had no settlers. Even the settled parts showed the wear of war. He described some lodgings as "pitiful" and grumbled about frequently losing his way.[56]

Nevertheless, the time alone gave him a chance to reflect. "Tho' I was disappointed in one of the objects which induced me to undertake this journey namely to examine into the situation, quality, and advantages of the Land which I hold upon the Ohio and Great Kanhawa," Washington wrote in a long entry near the end of his travel diary, "I am well pleased with my journey, as it has been the means of my obtaining a knowledge of the . . . temper and disposition of the Western Inhabitants."

Despite their indolence and isolation, Washington noted, these settlers could be brought into the sphere of American commerce and governance by extending "the inland Navigation as far as it can be done with convenience" in their direction. His explorations proved it possible, Washington assured himself, and suggested a plausible route up the Potomac's north branch and across a portage to headwaters of the Ohio on the Cheat River. "The more then the Navigation of the Patomack is investigated, and duly considered, the greater the advantages arising from them appear," Washington concluded. It became his cause.[57]

WITHIN WEEKS OF HIS RETURN to Mount Vernon, Washington sent a shower of letters about Potomac navigation to influential Virginians and Marylanders, beginning with Virginia governor Benjamin Harrison. These letters represented such a turning point in Washington's activities that in 1992 the modern editors of his papers introduced the first of them with the comment that it "marks his return to public life."[58] In this set of letters, Washington boasts of the profits that would flow from western navigation, warns of losing the West without it, and reports on his findings about the feasibility of using a Potomac River route. Unabashedly appealing to the nationalistic concern that largely moved him, he hailed Potomac River navigation as "the cement of interest, to bind all parts of the Union together by indissoluble bonds—especially that part of it, which lies immediately west of us."[59] Washington was careful not to disparage the James River alternative, however, because he could ill afford to alienate the powerful interests in Richmond favoring that rival route. He needed their support for state legislation incorporating and perhaps funding a Potomac navigation company. Washington felt so confident in his project that he did not care if canaling also went forward along the James River route.

At the time, Americans looked askance at private corporations because they enabled investors to limit personal liability for business debts and actions. Entrepreneurs, most Americans believed, should pay their obligations like everyone else or go to debtor's prison. No less a patriot than Robert Morris, the financier of the American Revolution, would land in prison after a particularly spectacular business failure in 1798. Laws providing for the forgiveness of debts through bankruptcy did not yet exist. Virginia, Maryland, and most other states only permitted the formation of corporations for public purposes—such as toll roads, bridges, and canals—but the state's legislature had to approve each one individually. Corporations must serve the people, Americans thought.

Washington did not want to go to prison if his navigation project defaulted on its debts, of course, so he needed Virginia and Maryland to incorporate a limited-liability company for it. That concern stood foremost in his mind when he initially wrote to Jefferson that he would consider leading the project only if doing so would not conflict with "that line of conduct with which I mean to glide gently down the stream of life."[60] Negotiating a satisfactory arrangement with two states would give Washington an object lesson in the value of assigning control over interstate commerce to the national government.

Pennsylvania posed another problem. While the Potomac segment of the proposed transit fell entirely in Virginia and Maryland, the trans-Appalachian portion to the Ohio River passed through Pennsylvania. Led by Morris, Philadelphia business leaders wanted to open the Schuylkill and Susquehanna Rivers for navigation, which would funnel western trade through their city. They could restrict the western reach of Potomac River navigation by having Pennsylvania bar the transit of goods across its land. "How an application to [the Pennsylvania] Legislature would be relished," Washington wrote in his initial letter to Harrison, "I will not undertake to decide; but of one thing I am almost certain, such an application would place that body in a very delicate situation."[61]

Accordingly, in subsequent letters about the project, Washington focused on the Potomac part and assumed that westerners would take care of the rest. In a private note, he even sketched out how, with two portages, they could get from the Ohio to the Potomac without passing through Pennsylvania. "Weak as they are at present, they would meet us half way," Washington wrote of westerners. "This is no Utopean Scheme," he affirmed. "It wants but a beginning."[62] Despite this boast, without one government possessing authority over interstate commerce, local interests could raise as many obstacles to Washington's project as the Great Falls of the Potomac did.

WITH A ROUGH PLAN IN MIND, Washington turned to getting approval from the Virginia and Maryland legislatures for a private toll route on the Potomac. To display support and obtain investors, an open invitation went out to "Gentlemen" of both states to attend a meeting on November 15, 1784, in Alexandria to discuss the project. "The objects of this meeting," the notice explained, "will be to form a company, and determine on the propriety of preferring a petition to their respective Assemblies, praying to be incorporated and favoured with such immunities, as to them may seem proper for such an undertaking."[63]

The results of this meeting delighted Washington. Not only did it attract a sizable number of potential investors, but they sent petitions to both legislatures urging the formation of a navigation company. Reflecting the same sense of national purpose that motivated Washington in pushing for the project, one newspaper account of the meeting noted, "The work of the Navigation of the Potomack is, perhaps, a Work of more political than commercial Consequences, as it will be one of the grandest Chains for preserving the federal Union." Also in accord with Washington's thinking, the newspaper added, "The Commerce and Riches, that must of Necessity pour down upon us, are too obvious to mention."[64] In this vein, in a letter to Madison discussing the meeting and responses to it, Washington made an observation that revealed much about his view of people and society: "The motives which predominate most in human affairs is self-love and self-interest."[65] In Washington's mind, the Potomac River project was a viable and worthwhile enterprise precisely because it benefited private investors and the country as a whole. That was how he had seen the American Revolution and that would be how he would see the Constitution: viable and worthwhile because they served both common and individual interests.

If Washington had any doubts about his political clout, the next few weeks should have put them to rest. At the time of the Alexandria meeting, both the Virginia and Maryland legislatures were in session. Washington shuttled between them. Despite resistance in Virginia from interests favoring a James River route and in Maryland from interests favoring navigation on the Susquehanna River to Baltimore, he got his way.

When it looked like the two states might pass different bills, and thus not create a single company, Washington urged that they appoint commissioners to agree on terms. "This would prevent dissimilar proceedings, as unproductive as no bill—save time—and bring matters at once to the point," he wrote to Madison on December 3.[66] No sooner asked than done. Virginia tapped Washington and two others. Maryland named an all-star delegation that included three signers of the Declaration of Independence and a Revolutionary War general.

Washington chaired the meetings, which quickly produced a bill granting everything he wanted. Each state legislature then passed the bill within days of receiving it. Under Washington's leadership, an issue that had languished in these two frequently feuding assemblies for more than a decade blew threw them both in less than two months. By the first week of 1785, the Potomac Company was chartered in both states. Each state also bought shares in the company and set aside funds to build the portage road.

With Washington drumming up interest, private funds flowed into the new company. He enthusiastically hyped the investment. "Men who can afford to lay a little while out of their money," he wrote to one potential investor, "are laying the foundation of the greatest returns of any speculation I know of in the world."[67] At the outset of the subscription campaign, he even wrote to Robert Morris—the richest person he knew but also the sponsor of a rival project—touting the benefits of investing in the Potomac Company. "I would hazard all the money I could raise upon the navigation of the [Potomac] river," Washington advised him. "I have no idea of a better opening . . . to make a fortune."[68] While Morris wisely declined and pushed on with his own project, others opened their purses.

Within six months, Washington could claim, "Of the £50,000 Sterling required for the Potomac navigation, upwards of £40,000, was subscribed before the middle of May, & increasing fast."[69] He bought five of the company's five hundred shares and was given fifty more by Virginia. At their first meeting in May, shareholders elected Washington as the company's president and Maryland's Thomas Johnson as its vice president.

For Washington, the presidency of the Potomac Company became a consuming occupation, though one that he pursued while also managing his plantation and investment properties. His retirement became even busier than before. "The earnestness with which he espouses the undertaking is hardly to be described," Madison commented about Washington's work for the Potomac Company, "and shows that a mind like his . . . cannot bear a vacancy."

Washington threw himself into deciding between cutting sluices through rapids or digging bypass canals around them, hiring supervisors and workers, and even overseeing the means of operation. On field trips, he frequently canoed down the river's wildest rapids in search of the best place for a channel or to inspect work in progress. "Retirement from the public walks of life has not been so productive of the leisure & ease as might have been expected," Washington wryly remarked to Benjamin Franklin.[70]

By the fall of 1785, when Washington sent this remark to Franklin, the company had separate teams of about fifty workers each cutting navigable channels through two of the Potomac's major rapids. The task involved blasting, digging, and pulling out rocks and boulders—and could be dangerous. Some men were blown to bits; many quit.

The company initially used newly arrived indentured servants from Europe for unskilled jobs, but so many of them ran away or died that it increasingly turned to black slaves. No free Americans wanted to do this work on the company's terms, but slaves eventually got it done. One of them, George Pointer, later recalled, "Yearly in the month of October, General Washington would come to view the progress of the works, and well I recall that at every Squad of workmen he passed, he would give a dollar to."[71] Later, the company turned to constructing bypass canals with lift locks around the river's two biggest falls.

Progress was sluggish, though: too slow for Washington. "In a boat we passed down the Seneca [rapids] to the place where the workmen were blowing Rocks," he wrote in one diary entry. "To me it seemed as if we had advanced but little, owing to the fewness, and sickliness of the hands."[72] Still, Washington remained optimistic about the project. During this period, visitors to Mount Vernon often commented that he would talk about little else. "The General sent the bottle about pretty freely after dinner, and gave success to the navigation of the Potomac for his toast, which he has very much at heart," one guest recalled. "When once he has begun anything, no obstacle or difficulty can come in his way."[73]

In fact, in his work on Potomac River navigation, Washington had more success moving human obstacles than physical ones. The project was far from finished in 1789, when he resigned as the Potomac

Company's president to take the helm of the new American government, and the completed waterway never fulfilled his hopes for it. No one made a fortune on Potomac Company stock; the Erie Canal became the main waterway to and from the West; railroads soon replaced canals in linking the union. Intractable physical impediments, like sheer falls, shallow rapids, and steep slopes, doomed Washington's grand vision for Potomac navigation.

Yet if he could not move mountains, the project proved he could move men. Before he stepped down, Washington followed up on his initial success in getting the company incorporated and funded, with a singular triumph in clearing away political obstacles to its operation through the adoption in 1785 of the landmark Potomac River Compact.

THE PROSPECT OF COMMERCIAL TRAFFIC on the Potomac brought to the fore long-simmering jurisdictional disputes between Virginia and Maryland. Under their colonial charters, Maryland claimed the river, but Virginia controlled its southern bank. The waterway might obscure or alter the boundary. Certainly it would cross it. Further, under the Articles of Confederation, each state was a republic unto itself. It could have its own rules and regulations, taxes and tariffs, and currency. Some states levied imposts on goods from other states. Unless the states cooperated, traveling along an interstate boundary like the Potomac River could impose problems for people and products.

Dealers in goods and services found it easier to stay in one state whenever possible. This situation hobbled the development of national markets even as it protected local businesses from interstate competition. So long as states remained sovereign over commerce, their lawmakers could regulate trade in ways that favored their state over the nation.

Late in 1784, Virginia and Maryland appointed commissioners to address political barriers to Potomac River commerce. They convened for a week of meetings at Alexandria on March 20, 1785, in the midst of a bitter early-spring snow squall. Ever watchful over matters impacting the Potomac Company, Washington soon invited them to move their deliberation to the warmth of nearby Mount Vernon.

A gracious and interested host who liberally lubricated his guests with good wine, Washington made sure that the commissioners reached agreement on critical matters of tolls, tariffs, and trade. They also agreed on shared contributions for navigational aids, common fishing rights, and cooperation in protecting travelers and prosecuting piracy. Virginians gained free access to a river formally within Maryland's domain. Recognizing that "it wou'd be of great Convenience to the Commerce & Dealings between the Citizens of the two States," the commissioners even recommended that coins "shou'd pass at the same Value" in Maryland and Virginia.[74]

The legislatures of both states ratified the thirteen clauses of this so-called Mount Vernon Compact—though not without some opponents objecting that, under the Articles of Confederation, Congress must approve any "treaty" between individual states. Madison served as floor manager for the compact in the Virginia legislature and received credit for its passage. Inspired by Washington's national vision, historian Joel Achenbach observed, "[t]he two states realized that this was not a zero-sum world after all."[75] Both could benefit from interstate cooperation, and those benefits could multiply if more states participated.

"We are either a United people, or we are not," Washington wrote to Madison shortly before Virginia's approval of the compact, and "if the former, let us, in all matters of general concern act as a nation."[76] Only a national government responding to constituent concerns from across the country could do so, he believed. State governments inevitably represented state interests.

Emboldened by this success, and allegedly at Washington's urging, Madison promptly called for a second convention on interstate commercial relations. At the time, trade disputes like those dividing Maryland and Virginia afflicted many states. Pennsylvania, Delaware, and New Jersey battled over their respective rights to use the Delaware River, for example, while New York, New Jersey, and Connecticut clashed over tariffs imposed by New York on goods entering New York Harbor bound for neighboring states and from those states entering New York. Within days after Virginia approved the Mount Vernon Compact, Madison proposed that its legislature authorize a general meeting on commercial regulations with delegates from all the states. Accordingly, in January 1786, Virginia issued a formal call for other states to send delegates to a convention at Annapolis in September authorized to consider "the trade and commerce of the United States [and] to consider how far an uniform system in their commercial intercourse and regulations might be necessary to their common interest and permanent harmony."[77] Pennsylvania, New York, New Jersey, and Delaware joined Virginia in sending delegates to Annapolis under these terms. In their resolutions, these five states differed only on whether the states or Congress had the ultimate authority to implement any resulting agreements.

Twelve delegates from these states assembled in Annapolis on September 11, 1786, including Madison and Governor Edmund Randolph of Virginia, John Dickinson representing Delaware, and Hamilton from New York. Four other states appointed delegates but they had not yet arrived and no one in Annapolis knew if they were coming. Four states did not name delegates. Those present chose Dickinson, an ardent nationalist with strong ties to Pennsylvania as well as Delaware, as the convention's chair, but they knew that they could not proceed with delegates from so few states. The issue over whether Congress or the states had authority over interstate compacts hung over their deliberations. If Congress needed to approve their work, the delegates feared, then nothing could get done anyway.

Further complicating matters, the proposed treaty with Spain had exploded over the right of Americans to use the Mississippi River. Spain, which controlled the river's mouth and western bank, wanted it closed; westerners and southerners demanded it open; northerners and easterners cared most about access to Spanish ports in the Americas. To the detriment of American trade with Spanish America, the dispute over using the Mississippi had stalled treaty negotiations between the two nations for years.

Only days before the Annapolis Convention, over the howls of southern members, Congress voted, seven states to five, to authorize Foreign Affairs Secretary John Jay to accept Spain's terms on the Mississippi. Treaty proponents argued that the United States lacked power to negotiate a better deal. Its opponents suspected that the northern states might be just as happy if closing the Mississippi inhibited development in the South and West. Indeed, some southerners saw it as a blatant attempt to use congressional authority over treaties for sectional advantage. They wanted to bring Congress into the negotiations and enforce a two-thirds rule for approving treaties. The Mississippi question and congressional power over treaties, already on the table because of their relationship to interstate commerce, became major issues at Annapolis. The treaty threatened to split the union, its opponents charged, and lose the West. Ultimately, Congress rejected the treaty.

Even before the delegates met, Madison, Hamilton, and other nationalists thought that any convention limited to commercial issues could not resolve the problems facing America, especially since, under the Articles of Confederation, Congress and all the states would need to approve whatever it did. Congress, they maintained, was part of the problem. It represented state rather than national interests. Only a thorough revision of the Articles, drafted by a specially called convention and ratified in a manner that would neither have to pass Congress nor require the approval of every state, could achieve the desired results. Nationalists in attendance wanted this first meeting to serve mainly as a prelude to a second one that, a month before going to Annapolis, Madison depicted as "a plenipotentiary convention for mending the Confederation."[78] As amended, they wanted that new constitution to establish a national government rather than a league of sovereign states. In fact, Hamilton had come to this view much earlier. As a twenty-five-year-old army officer in 1780, he had privately dismissed the Articles of Confederation as inadequate; suggested granting Congress supreme authority over such national matters as commerce, finance, and the military; and urged creating strong executive offices.

"By a plan of this kind, we should blend the advantages of a monarchy and a republic," Hamilton had written in 1780. He even had proposed calling a convention to draft it.[79] Now others were coming around to his point of view.

When the Annapolis meeting failed to attract delegates from enough states to proceed, and so could not achieve even its limited goals, Hamilton proposed that those present simply call for a second convention and go home. All told, the delegates met for only three days. Their closing resolution, drafted by Hamilton and approved by the delegates on September 14, urged their states to "use their endeavors to procure the concurrence of the other States, in the appointment of Commissioners, to meet at Philadelphia on the second Monday in May next, to take into consideration the situation of the United States, to devise such further provisions as shall appear to them necessary to render the constitution of the Federal Government adequate to the exigencies of the Union."[80] This proposed conclave, its proponents hoped, would be a true constitutional convention.

Some already charged that the Annapolis meeting could have attracted more delegates and achieved more results if Washington had participated, as he had for the Mount Vernon Compact. The challenge for nationalists now became getting him to Philadelphia in 1787 for the proposed grand convention.

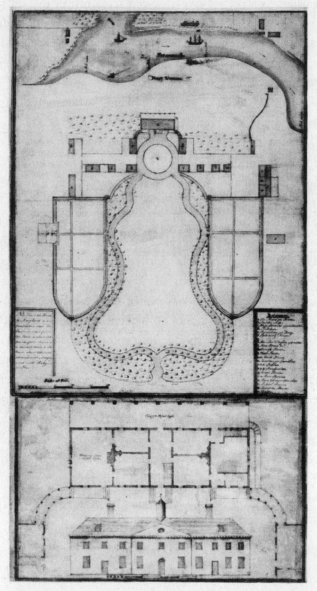

1787 diagram of the main house at Mount Vernon and its west lawn and gardens.

CHAPTER 3

To Go or Not to Go

JOHN JAY WAS a conservative revolutionary with nationalist leanings and close ties to Washington. In his politics, Jay represented but one faction within the internecine labyrinth of New York society. At the time, no other state was more divided than New York. Those splits dated from the late 1600s, when British conquerors imposed their rule over the Dutch patroons who had already established themselves in Manhattan and the Hudson Valley. Attracted by a spectacular natural harbor, rich farmland, and ethnic diversity, immigrants from other European countries and colonies soon joined the mix. And so many settlers brought or imported African slaves that by 1700 New York had more blacks than any other northern colony. In the resulting scramble for position, money and power mattered most. As the fair-haired child of a union between the son of a rich merchant of French Huguenot descent and the daughter of New York City's ethnically Dutch mayor, Jay had both. Educated at New York's King's College and trained in law, he was destined for a prominent role in society and government.

New York's political divisions became readily apparent during the Revolutionary War when the city remained the last stronghold of British rule in the colonies, even as radical patriots under Governor George Clinton ruled in Poughkeepsie. The state's delegation to the Continental Congress was so split, and its instructions were so indecisive, that it abstained on the epic vote for independence—the only delegation to do so. As a leading member of that divided delegation, Jay supported vigorous resistance to oppressive British laws but worked closely with Pennsylvania delegate John Dickinson to forestall a formal declaration of independence. Writing to John Adams, Jefferson would later recall of that historic time, "There you and I were together, and the Jays, and the Dickinsons, and the other anti-independents were arrayed against us. They cherished the monarchy of England; and we the rights of our countrymen."[1]

Once the die was cast, however, Jay sided with the patriots even as his brother backed the British. Linked by marriage to the powerful and wealthy Livingston clan of New Jersey and New York, Jay was elected president of the Continental Congress in 1778 and secretary of foreign affairs for the Confederation Congress in 1784. Between holding these two quasi-executive posts, he served as an American ambassador in Europe and helped to negotiate the treaty ending the war.

Jay experienced the central government's weakness firsthand while serving in all these positions. It particularly frustrated him as foreign affairs secretary. In dealing with Spain without an American army to strengthen his hand, for example, Jay was forced to concede closing the Mississippi River to American commerce in return for opening ports in the Spanish Caribbean—leading to charges that he had sacrificed the interests of western settlers to those of northeast shipowners. Further, he could not cajole Britain to abide by its treaty obligation to evacuate forts in the Northwest Territory so long as Congress remained powerless to force states and individuals to return property taken from Tories during the American Revolution as mandated by the same treaty. Indeed, some states continued to take Tory property after the war. To Jay—a devout Anglican by choice despite his French and Dutch Calvinist religious heritage—property rights, whether British or American, were sacrosanct.

Beyond his former loyalty to the British cross and crown, Jay's gravest hesitation about the Revolutionary War was that, by over-turning established authority, it might unleash leveling forces and lead to mob rule. Tall and thin with a high chin and hawk nose that made him appear to gaze down on others, Jay looked as much like an aristocrat as he acted. He increasingly felt that status imperiled by the rising tide of majority rule.

His every experience and instinct pushed Jay toward supporting a strong national government to right the situation. By 1786, with the rabble-rousing Clinton still ruling over New York, established property rights under assault from democratic factions in some states, and Congress unable to defend America's place on the world's stage, Jay grew ever more anxious for constitutional reform. He wrote to Jefferson in that year, "If faction should long bear down law and gov-ernment, tyranny may raise its head, or the more sober part of the people might even think of a King."[2] Only a balanced national gov-ernment with authority to protect property and project power could steer a republican middle course between democratic tyranny and monarchic rule, Jay believed.

And only George Washington, Jay thought, commanded suffi-cient popular respect to lead Americans to adopt and implement such a regime. Like other nationalists, he rallied around the General.

Even before the failed Annapolis Convention met in September 1786, Jay sent a desperate appeal to Washington begging him to emerge from his retirement long enough to back a more ambi-tious effort for constitutional reform than was already on the table. "Experience has pointed out Errors in our national Government, which call for Correction, and which threatened to blast the Fruit we expected from our 'Tree of Liberty,'" Jay warned. Although the Annapolis Convention might do some good in commercial matters, he wrote in March 1786, "an opinion begins to prevail that a general convention for revising the articles of Confederation would be expedient. Whether the People are yet ripe for such a Measure, or whether the System proposed to be attained by it, is only to be expected from Calamity & Commotion, is difficult to ascertain." To save "the Sovereignty and Independence which Providence has enabled You to be so greatly & gloriously instrumental in securing," Jay implored in a calculated reference to Washington's legacy, if a general convention is called, "I am fervent in my Wishes, that it may comport with the Line of Life you have marked out for yourself, to favor your country with your counsels on such an important & single occasion."[3]

Washington surely knew that, to make a difference, he could not come out of retirement simply for a single occasion. If he participated in a general convention to reform the national constitution, he would have to see the matter through or watch it fail. Further, even Jay conceded that the time might not yet be ripe for constitutional reform, and Washington did not want to expend his political capital prematurely. Franklin, he worried, had done just that by agreeing to become Pennsylvania's president in 1785, when its radically democratic constitution began running amok.[4] Any successful effort to reform the national government likely would need the combined support of Washington and Franklin, its advocates realized, and could scarcely afford any diminution in either man's prestige.

Thus, Washington put Jay off.

"I coincide perfectly in sentiments with you, my dear sir, that there are errors in our National Government which call for correction," Washington replied to Jay in May 1786, "but my fear is that the people are not yet sufficiently misled to retract from error!" Washington blamed the situation on ignorance among the people regarding the dangers to freedom and property from the excesses of democracy and wickedness by some who sought to take advantage of those excesses. "Ignorance & design are difficult to combat," he wrote. "Out of these proceed illiberality, *improper* jealousies, and a train of evils which oftentimes, in republican governments, must be sorely felt before they can be removed." Conceding that "something must be done, or the fabric must fall," Washington remained uncertain if the time had come to act. "I scarcely know what opinion to entertain of a general Convention," he cautioned Jay. "That it is necessary to revise, and amend the articles of Confederation, I entertain *no* doubt; but what may be the consequences of such an attempt *is* doubtful."

Washington preferred to wait until the calamitous consequences of the current course became clear to all people of goodwill. "Virtue, I fear, has, in a great degree, taken its departure from our Land, and the want of disposition to do justice is the source of the national embarrassments," he concluded.[5]

THE ANXIETY OVER CONSTITUTIONAL REFORM reflected in this exchange between an aristocratic New Yorker and a Virginia planter betrayed far more fundamental concerns than mere fears of losing the West, simple hopes for a national market economy, and plain desires to repay government creditors, though those issues certainly weighed heavily on both men. Their letters spoke in terms of calamity and commotion, loss of public virtue and disposition to do justice, and breakdown of the social fabric under the excesses of majority faction. Liberty itself was at risk, both men declared, much as it had been in 1776—but this time the threat came from within, which made it worse.

"Our affairs seem to lead to some crisis—some Revolution—something that I cannot foresee," Jay wrote back to Washington. "I am uneasy and apprehensive—more so than during the War."[6] Everything secured in the war was at risk, he warned.

Unlike the crisis leading up to the Revolutionary War, which exploded with the Battles of Lexington and Concord and had a single foreign source, the angst that bubbled over in these letters had built gradually in reaction to a pattern of perceived domestic abuses. "We are going and doing wrong, and therefore I look to Evils and Calamities," Jay wrote.[7] Oversimplified into single words, some blamed "democracy" for the country's woes; others blamed "debt." Jay blamed both.

To finance the Revolutionary War, Congress and the states had run up massive foreign and domestic debts that now, with peace, were falling due. Although some states had less debt or more resources than others, all of them at least had the power to tax citizens and impose tariffs to finance past debts and fund current services. Congress did not. It lacked the means to pay even interest on its debt, much less repay principal.

During a period of nationalist ascendancy from 1781 to 1783, Congress made two attempts to get the general government's fiscal house in order by passing measures to impose a 5 percent duty on imported goods—the first would have been collected by national agents; the second, in a concession to the states, would have been collected by state agents and transferred to Congress. Under the Articles of Confederation, however, all thirteen states needed to approve any national tax and neither plan gained universal assent. Congress was forced to rely on requisitions from the states, which often went unpaid.

In a 1786 letter to Jay, Washington lamented, "Requisitions are a perfect nihility where thirteen sovereign, independent, disunited States are in the habit of discussing & refusing compliance with them at their option."[8] Most of the nation's war-related debts were owed to Americans, however, and represented the collective obligations of all the states. If Congress failed to repay them, then the states could step in to take care of their own citizens and, by doing so, supplant Congress in the hearts, minds, and wallets of their people.

The scheme was simple and the results potentially debilitating for the national government. In every state, Congress owed money to public creditors: persons holding bonds or other securities issued during the war for money, goods, or services. Many of these securities, which originally went to a large number of lenders, suppliers, and veterans, had passed into the hands of a small number of speculators, who purchased them at a discount. In turn, the states owed annual requisitions to Congress and public creditors owed taxes to their states.

So long as Congress was unable to pay public creditors, the states could accept national securities from their citizens as payment for state taxes and apply them at face value toward their requisitions. Congress was obligated to use most of its revenue for debt financing anyway. By inserting itself as a middleman between Congress and public creditors, a state could ensure that its requisitions went to its own citizens rather than being distributed among foreign and domestic public creditors generally. Of course, if states accepted securities at face value for tax payments, speculators who purchased them at discount would stand to gain. Those speculators and their allies in government became the principal supporters of the scheme in many states. For them, it was profitable; for the states, it was efficient; for Congress, it was disastrous.

Congress might object to states meeting their requisitions by offsetting debt obligations rather than remitting hard money, but it could do little about it since many states did not pay their full requisitions and specie was scarce. The power to tax is the power to rule, every nationalist knew. Without it, Congress had to take what it could get from the states, and it was rarely hard money. One reckoning put the total amount of cash turned over to Congress by the states during the period from October 1786 to March 1787 at $663, or a mere 2 percent of the August 1786 requisition.[9]

EVER SINCE THE WAR BEGAN, hard money in the form of internationally accepted gold and silver coins had been in short supply throughout the states. At the time, Americans relied on other countries for specie, with Spain's gold dollar being especially popular. As these coins passed overseas to pay for imported goods and repay foreign loans, Congress tried to make up the deficit by printing paper dollars, called "Continentals," but stopped in 1779 after their value collapsed. By 1781, a Continental was worth half a cent and even Congress refused to take them.[10] During the war, state-issued paper money did not fare much better. Most suffered hyperinflation. People wanted hard money or paper backed by something of more certain value than a shaky government's doubtful promises. The states moved in to fill this monetary vacuum.

The attack on Congress's control over the national debt and money supply began in Pennsylvania, which had the country's most democratic state constitution. Adopted in the revolutionary fervor of 1776, less than three months after the Declaration of Independence, Pennsylvania's constitution abolished property qualifications for voting, established a one-house legislature with all seats elected annually, and gutted traditional checks and balances by having the state president, Supreme Executive Council, and judges appointed by the legislature for short terms and removable at will. More than in any other state, the people ruled in Pennsylvania—but they did so as a majority faction that was sensitive to shifts in popular opinion.

In 1782, when an all-but-bankrupt Congress stopped paying interest on its domestic debt, Pennsylvania began issuing state certificates of interest on that debt to public creditors in its state in place of the unpaid interest. It then credited these certificates toward its requisition instead of paying hard money to Congress. Once a certificate was issued, Congress no longer owed the interest covered by it, but Congress also stopped receiving the hard cash that it needed to pay its other creditors or fund ongoing operations. Further, until redeemed by the state, the certificates circulated as a form of paper money within Pennsylvania. This stimulated the cash-strapped local economy, which was depressed due to the lack of hard money and the collapse of other forms of paper money. The certificates retained value because Pennsylvania accepted them in payment of state taxes.

As Pennsylvania's Franklin famously observed during the 1780s, "in this world nothing can be said to be certain, except death and taxes."[11]

Emboldened by Pennsylvania's example, other states quickly adopted, adapted, or expanded on the scheme. New Hampshire and New Jersey began offering certificates or "revenue money" for unpaid interest within the year. By 1785, more than half the states had implemented some system of paying interest on their citizens' national securities. Once this ball started rolling, it was hard to stop, especially since it aggrandized the states.

Congress tried twice to regain control of its own debt. In 1784, it offered its own paper certificates, or "indents," in lieu of interest to public creditors, who then could redeem them through the states in payment of state taxes. Seeing nothing in this program for them, most states either refused to implement it or implemented it so poorly that it had little impact. A year later, Congress attempted to bar states from paying their requisitions with state interest certificates, but this backfired badly. Some states ignored the mandate; others, again led by Pennsylvania, got around it by calling in all or part of the national securities held by its citizens and exchanging them for state bonds that paid interest in the form of credits against state tax obligations. The states then fulfilled their requisitions by canceling the interest or principal owed by Congress on these securities.

By 1786, the states had assumed much of the total national debt, with Pennsylvania, New York, and Maryland alone holding nearly one-third of it. Congress was rapidly becoming irrelevant. By replacing state bonds for national securities, the loyalties of public creditors shifted from the nation to the states. And the flood of new state bonds, many of which were issued in small denominations and circulated almost like cash, addressed the urgent economic need for currency without involving Congress.

By 1785, severe deflation in the value of hard money had caused a nationwide recession that a well-regulated emission of paper credit could ameliorate. Many cautious Americans doubted, however, that elected state legislatures could regulate it well. They remembered the inflationary effects of printing too much unbacked paper money during the war. In a June 1786 letter to Washington, Jay described these paper-money skeptics as "the better kind of People—by which I mean the People who are orderly and industrious, who are content with their situations, and not uneasy in their Circumstances." This sort, he warned, "will be led by the Insecurity of Property" resulting from cheap paper money to question republican rule and "prepare their Minds for almost any change that may promise them Quiet & Security."[12] Washington agreed, and found it "much to be feared . . . that the better kind of people" might resort to a monarchy or worse. "We are apt to run from one extreme into another," he wrote back to Jay. "To anticipate & prevent disastrous contingencies would be the part of wisdom & patriotism."[13]

Jay's fears notwithstanding, the benefits from expanding the money supply through state-issued bonds and interest certificates revived popular demands for states to issue more paper money. The wartime experience with hyperinflation, which hit creditors like Washington especially hard, had soured many wealthy Americans on paper money. Having lent out money in pounds sterling prior to the Revolutionary War, for example, Washington was repaid during the war in depreciated paper money worth less than one-fourth its face value—and he never forgot it. In 1786, as demands for paper money grew, Washington depicted the practice of repaying hard cash with inflated paper money as "ungenerous, not to say dishonest." He would not do it to his creditors and did not want his debtors to do it to him. "Paper bills of credit," he complained, give "the shadow for the substance of a debt."[14]

Even less restrained in their words, Jay, James Madison, and many other leading nationalists denounced state-issued paper money in the strongest terms. Arguing against its issuance by his state in 1786, for example, Madison lectured Virginia's legislature that paper money would "destroy confidence between individuals" and "disgrace republican governments in the eyes of mankind."[15] Yet under the Articles of Confederation, Congress was as powerless to prevent states from issuing paper money as it was to stop an incoming tide. Creditors like Washington, who feared that cheap paper money would erode the value of their fixed investments, very much were swimming against that tide in trying to prevent state legislatures from authorizing it. At most, opponents could try to limit its use to paying taxes or have it secured by something of value, such as state-owned land.

The dam broke in 1786, when seven states issued paper money. "Pennsylvania & N. Carolina took the lead in this folly," Madison wrote in August to Jefferson, who was then serving as America's ambassador in Paris. Most of the initial emissions incorporated limits that helped them to hold value at least initially, but in debtor-controlled Rhode Island, which made its paper money legal tender for virtually all public and private debts, the bottom dropped out of the currency's value almost immediately and hard money was driven underground. "Supplies were withheld from the Market, the Shops were shut, popular meetings ensued, and the State remains in a sort of Convulsion," Madison informed Jefferson. "Depreciation is inevitable" in every state with paper money, Madison predicted, yet driven by popular factions, he feared that more states would join others in printing "this fictitious money."[16]

Madison perceived a pattern in the rush to paper. State governments with the fewest checks and balances tended to act first and in the most extreme manner. Pennsylvania and Rhode Island, for example, placed virtually all power in a single legislative chamber, with the executive and the judiciary serving all but at its pleasure. In contrast, Madison observed in his letter to Jefferson, Maryland held back because the state senate—presumably due to the long terms, indirect selection process, and property qualifications for its members—stood as "a bar to paper in that State." But as "the clamor for [paper money] is now universal, and as the periodical election of the Senate happens at this crisis," Madison added with his customary pessimism, Maryland's next senate would likely surrender.[17]

This experience confirmed Madison's view that America needed a balanced national government that could check the power of state excesses and majority factions. From Paris, Jefferson had sent Madison a shipment of treatises on government by European political philosophers, which arrived early in 1786. Now Madison began trolling through them in earnest for arguments in support of his view.

Expressing similar sentiments at the same time, Washington wrote to former congressman Theodorick Bland in August 1786, complaining about "the *present alarming troubles* in Rhode Island."[18] Writing to Jay on the same day, Washington added, "What a triumph for the advocates of despotism to find that we are incapable of governing ourselves, and that systems founded on the basis of equal liberty are merely ideal & fallacious! Would to God that wise measures may be taken in time to avert the consequences we have but too much reason to apprehend."[19]

For nationalists, the failure of paper money in states like Rhode Island and New Jersey became an object lesson in the dangers of excess democracy and a clarion call for a strong central government. Madison asked James Monroe earlier in 1786, "Is it possible with such an example before our eyes of impotency in the federal system, to remain skeptical with regard to the necessity of infusing more energy into it?"[20] Echoing these sentiments in his August letter to Jay, Washington wrote, "I do not conceive we can exist long as a nation, without having lodged somewhere a power which will pervade the whole Union in an energetic a manner." Significantly, he then added, "Retired as I am from the world, I frankly acknowledge I cannot feel myself an unconcerned spectator."[21]

IF WASHINGTON SAW RHODE ISLAND as the specter of democracy run amok, then Massachusetts soon appeared as the reality of it run riot. For him and many fellow nationalists, the debtors' insurrection that engulfed central and western Massachusetts beginning late in 1786 became the fire bell in the night awakening them in terror and calling them back to service.

Washington's exhaustive biographer, James Thomas Flexner, posits that the General first learned of the uprising from a September 23 article in the conservative *Pennsylvania Packet*, one of the many newspapers that he generally read. The article began by lamenting the situation in Rhode Island, where courts reportedly forced creditors to accept hundreds of pounds of paper money in repayment of old debt. "That 'Righteousness exalteth a people,' we believe is rather doubted in that state," the article quoted from Scripture. It then turned to events in Massachusetts, where the legislature had defeated popular proposals to print paper money and the courts strictly enforced obligations to repay debts in hard cash, which, given its shortage, was beyond the means of most debtors.

According to the article, armed bands under the command of former Revolutionary War officers had occupied the courthouses in Concord and Taunton during the September judicial term to stop debt collection and foreclosures. "I am going to give the court four hours to agree to our terms," the leader in Concord purportedly declared, "and if they do not I and my party will force them to it."[22] Both courts closed for the term. They would not meet again until December.

The *Pennsylvania Packet* article did not tell the half of it, but sensational reports soon reached Washington from other sources, filling in some details and exaggerating others. The two courthouse raids mentioned in the article were not the first during the September judicial term. Led by former officers, more than five hundred men from central and western Massachusetts—most of them farmers, many of them veterans, some of them armed—marched in military formation with fife and drum on August 29 to Northampton, where they stopped the court from meeting. Within a week, the scene repeated itself on a smaller scale but with similar results in Worcester. Concord, Taunton, and Great Barrington followed a week later. These raids shuttered most of the county courts west of Boston for the term. In many of the encounters, the local militia refused to defend the courts; in some, militiamen joined the insurrection. Participants included a cross section of the local community. Once the courts closed, the situation quieted down for a season.

As dramatic as they were, these events had precedent. Protests closed courts in many colonies during the years leading up to the American Revolution, and, in various forms, the practice continued after the war. When New Jersey refused to authorize paper money in 1786, for example, protesters blocked creditors' suits throughout the state. Vermonters, then in the process of revolting from New York rule, not only forced out New York judges but established their own hyperdemocratic state and local institutions. Suspicious fires destroyed courts in Washington's own state during the period. All told, historian Woody Holton estimates that debtor and taxpayer groups assaulted courthouses in about half the states.[23] Virtually every state experienced at least some violent resistance to the efforts by sheriffs to execute judgments, foreclose mortgages, or collect taxes.

The court closings in Massachusetts stood out mainly because of their number, extent, and coordination. By October, Washington had become sufficiently concerned about them that he wrote to his former aide, David Humphreys, who then lived in New England. "For Gods sake tell me, what is the cause of all these commotions?" he asked. "Do they proceed from licentiousness, British influence disseminated by the Tories, or real grievances which admit of redress?"[24] The responses that Washington received from his correspondents pointed him toward the first of his proposed answers; newspapers that he read suggested all three; modern historians have favored the last. Regardless of their cause, the commotions sufficiently shocked Washington to set him on the road to Philadelphia.

At the time, Massachusetts had one of the most balanced but least populistic constitutions in the country. Written largely by John Adams and adopted in 1780, it split the legislative power between a lower house that represented population and an upper house that represented wealth; created a powerful governor advised by an elite council; retained property qualifications for voting; and provided for appointed judges and sheriffs. Tilted toward urban eastern interests, the constitution was ratified in an improvised fashion that the state's rural western residents questioned. While John Hancock served as governor and worked to soften the system, these westerners went along. When the hard-line James Bowdoin replaced Hancock in 1785, westerners began to rebel, especially after Bowdoin pushed through a tax hike to pay Congress's oppressive requisition of 1785, which was the first to fund many of the most unpopular wartime debts, including the officers' commuted pensions. Even Madison feared that the requisition would "try the virtue of the States."[25] He was right. Many states refused to pay it in part or in whole, but not Massachusetts. Early in 1786, it imposed new, hard-money taxes on people and property, with revenue going to pay bondholders. After the eastern-dominated state legislature ignored petitions for relief, westerners closed the courthouses in September.

When the insurrection continued into the December judicial term despite political efforts to defuse it, Bowdoin got tough. Bypassing the local militia, which he did not trust, the governor raised private funds to hire a twenty-five-hundred-man army that relentlessly pursued the insurgents, whose largest force was then led by a decorated Revolutionary War captain named Daniel Shays. Singled out for his role in the uprising by its opponents, Shays became the rebellion's public face. On the advice of Secretary of War Henry Knox, the rich and portly Bostonian who had served as Washington's second in command during the Revolutionary War, Congress pitched in by expanding its forces for possible use in Massachusetts. From Congress, Henry Lee informed Washington that some members, "knowing your unbounded influence," wanted him to visit the insurgents and "bring them back to peace."[26] Washington shot back, "Influence is no government. Let us have one by which our lives, liberties, and properties will be secured."[27]

Having inspected some of the trouble spots following the September clashes, Knox took it upon himself to keep Washington apprised of developments in letters that by January arrived at Mount Vernon with every post. "The fine theoretical government of Massachusetts has given way," Knox wrote in a dark October message to Washington that depicted the insurgents as radical levelers who believed Americans should hold property in common and that anyone who "attempts opposition to this creed is an enemy to equality and justice, and ought to be swept from off the face of the earth." Knox estimated that these "desperate & unprincipled men" could field a force of fifteen thousand in New England alone. "Our government must be braced, changed, or altered to secure our lives and property."[28] In his letters, Knox damned these rebels as lawless people who "have never paid any, or but little taxes" and had "little or no property"—a classic European rabble. "Their first acts are to annihilate their courts of Justice, that is private debts. The Second, to abolish the public debt and the third is to have a division of property by means of the darling object of most of the States paper money," Knox added in December.[29]

Washington was horrified. "Good God!" he wrote to Knox, "there are combustibles in every State, which a spark may set fire to."[30] He perceived the country teetering on the brink of anarchy or mob rule.

The insurgency wilted before Bowdoin's army, which marched west from Boston under the command of Revolutionary War general Benjamin Lincoln in mid-January. Desperate for arms to resist the coming assault, the insurgents tried and failed to seize the national armory in Springfield before the army arrived. With the army on its way, they then retreated north to Petersham, where the army surprised and routed them amid a blinding snowstorm on February 4.

Many insurgent leaders fled to Vermont, where they found refuge; a few were caught in Massachusetts and hanged or imprisoned. Hundreds of participants in the insurrection faced indictments;

thousands of them lost the right to vote. In the next election, at least in part as a reaction against these heavy-handed reprisals, Hancock defeated Bowdoin in the contest for governor and Lincoln lost the race for lieutenant governor. The new legislature reduced direct taxes, enacted a moratorium on debts, and cut payments to public creditors. With these reforms, peace returned to Massachusetts.

Despite its outcome, Shays's Rebellion, as it has become known, haunted Washington. Without a strong national government, he feared that similar uprisings could flare up elsewhere. "I am mortified beyond expression whenever I view the clouds which have spread over the brightest morn that ever dawned upon any Country," he wrote Lee at the outset of the disturbances. "Precedents are dangerous things. Let the reins of government be braced in time & held with a steady hand."[31] To Humphreys, Washington later added, "It is but the other day we were shedding our blood to obtain the Constitutions under which we now live—Constitutions of our own choice and framing—and now we are unsheathing the Sword to overthrow them! The thing is so unaccountable, that I hardly know how to realize it."[32] He wondered if Britain secretly might have engineered the uprising in an effort to undermine the states and regain some of them. Certainly Washington worried that any domestic rebels would inevitably seek British aid. He was not alone. Reports circulated widely that British Canada offered asylum to Shays and support to Vermonters in their revolt from New York.

Events in New England caused Washington to doubt whether Americans were capable of self-government. "Who besides a tory could have foreseen, or a Briton predict them!" he wrote to Knox. "Notwithstanding the boasted virtue of America, we are far gone in every thing ignoble & bad."[33] And so to Madison, who was already thinking about a new national political structure, Washington wrote in November, "Thirteen Sovereignties pulling against each other, and all tugging at the federal head, will soon bring ruin to the whole; whereas a liberal, and energetic Constitution, well guarded & closely watched, to prevent incroachments, might restore us to that degree of respectability & consequence, to which we had a fair claim."[34]

Three months after the disturbances died down, Washington wrote to Lafayette about their ongoing impact on the campaign for constitutional reform. "These disorders are evident marks of a defective government," Washington asserted. "Indeed, the thinking part of the people of this Country are now so well satisfied of this fact that most of the Legislatures have appointed, & the rest it is said will appoint, delegates to meet at Philadelphia the second Monday in May next in general Convention of the States to revise, and correct the defects of the federal System."[35]

The Constitutional Convention represented the nationalists' response to Shays's Rebellion—but only in the sense that the uprising served as a critical, and for Washington perhaps an essential, final straw. The call for the convention had come months earlier in response to commercial and revenue concerns that predated the insurgency. Delegates to the failed Annapolis Convention on interstate commerce had issued it in September 1786, and several states had elected delegates before Shays's Rebellion reached a critical point. The paper-money crisis in Rhode Island added further impetus to the reform movement. Then Massachusetts exploded. The question remained: would Washington attend? Many thought that the convention would fail without him. He did not tip his hand to Lafayette.

WASHINGTON PLAYED HAMLET during late 1786 and early 1787 as he agonized over whether to attend the convention. The part came naturally to him. He had never been happier than during the past few years of honored retirement, and he had rarely been healthier. He had much to gain but more to lose by him returning to the public stage. So did the country.

The decision presented Washington with something of a chicken-and-egg dilemma. For his own sake and that of the country, he should not go unless the convention was likely to succeed, and yet it was not likely to succeed unless he went. No easy answer presented itself. Washington brooded over it for months with his most trusted correspondents. Meanwhile, his health deteriorated.

Virginia placed the decision directly on Washington's shoulders and left it there. In November, citing the "crisis" engulfing the confederacy, the state assembly authorized sending delegates to the proposed convention, making Virginia only the second state to do so.[36] A November 8 letter from Madison warned Washington that his name would likely stand atop the delegate list. "It will assist powerfully in marking the zeal of our Legislature, and its opinion of the magnitude of the occasion," Madison explained.[37]

Washington replied by return mail that "it is out of my power to do this" but gave an equivocating reason for his refusal. Given the urgency of revising "the federal System," he wrote, if the legislature asked him to serve as a delegate, he would obey "its call" but for the coincidence that the Society of the Cincinnati was meeting in Philadelphia one week prior to the convention. As a hereditary association of Revolutionary War officers and their eldest male descendants, the Cincinnati had aroused popular ire for its aristocratic pretensions. To distance himself from the society, Washington had announced that, for personal reasons, he could not attend its meeting or accept another term as its president. If he agreed to attend the Philadelphia convention, he could scarcely avoid the Cincinnati. So he must decline both.[38]

Washington's response failed to deter Virginia's general assembly. On December 4, it named him first on a list of delegates that included Madison, Governor Edmund Randolph, and four senior leaders of the American Revolution: Patrick Henry, George Mason, George Wythe, and John Blair. Randolph broke the unwelcome news to Washington in terms clearly calculated to appeal to the General's sense of service. Despite "the storms which threaten the United States," Randolph wrote, the country's "gloomy prospect still admits one ray of hope, that those, who began, carried on & consummated the revolution, can yet rescue America from the impending ruin."[39] Madison followed with a letter explaining why the legislature acted contrary to Washington's request. The convention's "pre-eminence over every other public object" might lead to a change of heart, he wrote, and "the advantage of having your name in the front of the appointment as a mark of the earnestness of Virginia, and an invitation to the most select characters from every part of the Confederacy, ought at all events to be made use of."[40]

These reasons gave Washington pause. In a brief note to Randolph, he expressed his desire to obey "the calls of my Country," but explained that "circumstances"—meaning the Cincinnati— would likely prevent him from attending the convention. He urged that someone "on whom greater reliance can be had" be appointed in his place.[41] Going into more detail about the Cincinnati, he again wrote to Madison, "It would be improper to let my appointment stand in the way of any other."[42]

Washington never flatly declined, however. Randolph took this as a yes, or at least not a no. In a second letter, he entreated Washington "not to decide on a refusal immediately"; let the offer stand. "Perhaps the obstacles, now in view, may be removed, before May," the governor suggested, or by then "every other consideration may seem of little weight, when compared with the crisis, which may then hang over the united states."[43] Taking a similar tact, Madison wrote separately to express his "wish that at least a door could be kept open for your acceptance hereafter, in case the gathering clouds should become so dark and menacing as to supersede every consideration."[44] Washington waited.

Virginia's delegate list had the desired effect. Newspapers throughout the states reprinted it, often with Washington's name in capital letters. When word reached Philadelphia, for example, the *Pennsylvania Herald* commented, "Every true patriot must be pleased with the very respectable delegation appointed by Virginia." Expressing hope "that the assembly of Pennsylvania will appoint some of her first political characters to meet those illustrious statesmen," the paper proposed Franklin, James Wilson, Robert Morris, and George Clymer—all signers of the Declaration of Independence—plus Thomas Mifflin, who presided over Congress at the war's end and accepted Washington's resignation. Such men, the *Herald* commented, "will undoubtedly be able to remove the defects of the confederation, produce a vigorous and energetic continental government, which will crush and destroy factions, subdue insurrections, revive public and private credit, disappoint our transatlantic enemies, and their lurking emissaries among us, and finally (to use an Indian phrase) endure 'while the sun shines, and the rivers flow.' "[45] The legislature complied on December 30 by tapping Morris, Wilson, Clymer, and Mifflin plus Gouverneur Morris and two others. Franklin was added later, when his health improved. Even with only three state delegations named by the end of 1786, the convention was already shaping up as a meeting for the ages.

Four more states named delegates to the convention by mid-February, when Congress reconvened for 1787. These seven states—a majority of the total—acted in response to the call issued by the Annapolis Convention, which troubled some nationalists who thought the call should come from Congress. "To me the Policy of such a Convention appears questionable," Jay wrote to Washington. "Their authority is to be derived from acts of the State Legislatures. Are the State Legislatures authorized either by themselves or others, to alter Constitutions? I think not." Congress should declare the current national government "inadequate to the Purposes for which it was instituted," Jay suggested, and invite the people through their states to act.[46] One of the states that had already named delegates conditioned their participation on Congress sanctioning the convention; four of the seven specified that Congress must approve of the convention's recommendations before they could take effect.

Washington, too, wanted Congress to confirm the call. It would enhance the convention's prospects of success. After considerable debate, rather than endorse the summons of the Annapolis Convention, Congress issued its own call for a convention "for the sole and express purpose of revising the Articles of Confederation." It named the same time and place as the prior summons, however, and authorized previously chosen delegates to serve.[47] Five more states promptly named delegates, adding such noted nationalists as Hamilton from New York and Dickinson from Delaware to the mix. Only radical Rhode Island refused.

WITH THE STAGE SET and most of the leading actors chosen, it remained for Washington to decide whether he would attend the convention and play the part reserved for him. Surely if he went, he would become the convention's presiding officer and public face. His initial instinct was to decline, and not only because of concerns about the Cincinnati but also because of his public commitment to retire from public life and his contentment with that choice.

But he was wavering. In December, he had asked for advice from Humphreys and Knox. Washington received long and detailed responses from both of them in early January, along with a similar letter from Jay. These confidants did not urge Washington to attend the convention, but they unwittingly gave him reason to go.

Conservative nationalists like Jay, Knox, and Humphreys typically blamed the nation's ills on some combination of Congress's weakness and excess democracy in the states. Writing from New England in the midst of Shays's Rebellion, for example, Knox and Humphreys had been so despondent about the nation's prospects that they did not think Washington should risk his reputation on a project with such slight chance of success. "I concur fully in sentiments with you, concerning the inexpediency of your attending the convention," Humphreys advised Washington. "If the people have not wisdom and virtue enough to govern themselves, or what is the same thing to suffer themselves to be governed by men of their own election; why then I must think it is in vain to struggle against the torrent, it is in vain to strive to compel mankind to be happy & free contrary to their inclinations." Knox added, "However strongly I wish for measures which would lead to national happiness and glory, yet I do not wish you to be concerned in any political operations, of which, there are such various opinions." Jay was equally doubtful of the convention's prospects but saw little harm in Washington going.[48]

Their pessimism sprang from a belief that the confederation was so hopelessly broken that merely revising the Articles could not save it. Yet the convention's call spoke only of proposing amendments to the Articles subject to approval by the states, not forming a new government. "Would the giving of any further Degree of Power to Congress do the Business?" Jay asked in his letter. "I am inclined to think it would not." An assembly of individuals representing sovereign states cannot govern, he wrote, because "as the many divide Blame and also divide Credit, too little a portion of either falls to each mans Share, to affect him strongly." Corruption follows, Jay concluded, as each "will collectively do or omit Things which individual Gentlemen in Private Capacities would not approve." Knox added the worry that the convention "might devise some expedients to brace up the present defective confederation so as just to keep us together, while it would prevent those exertions for a national character, which is esential to our happiness." The "only good" that could come out of this convention, Humphreys lamented, would be to show that "we cannot remain as a nation much longer in the present manner of administering our actual government." He had no hope that it could resolve America's problems.[49]

The United States needed a true national government with internal checks and authority over the states, Washington's correspondents agreed. "Let Congress legislate, let others execute, let others judge," Jay implored. Both Jay and Knox proposed splitting Congress into two houses, with members of an upper house chosen for life or long terms and members of a lower house elected for one- or two-year terms.

They also concurred on the need for an independent executive. Knox would have this "Governor General" elected by Congress for a seven-year term and entrusted with the power to veto laws. Jay would have the executive appoint judges. Based on their frustrations with the petty sovereignty of the states, all three men stressed the importance of consolidating power. The general government's authority should extend to "all national objects," Knox declared, "without any reference to the local governments." If necessary, the war secretary added, the army should compel compliance. Jay wrote of "the States retaining only so much [authority] as may be necessary for domestic Purposes; and all their principal Officers civil and military being commissioned and removable by the national Government." Humphreys warned that, whatever powers the national government gains on paper, without the ability to coerce obedience, "they are idle as the wind."[50]

For Washington, these letters offered the rough outline for a new government that, if formed, would justify him going to the convention. Yet none of his correspondents expected such a plan to emerge from Philadelphia. Indeed, Humphreys wrote, "I am as confident as I am in my own existence" that, due to its limited mandate and how the states instructed their delegates, nothing important would come from the convention.[51] Humphreys, Knox, and Jay could not even feel confidence in their own states. All three states—Connecticut, Massachusetts, and New York—in the end chose delegations that contained opponents of centralized power. New York did include Hamilton, who exceeded even Jay in zeal for a strong central government, but yoked him with two anti-nationalists, John Lansing Jr. and Robert Yates, and mandated that the concurrence of two delegates would govern the state's single vote at the proceedings. In effect, Hamilton could talk but not vote. In such a setting, Hamilton had one advantage over Jay. The high-minded Jay would likely feel bound by the convention's legal mandate and his state's instructions; a crafty partisan street fighter like Hamilton would not. As the list of participating states grew over the spring, Washington's enthusiasm for the convention rose notwithstanding Humphreys's caution that, if it did succeed with Washington in the chair, people would expect him to lead the new government.

Replying to these correspondents, Washington continued to profess his disinclination to go to the convention—yet his protests increasing lacked conviction. "It is not, *at this time*, my purpose to attend it," he wrote to Knox in February, but brushed aside concerns about the convention exceeding its mandate. "That which takes the shortest course to obtain [the needed governmental reforms] will, in my opinion, under present circumstances, be found best," he explained in Hamiltonian fashion. "Otherwise, like a house on fire, whilst the most regular mode of extinguishing it is contended for, the building is reduced to ashes." He said as much to Jay in March, while adding that he was "a good deal urged" to go.

To Humphrey, after relating the pros and cons of attending the convention, Washington raised a new factor: With his name now publicly listed among the delegates, would his withdrawal "be considered as an implied dereliction of Republicanism" or worse? Would some think that he did not want the convention to succeed? By this time, Washington was looking for reasons to go.[52]

In these letters, Washington endorsed the reforms proposed by Knox and Jay, and made them his own. "Those enumerated in your letter are so obvious, & sensibly felt that no logick can controvert," Washington told Jay. "But, is the public mind matured for such an important change?" Expressing similar sentiments to Knox, Washington stated his fear that "the political machine will yet be much tumbled & tossed, and possibly wrecked altogether, before such a system as you have defined, will be adopted." Jealous of their power, state officials "would give their weight of opposition to such a revolution," he predicted. "The People must feel before they will see or act under this new view of matters."

Nevertheless, he wrote to Jay, he wished to try the convention route and find out "what can be effected." It might represent "the last peaceable mode" of saving the republic; even in failure, it could show the way forward.[53] And should it devise a vigorous new constitution under his leadership, Knox now assured Washington, he would have doubly earned "the glorious republican epithet—The Father of Your Country."[54]

On March 28, scarcely forty days prior to the Convention's scheduled start, Washington relented—with a condition. "I have come to a resolution to go if my health will permit," he informed Randolph. In particular, Washington explained, "I have, of late, been so much afflicted with a rheumatic complaint in my shoulder that at times I can hardly able to raise my hand to my head, or turn myself in bed. This, consequently, might prevent my attendance."[55]

For Washington, at age fifty-five, health was an ongoing issue and one reason he repeatedly gave for his retirement from public life. He had suffered from dysentery, pleurisy, quinsy, severe headaches, fevers, and a mild case of smallpox in the past, and the quinsy and headaches periodically returned. As recently as 1785, he had complained to Knox that "heavy, & painful oppressions in the head, and other disagreeable sensations, often trouble me."[56] Washington's eyesight and hearing were also failing, and his teeth posed persistent and painful problems. Indeed, by the 1780s, his teeth had become so bad that he sought treatment from the itinerant French dentist Jean Pierre Le Moyer, first at army headquarters in Newburgh then on several occasions at Mount Vernon. Le Moyer specialized in the risky procedure of tooth transplants, which involved extracting a diseased tooth from a patient and replacing it with a healthy tooth obtained from a donor. Washington resorted to this procedure during the 1780s, with the healthy teeth coming from his slaves, who received thirteen shillings per tooth, or about one-third of what Le Moyer typically paid on the free market. Since Le Moyer visited Mount Vernon at least twice during the three months prior to Washington's decision to attend the Convention, the General's teeth may have been bothering him almost as much as his shoulder.[57]

Of course physical pain and illness offered compelling reasons to stay home, but in this case, health was part pretext. Five days *after* sending his conditional acceptance to Randolph, Washington wrote to Knox asking whether all the states would name delegates and if any would impose limiting instructions. In this letter, he spoke of only going to the convention if the delegates could reach beyond the Articles and "point out radical cures."[58] Should their authority be too limited, Washington could always use his health as an excuse to withdraw.[59]

WITH THE DECISION TENTATIVELY MADE, Washington called on Madison for the advice that would set the tone for all that followed. They had conferred in February when Madison visited Mount Vernon to encourage Washington to attend the convention. Now Washington wrote to Madison, "A thorough reform of the present system is indispensible . . . and with hand and heart I hope the business will be essayed in the full Convention." Fearing that some states might impose limits on their delegates, Washington reiterated his hope that the convention "would probe the defects of the Constitution to the bottom, and provide radical cures, whether they are agreed to or not." By doing so, the Convention's handiwork could become "a luminary, which sooner or later will shed its influence."[60]

Washington's words could not have found a more receptive reader than Madison. Scholarly and introspective, Madison had been working alone along similar lines for months and, with the convention approaching, now brought Washington, Randolph, and Jefferson into his thinking. In long letters to each and an even longer memorandum on the "vices" of the American state governments, he laid out his ideas for what became the Virginia Plan for a new constitution.

Struck by the similarities between Madison's proposals and those of Jay and Knox, Washington prepared an abstract comparing them.[61] All envisioned a national government with separate legislative, judicial, and executive branches. All would divide Congress into an elite upper house and a popular lower house. Madison elaborated more than the others on the judiciary. He viewed national courts as essential to avoid local bias in expounding national laws and deciding cases involving citizens of different states. Madison wrote less than the others about the executive. "I have scarcely ventured as yet to form my own opinion either of the manner in which it ought to be constituted or of the authorities with which it ought to be cloathed," he admitted to Washington.[62]

Like Jay and Knox, Madison was obsessed with reining in the states. "The national government should be armed with positive and compleat authority in all cases which require uniformity," he told Washington, "such as the regulation of trade." It must have an absolute veto over all state laws, he added, and state judges should swear to uphold the national constitution. He recommended placing state militias under national control and suggested that, as in colonial days, the general government should appoint state governors. Recognizing the inexpediency of abolishing the states altogether, however, Madison called for a federal system—"some middle ground," he called it—"which may at once support a due supremacy of the national authority, and not exclude the local authorities whenever they can be subordinately useful."[63] At least in areas under its domain, he maintained that the national government must have the power to act directly on the people and not just through the states.

More so than Jay or Knox, Madison supplied a classically liberal rationale for centralizing political power. All three men agreed that the states had ignored their duties to Congress, restricted commerce with other states, and abused the rights of citizens. Madison laid the blame on factions, chiefly majority ones. "In republican Government the majority however composed, ultimately give the law," he wrote in his memorandum and implied in his letters, and "what is to restrain them from unjust violations of the rights and interests of the minority, or of individuals?" Madison's examples suggested a particular concern with factions united by economic or religious passions.

Through state-issued paper money, he observed, debtor factions had devalued property rights. Religion, too, he warned, especially when "kindled into enthusiasm," is a "force like that of other passions" and "may become a motive to oppression." Common interests were "less apt to be felt" and majority factions "less easy to be formed" in large republics than small ones, Madison reasoned.[64] Increased size reduced the risk from faction. For example, he observed in his letter to Washington, "There has not been any moment since the peace at which the representatives of the union would have given an assent to paper money or any other measure of a kindred nature."[65]

Madison's letter encouraged Washington. It arrived only days after he grudgingly confirmed his intention to attend the convention. "I declare to you that my assent is given contrary to my judgment," Washington wrote to Randolph on April 9. "I have yielded however to what appeared to be the earnest wishes of my friends, and I will hope for the best."[66]

Soon Washington received three letters that gave substance to this hope. Expressing a desire to see him at the convention, Franklin advised Washington that "your Presence will be of the greatest Importance to the Success of the Measure."[67] In response to Washington's earlier request, Knox now reported that every state except Rhode Island would send delegates and none would carry excessively limiting instruction. "It is the general wish that you should attend," Knox wrote. "Your tried patriotism, and wisdom, would exceedingly facilitate the adoption of any important alterations that might be proposed by the convention of which you were a member, (& as I before hinted) and president."[68] Then came Madison's letter with its well-formed outline for a true national government. These letters reassured Washington that the convention would, in fact, consider the sort of radical cures for the nation's ills that he felt necessary. Nothing now could keep him away.

Nothing, that is, except his mother. The second wife of a wealthy planter, Mary Ball Washington survived her husband by nearly fifty years, giving her plenty of time to brood over how much of his estate he left to the sons of his first wife and how little he left to her. George, the eldest of her six children, was both the apple of her eye and a constant disappointment to her. She wanted a dutiful son who would care for his widowed mother; he wanted to cut her apron strings and make something of himself. She kept him from joining the British navy in 1746 and tried to stop him from serving under General Braddock during the French and Indian War in the position that propelled his military career. Disapproving of her son's choice in a wife, Mary skipped his wedding and never visited Mount Vernon. During the Revolutionary War, Mary complained so much about her son abandoning her for a cause that was none of his business that many dismissed her as a Loyalist. Despite having ample resources to get by, Mary regularly badgered her son for money. Responding to her pleas with yet another payment in early 1787, Washington harshly advised her that "happiness depends more upon the internal frame of a persons own mind than on the externals in the world."[69]

Shortly before his scheduled departure for the convention, Washington received word that his mother was dying. She wanted him at her bedside. The summons came late in the afternoon on April 26, just four days before he had planned to leave for Philadelphia. After dashing off a letter informing Knox that he would surely miss the meeting of the Cincinnati and probably the convention as well, Washington departed with the dawn for his mother's home in Fredericksburg, some fifty miles away. Riding at a gallop, he arrived in less than eight hours only to find his mother doing better than expected. His sister, who had fallen ill caring for their mother, had recovered. His mother, Washington wrote, "is some what amended."[70] She would live to see him become President.

Having already excused himself from the meeting of the Cincinnati, Washington stayed in Fredericksburg with his sister for three days, leisurely returned home, and then spent another week tending to matters on his plantation. His ties to Mount Vernon showed, as did his reluctance to leave it. Spring flowers still brightened the gardens and hung on some trees. Washington's own health had markedly improved. He could now travel without physical pain. Early on May 9, 1787, Washington finally set off by coach for Philadelphia. He sat inside the carriage, three liveried slaves rode outside, and trunks packed with enough clothes and supplies for a long stay were strapped in place. Washington had hoped to depart a day earlier, but the rain squalls that would dog his journey kept him from leaving. A clear morning dawned on the ninth, however, offering the promise of a better day. Washington's coach rolled away from Mount Vernon shortly after sunrise.

BOOK II

To, From, and In Philadelphia

1787

The State House in Philadelphia, site of the Constitutional Convention.

CHAPTER 4

The Center Holds

⁓

WASHINGTON'S 150-MILE JOURNEY to Philadelphia for the Convention took five days. Packed for a potentially long summer stay as the guest of honor in America's cultural capital, Washington traveled as fast as he could by carriage. This rarely averaged more than five miles an hour and often was much less. Heavy rain, muddy roads, and high winds particularly slowed his progress through Maryland. He complained of a violent headache and sick stomach. The storm had grown so bad by the time he reached the ferry at Havre de Grace on May 11 that, because of turbulence, he could not cross the Susquehanna River until the next day. Even then, Washington described the passage as difficult.

He dined and lodged quietly with friends or at public houses along the way, including one night in Baltimore with his former wartime aide, James McHenry, who would represent Maryland at the Convention. Washington traveled only with three trusted slaves: his mulatto valet, William Lee, who had cared for his personal needs for two decades; a groom named Giles; and Paris, a coachman. His wife remained at

Mount Vernon. "Mrs Washington is become too Domestick, and too attentive to two little Grand Children to leave home," he wrote ahead to Robert Morris.[1] She had urged him to stay home, too.

The hardship of Washington's relatively short trip through such a long-settled region of the country exemplified one of the challenges to forging a national government. Physically, America remained a string of separate states or groups of states. Each had begun as a virtual island of Europeans on a little-known shore already occupied by native people whom the newcomers wanted to drive out rather than live among or even subjugate. Starting with colonies in the Chesapeake Bay region, New England, the Hudson and Delaware valleys, Charleston, and Savannah, European settlement had expanded outward from these points but had not yet merged into a fully contiguous population even on the coast, much less in the interior.

Like spokes radiating from a common hub, the various colonies or regional groups of colonies were mainly connected through Britain before the Revolutionary War. Ten years later, land transport between the now independent states remained limited. Going from Virginia to Pennsylvania, Washington had to cross only from one grouping to the next. The roads were so bad farther south that delegates traveled to the Convention from the Carolinas and Georgia by ship. They could have sailed there just as easily from the British West Indies. Despite a brief episode of political unity during the war, physical separation kept the states apart.

Social, economic, and political factors aggravated the situation. Even though all of the Convention delegates were men of British, Irish, or northwestern European ancestry or birth—and nearly all had substantial means—the states they represented differed sharply. Savannah, Georgia, was all but a Caribbean port of call for Yankee sailors; Connecticut's pious Calvinist culture surely seemed frozen in time to enlightened Virginians like Washington and Madison. Great wealth came from trade and shipping in both "the eastern states," as New England was then called, and the mid-Atlantic commercial centers of

New York and Philadelphia; it was rooted in plantation agriculture farther south. Pennsylvania's boisterous egalitarian democracy stood in sharp contrast to South Carolina's staid republican aristocracy.

Above all, slavery and race divided North from South in America. A decade earlier, in 1776, every colony allowed slavery and nearly all the signers of the Declaration of Independence owned slaves; by 1787, Pennsylvania and the New England states had either ended slavery or mandated its gradual abolition. New York and New Jersey were moving in that direction. Only a few delegates from these states owned slaves at the time of the Convention. Some, like Franklin, were active in abolitionist societies.

In contrast, after some talk of manumission during the Revolutionary War, slavery had become more entrenched than ever in the South. Virtually every delegate from the region possessed slaves. Although he had privately expressed his "wish to get quit of Negroes" during the Revolutionary War, Washington owned more than a hundred slaves in 1787 and controlled almost two hundred more inherited as dower slaves by his wife, making him one of the largest slave owners in Virginia.[2] Utterly untroubled by the institution, the Pinckneys of South Carolina, General Charles Cotesworth and his cousin Charles, each owned between two and three hundred slaves. Race mirrored slavery, with few blacks in the North and many in the South. Indeed, black slaves made up more than one-third of the population in most southern states and nearly half the people in South Carolina. As the Convention would show, these differences mattered.

His five-day trip from rural, slaveholding Virginia to cosmopolitan Philadelphia gave Washington time to meditate on what lay ahead. He was not optimistic about the prospects for the Convention. First, Washington doubted whether it could achieve anything of substance. Conditions in the states might need to grow much worse before the public would accept a true national government, he feared, and by then it could be too late to save the union. Petty state politicians, jealous of one another's power, would surely try to derail any significant reforms.

Further, far from seeking power for himself, Washington dreaded his own growing national role. "It was not until after a long struggle I could obtain my own consent to appear again in a public theatre," he wrote to Robert Morris just four days before leaving for the Convention. "My first remaining wish being, to glide gently down the stream of life in tranquil retirement till I shall arrive at the world of Sperits."[3]

Finally, Washington recognized the revolutionary nature of the reforms needed. Only "radical cures" would do, he repeatedly told his correspondents during the months leading up to the Convention, and only the genuine possibility of fundamental changes had lured him from retirement—but Washington was no radical and did not enjoy promoting such measures.[4] He would have sooner stayed home.

Yet here he was in mid-May of his fifty-fifth year, slogging over muddy roads in a rain-soaked, windblown carriage, traveling without family or friends to Philadelphia. Because Washington had not announced his route or schedule, his passage through various towns came as a surprise to local citizens. Unlike during his celebratory ride through Philadelphia to Mount Vernon four years earlier to resign his military commission and retire from public life, people did not turn out en masse to hail him along the way.

Americans knew why Washington was going to Philadelphia, however, and they excitedly discussed its significance. "It is with particular satisfaction we inform the public, that our illustrious fellow Citizen, GEORGE WASHINGTON, Esquire, has consented to serve on the ensuing Federal Convention," the *Connecticut Journal* reported on May 2. "What happy consequence may not all the true friends to federal government promise themselves, from the united zeal, policy, and ability of so *august an assembly*?"[5] Calling him "the American Fabius" after the legendary Roman general and statesman, a nationalist paper in Rhode Island printed a poem on May 5 about Washington's much-anticipated arrival in Philadelphia:

The hero comes, each voice resound his praise,
No envious shafts can dare to chill his rays;
All hail! great man! who, for thy country's cause,
Flew at her call for to protect the laws.

Following more than a dozen lines hailing Washington's part in winning the war, this poem closed with a couplet about his expected role at the Convention in securing the peace:

But fly once more the Senate house with grace,
And crown the States with everlasting peace.[6]

"A union of abilities of so distinguished a body of men, among whom will be a FRANKLIN and a WASHINGTON, cannot but produce the most salutary measures," the *New Hampshire Gazette* commented on the Convention later in May. "Their names affixed . . . will stamp a confidence in them, which the narrow-soul'd, antifederalist politicians in the several States, who by their influence, have hitherto d[amn]'d us as a nation, will not dare attack."[7]

These and other widely circulated accounts show that, even before it began, nationalists expected radical cures from the Convention. "Upon the events of this great council, indeed, depends every thing that can be essential to the dignity and stability of the national character," the *Maryland Chronicle* noted in an article dated on the very day that Washington passed through Baltimore.[8] He was greeted in Philadelphia with an essay in one leading local paper that proposed giving Congress complete power over "those things which alike concern all the states."[9]

With Washington clearly in mind to head the Convention, other essays commented on the need for an independent executive as well as an empowered Congress. Some also called for national courts.[10] "The more we abridge the states of their sovereignty, and the more supreme power we concentrate in an Assembly of the States," an essayist in a

Philadelphia newspaper observed in late May, "the more safety, liberty, and prosperity will be enjoyed by each of the states."[11] Virginia's anti-nationalist former governor Patrick Henry later reportedly commented that he declined his election to serve as a delegate to the Convention because "he smelt a rat" in Philadelphia.[12] If by this he meant a loss of states' rights, then others caught the scent and found it sweet.

The young country's only national journal, the *American Museum*, devoted its April 1787 issue to the coming Convention. As a subscriber, Washington possibly read it on his way to Philadelphia. A lead article depicted the nation as "a headless body, where the tremulous motion of the severed nerves, is the only sign of remaining life." It called for giving Congress control over interstate and international commerce, establishing a national judiciary, and, most of all, creating an independent executive. "None of our political articles supposed it possible to make a good constitution, without placing a governor at the head," the article noted about state governments. "Yet when they united their talents to construct the federal machine, they left out the main spring upon which the continuance of its motion must depend."[13] Washington surely read these words knowing that he was expected to become that mainspring in any new national government. Succeeding issues of the journal reprinted several of the General's earlier calls for a strong central government along with essays and poems praising him. Published by Irish émigré Mathew Carey under Franklin's sponsorship with funds from Lafayette, the *American Museum* gave voice to the same sort of sentiments that gave rise to the Convention. It counted about half of the delegates among its subscribers, including at least one from every state except New Hampshire, and broadcast their nationalist ideals across the land.

EVEN THOUGH THE RAIN continued to pelt down, the trip brightened considerably as Washington approached Philadelphia on Sunday, May 13. He slept the night before in Wilmington, Delaware, at a popular inn operated by Patrick O'Flynn, who had served as a captain during the war. There, Virginia legislator Francis Corbin joined Washington for the final leg of his trip. An official delegation met them just across the state line in Chester, Pennsylvania. Thomas Mifflin, who as president of Congress received Washington's resignation in 1783 and would succeed Franklin as president of Pennsylvania in 1788, headed the delegation. The seven-member group included Washington's old comrades Henry Knox and David Humphreys, then in Philadelphia for the meeting of the Cincinnati, and one of his former staff officers, William Jackson, who used the occasion to lobby for the post of Convention secretary.[14] After dining at Chester's elegant Columbia Hotel, where Lafayette had recovered from wounds sustained in the Battle of Brandywine, the party traveled the remaining twenty miles to the city. Everything must have seemed familiar to Washington. After three years in retreat at rural Mount Vernon, this may have felt like returning to a comfortable second home in the city.

If so, that sensation could have only increased as Washington entered Philadelphia. From Gray's Ferry on the Schuylkill River, mounted dragoons under the command of another friendly face, Samuel Miles, escorted the General's coach to town. As deputy quartermaster during the Revolutionary War, Miles had arranged transport for Washington's army to the decisive Battle of Yorktown. To mark the General's arrival into the city proper, cannons fired thirteen rounds in the so-called federal salute and the great bells of towering Christ Church, the country's chief Episcopal edifice, peeled loudly. No other delegate received an official welcome.

"Notwithstanding the badness of the weather great numbers of respectable citizens assembled in the streets to hail him as he passed," the *Pennsylvania Herald* reported on Washington's entry into the city.[15] "This great patriot will never think his duty performed, while any thing remains to be done."[16] Another local newspaper marked the occasion with a poem on the nation's plight and Washington's prospective role in remedying it, concluding with the stanza:

> *Dry up your tears, ye maidens fair!*
> *With finest flowers adorn your hair!*
> *Your war-try'd hero comes;*
> *He comes, and grace sits on his brow!*
> *Bow down, ye tyrants, lowly bow,*
> *Sound trumpets, fifes and drums!*[17]

In what resembled a parade, Washington's carriage, accompanying dignitaries, and mounted troops wound their way through town to a popular boardinghouse on Market Street operated by Mary House. Madison had already settled there and Edmund Randolph was expected soon. A block from the State House, where the Convention would meet, these stylish lodgings served as the nerve center for Virginia's delegation. Robert Morris waited among the well-wishers to spirit Washington away, however. The General would stay a few doors west on Market, Morris insisted, in his mansion—one of the finest in Philadelphia and equal to some of the best in London. With ample room for the General's valet, horses, and carriage, Morris's estate became Washington's home for the Convention.

Even before settling in, Washington called on Franklin. A world-renowned inventor, natural philosopher, and diplomat who had coauthored the Declaration of Independence, secured the alliance with France, and brokered the peace with Britain, the "Sage of Philadelphia" was Washington's sole peer in popular esteem. Only by pulling together could they hope to win public approval for fundamentally reforming the confederation.

Despite their mutual admiration, because Franklin had spent most of the war in France and Washington had spent it in the field, the two men hardly knew each other except by reputation. Based on his frustrations representing the United States in Europe, Franklin supported a strong general government, but, perhaps due to his humble origins and common touch, he trusted democracy more than Washington, Hamilton, and many other prominent nationalists. Washington and Franklin needed to understand each other and could not work at cross-purposes or else the Convention would surely fail.

Much as when Franklin embraced Voltaire at the Academy of Sciences in Paris two decades earlier, this was a meeting for the ages. Unfortunately for later historians, it was a private encounter, and no one recorded what happened. Richard Beeman speculates that the two men sipped wine in Franklin's garden and toured the house and library.[18] Surely they discussed the Convention and, despite their differences, established a rapport.

A generation older than Washington and crippled by gout and kidney stones, Franklin nevertheless retained more boyish enthusiasm than the Virginian. Social magnets, both men charmed the ladies—though Franklin purportedly took them to bed while Washington danced them into delirium. Both also enjoyed the company of men, with Franklin drawing them into witty conversation and Washington keeping them rapt at a distance. Ever puckish, Gouverneur Morris once allegedly bet Hamilton that he could greet Washington with a gentle backslap. Morris won the bet but received such a glare from the General that he regretted the incident.[19] In contrast, Franklin readily accepted hugs and kisses, as he had from Voltaire. "How charming," John Adams grumbled at the sight.[20] A born organizer, in advance of the Convention Franklin formed a biweekly discussion group on republican government. Seven of his state's eight Convention delegates joined.[21] Except perhaps for Madison and the Virginians, thanks in part to Franklin, Pennsylvania's delegation was the best prepared for the Convention.

"THIS BEING THE DAY appointed for the Convention to meet," Washington wrote in his diary for Monday, May 14, "such members as were in town assembled at the State House."[22] That meant only Washington, Madison, and the Pennsylvanians. No others had arrived. Those present agreed to meet again at eleven o'clock on the following day. By then, a few delegates from Delaware, New Jersey, and North Carolina had trickled in, but not enough to proceed.

To vote, every state except Maryland required the presence of at least half of its delegates; to conduct business, the Convention needed at least seven voting states. For the first two days, only Pennsylvania qualified. Governor Randolph arrived late on the fifteenth to augment the Virginia delegation, followed by the rest of its members by May 17. Still, that made only two states represented out of a baker's dozen.

Prospects looked bleak, but the slowly growing band kept reassembling at the State House each day except Sunday, only to disburse for lack of a quorum. The delay "is highly vexatious to those who are idly, & expensively spending their time here," Washington complained on May 17.[23] On one such idle day, he dined with the assembled members of the Cincinnati and reluctantly accepted their reelection as the society's president, which was just what he had hoped to avoid.

Franklin hosted a dinner for the assembling delegates at his home on May 16. Despite having become a connoisseur of fine wine during his time in France, Franklin served porter—a strong, dark beer then associated with working-class Englishmen. Despite lightheartedly referring to the delegates as "un assemblée des notables," Franklin may have wanted to bring them down to earth by dispensing a commoner's beverage. In any event, the results pleased him. "When the cask was broached," Franklin reported to the brewer in London, "the company agreed unanimously, that it was the best porter they had ever tasted." Even his gout and kidney stones seemed under control since he commented in the letter that they "have not yet deprived me of my natural cheerfulness, my delight in books, and enjoyment of social conversation."[24]

Holding the dinner on May 16 limited it mainly to delegates from Virginia and Pennsylvania—but that proved fortuitous. Those two delegations bonded and, while waiting for others to arrive, met together regularly to frame a draft plan for a true national government. The combined group contained the three delegates with the most advanced ideas on the topic: Madison; Gouverneur Morris, who had moved from New York to Philadelphia during the Revolutionary War and represented Pennsylvania at the Convention; and the Scottish-born Philadelphia lawyer James Wilson.

Prior to the Convention, Washington personally knew Madison and Gouverneur Morris quite well; he mainly knew Wilson by his reputation as a legal scholar. Indeed, three years earlier, when Washington's nephew Bushrod opted to study law, Washington recommended and paid for him to study under Wilson. All three were notably brilliant: Madison and Wilson in a bookish sort of way that displayed itself best in writing and committee work; Morris, in contrast, had a wit that could bedazzle people in any setting. Less scholarly and not as quick, Washington relied on these three delegates during the Convention even though he was somewhat put off by Morris's showmanship and would later tire of Madison's intrigues.

Wilson had a different Achilles' heel: money, or rather the lack of it. Born into a pious Scottish family and educated for the ministry at St. Andrews, Wilson sought his fortune in America but, never satisfied with a lawyer's income, always seemed a day late or a dollar short in the get-rich schemes that would eventually land him in debtor's prison. Creditors were already hounding him in 1787, but this did not stop him from playing a leading role with Madison and Morris at the Convention.

By the time a quorum assembled, the Virginia and Pennsylvania delegations had cobbled together the rough outline for a new plan of government. It became known as the "Virginia Plan" because Virginia governor Edmund Randolph introduced it at the Convention. Although few records survive of the informal meetings that generated it, Washington participated throughout and endorsed the end product. Before leaving Mount Vernon, he worked through the preliminary plans for union offered to him by Madison, Henry Knox, and John Jay, which roughly anticipate the Virginia Plan, and consolidated them into a single handwritten abstract.[25] In a May 20 letter to his eldest son, senior Virginia delegate George Mason stated that all members of his state's delegation, which would therefore include Washington, met for two or three hours every day to draft the final proposed plan. He noted that it already had support from other principal states, which at that point must have meant Pennsylvania.[26] Beeman gives equal credit to the Pennsylvanians, particularly Morris and Wilson, for preparing the plan.[27] Two other states, South Carolina and New York, were represented at the Convention by the twentieth, but their delegates apparently played little part in drafting it.

———

AS MASON DEPICTED the still-forming plan in his letter, nothing less than a revolution in government was brewing. "The most prevalent Idea," he wrote, "seems to be a total Alternation of the present federal System and substituting a great National Council, or Parliament, consisting of two Branches of the Legislature, founded upon the Principles of equal proportionate Representation, with full legislative Powers upon all the Objects of the Union." In two phrases, this one sentence effectively summarized the Virginia Plan.

First, people would replace states as the building blocks of a national republic. Under the existing confederation, each state had one vote in Congress even though small ones like Delaware and Rhode Island had less than one-tenth as many people as Virginia and one-seventh as many as Pennsylvania. Under the new plan, representation would be proportional to population or wealth. The United States would become a government of the people rather than of the states. The Pennsylvania delegates also wanted proportionate representation at the Convention itself, but the Virginians feared that pushing for it

Romanticized nineteenth-century portrayal of Washington's emotional farewell to his Revolutionary War officers at Fraunces Tavern in New York on December 4, 1783.

John Trumbull's classic painting for the U.S. Capitol rotunda of Washington resigning his commission as commander in chief of the Continental Army on December 23, 1783.

Martha Washington, 1772.

George Washington, 1785.

West Front of Mount Vernon, c. 1787–1791.

The Washington family at Mount Vernon, showing George and Martha
Washington; Martha's grandchildren George Washington Parke Custis and
Eleanor Parke Custis; and one of Washington's slaves, probably William Lee, 1798.

Robert Morris, c. 1785.

Elizabeth Welling Powel, c. 1793.

Benjamin Franklin, 1787.

Gouverneur Morris, 1783.

Henry Knox, later reproduction from portrait, c. 1805.

George Clinton, nineteenth-century engraving of 1802 painting.

James Wilson, drawing from original portrait, c. 1825.

Alexander Hamilton, later reproduction of 1792 portrait.

ABOVE: Howard Chandler Christy's classic painting for the U.S. Capitol of Washington presiding over the signing of the Constitution on September 17, 1787.

LEFT: First public printing of the United States Constitution: *Pennsylvania Packet*, September 19, 1787.

James Madison, c. 1828, lithograph from portrait painted c. 1805–1807.

John Jay, later reproduction of 1794 portrait.

Satirical engraving by federalist Amos Doolittle depicting the battle between urban federalists and rural antifederalists over ratification of the Constitution in Connecticut, 1787. One federalist, pulling left, shouts "Comply with Congress"; one antifederalist, pulling right, replies "Success to Shays."

Richard Henry Lee, c. 1820, engraving from a drawing based on an original miniature.

Patrick Henry, c. 1891, copy of a portrait based on a 1791 miniature.

Contemporary etching of the arrival of Washington at the laurel-bedecked Gray's Ferry Bridge near Philadelphia on his inaugural journey, April 20, 1789.

Nineteenth-century print of Washington's landing by ceremonial barge at New York City for his inauguration as President, April 23, 1789.

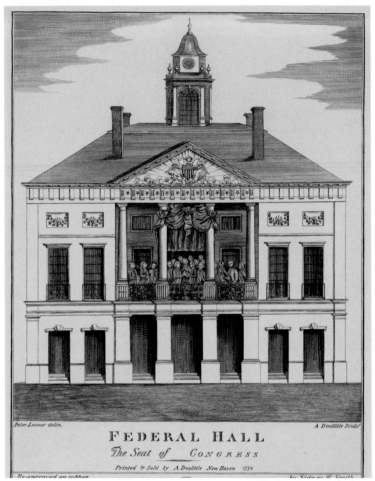

FEDERAL HALL
The Seat of CONGRESS

Peter Lacour delin.   *A Doolittle Sculpt*

Printed & Sold by A Doolittle New Haven 1790

Re-engraved on copper   *by Sidney L. Smith*

Engraving of the only known live sketch of
Washington's inauguration at Federal Hall,
April 30, 1789.

Bust of Washington made at Mount
Vernon from a live mask by French
sculptor Jean-Antoine Houdon in 1785.

might cause a fatal divide between small and large states at the outset. Better to wait.

Second, Congress would no longer go hat-in-hand to the states for everything. On matters of national interests, it would either dictate to the states or bypass them altogether in dealing with the people. To buttress the new government's total control over national issues, Mason noted, the plan would empower Congress to veto state laws deemed "contrary to the Interest of the federal Union." When held by the king over the colonies, this was one of the powers cited in the Declaration of Independence to justify revolution. The Virginia Plan would give it to Congress. Yet about this power and the plan in general, Mason predicted in his letter that "with a proper Degree of Coolness, Liberality & Candour (very rare Commodities by the Bye) I doubt not but it may be effected."[28]

Both in this letter to his son and in one sent earlier to Richard Henry Lee, Mason ascribed the delegates' willingness to adopt such radical measures to recent abuses by the states, particularly their assault on property rights through the emission of paper money. "Knaves assure, and fools believe, that calling paper money, and making it tender, is the way to be rich and happy," Mason wrote to Lee, "thus the national mind is kept in constant ferment; and the public councils in continual disturbance by the intrigues of wicked men, for fraudulent purposes." Giving Congress the power to veto state laws and rendering "*ipso facto* void" any state law that contravened national policy should resolve the matter, Mason suggested. And since the problems had been centered in the eastern states, he predicted that those traditional "republican" states would be the first to agree. "However extraordinary this may at first seem," Mason wrote to his son in Virginia, "it may, I think, be accounted for, from a very common & natural Impulse of the human Mind. Men disappointed . . . are very apt to run into the opposite Extreme; and the People of the Eastern States, setting out with more republican Principles, have consequently been more disappointed than we have been."[29]

Mason here sounded like Madison. A month earlier, in a letter to Washington, Madison had baldly asserted that Congress would never emit devaluated paper money. Such faith in the national legislature fit Madison's theory that, in a republic, majority factions posed the gravest threat to individual and minority rights. To reduce the danger of majority factions forming or taking control, he proposed enlarging the republic and making it less homogeneous. This became his libertarian rationale for national supremacy under the Virginia Plan. It had the advantage of not relying on the supposed "republican virtue" either of citizens, as Jefferson did with his vision of republican yeoman farmers supporting the common good, or of leaders, as Washington and Adams did with their notions of enlightened solons disinterestedly dispensing justice.

Madison viewed his approach as a realistic way to secure good laws from self-interested voters and legislators. Simply check and balance their interests. Of course, except for the romanticized examples of remote Swiss cantons and ancient Greek city-states, the founders had no examples of effective republican rule to draw on in framing their governments. They dreamed of creating something better in the New World than the monarchies that still ruled the Old World, but none of them knew how to do it.

When Mason joined the patriot cause before the American Revolution, colonial governors, the king, and Parliament posed the greatest threat to freedom while colonial legislatures served as bulwarks of liberty. Running to the opposite extreme, Revolutionary Era Americans entrusted state legislatures with near-total power and circumscribed their governors and the confederation government. Pennsylvania went so far as to place legislative power in one hyper-representative chamber over the strenuous and continuing opposition of Robert Morris and his conservative, business-minded partisans.

Similarly, at the federal level, the Articles of Confederation united legislative, executive, and judicial functions in a one-house Congress. Once the vices of the republican extreme became apparent in the states, the Virginia Plan sought to shift substantial power to the national level and check Congress's representative lower house with an elite senate whose members served terms of "sufficient [length] to ensure their independency."[30] Both moves, Madison posited, would lessen the risk of majority faction. Unlike Mason, Madison had matured politically during the postrevolutionary period of state legislative supremacy rather than the pre–Revolutionary Era of abuses by the king and Parliament.

Madison's scheme did not initially focus on the executive's role in checking the legislature. Indeed, in his April 16 letter to Washington, Madison maintained that he had not formed an opinion on the structure or authority of the executive branch. This may be where Morris and Wilson contributed to the emerging plan—it certainly was where they would play the most significant role during the Convention. They had lived under the emasculated presidency of Pennsylvania's radically republican constitution of 1776, and witnessed its failings. Further, Gouverneur Morris had worked closely with Robert Morris during the darkest days of the Revolutionary War in trying to forge an effective executive office of finance for Congress, only to see it crumble once the exigency of war gave way to the lethargy of peace.

Already in his May 20 letter to his son and one the next day to Virginian Arthur Lee, Mason noted that the Virginia Plan would establish a "national Executive" separate from Congress, which represented a radical departure from the Articles of Confederation.[31] As proposed, the Virginia Plan ultimately provided for a single executive possessing all of the executive rights formerly vested in Congress plus a general authority to execute the nation's law. To ensure independence of action, the executive, although chosen by Congress, would serve a fixed single term. This sketch served as the starting point for what became prolonged deliberations over the American presidency.

No one should have been discouraged by the progress made by the Virginia delegates during the days waiting in Philadelphia for a quorum to arrive. By having a plan ready for introduction at the outset, they gained the initiative. Washington, however, despised delay. On May 20—the same day that Mason wrote so optimistically to his son about the emerging Virginia Plan—Washington groused about the Convention's late start. "Not more than four states were represented yesterday. If more are come in since it is unknown to me," Washington grumbled in a letter to Arthur Lee. "These delays greatly impede public measures, and serve to sour the temper of the punctual members who do not like to idle away their time."[32] In so saying, he certainly spoke to his own sour mood.

During this period, Washington wrote his longest and most heartfelt letters to the nephew who managed Mount Vernon in his absence. He sent one almost every week. "I hope the fine rains which have watered this part of the country," Washington wrote in one, "were not unproductive as they hovered over you. All nature seems alive from the effect of them."[33] These letters leave little doubt that, as much as he obviously enjoyed the social scene in Philadelphia, Washington also missed his pastoral life in Virginia.

WITH FOUR STATES REPRESENTED by May 20, the Convention stood more than halfway to securing a quorum but far shy of the number of states realistically required to get anything done. The twentieth also marked the first Sunday after the Convention's scheduled starting date. Instead of gathering again at the State House, as they had done every day since May 14, all of the Virginia delegates except Washington went to church together. They made a telling choice of service to attend. Although none of them were Roman Catholics, they went to Mass.

Prior to the Revolutionary War, Catholics were persecuted in every colony. They could not vote or hold public office anywhere— not even in Maryland, which was founded as a haven for Catholics, or in famously tolerant Rhode Island, where even atheists had rights. Massachusetts made it a capital offense for priests to proselytize or say Mass. The colonists' special concern with Catholics was as much political as spiritual. It stemmed in part from Protestant England's long warfare with Catholic France and the widespread Protestant perception that all Catholics obeyed the pope and his worldwide network of prelates and priests on matters both spiritual and temporal.

Overt anti-Catholicism abated during the war, especially after the United States allied with France, but it did not end. At New York's constitutional convention in 1777, for example, John Jay sought to maintain his state's ban on Catholics holding office, and, although he failed to secure such a provision in the new state constitution, he obtained a state law to that effect in 1788. At the time of the Convention, Massachusetts had yet to witness its first public Mass.

With only about thirty-five thousand adherents in all of the states, Catholicism was a foreign religion to most Americans. Even in Maryland, New York City, and eastern Pennsylvania, where most American Catholics lived, they remained a distinct and somewhat insular minority. Their numbers were growing, however, as a rising tide of Irish Catholics sought refuge from British rule in the newly independent United States. That the delegates chose to attend Catholic Mass during their first Sunday in Philadelphia, even though the city boasted America's leading Episcopal church and was hosting a national Presbyterian convention, gave Catholics a reason to hope that a strong national union might support their rights more than the individual states had done so.

The invitation to Mass likely came from Pennsylvania's lone Catholic delegate, Thomas Fitzsimons, a wealthy Irish-American merchant and ardent nationalist who had served as an officer in his state's home guard during the Revolutionary War. Maryland also sent a Catholic to the Convention, Daniel Carroll, but he had not yet arrived. Explaining the decision to attend Mass, Mason wrote to his son that it was "more out of Compliment than Religion, & more out of Curiosity than compliment." Unless they traveled, Virginians would have known few Catholics. Commenting on the service, Mason described the "preacher" as a foreigner, his "delivery" as faulty, and his "sermon" as trivial. "While I was pleased with the Air of Solemnity so generally deffused thro' the Church," Mason added, "I was somewhat disgusted with the frequent Tinckling of a little Bell; which put me in Mind of the drawing up of the Curtain for a Puppet-Shew."[34] Still, the delegates' attendance was widely noted.

More notably, Washington attended Catholic Mass on the following Sunday. He had skipped the previous service but, after hearing about it, led a delegation of leading Philadelphia Protestants on May 27 to St. Mary's Chapel, which stood two blocks from Fitzsimons's home and within easy walking distance of Washington's residence for the Convention. "The anthems and other solemn pieces of music performed on this occasion were admirably adopted to diffuse a spirit of devotion throughout a very crowded congregation," the *Pennsylvania Herald* reported in an article reprinted in newspapers across the country.[35]

The event merited all of the attention it received. Despite his respect for religion's role in civil society and belief in divine providence, Washington rarely went to church during this period of his life. Indeed, he attended Sunday worship services on only one other occasion during the Convention, and this was when an old friend preached at Christ's Church. Therefore, his attendance at a Catholic Mass sent a clear message.[36] During the Revolutionary War, he had welcomed both French and Polish Catholics into the American officer corps, from Lafayette to Casimir Pulaski, and developed lasting friendships with some of them. Now he could reciprocate by standing with American Catholics. "Being no bigot myself to any mode of worship," Washington wrote to Lafayette later in 1787, "I am disposed to endulge the professors of Christianity in the church, that road to heaven which to them shall seem the most direct."[37]

WASHINGTON'S VISIT TO PHILADELPHIA'S leading Catholic parish came at a propitious moment. During the previous week, enough delegates had arrived from Delaware, North Carolina, and New Jersey to allow the assembly to convene on Friday, May 25, with a bare majority of seven states represented and one deputy each from two others. The emergence of the Virginia Plan may have hurried them along. When Delaware's George Read saw either that plan or a somewhat similar one by South Carolina's Charles Pinckney, he urged his colleague John Dickinson to come fast. "By this plan our State may have a representation in the House of Delegates of one member in eighty," ever-vigilant Read warned on May 21. "I suspect it to be of importance to the small States that their deputies should keep a strict watch upon the movements and propositions from the larger States, who will probably combine to swallow up the smaller ones." He implored Dickinson, "If you have any wish to assist in guarding against such attempts, you will be speedy in your attendance."

Similar pleas may have gone out to New Jersey delegates. Many delegates from these two small states lived within a few hours' ride of Philadelphia; some were waiting at home for the Convention to begin. Once the extent of the proposed reforms became evident, they came quickly. Three other small states had not even named delegates yet. One of them, Maryland, now did so with dispatch and sent them scurrying to Philadelphia.

With just seven states represented and only twenty-nine delegates present on the twenty-fifth, the Convention could do little more than formally convene and prepare for future deliberations. Mainly, that meant electing a presiding officer. As president of the host state, Franklin wanted to perform the happy act of formally nominating Washington as the Convention's president. Kidney stones and a persistent rain kept Franklin home, however. The task fell to Pennsylvania's next most senior delegate, Robert Morris, who stated that he did so on behalf of his entire delegation. South Carolina's senior delegate and former governor John Rutledge seconded the nomination and urged the Convention to accept it unanimously. It did. Morris and Rutledge then escorted Washington to the Speaker's chair: a finely carved seat with a half sun painted on its crown. It stood behind a draped desk on the dais at the front of the State Assembly Room.

After sitting, Washington accepted the "honor," as he called it, "conferred on him" by the Convention, noted the "novelty" of the president's role for him, and asked "the indulgence of the House toward the involuntary errors which his inexperience might occasion." He had not asked to preside over the Convention but surely expected to do so. If "he felt himself embarrassed" with the honor, as he reportedly said at the time, it surely was a fleeting feeling.[38] Washington was comfortable with command. Being persuaded that only a strong general government could save the union, he was ready to play whatever part was required of him to secure that end.

Henceforth, as Washington realized perhaps more than anyone, he no longer represented merely himself, the army, or Virginia. He represented the nation, and on him its future rested. That made it all the more noteworthy that he chose, as his first public outing on the following Sunday, to attend Catholic Mass. Washington had an instinctive sense of theater. He spoke more through actions than words. And now he was acting on behalf of the nation.

Three more brief business items came before the rump convention on that initial Friday. First it chose Washington's former aide, William Jackson, as the Convention's secretary. Balloting by state, the delegates picked Jackson over Franklin's grandson, Temple, by a margin of five to two. Then one member from each state presented the credentials for his delegation. Finally, before adjourning for the week, the Convention appointed a committee chaired by Virginia legal scholar George Wythe to draft standing rules for the assembly. At a time when Americans typically worked six days each week, not meeting on the first Saturday suggested that the delegates still felt that their numbers remained too low to tackle substantive matters. Thereafter, they met on Saturdays.

In presenting the credentials from his state, George Read made a point of stating that Delaware had barred its delegation from supporting any change in the policy of equal representation for every state in Congress. This caught the attention of every delegate. It appeared in all their surviving notes.[39] Mason promptly wrote home, "Delaware has tied up the hands of her deputies by an express direction to retain the principle . . . of each State having the same vote."[40] A member of the Continental Congress from Delaware, Read had voted against independence in 1776 but supported that decision once made. Fundamentally conservative, he favored a strong national government but wanted his small state to have as much say in it as any large one. His opening salvo suggested that the chief controversy at this Convention would not involve whether Congress received more power but rather who would wield it.

———

MONDAY BROUGHT NINE MORE DELEGATES and two added states, Massachusetts and Connecticut. Although the comings and goings of delegates meant that not every state remained represented at all times, the total never again dropped below eight or rose higher than twelve. The Convention could proceed.

Unable to walk steadily that day, Franklin arrived in a sedan chair carried by two trustworthy convicts assigned to transport the state's chief executive on official business. The mode of travel further added to his aura. "Dr. Franklin is well known to be the greatest phylosopher of the present age," Georgia delegate William Pierce wrote from the Convention. "The very heavens obey him, and the Clouds yield up their Lightning to be imprisoned in his rod."[41]

Others arrived on foot, but more than a few of them had a reputation that commanded widespread respect. Of those by now assembled—beyond Washington, Madison, Hamilton, Mifflin, and the two Morrises—the delegates included four past or present state governors, a half dozen past or present members of Congress, and such well-known Revolutionary Era leaders as Mason, Wilson, Wythe, and General Pinckney. Among American political figures with a nationalist bent, this indeed constituted "un assemblée des notables," as Franklin had said.[42]

The delegates began the new week by debating draft rules proposed by Wythe's committee. In line with conventional parliamentary practice, these rules placed substantial authority in Washington, as president, to maintain order. One look or word from him could command respect, which the rebellious officers at Newburgh had learned to their dismay in 1783. As expected, the rules provided for the delegates to vote by state, one equal vote for each, with seven states required for a quorum. Every member wishing to speak would address Washington first and all would rise when he entered the hall each day. "When the House shall adjourn," the rules added, "every Member shall stand in his place until the President pass him."[43]

The most significant rules did not come from the committee, but were suggested from the floor on Monday and adopted on Tuesday. Rufus King of Massachusetts objected that recording the votes of individual members might hinder them from changing their opinions and North Carolina's Richard Dobbs Spaight urged that any member be allowed to request that the Convention revisit matters previously decided. These variations from normal parliamentary procedure allowed delegates to play with new ideas and take tentative positions. Of even greater import, Pierce Butler of South Carolina moved that the Convention keep its proceedings secret. The final rules provided that "no copy be taken of any entry on the journal" and that "nothing spoken in the House be printed, or otherwise published, or communicated without leave."[44] These added rules allowed the Convention to build internal consensus without outside interference.

"No Constitution ever would have been adopted by the Convention if the debates had been public," Madison later commented.[45] He was probably right.

Washington scrupulously followed the secrecy rule in public discourse and private writings. "No Com[municatio]ns without doors," he wrote in his personal diary for May 29, and never again disclosed details of the deliberations even in it.[46]

When one delegate accidentally breached the secrecy rule by mislaying a copy of the Virginia Plan, Washington's stern supervision of the deliberations showed itself. "I am sorry to find that some one Member of this Body, has been so neglectful of the secrets of the Convention as to drop in the State House a copy of their proceedings," Washington lectured the members after another delegate found it. "I must entreat Gentlemen to be more careful, lest our transactions get into the News Papers, and disturb the public repose by premature speculations." He then threw down the offending document, directed its unnamed owner to claim it, bowed to the members, and marched from the room as they stood cowering at their seats.

"It is something remarkable that no Person ever owned the Paper," observed Georgia's Pierce, who later privately expressed great relief in confirming that it was not his copy.[47] Other delegates also jotted down some firsthand observations about the Convention in private journals or letters that subsequently became public, but the only comprehensive account of the closed-door sessions appeared in the copious daily notes taken by Madison, which he vowed to keep confidential until the last delegate died.[48] As it turned out, passing at age eighty-five in 1836, he was that final survivor.

Two key delegates well known by Washington checked in for the first time on Tuesday morning, just in time to vote on the proposed added rules. Delaware's John Dickinson and Elbridge Gerry of Massachusetts had served together in 1776 at the Continental Congress, where the ever-cautious Dickinson dragged his feet on independence while the more progressive Gerry ran on ahead. "If every Man here was a Gerry, the Liberties of America would be safe against the Gates of Earth and Hell," John Adams had said at that time.[49] Both now came to Philadelphia open to strengthening the confederation but with Dickinson protective of a role for small states in that union and Gerry worried about individual rights under any regime. Neither would likely rubber-stamp the Virginia Plan but no sooner had they arrived than it took center stage.

ON TUESDAY MORNING, after the Convention had committed itself to secrecy, the Virginia delegation dropped its bombshell. Having participated in preparing it, Washington clearly conspired in the timing of its delivery. To begin "the main business" of the Convention, as Madison termed it in his notes, Washington called on Randolph.[50] The Virginia governor then presented his delegation's plan for a new national government. Once he took the floor, Randolph held it for most of the day and left no doubt about his state's radical intentions.

As presented by Randolph, the fifteen numbered resolutions that became known as "the Virginia Plan" contained the outline for a "national" government composed of a two-house legislature, some sort of chief executive, and a judiciary with supreme and inferior courts. This represented the Virginia delegation's radical cure for America's woefully inadequate central government. Citing the commercial discord among the states, the rebellion in Massachusetts, "the havoc of paper money," and the failure to pay the nation's debts, Randolph argued that the existing confederation did not work. It raised "the prospect of anarchy from the laxity of government every where." Further, he added, "there were many advantages, which the U.S. might acquire, which were not attainable under the confederation—such as a productive impost—counteraction of the commercial regulations of other nations—pushing of commerce." The hope, Randolph declared, lay in a national government with power to legislate on matters of general concern, compel obedience to its laws, and veto state laws that contravene its purposes.

William Paterson, a pro-state delegate from New Jersey, captured the speech's essence in a scribble: "Sovereignty is the integral Thing—We ought to be one Nation."[51]

Virginia had staked its ground, forcing others to respond. No delegate could doubt where Washington stood. He remained a voting member of Virginia's delegation, called on Randolph to speak first, and never suffered any interruption of what Yates depicted as the governor's "long and elaborate speech."[52] Clearly Washington sided with Virginia and the Virginia Plan. In doing so, he had helped to hijack the Convention. Congress had endorsed this gathering as a meeting to draft amendments to the confederation; Washington's Virginia instead proposed using it to scrap the existing government and forge a nation.

This took time to digest. It also might require a more fluid format than even the Convention's revised rule permitted. Thus, when Randolph finished, the delegates resolved to reconvene the next morning as a committee of the whole "appointed to consider the State of the American Union." This removed Washington from the chair and put him on the floor with the Virginia delegation for so long as the delegates met as a committee. To chair that committee, the members chose Massachusetts delegate Nathaniel Gorham, who had presided over Congress when the issue of the Philadelphia Convention first arose in 1786 and never took a strong position for or against it. He was, however, a nationalist.

RANDOLPH'S SPEECH MAY HAVE RUN ON until nearly four o'clock, when the delegates typically adjourned for dinner. Certainly the Convention did little else after hearing Randolph on that first Tuesday. Keeping to a schedule of meeting from 10 A.M. to about 4 P.M., six days each week, left time each evening for members to meet informally, attend to personal business, and socialize—all of which were necessary for a successful Convention. On this momentous day, Washington dined at "home," as he now called the Morris mansion in his diary, and then escorted Mary Morris to a benefit concert at City Tavern, one of Philadelphia's finest venues.

Sometime that night he likely also worked on the long letter that he posted the next day to Jefferson. "The business of this Convention is as yet too much in embryo to form any opinion of the result," Washington wrote. "That something is necessary, all will agree; for the situation of the General Government (if it can be called a government) is shaken to its foundations—and liable to be overset by every blast. In a word, it is at an end, and unless a remedy is soon applied, anarchy & confusion will inevitably ensue."[53] These worried words echoed Randolph's urgent speech. It also suggested that Washington still remained in doubt about how the delegates would respond.

Although the next day, Wednesday, did not dispel Washington's doubts, it opened the door for the sort of radical cures that he wanted. Fittingly, the day marked the entrance of the last major player to arrive onstage: Connecticut's sixty-six-year-old Roger Sherman. No delegate except Franklin had served the public longer than Sherman. And besides Franklin, Sherman was the only delegate from a true working-class background. Unlike the urbane Franklin, however, despite years of service in Congress and for his state, the rustic Sherman could still pass for a New England worker awkwardly dressed in an ill-fitting suit. Crude in speech and angular in shape, he was once depicted by John Adams as "the reverse of grace." At the Convention, Pierce called him "grotesque and laughable." Yet neither underestimated him. In 1777, Adams characterized Sherman "as honest as an angel, and as firm in the cause of American independence as Mount Atlas." A decade later, Pierce wrote about Sherman, "No Man has a better Heart or a clearer Head."[54] But he was an old-school patriot from a small state and suspicious of centralized power. After Connecticut tapped Sherman for the Convention, one Hartford nationalist warned the ultranationalist Rufus King, "He is as cunning as the Devil, and if you attack him, you ought to know him well."[55] Angel and devil: both sides of Roger Sherman soon showed themselves in Philadelphia.

NATIONALISTS IN THE VIRGINIA and Pennsylvania delegations must have conspired on Tuesday night to present a united front on Wednesday. They entered with a joint strategy to focus debate on the issue of national versus state sovereignty. As Madison reported it, Randolph "moved on the suggestion of" Gouverneur Morris that the delegates preface consideration of the fifteen resolutions comprising the Virginia Plan by debating a single fundamental resolve: "That a *national* government ought to be established consisting of a *supreme* legislative, judicial and executive." Initially, they offered this resolve with two others declaring that any "merely federal" government, like the one linking sovereign states by the treatylike Articles of Confederation, could not achieve the Articles' express purposes of providing for "common defense, security of liberty, and general welfare," but quickly agreed that the one resolve would suffice.[56]

Surviving accounts differ on what happened next but clearly a fierce debate ensued. "Mr. Charles Pinckney wanted to know of Mr. Randolph whether he meant to abolish the State Governments altogether," Madison wrote. Pinckney's cousin, General Charles Cotesworth Pinckney, denounced the proposed resolution as beyond the scope of the Convention's call.

Gerry agreed. "A distinction has been made between a *federal* and *national* government," he complained. "We ought not to determine that there is this distinction or if we do, it is questionable not only whether this convention can propose a government totally different or whether Congress itself would have a right to pass such a resolution."[57] Despite fears of state excesses, Gerry still favored a federal system.

Randolph and Morris parried these blows as best they could. His resolution would not abolish the states, the Virginia governor asserted, only take from them such sovereignty as hinders the general government from achieving its legitimate objectives. Morris questioned whether the Convention could make any meaningful distinction between a federal and national system anyway. If by "federal," delegates meant "a mere compact resting on the good faith of the parties," then that could not secure the confederation's stated purposes. If "federal" instead meant a government that "has a right to compel every part to do its duty," then the United States lacked one. "In all communities there must be one supreme power, and only one," Morris stated. The result of leaving sovereignty with the states portended disaster. "We had better take [one] supreme government now, than a despot twenty years hence—for come he must," Morris warned.[58]

Washington sat silent in the hall but surely spoke in private. "Persuaded I am that the primary cause of all our disorders lies in the different State Governments," he soon wrote to a fellow nationalist in Virginia, "and in the tenacity of that power which pervades the whole of their systems." So long as states retained "independent sovereignty," Washington predicted, the country would remain weak.[59]

In addition to defending the states, opponents attacked the Virginia Plan's open-ended grant of power to Congress. Conceding "that additional powers were necessary, particularly that of raising money which would involve many other powers," Sherman stated that he was not "disposed to Make too great inroads on the existing system." For narrow-minded reformers, merely empowering Congress to impose a tariff on imports would suffice.

Agreeing with Sherman, Dickinson urged that, instead of debating the broad Virginia Plan, the delegates should simply decide what added powers they should vest in Congress. "We may resolve," he said, "that the confederation is defective; and then proceed to the definition of such powers as may be thought adequate to the objects for which it was instituted." When Dickinson's Delaware colleague George Read then moved to defer consideration of Randolph's motion until after debate on Dickinson's resolve, the Convention stood at a crossroads.

Every delegate understood the choice. "The object of the motion from Virginia [is] an establishment that is to act upon the whole people of the U.S.," Rufus King noted. "The object of the motion from Delaware seems to have application merely to the strengthening of the confederation by some additional powers."[60] The delegates must choose, King all but said, and the country needed more than Dickinson's approach allowed. If not yet fully convinced on all aspects of the Virginia Plan, at least many delegates already rejected the idea of merely amending the Articles of Confederation by granting added powers to Congress. Read's motion lost on a tie vote, four to four, with Virginia voting no. The delegates returned to Randolph's introductory resolve, which immediately passed with six states voting yes, New York divided, and only Sherman's Connecticut voting no. Once its motion had lost, even Delaware voted aye.[61] That settled, the Convention then moved on to the fifteen resolutions comprising the full Virginia Plan, which they took up, debated, revised, and expanded over the ensuing weeks.

The historic vote in favor of Randolph's first resolve, which set the stage for all that followed, represented the high-water mark of nationalist influence at the Convention. With the delegates sitting as a committee of the whole for three more weeks and then in convention with Washington in the chair for three long months, Sherman, Dickinson, Paterson, Read, Yates, Gerry, and other critics steadily chipped away at the Virginia Plan. The addition of John Lansing tipped the balance of New York's three-member delegation in their favor after June 2. They gained another key ally on June 9 when Maryland's clever but cantankerous Luther Martin took his seat. The arrival of representatives from New Hampshire on July 23 added to the mix. These anti-nationalist and small-state delegates often had the past abuses of British imperial policy forefront in their minds.

Focused instead on recent instances of states run riot and flanked by a shifting array of allies that often included Massachusetts and sometimes the Carolinas, Georgia, or other states, the Virginia and Pennsylvania delegations, representing America's two largest states, formed a virtual phalanx to defend the core concept of a supreme national government. Both sides claimed the moral high ground of liberty and justice for all free men.

One by one, the accoutrements of extreme nationalism fell away from the Constitution being crafted from the Virginia Plan, leaving the framework for a mixed government that remains susceptible to differing interpretations. The Virginia Plan would have empowered the national government "to call forth the full force of the Union" against states that failed to obey its commands. Even Madison could not stomach this and, on May 30, moved that it be struck. "The use of force against a State," he observed, "would probably be considered by the party attacked as a dissolution of all previous compacts by which it might be bound." He fought harder to retain authority for Congress to veto state laws but could only get three states to agree. Instead, the Convention left the defense of national supremacy to the courts, with its final draft providing that the Constitution, laws, and treaties of the United States "shall be the supreme Law of the Land; and the Judges in every State shall be bound thereby."

Led by Sherman and Martin, the extreme anti-nationalists tried to strike the provision for inferior national courts, so that state judges would rule on the validity of state laws subject only to appeal to a national supreme court. Arguing the obvious—that "inferior courts are essential to render the authority of the National Legislature effective"—nationalists secured the compromise that Congress at least *could* create lower national courts.[62]

WHILE THESE COMPROMISES ENSURED that the general government would not rule over the states by force and veto like the

British king and Parliament had reigned over the colonies, questions persisted about the extent of its power. Using their fluid procedural rules, the delegates repeatedly revisited the issue of whether the Constitution would invest the general government with open-ended power over "all cases to which the separate States are incompetent," as the Virginia Plan provided, or enumerated powers as Sherman, Dickinson, and other states' rights advocates wanted.[63]

When delegates first debated this provision on May 31, even members from Virginia admitted to having some qualms. Madison recorded himself as saying that "he had brought with him into the Convention a strong bias in favor of enumeration and definition of the powers necessary to be exercised by the national Legislature; but had also brought doubts about its practicability." His frustration with the inadequate grant of power under the Articles of Confederation made him doubt that any current drafters could anticipate future needs. For his part, Randolph "disclaimed any intention to give indefinite powers to the national Legislature."[64]

Washington again remained silent but soon wrote privately, "The Men who oppose a strong & energetic [national] government are, in my opinion, narrow minded politicians, or are under the influence of local views."[65]

Of all the delegates, it was Hamilton and Wilson—two pro-business nationalists from large commercial states—who most vocally defended an open-ended grant of power to Congress. On June 18, for example, after New Jersey proposed an enumerated list of powers in its alternate plan for a federal government, Hamilton exploded. "The general power . . . must swallow up the State powers, otherwise it will be swallowed up by them," he declared. "Between the National & State Legislatures," he later added, "the former must therefore have indefinite authority." It was then that Hamilton famously asserted that the centralized British government, with its aristocratic House of Lords and strong monarchy, "was the best in the world" and declared that nothing "short of it would do in America."

Wilson was more discreet. Distancing himself from Hamilton's extreme remarks, he still argued that the states should only survive as "lesser jurisdictions" or a "subdivision" of the nation.[66] When the New Jersey Plan garnered only three votes, the Convention was left with the Virginia Plan's language on national power. In an apparent nod to state-minded delegates, however, the Convention then passed a motion by Connecticut's Oliver Ellsworth deleting the opening reference to "a *national* government" from the Virginia Plan.[67] With this, the word "national" vanished from the emerging Constitution, and never returned.

In late July, without resolving an enumerated list of powers, the Convention sent the Virginia Plan's provision on congressional power along with all else that it had passed to a Committee of Detail, composed of Randolph, Wilson, Gorham, Ellsworth, and Rutledge, charged with weaving them into a single constitution. There, Randolph tried his hand at composing an enumeration of powers to replace the Virginia Plan's open-ended grant. His initial list then bounced around the committee until it included, among others, the power to lay and collect taxes; regulate international and interstate commerce; raise armies; and, in a sweeping final clause presumably added by Wilson, make "all laws that shall be necessary and proper for carrying into execution the forgoing powers."[68] Although Washington did not serve on this committee, its listing of enumerated powers mirrored the main concerns that he had expressed about limits on congressional power under the old confederation.

Madison accepted the list, too, but, along with the other compromises, it left him concerned about the government's authority. Privately, he worried that the Constitution would "neither effectually *answer* its *national object* nor prevent the local *mischiefs* which every where *excite disgusts* against the *state governments*."[69] Later, putting the best public face on the overall document, Madison depicted the new government as "of a mixed character, presenting at least as many *federal* as *national* features."[70]

From start to finish, Washington presided at the Convention without expressing his views on the proper extent of the general government's power. He did not need to. Ever since his 1783 Circular to the States, which was then the country's best-known public document other than the Declaration of Independence, Washington stood as the personification of nationalism in the United States. His daily presence on the dais spoke louder than the speeches of anyone in the hall. As Madison had planned, it gave weight to the Virginia Plan, which implicitly bore Washington's imprimatur. And when Randolph drafted an enumeration of powers that the Virginia delegation supported, it included every one that Washington had publicly endorsed.

No issue mattered more to him than the new government's supreme power and sovereignty. There were other topics for the members to address: some so divisive as to nearly derail the Convention; others that every delegate knew would directly impact Washington should he lead the resulting government. They would look to him on these issues, too, and he in turn helped to shape the outcome, but national supremacy mattered most to him. "Vain is it to look for respect from abroad, or tranquility at home," Washington wrote to Lafayette one day before the delegates approved the committee's list of enumerated powers, "till the wisdom and force of the Union can be more concentred."[71]

Charles Willson Peale's likeness of George Washington, sketched and printed in Philadelphia during the Constitutional Convention.

CHAPTER 5

In His Image

❧

REMARKABLY LITTLE INFORMATION LEAKED about the ongoing deliberations at the Convention. Indeed, once the thirty-eight delegates adopted the secrecy rule, news from the Convention virtually ceased. Later arriving delegates, even those from states not yet represented when the rule was adopted, obeyed it. Early departing delegates, even those who left in protest that the Convention had exceeded its mandate, obeyed it.

Historians have speculated that the states' rights patriot-agitator from Virginia, Patrick Henry, had he known what was afoot, would have ridden to the Convention, taken his seat, and denounced the nationalist plan offered by his state's delegation.[1] Yet, although Henry stayed away because he opposed the proceedings, no certain word of the Virginia Plan and its radical extent reached him. This remained true even after New York's two anti-nationalist delegates, Robert Yates and John Lansing, stormed out of the Convention on July 10. Although committed to fight ratification of any nationalist Constitution emerging from the Convention, they did not publicly expose the extralegal nature of the proceedings. Even though Lansing had not been present to vote on the secrecy rule, he obeyed it.

Nearly a hundred newspapers then existed in the United States, with a full dozen operating in Philadelphia. They were hungry for content and eagerly reprinted stories lifted from other papers, especially about politics. Any news from the Convention would have quickly spread through the states, but after the initial reports of delegates assembling and their selection of Washington as president, the reliable accounts stopped.

The few articles about the Convention that did appear were either hopelessly vague or simply wrong. Conflicting reports of the Convention's progress appeared in June, for example. "Though the particular arguments, debates, and decisions that take place in the federal Convention are considered as matters of secrecy," one widely republished article reported, "we understand, in general, that there exists a very great *diversity* of opinion amongst the members."[2] About the same time, another popular account stated, "We hear that the greatest *unanimity* subsists in the councils of the Federal Convention."[3] The most specific news appearing in widely circulating articles during the summer were wildly inaccurate reports that the delegates had voted to expel Rhode Island from the union and considered inviting George III's second son, the Duke of York and Albany, to become America's king.[4]

One early report from Philadelphia did hit the mark. "Such circumspection and secrecy mark the proceedings of the federal Convention," a June 2 article in the *Evening Herald* noted, "that the members find it difficult to acquire a habit of communication even among themselves, and are so cautious in defeating the curiosity of the public, that all debate is suspended upon the entrance of their own inferior officers." While the writer conceded the "propriety" of such secrecy, he urged the delegates to act with "dispatch, as the anxiety of the people must be necessarily increased, by every appearance of mystery in conducting this important business."[5]

Not everyone accepted the secrecy rule so readily. Commenting from Paris, Jefferson complained that it set an "abominable" precedent in a free society. "Nothing can justify this example," he wrote about the delegates, "but the innocence of their intentions, & ignorance of the value of public discussions."[6] Nevertheless the practice persisted for four months as the delegates wrangled behind closed doors and shuttered windows during a predictably hot and humid Philadelphia summer.

The silence engulfing the Convention especially limits what is known about Washington because, as the presiding officer, he rarely spoke on substantive matters inside the Assembly Room, where Madison dutifully recorded the debate. Washington did talk privately with other members, of course, and voted with the Virginia delegation.[7] He also supervised the floor debate and called on members when they spoke at the Convention. But no one recorded these utterances and, scrupulously obeying the secrecy rule, Washington did not repeat them in any surviving letters or other writings. The other members likely knew where he stood on significant matters but beyond his oft-stated desire to create a true national government with power to tax, maintain an army, and regulate interstate and international commerce—positions that he had publicly championed since 1783—the record of his specific contributions to the Constitution remains frustratingly oblique. We can only surmise those details from the clues available to us.[8]

The public silence was all the more remarkable because the members of the Convention otherwise did not act like Catholic cardinals sequestered to elect a pope. Quite to the contrary, they enjoyed an active social life in Philadelphia. Many of them regularly dined in clubs, drank at taverns, attended evening teas and balls, and went to concerts and plays. Such outings were particularly common for Washington, who was the lion of the summer season in Philadelphia high society.

And what a season it was. Never before or since has such a large share of the country's political, economic, and cultural elite gathered in one place for so long. As the wealthiest and most culturally sophisticated American city of the day, Philadelphia was ready, willing, and able to host them. In some of these social settings, at least among themselves and possibly within a discreet inner circle, the delegates discussed issues that they debated at the Convention.

IMITATING PARISIAN HIGH SOCIETY, a salon scene dominated by wealthy, independent-minded, married women flourished in Philadelphia during the 1780s. These ladies would invite large gatherings for evenings of tea and conversation in their parlors. During the summer of 1787, Washington was the most sought-after guest for such events and, according to his diary, he frequently attended them. Two or three evenings in a typical week, it records him having "tea" at the mansion of the Powels, the Binghams, or some other prominent Philadelphia couples.[9] For Washington, teas or dinners in "a very large Company" sometimes also occurred "at home" with the Morrises.[10] What he wrote of one evening out at the lavish in-town home of the lawyer Benjamin Chew and his independently wealthy, once-widowed wife, Elizabeth, Washington could have said about other evenings as well: "Drank Tea there in a very large circle of ladies."[11] He clearly enjoyed their attention, and they his. A leading figure in Virginia's social scene since his marriage to the rich widow Martha Custis in 1759, Washington excelled in polite conversation at tea, over drinks, or while dining.

At many of these Philadelphia teas, it was the wives who charmed. Elizabeth Powel, for example, was famously spirited. "She plays the leading role in the family—*la prima figura*, as the Italians say," Washington's friend the Marquis de Chastellux wrote about her during his visit in 1780. "She has wit and good memory, speaks well and talks a great deal." Washington particularly enjoyed her company. He spent at least fifteen evenings at the Powels' during the Convention, wrote to Elizabeth frequently, and accompanied her to plays and concerts. "What chiefly distinguishes her," Chastellux observed, was "her taste for conversation and the truly European manner in which she used her wit and knowledge." Elizabeth Powel would later comment about the summer of 1787 that she "associated with the most respectable, influential Members of the Convention that framed the Constitution, and that the all important Subject was frequently discussed at our House."[12] A discreet hostess, she kept any conversations about the Constitution confidential.

Robert Morris's wife, Mary, and Anne Bingham, daughter of the colonial mayor Thomas Willing and wife of the merchant-prince William Bingham, were every bit as engaging and politically astute as Elizabeth Powel. Washington often attended plays, concerts, and other cultural events with Mary Morris, and spent at least six evenings at the Binghams' house, which many thought the finest mansion in town. With two formal parlors, a grand ballroom, and a marble central hall, even Washington remarked on its "great splendor."[13]

Because they never published their political views, it is unclear how these women may have influenced the Convention. In all likelihood, they were conservative nationalists who favored a strong executive and hoped that Washington would fill the role.[14] Consider some evidence. Mary Morris's husband, Robert, was the leading nationalist in the Confederation Congress and architect of its effort to create executive offices. Anne Bingham's father, Thomas Willing, was a conservative member of the Continental Congress who voted against independence and later presided over the nationalists' Bank of the United States; her husband, William, would become an arch-nationalist United States senator. Elizabeth Chew's husband, Benjamin, worked for Pennsylvania's British proprietors before the Revolutionary War and was detained by patriot authorities during it. Elizabeth Powel remained in Philadelphia throughout the British occupation of 1777–78 with her husband Samuel, the mayor, widely suspected of Tory sympathies. Later, she helped to persuade Washington to serve a second term as President.

Given the leanings of their hosts, these Philadelphia salons of the 1780s were more likely modeled after those of Louis XVI's Paris than a model for those of revolutionary France. It then may have been with a twinkle in his eye that, when asked by Elizabeth Powel at the Convention's end about what sort of government the delegates had created, Franklin reportedly replied, "A republic, madam, if you can keep it."[15] Like some of the delegates, she may have wanted a less republican government than Franklin did.

ONCE THE CONVENTION AGREED to form a sovereign general government with three separate branches, its focus shifted to the balance of power among those branches. In the delegates' eyes, the presidency would possess basic executive authority, the future House of Representatives would hold broad legislative power, and the Supreme Court would play a purely judicial role. The Senate proved more problematic, however, and that inevitably impacted the other branches, especially the presidency.

Prior to the Revolutionary War, most colonial governors were appointed by the king and advised by a council composed of leading local citizens. This council typically served both as a valued check on a governor's exercise of executive authority, including in the appointment of officers, and as an upper legislative house akin to the British House of Lords. As such, it had executive and legislative functions. Some delegates saw the Senate playing this dual role in the new central government, and therefore wanted it to have a say in the appointment of judges and officers, the drafting of treaties, and the execution of policy as well as in the passage of legislation. Others saw less reason to restrain the executive authority of a chosen American President than a royally appointed governor but still favored a bicameral legislature. The delegates battled for months over the precise balance of power among the branches, particularly between the President and the Senate. In his prize-winning history of the Constitution, Jack Rakove equated this task to solving a complex equation with a large number of dependent variables. "Change the value of one, and the values shift throughout," he wrote.[16]

Since everyone presumed that Washington would become the new government's first executive, no one could conceive of the position without thinking about him in it. Indeed, within the year, Pierce Butler flatly stated that his colleagues at the Convention "shaped their Ideas and Powers to be given to the President, by their opinions of [Washington's] Virtue."[17] Although many members looked beyond Washington in crafting the executive, their faith in his virtue likely made them more open to strengthening the office.

The presidency was the Convention's most original creation. Groping for analogies while debating it, delegates at various times alluded to the Venetian Republic's doge, the Holy Roman Emperor, the king of Poland, the consuls of ancient Rome, and even the pope as examples of political leaders chosen by some sort of elite electorate. None of these analogies fit. The American presidency was something new under the sun.

For Congress, in contrast, the delegates needed only look to their state legislatures. From the beginning, they leaned toward a two-chamber Congress with a broadly representative lower house, elected by popular vote and allocated by population, much like the lower house of every state's legislature. The upper house was trickier, but for it, too, the delegates could build on the experience of state governments, most of which had some sort of senate or council with mixed executive and legislative functions and whose members were chosen by a narrower electorate and for longer terms than members of the state's lower house. The puzzle here came in fixing the proper balance of executive and legislative duties for a national senate and determining how to allocate and choose its members. The states offered poorer precedents for the presidency, as quickly became clear.

HAVING AGREED TO BEGIN their deliberations by working through the Virginia Plan as a committee of the whole, the delegates reached the plan's two resolutions regarding the executive on June 1. The longer of these called for a "National Executive" chosen by Congress for a single term of some fixed but unspecified length. "Besides a general authority to execute the national laws," it stated, this officer "ought to enjoy the Executive rights vested in Congress by the Confederation." The shorter one provided a limited means of vetoing bills passed by Congress.[18]

If these "Executive rights" included all those once held by the British monarch and later vested in Congress, the two resolutions gave considerable power to the executive. In addition to executing laws, the king held direct authority over war and peace, the military, foreign affairs, appointing officers and judges, convening and proroguing Parliament, and granting pardons, to name just a few. Since the Articles of Confederation vested power over war, peace, foreign affairs, and appointing officers in Congress, these powers might go to the executive under the Virginia Plan. Then again, they might not. The resolutions were frustratingly vague on such matters.

Perhaps because Washington was sitting among them, when the delegates reached these resolutions, they fell unusually silent. Even Sherman, Gerry, and Dickinson said nothing. After brief comments by two supporters of a strong executive, Madison wrote in his notes, "a considerable pause ensued" and the chair asked if the delegates were ready to vote. With the provisions coming from Washington's delegation, no one seemed inclined to dispute them. Washington would be the first President, of course, and the delegates appeared reluctant to cross him.[19] But who would follow Washington? Franklin broke the silence. Observing that the structure of the executive is "of great importance," he urged the delegates to "deliver their sentiments on it before the question was put."[20] Franklin's comment burst the dam and debate flooded the room. Four days later, with the discussion still going strong, Franklin would add with reference to Washington and the debate over the executive, "The first man, put at the helm would be a good one. No body knows what sort may come afterwards. The executive will always be increasing here, as elsewhere, till it ends in a monarchy."[21]

That was the rub. The colonies had revolted in part against abuses by a monarch and his appointed governors. "The history of the present King of Great Britain," the Declaration of Independence asserted, "is a history of repeated injuries and usurpations, all having in direct object the establishment of an absolute Tyranny over these States."[22]

An injury once suffered is a lesson long learned. Upon removing their royal governors, many of the newly independent states limited executive power by having their governors elected by legislators for short terms and requiring them to act in consort with counselors or senators. Most lost the veto power. The post was so emaciated in Pennsylvania that Washington questioned Franklin's decision to accept it.[23]

The inefficiencies, corruption, and demagoguery associated with unchecked legislative power in some states caused a reaction. New York and Massachusetts soon restored a measure of executive independence by having their governors elected by popular vote and arming them with a limited power to veto bills. At the Convention, the debate over executive authority was further complicated by the added powers over war, peace, and foreign policy, which governors never held but traditionally were lodged directly in the monarch. The prospect of such awesome powers passing to a national executive forced the delegates to reflect on their experiences under King George III. Franklin was right: the delegates had much to consider in crafting the presidency.

THE MEMBERS DEBATED the executive at length three separate times during the Convention: early June, mid-July, and early September. During the first of these occasions, they raised virtually all of the issues about the presidency that would later occupy them, but they had trouble even resolving whether one person or a committee should hold the office. With Washington in the room, a unitary executive should have seemed obvious to all, especially since every state had but one governor. Fearful of investing too much power in any single person, however, some delegates—including two within Washington's own delegation—favored an executive triumvirate like those of late republican Rome. Denouncing a single executive as "the fetus of monarchy," Randolph averred that "the people" would oppose it.[24] Further, Mason added, an executive troika could better represent the country's three regions—North, middle, and South—than any one ruler could.[25]

These comments on a single executive, coming as they did from old friends, surely vexed Washington, who prided himself on his republican virtue, public support, and unbiased nationalism. Every delegate who knew him well must have understood that Washington would neither consent to serve as one member of an executive triumvirate nor be suited for such a post. While he remained silently seated next to Randolph and Mason, others rallied to defend the sort of unitary executive that Washington was so clearly qualified to fill. "Delay, divisions and dissentions arise from an executive consisting of many," Butler warned.[26] "Unity in the Executive" promotes "vigor and dispatch" in office, Wilson added, and by fixing responsibility on one person, served as "the best safeguard against tyranny."[27] Gerry stressed that a troika would be particularly troublesome in war. "It would be a general with three heads," he declared.[28]

While these positions came out in the course of the formal debate, delegates discussed them on other occasions as well. Like Washington, some members regularly attended evening teas and balls, where they could talk in semiprivate settings. Even those delegates who did not circulate in high society inevitably spent considerable time together outside the Assembly Room. Most of them lived tightly packed into a handful of the city's best boardinghouses—such as those run by Mary House or Mary Dailey—and inns, where they dined at common tables. City Tavern, Indian Queen, Springsbury Manor, and other public dining halls also hosted informal "clubs" at which delegates could gather for dinner. Significantly, these lodging and dining arrangements did not segregate along state, regional, or ideological lines, but instead threw delegates together in a social and partisan mix that encouraged them to share ideas and build relationships.

As much as he enjoyed life at the Morris mansion, where he could dine in elegance every day, Washington frequently ate "in club" with other members. Indeed, on June 2, after the extent of disagreement over the power, structure, and selection of the executive first became apparent, Washington ate with the club at City Tavern, where the subject of the day's heated debate likely came up and surely remained on everyone's mind. While in session earlier that day, the delegates raised and could not resolve whether the United States should have one executive officer or three. Reminiscent of debates held in the same room over independence in 1776, some members had returned to first principles regarding the executive. Warning of the "natural inclination in mankind to Kingly Government," Franklin favored measures to avoid "nourish[ing] the fetus of a King." John Dickinson, Franklin's nemesis on the issue of independence in 1776, replied "that a firm Executive could only exist in a limited monarchy."[29] The delegates stood far apart.

Now, later that evening, as many of those members casually dined with the man who would be that king, Washington's presence must have reassured them. As a frequent guest at City Tavern, Pierce Butler may have been present. If so, it might explain his later comment that powers vested in the chief executive under the Constitution would not "have been so great had not many of the members cast their eyes toward General Washington as President."[30] At the Convention's next session, the states voted by a margin of seven to three for a single executive and, unlike most of their decisions, never revisited it. Virginia joined the majority, with Washington casting the deciding vote within its five-member delegation.[31]

HAVING A SINGLE EXECUTIVE did not settle either the extent of executive powers or whether their exercise would require the advice or consent of an executive counsel, or senate. At this early stage of the proceedings, the delegates simply agreed that those powers should be enumerated in the Constitution and would include a limited veto over legislation, which Congress could override by a two-thirds vote.[32] Led by Wilson and Madison, even the most ardent supporters of a strong presidency consistently maintained that, in a republic, the executive should not decide matters of war and peace. "The only powers he conceived strictly Executive were those of executing the laws," Wilson observed at the outset, "and appointing officers not appertaining to and appointed by the Legislature." Extending these powers to war and peace, Charles Pinckney added, "would render the Executive a Monarchy, of the worst kind, towit an elective one."[33]

When first debating the executive in early June, many of the members knew Washington only by reputation and no consensus had yet emerged on the nature or structure of the general government. Madison, Wilson, Gouverneur Morris, and Charles Pinckney, for example, came to the Convention committed to forming a true national government founded on proportionate representation in Congress and an independent executive under the control of a single individual. Pinckney's initial plan used the term "President" for the executive officer and, after much back-and-forth over the title, it became the one that stuck. Under the Virginia Plan, Congress would choose this officer for a single fixed term but, to separate power, Wilson always wanted the President elected by the people or by independent electors and eligible for reelection.

Morris and Madison quickly came around to Wilson's view on presidential selection but, until nearly the Convention's end, most delegates favored having Congress pick the executive for a single seven-year term. With such a long term, however, they worried about what to do if problems arose. This led them in June to add a means for impeachment and removal.[34] The following month, when the Convention next debated the presidency, Mason spoke for a shrinking majority when he pronounced "that an election by the National

Legislature as originally proposed was the best. If it was liable to objections, it was liable to fewer than the others."[35] By then, however, this method survived with only six states still backing it and five states opposed or not voting. Washington joined Madison in voting no, which split Virginia's delegation and kept it from casting a vote.[36] The tension in that small group, particularly between Washington and Mason, must have been palpable. With the presumptive first President opposed, the issue was ripe for reconsideration.

Three middle-state delegations—New York, New Jersey, and Delaware—proved particularly resistant to any reforms that would significantly strengthen the presidency. Together with half of the Maryland delegation, they formed a block committed to preserve an equal say for each state in Congress and in choosing the executive. From the outset, Connecticut's Roger Sherman pushed for the compromise of having one house of Congress represent people and another represent states, but, depicting the executive as "nothing more than an institution for carrying the will of the Legislature into effect," he wanted the President to serve without a fixed term at the whim of Congress.[37] If followed, this would have created something akin to a parliamentary republic. By September, Wilson could rightly say about the presidency, "It is in truth the most difficult of all on which we have had to decide."[38]

WITH LITTLE MORE SETTLED about the presidency than that only one person would fill it a time and the delegates moving on to other issues, Washington took Sunday, June 10, to visit Bartram's Garden, on the Schuylkill River about three miles from Philadelphia. Founded by John Bartram in 1728 as the first commercial nursery in the colonies, the garden became an international clearinghouse for American plants. Bartram and his sons John Jr. and William traveled through the colonies gathering seeds and cuttings for propagation and sale. They returned with hundreds of previously unknown species, including a widely celebrated small flowering tree that William named *Franklinia* for Philadelphia's first citizen. John's knack for finding new species led George III to name him as the King's Botanist for North America. Following John's death in 1777, John Jr. ran the garden while William gathered plants. When Washington visited in 1787, William was in the midst of turning the journal of his latest collecting trip into a lyrical and lasting book, *Travels Through North & South Carolina, Georgia, [and] East and West Florida*, which was destined to inspire a generation of nature writers and poets. After the volume failed to find a publisher, Washington helped to underwrite its first printing in 1791.

Three days earlier, the cool, rainy Pennsylvania spring had abruptly given way to a hot, humid Philadelphia summer, making that Sunday an ideal time for Washington to escape the city. Accustomed to the large, formal plantings at Virginia's grand estates, he privately expressed disappointment with the small size and functional arrangement of Bartram's Garden, but was delighted by its many curious and exotic plants.[39] He returned again in September, when different flowers bloomed, and subsequently ordered hundreds of plants for Mount Vernon from the Bartrams. On his first trip to the garden, Washington also stopped by a nearby farm to examine the effect of using gypsum as fertilizer. Taking notes on the process, he soon introduced it at Mount Vernon.

Anyone watching Washington on that steamy Sunday in June would be hard-pressed to see him as a would-be Caesar conspiring to create an imperial presidency for himself. He played the Cincinnatus, more interested in plants than power. After observing him up close as President, John Adams later described Washington as the finest political actor he ever saw—but these pastoral pursuits were not for show. That very evening, with the spring rains finally over, he penned meticulous instructions to his nephew on planting the summer crops at Mount Vernon. "Delay no more," he wrote about the turnips, "that the whole may be put in before the season is too far advanced."[40] As other delegates fretted over the Constitution, Washington worried about turnip plants. He likely talked about them and other agricultural matters with the members who owned farms. During the course of the summer, he also visited nearby vineyards, gristmills, and even a bee yard—peppering their owners with practical questions in each instance. This facet of Washington's character appealed to republicans wary of a national power grab. Yet as much as he cared about his plantation, Washington was determined to see the process through at the Convention and was one of the few delegates never to miss a session. "There is not the smallest prospect of my returning before harvest," he wrote to his nephew in early June, "and God knows how long it may be after it."[41]

BOGGED DOWN IN DETAILS, once the delegates deferred further consideration of the executive on June 9, the Senate took center stage in their deliberations. The nationalistic Virginia Plan called for proportional representation in both house of Congress, with the plan's most ardent and insightful proponents viewing population as the *only* just way to allocate seats. They foresaw the United States as a nation of people rather than a confederation of states. "As all authority was derived from the people," Wilson explained early on, "equal numbers of people ought to have an equal number of representatives."[42]

While a majority of delegations accepted this nationalist viewpoint, a determined minority made up mainly of small states clung to the federalist fundamental of equal representation for every state. Motivated by some mix of high ideals and state interest, most members of these delegations wanted merely an enhanced confederation of sovereign states. "Let them unite if they please," New Jersey's William Paterson said on June 9 of the states favoring proportional representation, "but let them remember that they have no authority to compel the others to unite. New Jersey would be swallowed up. I would rather submit to a Monarch, to a despot, than to such a fate."[43] The New Jersey, Delaware, and New York delegations backed

Paterson on this key point, as did half of the delegates from Maryland.

Seeking compromise, Connecticut's delegation proposed having proportional representation in Congress's lower house and equal representation in the Senate, but such a novel and unprincipled mishmash only slowly won favor at the Convention. The battle for representation went on for weeks, first in the committee of the whole with Washington sitting as a member of Virginia's delegation and later, after June 19, at the Convention with him presiding. A fight over deep principle with profound practical implications, it was the one clash that threatened to derail the Convention.

"Can we forget for whom we are forming a Government? Is it for *men*, or for the imaginary beings called *States*?" Wilson asked for the nationalists.[44] He objected to a majority of the states having power to set the nation's course when those states contained a minority of its people and wealth: they could easily abuse their power.

Other delegates saw their rights and welfare flowing from the states and did not want to disenfranchise them. "A general government will never grant me this," Oliver Ellsworth said of his domestic happiness, "as it cannot know my wants or relieve my distress."[45] Jonathan Dayton of New Jersey dismissed Connecticut's proposed compromise as "a novelty, an amphibious monster . . . that never would be rec[eive]d by the people."[46]

Franklin, though, was not so sure. Looking at both sides in his folksy, pragmatic way, he noted, "If a proportional representation takes place, the small States contend that their liberties will be in danger. If an equality of votes is to be put in its place, the large States say their money will be in danger." Like a carpenter making a table from planks of uneven length, he would add or subtract a little from each to make a good fit.[47]

By Saturday, June 30, some big-state nationalists wanted to call the bluff of those demanding equal representation. "If a minority should refuse their assent to the new plan of a general government," Wilson asserted, "and if they will have their own will, and without it separate the union, let it be done." It could not happen on better grounds, he added.[48]

Madison and Rufus King agreed. If the Convention caved on this point, King declared, then "our business here is at an end."[49] Delaware's impetuous Gunning Bedford Jr. shot back, "The Large States dare not dissolve the confederation. If they do the small ones will find some foreign ally . . . who will take them by the hand and do them justice." Turning to the nationalists, he said with emphasis, "*I do not, gentleman, trust you*."[50] The delegates adjourned for the week in disarray with a vote on the so-called Connecticut Compromise scheduled for Monday.

Watching the increasingly bitter debate from the chair, Washington nearly lost hope. That evening, he dined with delegates in club at Springsbury Manor and the next day met with Gouverneur and Robert Morris. According to an account of that meeting by the first editor of Washington's papers, the perspicacious Jared Sparks, who later became president of Harvard, all three were dejected by the "deplorable state of things at the Convention." They complained of conflicting opinions "obstinately adhered to" and members threatening to leave. "At this alarming crisis," the account noted, "a dissolution of the Convention was hourly to be apprehended."[51]

Hamilton in fact had departed on the thirtieth, and the other New York delegates soon followed him home. "I am seriously and deeply distressed at the aspect of the Councils which prevailed when I left Philadelphia," he wrote to Washington. "I fear we shall let slip the golden opportunity of rescuing the American empire from disunion anarchy and misery."[52] Washington replied in near anguish: "I *almost* dispair of seeing favourable issue to the proceedings of the Convention, and do therefore repent having had any agency in the business."[53] Firmly in the nationalist camp, Washington presumably favored proportional representation in Congress but, like Franklin, was probably willing to take from both sides to save the middle. Indeed, from this point on, all of Washington's actions can most easily be seen as the efforts of a determined leader trying to achieve meaningful consensus.

On July 2, when delegates finally voted on the Connecticut Compromise, the Convention deadlocked: five to five with one state split. Virginia voted no. Declaring "we are now a full stop," Sherman backed a motion to commit the matter to a committee with one member from each state, where cooler heads might prevail. "Something must be done, or we shall disappoint not only America, but the whole world," Gerry pleaded. As he saw it, not only the Convention, but the country, hung in the balance. "If we do nothing, it appears to me we must have war and confusion—for the old confederation would be at an end." Led by Madison and Wilson, most big-state nationalists opposed the move but, perhaps influenced by his meeting with Washington, Gouverneur Morris endorsed the motion and it passed with Virginia voting yes.[54] The delegates then stacked the committee with moderates like Franklin and Gerry from big states and hardliners like Paterson and Bedford from small ones. A vocal critic of centralized power, Gerry chaired the committee.

With its most divisive issue in the hands of this so-called Grand Committee, the Convention recessed early for Independence Day. "Happy indeed would it be if the Convention shall be able to recommend such a firm and permanent Government for this Union, as all who live under it may be Secure in their lives, liberty and property," Washington wrote on July 1 to a confidant in Virginia, "but what will be the final result of its deliberations, the book of fate must disclose." Alluding to the ongoing debates, he warned, "Whilst the local views of each State and the separate interests by which they are too much govern'd will not yield to a more enlarged scale of politicks; incompatibility in the laws of different States, and disrespect to those of the general government must render the situation of this great Country weak, inefficient and disgraceful."[55]

THE FOURTH OF JULY never came at a more opportune time. And never before or since did so many of the country's founders gather at one place for the occasion. In its galaxy of patriot luminaries, it outshone even the first Fourth in Philadelphia, which lacked Washington and much of America's military elite. Among the delegates in attendance on July 4, the Convention included six signers of the Declaration of Independence. And of the fifty-five delegates who attended the Convention at some point, nearly three-fourths had represented their states in Congress during the Revolutionary War and more than half had served in the Continental Army or wartime state militias. Among delegates with military service, six endured the grim winter of 1777–78 at Valley Forge, five engaged in the brutal southern campaigns of 1779–81, and five participated in the decisive victory at Yorktown in 1781. Franklin, of course, made that final victory possible by brokering the alliance with France. Every delegate could reflect on personal sacrifices endured or witnessed for independence. To them, the Fourth held sacred significance. Further, many patriot notables lived in Philadelphia, including two added signers of the Declaration of Independence, and an array of Revolutionary War officers assembled in the city on that Independence Day for the annual meeting of the state's chapter of the Cincinnati.

Festivities began before dawn with the assembling of the city's militia and ended after dark in a stunning display of fireworks. The infantry shot its first feu de joie at 6 A.M., surely waking much of the city. Artillery followed with three times thirteen rounds of cannon fire. Church bells rang through the morning and troops paraded to martial music. At eleven, Washington, and many delegates and other dignitaries, attended a patriotic oration at the Reformed Calvinist Church, where the speaker predicted "the stately fabric of a free and vigorous government rising out of the wisdom of a Federal Convention" as if it were predestined to happen. The afternoon was marked by "entertainments" at various taverns, where, as one newspaper wrote, "different parties from the city and Jersey met with mutual congratulations, and spent the remainder of the day with liberality and good humour."

Washington joined the party at Epple's Tavern before retiring to the Powel's home for evening tea. Formal toasts of the day typically included ones to Washington, Franklin, and the Convention: "May they recommend, and the United States adopt, such a plan, as will secure the happiness of America," proclaimed the party at Preston's Tavern. Had these revelers known of the discord within the Convention, they might not have cheered so loudly.[56]

The spirit of the day likely reminded the delegates of the cords already binding the states and prodded them to seek some way forward. For weeks following the Fourth, Philadelphia's newspapers carried accounts of Independence Day orations and toasts from nearby towns and neighboring states. Everywhere, it seemed, Americans were looking toward Washington and the Convention. "The Grand Convention, may they form a constitution for an eternal republic," one of the thirteen toasts at New Jersey's capital declared, while in New York, citizens hailed, "The Convention in Philadelphia, may an energetic federal government be the results of their councils." From nearby Lancaster, the first toast was to the Fourth, the second to Congress, the third to Washington, "the Father and Savior of his Country," the eighth to Franklin, and the ninth to "the members of the present Convention: May they do as much towards the *support* of our Independence, as their virtuous President did towards establishing it." The sentiments were similar across the land. "The Convention now sitting," remarked one correspondent in Philadelphia's *Independent Gazetteer* on July 6, "stands remarkable and alone in political history." Where before governments were forced on people, "it still seems singular to see an authority . . . presiding tacitly over the confederation of the states by voluntary election."[57]

With an insatiable public demand for his image, Washington used this pause in the proceedings to sit for artist Charles Willson Peale, the leading portraitist of the revolutionary generation. Washington had sat for Peale five prior times, beginning in 1772, when Peale portrayed him as a boyish-looking militia officer. In all, from seven sittings spread over twenty-three years, Peale would make sixty paintings and numerous prints of Washington. In Peale's earlier portraits of him, Washington appeared younger than his age with a smooth, confident face and eyes generally looking away, as if into the future. The portrait from the Convention depicts a much older man, with some wrinkles and a slightly sagging jaw, but still in a crisp officer's uniform and now staring straight ahead with large, firm, fixed eyes. Peale's mezzotint print from this sitting reads, "His Excel: G: Washington Esq: L.L.D. Late Commander in Chief of the Armies of the U.S. of America & President of the Convention of 1787." Already, Washington's role at the Convention vied with his military service as worthy of note on a commercial print, which Peale offered for sale at one dollar per copy even before the proceedings ended.[58] The only image of Washington drawn at the Convention, and one made at a low point in the deliberations, Peale's print shows him weary but determined: a general who won a war of attrition with a world power by never surrendering.

WHILE WASHINGTON POSED, Franklin worked his mediating magic in the Grand Committee. Hosting committee members for dinner on July 2 and then meeting with them at the State House on the third, Franklin proposed his version of the Connecticut Compromise. For small states, he offered "an equal vote" for every state in the Senate; for large states, he offered one member in the future House of Representatives "for every forty thousand inhabitants" plus the concession that all bills raising or spending money would originate in this lower house and could not be amended by the Senate. Presumably, this arrangement would protect the small states' liberty and the large states' money. Although each side objected to some part of the compromise, the committee agreed to submit it to the Convention, as Gerry explained, "merely in order that some ground of accommodation might be proposed."[59] After more bitter debate and some minor amendments, the Convention narrowly passed the compromise on July 16 and never looked back. Franklin's greased language left three open issues: how would the limits on money bills operate, who are "inhabitants" for purposes of apportioning the House, and what constitutes an equal vote in the Senate. In the further debate, Washington deftly played a conciliating role.

Surprisingly, the concession on money bills split the big-state delegates. Although intended to limit the power of the small-state-dominated Senate, some big-state nationalists like Wilson, Madison, and Gouverneur Morris feared that the provision would undermine that body's ability to check democratic excess in the lower house. In August, after the bar against the Senate originating or amending money bills was included in the draft constitution compiled from provisions already approved by the Convention, these delegates pushed to remove it. Other big-state delegates viewed the concession as essential to their states' interests, however. "To strike out the section, was to unhinge the compromise of which it made a part," Virginia's George Mason complained.

Casting the deciding vote in a divided Virginia delegation, Washington first voted to strike the provision, but when the issue came up again five days later, he switched sides and carried Virginia with him. "He disapproved & till now voted against," Madison wrote, but "gave up his judgment, he said, because it was not very material weight with him & was made an essential point with others, who if disappointed, might be less cordial in other points of real weight."[60] Ultimately, the Convention settled on language that surely pleased Washington: "All Bills for raising revenue shall originate in the House of Representatives: but the Senate may propose or concur with amendments as on other bills."[61]

The Grand Committee's proposal to apportion the House of Representatives based on the number of a state's "inhabitants" reopened the explosive issue of slavery. When the delegates originally accepted the principle of proportional representation for Congress, they simply agreed to allocate seats "according to *some* equitable ratio of representation," which many believed should factor in both people and property since government was instituted to protect both.[62] As a practical matter, because they had relatively more slaves and fewer free people than their northern counterparts, southern states would lose power under any allocation based strictly on free inhabitants. Factoring in property could help to equalize representation between North and South, but counting slaves as people would produce similar results. The problem with the later approach was, as some northern delegates noted, the South treated slaves as property, not people. If people were the sole basis for representation, Gerry bluntly asked when this issue first arose, "Why then should the blacks, who were property in the South, be in the rule of representation more than the cattle & horses of the North?"[63]

In mid-June, when many delegates were still thinking in terms of an "equitable ratio" that factored in property as well as people, they easily accepted a plan proposed by Wilson and seconded by Charles Pinckney to apportion congressional seats among the states in proportion to the whole number of their free inhabitants plus "three fifths of all other persons," meaning slaves.[64] In devising this now shocking formula, the delegates were not thinking of slaves as having three-fifths of the moral worth of free persons but, in even less human terms, as having three-fifths of the property value of free people. Astonishing as it seems today, the so-called three-fifths compromise initially passed with only Gerry speaking against it, and he couched his opposition in terms of not wanting slaves "put upon the Footing of freemen."[65] Even Gouverneur Morris, who opposed expressly counting slaves for purposes of representation, accepted doing so as a rough gauge of property.[66]

By mid-July, after Gerry's Grand Committee proposed and the Convention agreed to allocate House seats based on population with one representative for each forty thousand inhabitants, no one could disguise the three-fifths rule as merely a means to factor in the relative worth of southern property. "Individuals" could only mean people. With tensions raised by the battle over equal representation, other northerners now joined Gerry in arguing that slaves should not count at all because their states treated them as property. "Has a man in Virginia a number of votes in proportion to the number of his slaves" Paterson asked in a rhetorical question addressed directly to Washington, "and if Negroes are not represented in the states to which they belong, why should they be represented in the General Government?"[67] Even Wilson, who had proposed the compromise, observed that "the blending of the blacks with the whites" in allocating seats would "give disgust to the people of Pen[nsylvani]a."[68] South Carolina's Pierce Butler and Charles Pinckney responded by demanding that slaves count as whole people despite their lack of rights. "The security that the South[er]n States want is that their negroes not be taken from them," Butler thundered.[69] Virtually no one expressed concern for the slaves. They became white men's pawns in a North-South power struggle over representation.

For those delegates principally concerned with preserving what had been gained to this point, the goal became getting the delegations back to the three-fifths compromise. Randolph, Madison, Ellsworth, and Charles Pinckney all tried at different points, and eventually succeeded after a week of wrangling. Washington played a part when, in the midst of this debate, a committee chaired by Gouverneur Morris proposed an initial allocation of House seats. Challenged by delegates who thought their states underrepresented, Morris explained that his committee used an estimate—really "little more than a guess," he said—of population and property in allocating seats.[70]

Washington promptly created another committee, which made a new allocation using the three-fifths compromise.[71] In a similarly pragmatic move made near the Convention's end, when some members urged that the limit on the number of representatives per state be lowered from no more than one for every forty thousand inhabitants to no more than one for every thirty thousand, Washington broke his silence on substantive issues. "It was much to be desired that the objections to the plan recommended might be made as few as possible," he stated, and this change accommodated a general inse-curity "for the rights & interests of the people."[72] With Washington's endorsement, the amendment passed unanimously.

Two added issues relating to slavery arose in late August, as Washington and other delegates pushed toward adjournment. The first involved imposing a twenty-year ban on Congress's power to bar the importation of slaves; the second related to a proposed clause requiring free states to return fugitive slaves to their masters in slave states. By this time, Washington had new hope that the Convention would soon end successfully. "By slow, I wish I could add & sure, movements, the business of the Convention progresses," he wrote to Henry Knox on August 19. "I am fully persuaded," he added about the emerging Constitution, "it is the best that can be obtained at the present moment, under such diversity of ideas as prevail."[73]

Then, two days later, Charles Pinckney threatened that South Carolina would never ratify that document if it allowed Congress to limit the slave trade. Others made similar threats on behalf of the lower South states of Georgia and North Carolina, where demand for new slaves remained high.[74] With Washington presiding, the delegates agreed to restrict congressional power over this form of international commerce. Analyzing the debate, historian Paul Finkelman concluded that the Carolinas and Georgia would not have walked over this mat-ter.[75] No states cared enough to test them, however, though Virginia and three other states voted to hold the restriction to twelve years.[76]

For all the future horror that it caused, the Fugitive Slave Clause generated even less controversy at the Convention than the slave-trade provision. Butler raised the matter on August 28, and the clause passed without debate or opposition on the next day. Decades later, it would contribute to the crises leading toward the Civil War, but northern delegates seemed more intent on stitching the Constitution together than keeping it from later falling apart. Perhaps they feared that, had they resisted, their slave-state counterparts might again threaten to defeat the Constitution, with the threats coming from upper as well as lower South delegates.[77] And the upper South included Virginia, where, due to the proximity of Pennsylvania, runaway slaves were a major worry. They posed a personal problem for Washington, who doggedly pursued fugitives from Mount Vernon. He likely favored the clause, and if so, his support would carry weight. "His strong personal commitment to the status quo of slavery made the topic especially difficult," historian Fritz Hirschfeld concludes from his analysis of this issue. "There was probably not a single representative at the convention who was willing to provoke Washington on this sensitive topic."[78] In its provisions on slavery as much as in its conception of the presidency, the Constitution was crafted in Washington's image.[79]

A third issue left open by the compromise on representation involved how a state would receive its "equal vote" in the Senate. Under the Articles of Confederation, each state had one vote in Congress and could instruct its representatives how to cast it. These members served at the pleasure of their state's legislature and truly represented the state's interests. Some Convention delegates thought that the Senate should operate in a similar fashion but nationalists like Madison and Hamilton envisioned it as a quasi-aristocratic body whose members served long, staggered terms. These independent senators would serve as a check on the popularly elected House of Representatives. An elite Senate could also act in a quasi-executive fashion somewhat like the governor's councils that still existed in some states and formerly were common in the colonies.

Seizing the initiative on July 23, Gouverneur Morris and Rufus King moved that the Senate consist of a fixed number of members from each state—the Convention set this figure at two—who would serve six-year terms and vote individually.[80] Although appointed by state legislatures, their long terms and independent votes would create, as Randolph depicted it, "the countenance of an aristocracy." Mason was blunter about these senators. "Chosen by the States for 6 years," he noted, they "will probably settle themselves at the seat of Gov[ernmen]t [and] will pursue schemes for their own aggran-dizement."[81] Over time, in practice if not in theory, the result might approach what Hamilton had in mind for the Senate—an American House of Lords.[82] Not surprisingly, nineteen of the Convention's fifty-five delegates, including both Morrises, later became senators.

With New York's anti-nationalists having already departed in disgust, the only opposition to individual voting by senators came from the Maryland delegates still committed to preserving a con-federation of states. Luther Martin denounced it "as departing from the idea of the *States* being represented" while Daniel Carroll added that "he did not wish so hastily to make so material an innovation."[83] Their state was outvoted, ten to one.

BY THE LAST WEEK OF JULY, when the delegates resolved the Senate's structure and reconfirmed their earlier decision to have the President chosen by Congress for a single seven-year term, the Con-vention had at least tentatively and in a piecemeal fashion approved the component parts for a complete plan of government. On July 26, after referring all of the various provisions passed so far to the five-member Committee of Detail charged with arranging them into a unified document, the Convention adjourned for ten days. Having been cooped up in the Assembly Room for two months with windows shuttered and doors closed for secrecy, many of the members took advantage of this long recess to get out of Philadelphia, which was notorious for foul air and pestilence in summer. Some from nearby states went home; some living farther afield headed to New York. Washington considered a trip to New York, where he could confer with Jay and Hamilton, but his carriage was undergoing repairs, and he did not want to borrow one.[84] He went fishing instead. In fact, during this brief recess, Washington took two fishing trips, both to nearby locations that held powerful memories.

On Monday, he went with Gouverneur Morris to a popular trout stream near Valley Forge. They traveled in Morris's light, open carriage pulled by Washington's two powerful horses and stayed for two nights in a farmhouse near the Revolutionary Army's old winter encampment. One day, Washington toured the breastworks—"which were in Ruins," he noted—before fishing.[85] It was his first visit to the site in summer; trees and crops now grew on ground that his men had stripped bare for firewood and building materials. Meeting some farmers, he talked with them about growing buckwheat and using it to fatten livestock. In an uncharacteristically playful mood on his way out of town, Washington declined Elizabeth Powel's invitation to the play *The School for Scandal*, with a note expressing regret that fishing would force him to miss his chance "to receive a lesson in the School for Scandal."[86]

Scarcely a day after returning to Philadelphia, Washington left again, this time with Gouverneur and Robert Morris on a two-day fishing trip to Trenton, the sight of the General's first battlefield victory. The party stayed with Gouverneur Morris's sister and her husband, a former Revolutionary War officer who owned an ironworks near the falls of the Delaware River. One afternoon, the party dined with John Dickinson's brother, who had fought with Washington as a general in New Jersey's revolutionary militia. Every place that he went in and around Philadelphia, it seemed, reminded Washington of service and sacrifice for cause and country. He returned to the Convention with a renewed sense of mission.

While Washington fished, the Committee of Detail fleshed out a draft constitution from the provisions already passed by the Convention and its sense of what the delegates wanted. When it turned to composing the articles on the presidency and Senate, this enterprise became particularly creative. At the outset, the big-state nationalists envisioned a proportionally representative senate as both a check on the entire system and the guardian of national interests. Like the governor's councils of colonial days, it would have executive, legislative, and judicial functions. Early on, perhaps only Wilson fully appreciated the role that a President—especially one like

Washington—could play as a check on Congress and as a national-izing force. It took time for the delegates to realize how their decision to have states appoint senators impacted the balance. Working as it did with many early-adopted provisions, the Committee of Detail—which included Randolph, who earlier had denounced the unitary executive as "the fetus of monarchy" and still depicted the presidency as "the form at least of a little monarch"[87]—produced draft articles giving more power to the Senate and less to the President than the delegates, on further reflection, might want. Also by this time, they knew Washington better and perhaps trusted him more to define the President's role by his practice.

THE COMMITTEE'S DRAFT CONSTITUTION presented a snap-shot of where matters stood in early August. The President, elected by Congress for a single seven-year term, would execute the nation's laws, "appoint officers in all cases not otherwise provided by this Con-stitution," possess a limited veto over legislation, receive ambassadors, hold the pardon power, and serve as commander in chief of the armed forces.[88] Washington had served as commander in chief during the Revolutionary War, of course, and always conceived that post as under the civilian control of Congress. Power over war and peace, or at least the power to declare war and make peace, remained with Congress.[89] The Senate, with two members named by each state's legislature for six-year terms, would act as a coequal house of the legislature, appoint ambassadors and Supreme Court judges, make treaties, and serve as a court for disputes between states. These articles provided the starting point for the Convention's concluding deliberations on the separation of powers, which extended into early September as weary delegates raced toward adjournment. During this final stage of the proceedings, the presidency gained power at the Senate's expense.[90]

The resulting changes in the power balance among branches, which laid the foundation for the American presidency, began with concerns over the Senate. Some delegates thought that the committee, by giving so much power to the Senate, created an aristocracy, which Mason defined as "government of the few over the many."[91] Even Dickinson conceded that, if the plan went forward, "Aristocracy will be the watchword; the Shibboleth among its adversaries."[92] Others soured on the Senate after it became the agency of the states rather than proportionally representative of the nation as a whole. They foresaw it perpetuating the failings of the Confederation Congress by favoring state over national interests.[93] In light of the recent uproar caused by a bare majority of states in Congress agreeing to negotiate a treaty with Spain on terms that many southerners viewed as crippling to their region's interests, this concern especially applied to treaty-making. "The Senate represented the States alone," Madison argued, "and that for this as well as other obvious reasons it was proper that the President should be an agent in Treaties."[94] As far as entrusting it with the power to make appointments, Gouverneur Morris denounced the Senate "as too numerous for the purpose; as subject to cabal; and as devoid of responsibility."[95] Few of the committee's proposals on these particular points made it into the final constitution.

While the members accepted many parts of the Committee of Detail's draft constitution, they deferred action on several key provisions relating to the presidency and Senate. Reaching an impasse, on August 31 they referred these postponed parts, which included basic matters regarding presidential selection and executive power, to a committee with one member from each state. It included such leading nationalists as Madison, King, and Gouverneur Morris. This committee revived the idea of using electors to choose the President, which Madison and Morris had long favored, and proposed that the President make treaties and appoint judges, ambassadors, and other major officers "with the advice and consent of the Senate": a formula suggested earlier by delegates from Massachusetts based on how their state chose judges.[96] Although no member attempted to define "advice and consent," various comments suggested that the Senate still would have a meaningful role in the process. "As the President was to nominate, there would be responsibility" Morris explained, "as the Senate was to concur, there would be security."[97] Also in line with nationalists' aspirations, the committee fortified the taxing power by adding expansive language authorizing Congress to lay and collect taxes "to pay the debts and provide for the common defense and general welfare of the United States."[98] With members anxious to finish, the Convention accepted these fundamental changes with little debate and almost no dissent.[99]

So long as Congress elected the President, the delegates had limited the President to a single long term. Otherwise, they feared the executive would come under the sway of the legislators who could reappoint him. Using independent electors to pick the President opened the door for short, multiple terms, which most delegates always believed would encourage better behavior in office.[100] Accordingly, the committee also proposed a four-year term for the President with no limits on reelection. Indeed, in presenting the electoral system to the Convention, one committee member stated that its "object . . . was to get rid of ineligibility, which was attached to the mode of election by the Legislature, & to render the Executive independent of the Legislature."[101] With this critical final adjustment, the Convention struck its ultimate balance between executive and legislative power, and gave birth to the American presidency.

On September 9, one day after the last of these postponed parts passed the Convention, Washington wrote to his nephew in Virginia. "This," he began, "is probably the last letter I shall write you from this place; as the probability is, that the Convention will have completed the business which brought the delegates together, in the course of this week." In case anyone doubted his impatience for the Convention's end, Washington added, "God grant I may not be disappointed in this expectation, as I am quite homesick."[102] A few matters remained to wrap up, but none of them particularly concerned Washington. He was eager to send the Convention's work to the states for ratification knowing that the future of his country and, in all likelihood, the next stage of his life would turn on their decision.

Howard Chandler Christy's 1940 painting of the signing of the United States Constitution.

CHAPTER 6

"Little Short of a Miracle"

"WE THE PEOPLE OF THE UNITED STATES," the Constitution's late-added Preamble declares, "in Order to form a more perfect Union, establish Justice, insure domestic Tranquility, provide for the common Defense, promote the general Welfare, and secure the Blessings of Liberty to ourselves and our Posterity, do ordain and establish this CONSTITUTION for the United States of America."[1] The handiwork of Gouverneur Morris,[2] the Preamble's one long sentence—perhaps the most famous single sentence of modern times—captured the nationalists' goals without immediately provoking their opponents' ire.[3]

In context, the Preamble's first seven words presented an ambiguity that ran through the Constitution. Morris and other nationalists, including Washington, could read it to say that the document emanated from the people of a vast new entity called the United States. Given the vagaries of capitalization at the time, however, Sherman, New Jersey's William Paterson, Delaware's Gunning Bedford, and other states'-rights-minded delegates could read it as saying that the document came from the people of various sovereign, federally united, states.[4] From this opening ambiguity through its purposeful appeals to justice, domestic tranquility, common defense, general welfare, and liberty, the Preamble encapsulated the framers' hopes for the government that they had crafted during nearly four months of intense negotiations.

Added without debate during the Convention's final days, Morris's lyrical Preamble replaced a functional one composed by the Committee of Detail as part of its draft constitution and unanimously approved by the delegates on August 7. This earlier preamble simply listed all thirteen states and stated that the people of those states ordained the Constitution for themselves and their posterity. It neither mentioned the United States nor suggested any noble purposes.[5] The inclusion of Rhode Island in the list was debatable. That small state had boycotted the Convention; the Constitution, upon ratification by the other states, would take effect without it. The delegates might as well have listed Vermont since its addition to the union was then at least as likely as the incorporation of Rhode Island.[6] In this and other respects, the Committee of Detail's entire constitution, while useful as a framework for debate, lacked an authoritative style and harmonious structure. A month of piecemeal amendments had further disordered it.

With virtually every issue settled by the second week of September, the Constitution desperately needed a "last polish," as one delegate termed it.[7] The task fell to a five-member committee charged with revising the document's style and structure without altering its content. Morris penned the Preamble as one member of this so-called Committee of Style and Arrangement. He worked with the other members in reorganizing a hodgepodge of twenty-three articles into a melody of seven: one for each of the three branches and four dealing with such miscellaneous matters as requirements for states and statehood, constitutional supremacy, and the process for ratifying and amending the Constitution.[8]

Compared to state constitutions and the later constitutions of most nations, the committee's draft was brief—essentially a backbone for a government rather than a detailed plan. It ran only four pages in the printed version distributed to the delegates for their closing deliberations. In its revisions, the Committee of Style followed the first rule of the Committee of Detail: "To insert essential principles only, lest the operations of government should be clogged by rendering those provisions permanent and unalterable, which ought to be accommodated to time and events."[9]

Washington's closest allies at the Convention dominated the Committee of Style. Not only was Morris its most active member and scribe, but Madison and Hamilton—the latter back from New York for the Convention's close—served on it, too.[10] Washington had collaborated with all three for years in trying to forge a more perfect union. A fourth big-state nationalist, Rufus King, and the most nationalistic of the Connecticut compromisers, William Samuel Johnson, rounded out the committee.

While the committee's ideological imbalance remains puzzling, it exemplified the revival of nationalists' fortunes within the Convention.[11] After their initial success in getting the delegates to use the nationalistic Virginia Plan as the starting point for deliberations, Madison, Morris, Hamilton, King, and the other big-state nationalists suffered a series of setbacks in the composition of the Senate and the nature of the executive. By late June, even the Virginia Plan's reference to a "national government" was dropped from the evolving constitution.[12]

The Committee of Style's limited charge restricted its ability to give a robust nationalistic tilt to the document, but at least its members would not permit further erosion on this score and, in the case of the Preamble, put a nationalistic gloss on the Constitution's most widely read section. As such, the committee extended the nationalists' resurgence that began in late July when the Committee of Detail included the sweeping Necessary and Proper Clause among Congress's enumerated powers and stretched into early September with the decisions to free the executive from election by Congress and shift substantial power from the state-controlled Senate to this nationally elected President. Then the Convention added language specifying that Congress could tax (and presumably spend) for the "general welfare"—a phrase that had appeared in the old Articles of Confederation, but not in reference to taxation.[13] With its expansive Preamble, the Committee of Style reiterated the authority for the new government to "promote the general welfare" and replaced the people of the thirteen states with the people of the United States as the source of governmental authority.[14] Washington seemed pleased. From July to September, he went from expressing "despair" over the Convention to depicting its product as "the best that could be obtained."[15]

The committee had two other chances to advance nationalism at the Convention and, with Washington's aid, made the most of both. Writing for the committee, Morris penned a cover letter from Washington for transmitting the Constitution to Congress. "The friends of our country have long seen and desired, that the power of making war, peace, and treaties, that of levying money and regulating commerce, and the corresponding executive and judiciary authorities should be *fully* and effectually vested in the general government," the letter stated. "It is obviously impracticable in the federal government of these States, to secure all rights of independent sovereignty to each, and yet provide for the interests and safety of all." These factors, the letter claimed, justified "the *consolidation* of our Union, in which is involved our prosperity, felicity, safety, perhaps our *national* existence."[16] This letter, approved in Convention and signed by Washington, effectively opened the public campaign for ratification.

The Style Committee also proposed two resolutions for the Convention to submit to Congress. The first requested that Congress forward the Constitution to the states for ratification. The second asked that, if the states ratified the document, Congress set a time for choosing presidential electors and a date for the new government to assume power. Washington's signature on the transmittal letter and accompanying resolutions ensured they would command attention. Indeed, they made it look as if the Constitution came from him.

ONCE THE DELEGATES RECEIVED the Committee of Style's report on September 12, the Convention raced toward closure. For three more days, the members wrangled over details in the committee's draft, changing a word here or a phrase there but rejecting all major amendments, including the motion by Gerry and Mason to add a bill of rights, which—remarkably in retrospect—failed to gain the support of even a single state.[17] The key compromises on representation, slavery, national power, and the presidency in place, a majority of the members in every delegation seemed unwilling to consider anything potentially disruptive or time-consuming. No bill of rights was needed, Sherman argued and others apparently agreed, because the new government would hold only enumerated, not unlimited, powers. "The State Declarations of Rights are not repealed by this Constitution; and being in force are sufficient," he said.[18]

It was not just the nationalists' constitution anymore, though they got much of what they wanted. The small states had equal representation in a powerful senate, the slave states had guarantees for their peculiar institution, and the commercial states had assured access to national markets. There would be money to pay bondholders, maintain an army, and provide for the general welfare. Property rights were secured, domestic order imposed, and state-issued paper money curtailed. Reflecting the broad consensus, particularly the compromise on representation, supporters of the Constitution began calling themselves federalists rather than nationalists. Opponents, who typically favored a system like the old confederation but with enhanced powers, ironically became known as antifederalists. While Washington hated partisan faction and saw himself rising above it, he inevitably became the living embodiment of federalism.

With a respectable result assured once the Committee of Style reported, Washington appeared to enjoy himself more than ever during the Convention's final week. Determined not to waste his reputation and political capital on a failed venture, he had resisted going to Philadelphia until he had some hope that the Convention might succeed and, as recently as July, had regretted doing so when the effort appeared on the brink of failure. But composing a meaningful plan of national union and offering it to the states, Washington believed, was a sufficient accomplishment to justify his participation even if the states did not immediately ratify it. "Conduct like this," he had written to Madison in March when announcing his willingness to attend the Convention, "will stamp wisdom and dignity on the proceedings and . . . sooner or later will shed its influence."[19]

Clearly in a celebratory mood, Washington kept a full social schedule during the Convention's closing days. On Wednesday the twelfth, with the Committee of Style's Constitution complete, he dined with Franklin one last time and had tea with the artist Robert Edge Pine, who had painted the General's portrait two years earlier and now wanted to touch up that work. On Thursday, Washington joined a dinner party at the home of Pennsylvania vice president Charles Biddle, whose son Nicholas would later lead the nationalist Bank of the United States, and then went to tea at Elizabeth and Samuel Powel's mansion. On Friday, delegates accompanied Washington to a raucous dinner party given in his honor at City Tavern by Philadelphia's elite light-horse cavalry. The revelers consumed considerable quantities of Madeira, claret, porter, beer, rum punch, and other alcoholic beverages, and ultimately received a substantial bill for breakage from the management.[20] From there, presumably along with Pennsylvania delegate George Clymer, Washington went to an after-party at the home of Clymer's brother-in-law, Samuel Meredith, a wealthy merchant who later served as treasurer of the United States in the first two federal administrations.

With the Convention's end in sight, the delegates remained in session later on Saturday than on any other day: until 6 P.M. By then they had completed voting on the Constitution. The tally by states was unanimous, though some individual members dissented. In fact, two of Virginia's five remaining delegates—Mason and Randolph— renounced the document for giving too much power to Congress, imposing too few constraints on the President, and falling to include a bill of rights. Mason had already dramatically vowed that he "would sooner chop off his right hand than put it to the Constitution as it now stands."[21] As the arguments swirled around him on this final day of debate, Mason expanded his stated objections into a written list that would circulate widely.

By their positions, Mason and Randolph forced Washington to cast the deciding vote in his own state's delegation. Without him, unanimity would have been lost. Of course, Rhode Island never joined the Convention and New York lost a quorum when its two anti-nationalist members, Lansing and Yates, departed on July 10, so the final vote was eleven states to none. Still, the Constitution's proponents made the most of the unanimous vote by the remaining states. It propelled their drive for ratification.[22] After the vote, the delegates recessed until Monday, when they would return to sign a parchment copy of the engrossed document. His role at the Convention nearly over, Washington retired to his rooms at Robert Morris's home for a late supper. He spent the next day, Sunday, catching up on personal correspondence and dining at the Morrises' country estate, The Hills.

AS THE TWO LARGER-THAN-LIFE LEADERS whose support made the Convention and Constitution credible, Washington and Franklin were to take center stage on Monday for the signing. They do so in the monumental painting of the event by Howard Chandler Christy that, in the depths of the Great Depression, a later Congress commissioned for the United States Capitol. The shutters are symbolically open and drapes pulled to reveal a bright new day that backlights the figures in an almost holy aura; Franklin sits facing the viewer at center surrounded by the other signers. Washington stands alone in near profile to the viewer's right, towering over all others as he surveys the scene from an overly elevated dais.

Christy invented the arrangement of characters and tinkered with the cast, but his painting's spirit rings true. Washington oversaw the signing much as he had the Convention by supervising events from his elevated chair. Franklin was given the day's lead speaking role, though frailty forced him to hand over his remarks to Wilson for reading. While his speech soon found its way into the press—as did the Constitution, final resolutions, and transmittal letter signed by Washington—the public remained barred from the Assembly Room, its shutters and drapes stayed closed, and other records were kept secret. Indeed, to maintain secrecy at least through ratification, on this final day the Convention directed Washington to hold its journals and records until instructed otherwise by a Congress formed under the new Constitution. King openly worried that "if suffered to be made public, a bad use would be made of them by those who would wish to prevent the adoption of the Constitution."[23]

At the final session, Washington called on Franklin first. Suspicious of aristocracy, Franklin's state constitution for Pennsylvania had a hyperrepresentative assembly, no senate, and weak executive—all features he had championed without success at the Convention.[24] Still, he was ready to close ranks behind the Constitution and used his speech to entreat others to follow suit. "I agree to this Constitution with all its faults, if they be such; because I think a general Government necessary for us, and there is no form of Government but what may be a blessing to the people if well administered, and believe farther that this is likely to be well administered for a course of years," he explained with a verbal nod toward Washington as the presumed first President. The alternative, Franklin said, was disunion, with the states "only to meet hereafter for the purpose of cutting one another's throats." Observing that "much of the strength & efficiency of any Government in procuring and securing the happiness to the people depends on the general opinion of the goodness of the Government," he urged the delegates to "act heartily and unanimously in recommending this Constitution." To gain that end, he moved that by signing, members attest to "the unanimous consent of *the States* present," rather than to their personal support for the document.[25]

Franklin's motion, which the Convention adopted, appeased some dissenters but not the three principal ones: Mason, Gerry, and Randolph. Complicating the last day, they reiterated in brief the objections that they had stated at length prior to the final vote on Saturday. On one or both occasions, each of them condemned what Randolph deplored as "the indefinite and dangerous power given by the Constitution to Congress," with Gerry focusing his angst on the Necessary and Proper Clause. To Washington's likely annoyance, the Virginians again railed against the unitary executive, which Randolph had denounced from the outset as the fetus of monarchy. They wanted an executive council with regional representation to advise and circumscribe the President. Mason also decried the lack of a bill of rights and predicted that the new government "would end either in monarchy, or a tyrannical aristocracy."[26]

By this point if not before, Washington must have glared down at Mason, his old friend, even as Mason, by the Convention's rules, addressed his remarks to Washington as President. Neighbors in Virginia, their relationship never recovered from the strains of the Convention and subsequent ratification fight.[27] Randolph, in contrast to Mason, wavered even as he spoke by conceding that his decision not to sign "might be the most awful of his life" and saying that he might still support ratification in Virginia.[28]

In what represented a continuation of exchanges that began during the debate on Saturday and probably went on in private throughout the weekend, Washington and other federalists tried to win over the dissenters. Hamilton and Gouverneur Morris contended that they, too, had objections to the Constitution—with Hamilton going so far as to say that "no man's ideas were more remote from the plan than his"—but would sign it anyway because, in the words of both, the alternative was "anarchy."[29] Hamilton and Morris viewed the proposed government as too weak rather than too strong, however, so their willingness to sign could hardly help to appease the dissenters.

Franklin tried to assure the dissenters that his earlier remarks on compromise were not aimed at them, but Gerry shot back that he could not think otherwise. At Washington's urging, the Convention passed a late amendment designed to address one of Mason's objections by allowing for a larger House of Representatives.[30] It was a minor change, though, and not likely to win over the dissenters unless they were looking for an excuse to retreat. When they did not relent, the signing proceeded without them. The official journal, which did not record individual comments or votes, never mentioned their dissent and Christy totally omitted them from his romanticized portrayal of the event.[31]

Although observed by no one except the Convention's members and officers, the signing may have felt as historic to them as it looks in Christy's painting. Washington signed first and above the rest in a bold, large hand somewhat reminiscent of John Hancock's already well-known signature on the Declaration of Independence: "G°: Washington, Presid[t] and Deputy from Virginia." Then the other thirty-eight signers filed forward by state beginning with New Hampshire's John Langdon and proceeding southward to Abraham Baldwin of Georgia. One by one, they mounted the dais where Washington sat and added their signatures to the document. Even though New York had not voted on the Constitution, Hamilton signed as the state's lone remaining delegate and won a central seat in Christy's picture. Unable to attend the closing session, Dickinson also gained a place in the painting by having another delegate sign for him.

While the last members were signing, Franklin looked at the half sun adorning the crown of Washington's chair. "I have," he said to those near him, "often in the course of the Session, and the vicissitudes of my hopes and fears as to its issue, looked at that behind the President without being able to tell whether it was rising or setting: But now at length I have the happiness to know that it is a rising and not a setting Sun."[32] Madison chose this anecdote involving the Sage of Philadelphia and Washington's chair to close his meticulously edited *Notes of the Federal Convention*. After relating it, Madison's *Notes* simply conclude that, once the last members signed, "the Convention dissolved itself."[33]

Elaborating only slightly, Washington reported in his diary, "The Members adjourned to the City Tavern, dined together and took a cordial leave." In the privacy of that diary, which typically contained a matter-of-fact account of events, Washington also added that, after dinner, he "retired to meditate on the momentous work which had been executed."[34] The product of that labor—the Constitution—*if* sent to the state legislatures by Congress, and *if* then referred by those legislatures to state ratifying conventions, and *if* finally ratified by at least nine of those conventions, would transform the rest of his life and his country forever. The first step finished, still more momentous works lay ahead.

WASHINGTON WASTED LITTLE TIME in departing Philadelphia. On the morning after the signing, he mailed brief letters to Jefferson and Lafayette in France, enclosing a copy of the Constitution with each. "It is now a Child of fortune, to be fostered by some and buffited by others," he wrote, "if it be good I suppose it will work its way good—if bad it will recoil on the Framers."[35] Then, about 1 P.M., Washington dined with Robert and Gouverneur Morris, who afterward rode with him as far as Gray's Ferry on the Schuylkill River just south of the city, where he left them and Philadelphia behind.

In his grand, two-horse, enclosed carriage with liveried attendants, the trip to Mount Vernon took nearly five days. John Blair, the

quietest of the Virginia delegates, joined Washington for the journey. Respected in Virginia for his well-connected family, vast fortune, and legal training at London's Middle Temple, Blair was, as
one fellow delegate noted, "no orator."[36] Although he rarely spoke
at the Convention, Blair's continued presence proved crucial after
George Wythe left in June to join his dying wife and James McClurg
went home in July. Without Blair's steady support of their nationalist
positions, Washington and Madison would have lost control of their
own delegation and Virginia might not have backed the Constitution.
History turns on such contingencies. As it was, Virginia normally
voted with Washington on motions favoring a strong general government and powerful, independent executive.

With Blair along, Washington seemed to enjoy the journey home. The only difficulty came when one of the horses pulling Washington's coach broke through the rotten planks of an old
wooden bridge over the Elk River in Maryland. Late summer rains
had swollen the river, leading an impatient Washington to try the
long-disused span rather than wait for the ford to become passable.
If the other horse had gone, too, the carriage would have followed
and been swept into the swift current. Such was Washington's stature that newspaper accounts of the episode spoke of his "providential
preservation . . . for the great and important purpose" of establishing the new government.[37] Actually, Washington had disembarked
from his coach before it crossed the derelict bridge and had safely
witnessed the drama from the rain-soaked bank. The press, however,
presented him on the precipice looking down, much as it had so often
portrayed him during his earlier military engagements.

After three more days and no further incidents, Washington
reached Mount Vernon by sunset on the first day of fall, September 22,
1787. He had been away from his plantation for an entire season—one
of the worst summers on record for farming in the Potomac region
due to an unprecedented drought.[38] Resuming the Cincinnatus role
that suited him so well, Washington vowed to focus his full attention

on domestic affairs—his farm and family—but broke his word almost immediately.

Washington had so much time and reputation invested in the Constitution, and believed so strongly that his country could not survive without it, that its progress consumed him even as he resumed day-to-day management of Mount Vernon. Although he had written to Lafayette on the eighteenth about the Constitution that "the General opinion on, or reception of it is not for me to decide," and he genuinely embraced the role of a disinterested republican patrician responding to the call of the people, Washington could not refrain from exerting his influence in this case. Like most other federalists at the Convention, he was convinced that the choice lay between the Constitution and chaos: the preservation of liberty and property required ratification. Washington could not keep his self-imposed promise to Lafayette that he would not "say anything for or against" the Constitution.[39] Two days after reaching Mount Vernon, he sent copies of the document to three former Virginia governors along with identical letters urging them to support it. "I sincerely believe it is the best that could be obtained at his time," Washington wrote. "If nothing had been agreed to by [the Convention] anarchy would soon have ensued."[40] With Mason and Randolph opposed, Washington feared that the Constitution would face strong headwinds in Virginia.[41]

ONCE THE CONVENTION ADJOURNED, news of the Constitution and calls for its ratification quickly spread across the country. Countless newspapers printed the Convention's transmittal letter to Congress as if its pleas for ratification came directly from Washington. Some articles credited the Constitution itself to him or trumpeted his support as reason alone to ratify it. "Is it possible that the deliverer of our country would have recommended an unsafe form of government?" a widely reprinted article from the *Pennsylvania Gazette* asked in early October.[42]

South Carolina's *Columbian Herald* celebrated the news from Philadelphia with new lyrics to an old song. After extolling the proposed constitution as a boon to trade, prosperity, liberty, and order, the tune's final verse concluded:

> *That these are the blessings, Columbia knows—*
> *The blessings the Fed'ral CONVENTION bestows.*
> *O! then let the People confirm what is done*
> *By FRANKLIN the sage, and by brave WASHINGTON.*[43]

Reporting that the state's popular governor, John Hancock, would back ratification, the *Massachusetts Centinel* asked a rhetorical question that suggested how much the processes might turn on the opinions of great men: "Let it but appear that a HANCOCK, a WASHINGTON, and a FRANKLIN approve the new government, and who will not embrace it?"[44] Everywhere, early reports sounded much the same. Supporters would rely on trust in Washington, other framers, and local supporters to carry the Constitution.[45]

Washington knew the role that his name and reputation were playing in the campaign for ratification. He received and read newspapers from around the country almost daily, and closely followed the unfolding drama in them and through private correspondence. These newspapers and letters carried endless references to Washington's central role at the Convention. "Indeed I am convinced that if you had not attended the Convention," Gouverneur Morris wrote to Washington in October, "and the same paper had been handed out to the World, it would have met with a colder Reception, fewer and weaker Advocates, and with more and more strenuous opponents."[46] Rather than question his intentions in signing the Constitution—clearly a hard sell in America—some opponents resorted to claiming that Washington had been duped into supporting it—which was scarcely more effective.[47] "The universal popularity of General Washington," Hamilton said at the time, was the strongest factor in the federalists' favor going into the ratification contests.[48]

Most people probably cared less that Washington had signed the Constitution than that he would likely lead the government under it. No sooner had the Convention issued its Constitution in September than the *Pennsylvania Gazette* proclaimed, "GEORGE WASHINGTON has already been destined, by a thousand voices, to fill the place of the first President."[49] If anything, the *Gazette*'s count was far too low. People everywhere, when they heard about the proposed new government for the United States, commonly assumed and generally expected Washington to lead it.[50] "What will tend, perhaps, more than any thing to the adoption of the new system," David Humphreys wrote to Washington upon first reading the Constitution in September, "will be an universal opinion of your being elected President."[51] No doubt Washington saw it coming and, without coveting or courting the position, never denied that he would accept it. "Should the Idea prevail that you would not accept the Presidency," Morris warned in his October letter about the Constitution's prospect, "it would prove fatal in many Parts."[52] By silence on this score, Washington again played his part. Even with him in their camp, however, federalists faced the daunting task of securing ratification for their radical centralization of power.

THE CONFEDERATION CONGRESS PRESENTED the first hurdle. As understood from the outset, upon completing its work, the Convention transmitted the finished Constitution to Congress, which had been idling away the summer in New York. With ten of its members serving as delegates to the Convention, Congress lacked a quorum most days. Washington and other federalists considered it an irrelevancy anyway: the relic of a failed confederation. Then, on September 20, Convention secretary William Jackson rode into town with copies of the Constitution, resolutions from the Convention, and Washington's transmittal letter.

Congress sprang to life, if only to receive its death warrant. Four of its members had arrived from the Convention by then, bringing the number of states represented to nine. The number reached eleven by the twenty-sixth, when Congress formally took up the matter.[53] By this time, Virginia congressman Richard Henry Lee had received letters from Mason and Randolph outlining their objections to the Constitution and was primed to take up their fight. Madison then resumed his seat as one of Virginia's five members of Congress and, along with fellow Convention delegates King and Gorham from Massachusetts, Butler of South Carolina, and Johnson from Connecticut, readied the response. An epic clash was brewing that would inevitably engage Washington.

Lee was no ordinary naysayer. Having led the chorus of noes to George III in 1776 by introducing the resolution in Congress for independence, Lee was more than willing to take on George Washington when he disagreed with him. Lee *may* have considered Washington an equal, but never a superior to whom he should defer.[54] Born a month apart, Lee and Washington had entered the Virginia House of Burgesses together in 1758, and remained members until that body elected both of them to the First Continental Congress in 1774. Lee had served off and on in Congress ever since, including a stint as its president, and worked with Washington on many matters. They corresponded frequently. Like Mason's, Lee's voice carried weight in Virginia and beyond.

The Constitution posed a problem for Congress, which had authorized the Convention only to propose amendments to the Articles of Confederation. Amending the Articles required the consent of Congress and approval by all thirteen state legislatures.[55] Instead, the Convention had drafted a new plan of government that would take effect upon ratification by "the conventions of nine states."[56] At the Convention, Washington favored an even lower number of states: seven, a bare majority.[57] Rather than ask Congress to approve the plan, the Convention simply requested that it submit the Constitution for ratification to conventions of delegates "chosen in each State by the People thereof, under the recommendations of its Legislature."[58]

Faced with the difference between what Congress authorized and what the Convention did, members debated how to proceed. Lee and other skeptics moved that Congress send the Constitution to the states for consideration with some sort of disclaimer stating that it did not comply with the procedures for amending the Articles of Confederation. Anything less, Lee's resolution suggested, would not be "respectful" to a Convention of twelve states chaired by Washington; anything more would exceed Congress's authority. Your motion "is not respectful to the Constitution," Madison shot back at Lee. It "implies a disagreement." He favored an alternative resolution offered by Washington's friend Edward Carrington, a founding member of the Cincinnati, asking that Congress take up the Constitution, agree to it as written, and send it to the states with the request that they "speedily" hold ratifying conventions. This surpassed even what the Convention had requested, but Gorham, Johnson, King, and the other former delegates rallied behind it.[59]

Madison's response left Lee an opening. To take up and approve the document, Lee argued, "implies a right to consider [it] on the whole or part," and amend it. He then offered a list of amendments largely borrowed from Mason, beginning with an expansive bill of rights, through an executive council both to advise the President and to replace the Senate in confirming appointments, and concluding with an expanded lower house of Congress and a proportionally representative Senate.[60] Lee had overplayed his hand. Even his fellow skeptics realized that Congress could not reopen the basic compromises made in Philadelphia without derailing the Constitution. After two days of wrangling, Congress took a middle course by resolving "unanimously" to transmit the Constitution to every state legislature for submission "to a convention of Delegates chosen in each state by the people."[61] Neither side clearly won but battle lines were clearly drawn.

THE RESULT SATISFIED WASHINGTON. He received a one-sided report of the dustup in Congress from Madison, but the episode largely stayed out of the press for months. Congress met in private and, even though members could disclose what happened, none of them publicized it until December. Indeed, far from questioning its prospects, one of the few articles about the Constitution in any New York newspaper during the congressional debates simply predicted that Washington's election as the first President "would doubtless be unanimous."[62] Congress's official journal included none of the acrimonious discussion and, after the vote on Lee's motion was stricken from the record, contained scarcely a whiff of dissent.[63] "I am better pleased that the proceedings of the Convention is handled from Congress by a unanimous vote (feeble as it is) than if it had appeared under stronger marks of approbation without it," Washington wrote back to Madison in October. "Not everyone has opportunities to peep behind the curtain; and as the multitude often judge from externals, the appearance of unanimity in that body, on the occas[io]n, will be of great importance."[64] ⟶

By this point, Washington had many reasons to be pleased. In her prize-winning history of the ratification, Pauline Maier observed that, due to the influx of newspapers, letters, and visitors, "Mount Vernon became a fine vantage point for watching the drama unfold."[65] During the first month after Washington's return, virtually every report reaching Mount Vernon boded well for ratification. Most American newspapers published both the Constitution and Washington's transmittal letter without comment, which gave an appearance of approval. "From what I hear," Humphreys reported to Washington in late September on ratification, "opposition will be less than was apprehended."[66] By early October, Knox fairly gushed to Washington about the Constitution. "The people of Boston are in raptures with it," he wrote. "The people of Jersey and Connecticut . . . embrace it with ardor."[67] Departing from his customary cynicism about the voice of the people, Hamilton soon sent word from New York, "The New Constitution is as popular in this City as is possible for any thing to be—and the prospect thus far is favourable to it throughout the state."[68] Also in mid-October, Madison advised Washington from Congress, "The Reports continue to be rather favorable . . . from *every* quarter."[69] When General Pinckney visited Mount Vernon in October on his way home from the Convention, he likely vouched for South Carolina as only a Pinckney could.[70]

From his Mount Vernon retreat, Washington often replied to correspondents with stories about responses to the Constitution in his part of Virginia. "In Alexandria," he informed Hamilton, "and some of the adjacent Counties, it has been embraced with an enthusiastic warmth of which I had no conception."[71] He seemed especially pleased when voters in his county instructed their legislators to support calling a ratifying convention.[72] One of those legislators, Washington all but chuckled in a note to Madison, was Mason. And Randolph, Washington wrote, now "wishes he had been among the subscribing members" at the Convention.

In the afterglow of the Convention, Washington allowed himself to hope that even Patrick Henry might support ratification and depicted Richard Henry Lee and Mason as isolated. "It may be asked which of them gives the tone?" Washington commented on Lee and Mason. "Without hesitation I say the latter; because the latter, I believe, will receive it from no one. He has, I am informed, rendered himself obnoxious in Philadelphia by the pains he took to disseminate his objections . . . [and] his conduct is not less reprobated in this County."[73] Letters to Washington from both men explaining their dissent did little to appease him.[74] Their opposition seemed to steel his resolve, which only increased after Henry told him that he, too, opposed ratification. By this point, Washington identified with the

Constitution and tended to take criticism of it personally.

These letters of dissent from three fellow Virginians had common threads. Unlike Yates, Lansing, and Maryland's Luther Martin, who had stormed out of the Convention implacably opposed to the emerging new union, Mason and Lee recognized the need for an enhanced general government and claimed to favor much in the new Constitution. Henry was less conciliatory but offered to keep an open mind.[75] Each letter had a cordial, respectful tone. Yet all three of these Revolutionary Era leaders concluded that the Constitution contained fundamental flaws that should be addressed *prior* to ratification.

Henry, Lee, and Mason wanted a bill of rights to protect individual liberties from the new government and adjustments to the balance of power both among its branches and between it and the states. Mason harped on the refusal of federalists to consider his amendments during the final days of the Convention, and Lee picked up this lament after Congress acted in a similar fashion. "It was with us, as with you, this or nothing," Lee complained to Mason following Congress's action. "In this state of things the Patriot voice is raised in vain for such changes and securities as Reason and Experience prove to be necessary against the encroachments of power upon the indispensable rights of human nature."[76]

Further, these dissenters feared, federalists would bar amendments to the Constitution at state ratifying conventions, too. "It was improper to say to the people, take this or nothing," Mason implored fellow delegates at the Convention.[77] In Congress, Lee compared it to "presenting a hungry man 50 dishes and insisting he should eat all or none." Forewarned by Mason, Lee asked the Convention delegates in Congress, "Is it the Idea of the Convention that not only Congress but the States must agree in the whole, or else to reject it—and . . . [that] amendments are precluded?"[78] They never gave him a clear answer. Madison, King, and Johnson said that Congress could not amend the Convention's constitution because that would create two plans for the states: the original and the revised. They left the issue of state-by-state amendments hanging.

By circulating their objections and proposed revisions, Mason, Lee, and Henry hoped to encourage a coordinated response by the states. Gerry joined them in this mission, as did a fractious mix of big-government skeptics and states' rights advocates. To stop the federalist juggernaut, they needed to prevail in five of the thirteen states or, for all practical purposes, any two of the big four: Pennsylvania, Massachusetts, New York, or Washington's Virginia. Like it or not, the clash would draw in Washington.

THE KEYSTONE STATE of Pennsylvania came first. Meeting upstairs in the State House while the Convention occupied the first-floor Assembly Room, the state's legislature had less than two weeks left in its annual session when the delegates signed the Constitution on September 17. On that same day, with the ink hardly dry on the Constitution downstairs, Pennsylvania's eight delegates to the Convention delivered a joint letter to their Assembly stating that they "were ready to report" on the proposed new federal government.[79] One of those delegates who also served in the Assembly, Thomas Fitzsimons, suggested making that full report on the next morning, which was before the new constitution would even reach Congress in New York. The Assembly agreed and the race to ratify began.

Sitting in seats that Convention delegates had occupied a day earlier, members of the Pennsylvania Assembly, with the room's shutters now open and a large audience in the gallery, heard the Constitution and Washington's transmittal letter read publicly for the first time. As senior delegate and president of the state, Franklin delivered a copy of the Constitution to the Assembly and proposed that Pennsylvania donate a ten-mile-square tract of land as a seat for the new federal government. Another Convention delegate, Thomas Mifflin, who served as the Assembly's Speaker, then read the Constitution aloud as members followed along on printed copies. Philadelphia's federalist-leaning newspapers hailed the event as historic.

Carefully orchestrated petitions from voters soon began flooding the Assembly requesting that it quickly call a ratifying convention. On September 28, with one day left in the session, Convention delegate and Assembly member George Clymer moved separate resolutions for the election of deputies to a state ratifying convention and the subsequent convening of that body. Unless the resolutions passed by the next day, however, the calling of the convention would have to wait until the Assembly's next session, when a new group of members would meet following the October state elections. The current Assembly favored ratification; the new one might not.

State constitutional issues already split Pennsylvania politics into two distinct parties. One party, rooted in rural central and western Pennsylvania, supported the existing state constitution, which centered power in a locally representative one-house legislature. Another party, tied to Philadelphia's commercial interests, sought a new, balanced government with a two-house legislature and independent executive. The reformers held a majority in the Assembly and stacked the state's federal Convention delegation with its partisans.[80] Franklin had a foot in each camp but the other Convention delegates despised the old state constitution as much as they wanted a new federal one. Their thinking on state constitutional issues informed their essential contributions to the federal Convention. In contrast, backers of the old state constitution, excluded from the Convention, brought skeptical eyes to the proposed federal government, with its two-house legislature, strong executive, and elite senate. The lack of a bill of rights heightened their concerns. Mason's written objections found a ready audience in members of this group and circulated widely among them.

Clymer's last-minute resolutions caught minority members by surprise, or so they said.[81] They had some inkling of what was brewing at the Convention during the summer and, following its adjournment on September 17, over a week to digest the new federal Constitution.

They maintained, however, that states could not call ratifying conventions until Congress authorized them. This would push the matter over to the next session. After all, they argued, Congress might amend the Constitution. Rather than comment on the document, these skeptics initially raised procedural concerns and asked for time so that voters in remote districts could hear about the proposal first. No petitions had come from their constituents. Every Assembly member representing the western counties where Washington owned land opposed Clymer's motions.

Undeterred, federalists pushed for an immediate vote on calling a ratifying convention and offered to defer the vote on when and where to hold it only until after a midday break. The people wanted a new federal constitution, Daniel Clymer argued in support of his cousin's resolutions, and Congress had no say in the matter. The Convention simply referred the Constitution to Congress as a means to convey it to the states, he claimed. Even the states could not amend it. "They must adopt it *in toto* or refuse altogether," Clymer said, "for it must be a plan that is formed by the United States, which can be agreeable to all, and not one formed upon the narrow policy and convenience of any one particular state." Then he invoked Washington and the other framers—"the collective wisdom of a continent," he called them—as the authority for the document: "a venerable band of patriots, worthies, heroes, legislators and philosophers—the admiration of a world."[82] The deification of the Convention had begun, but strictly for partisan purposes.

With members already split into factions over state issues, Clymer's first resolution passed on a near party-line vote. Without hope of defeating the second resolution, its opponents sought to delay it by boycotting the afternoon session. This deprived the Assembly of a quorum. The sergeant at arms attempted to retrieve the seceding members. When these so-called seceders refused to return, the Assembly recessed until the next morning. With nineteen members still absent on September 28 and the session scheduled to end that day, the sergeant at arms forcibly brought in two seceders—enough to make a quorum—and held them until the second resolution passed. Under its terms, Pennsylvania's ratifying convention would convene in federalist-friendly Philadelphia on November 20. The means used to call it, however, unleashed the first round of pamphlets and articles opposing ratification. Indeed, to explain their actions, the seceders themselves promptly published a broadside critical of the Constitution. Raising many of the same concerns as Mason, it asked voters if the proposed "continental government" would be "likely to lessen your burthens or increase your taxes or . . . be competent to attend to your local concerns?"[83]

Despite the rising opposition, Washington welcomed events in Pennsylvania. He read about them mainly through the filter of federalist newspapers, most likely the daily *Pennsylvania Packet* and weekly *Pennsylvania Gazette*, which he received at Mount Vernon. Initially blaming outsiders for arousing the dissent, Washington complained that Mason in particular took "pains . . . to disseminate his objections among some of the leaders of the seceding members of the legislature."[84] While in Philadelphia, Washington associated almost exclusively with leaders of the reform party—Wilson, Fitzsimons, George Clymer, Robert Morris, and the like—and saw the dispute through their eyes. The seceders, in contrast, surely reminded Washington of those unruly tenants and squatters on his lands in Pennsylvania, who he kept at a distance.

The always aristocratic and often overly dramatic Gouverneur Morris sharpened Washington's view of the situation. "With Respect to this State," he wrote to Washington on October 30 about the prospects for ratification in Pennsylvania, "I dread the cold and sour Temper of the back Counties, and still more the wicked Industry of those who have long habituated themselves to live on the Public, and cannot hear the Idea of being removed from the Power and Profit of State Government."[85] Morris was speaking of the plebeian party, of course, but a similar depiction of profiting from the public trough applied to his patrician partisans as well. Such was Pennsylvania.

As he grew to identify more completely with the Constitution, Washington increasingly shared Gouverneur Morris's outlook regarding the opposition in Pennsylvania and elsewhere. He soon wrote from Mount Vernon to his nephew about those resisting ratification, "Their objections are better calculated to alarm the fears, than to convince the judgment of readers. They build them upon principles which do not exist in the Constitution—which the known & literal sense of it, does not support them in; and this too, after being flatly told that they are treading on untenable ground."[86] Of course, for months, Washington, Hamilton, and other federalists had warned of anarchy and disunion should the Convention falter or the Constitution fail. Both sides appealed to emotion as much as reason to advance their cause.

As opposition to the Constitution emerged, Washington enlisted supporters to defend it. "Much will depend," he wrote to Humphreys in mid-October, "on literary abilities, & the recommendation of it by good pens."[87] An early October speech by Wilson refuting the seceders' claims so delighted Washington that he distributed copies of it to others. Wilson's speech, he wrote to a trusted federalist confidant, David Stuart, "will place the most of Colo. Mason's objection in their true point of light." He urged Stuart to republish it widely "if you can get it done."[88] While never putting his own pen to this public use, Washington encouraged others to publish essays on behalf of ratification and privately endorsed their best efforts.

THE RUN-UP TO THE Pennsylvania ratifying convention in late November spawned the first sustained public airing of federalist and antifederalist arguments. This debate intensified when Delaware and New Jersey set their ratifying conventions for early December. Since all three states largely revolved around Philadelphia, the debate centered in its newspapers. Most of these papers favored ratification but two leaned against it and one, the *Independent Gazetteer*, printed contributions from both sides. Newspapers at the time rarely spoke with an objective voice: they mainly contained public notices, paid advertising, articles lifted from other papers, letters to the editor, and contributed essays. As the Pennsylvania convention neared, the letters and essays more and more consisted of pleas for or against ratification written under pseudonyms, such as "An American Citizen" and "A Plain Citizen" for federalists or "Centinel" and "An Old Whig" from antifederalists. Washington's stance on the Constitution and prospective role as President figured conspicuously in the exchange.

From start to finish, the federalist case for ratification in Pennsylvania relied on public trust in Washington and, to a lesser extent, Franklin.[89] In a widely reprinted essay from the *Independent Gazetteer*, "Centinel" attempted to counter this argument by portraying these framers as the unwitting tools of special interests. "I would be very far from insinuating that the two illustrious personages alluded to, have not the welfare of their country at heart," he wrote, "but that the unsuspecting goodness and zeal of the one, has been imposed on; . . . and that the weakness and indecision attendant on old age, has been practiced on in the other."[90] Writing in the *Independent Gazetteer*, another antifederalist questioned if "both or either of those distinguished patriots" even backed the Constitution. Since their signatures on the document only attested to the unanimity of the states in supporting it, he argued, "It is not unfair to suppose that both General Washington and Dr. Franklin were in the minority on several great questions."[91]

The federalist response came fast and furious. Within days of Centinel's first blast, a letter to the *Independent Gazetteer* denounced the antifederalists: "They do not reason, but abuse—General *Washington*, they (in effect) say, is a dupe, and Doctor *Franklin*, an old fool— vide the *Centinel*."[92] Many like it appeared.[93] In his own defense, Centinel asked in a second essay, "Is it derogating from the character of the *illustrious* and *highly revered* WASHINGTON, to suppose him fallible on a subject that must be in a great measure novel to him?"[94] This only elicited more attacks.[95] "Not even the illustrious SAVIOUR OF HIS COUNTRY has been exempted from the most illiberal torrents of abuse, that envy or malice, could suggest," roared "A Plain Citizen" in reply.[96] Try as he might to stay out of it, Washington could not escape a prominent part in Pennsylvania's ratification debate.

Writers on both sides of this partisan debate assumed that Washington would become the first President. For some, this represented reason enough to ratify the Constitution.[97] Anticipating charges that the office was too monarchical, Tench Coxe, a Philadelphia entrepreneur friendly with Washington, took up its defense in the first installment of an early series of essays published under the name "An American Citizen." Starting with Washington's well-known argument that America needed a "national government" to preserve "liberty, property, and the union," Coxe presented the presidency at its "head" as a fundamentally republican institution. Britain's hereditary monarchs, he noted, appoint bishops and lords, hold legislative and judicial power, and rule for life. "In America our President will not only be *without* these influencing advantages," Coxe wrote, "*but* . . . will always be *one of the people* at the end of four years." He can be removed from office, cannot dissolve Congress, and is elected "by the people" through electors. Senators must approve his appointees and all treaties. "Our President will fall very far short indeed of any prince," Coxe concluded, and "whatever dignity or authority he possesses is . . . *transiently vested in him by the people themselves for their own happiness*."[98]

Not so, "An Old Whig" charged in the *Independent Gazetteer*. "Our future President will be as much a king as the king in Great Britain." Both have "the power of making all the *great men*," he noted, and the President will also serve as commander in chief. While trusting Washington with the "use of great power," the author warned that, if a future President lacked Washington's virtue, moderation, and love of liberty, then "this country will be involved at once in war and tyranny." Indeed, this critic predicted that within a generation some President with less republican virtue than Washington would, like Caesar, use his position to seize total power. Simply put, the essay suggested, a position created for Washington could not be trusted to most mortals.[99] "If we are not prepared to *receive a king*," this "Old Whig" concluded, "let us call another convention to revise the proposed constitution."[100]

These public debates would set the stage for much that followed in American politics, beginning with the emergence of two distinct national political parties during the 1790s and the bitter federal election of 1800, but at the time they had little impact on the immediate question before voters. With Pennsylvanians already divided into two entrenched factions over state constitutional issues that tracked concerns raised by the federal Constitution, events played out along party lines with predictable results. Backers of the old state constitution gained seats in the October Assembly elections, but not enough to wrest control of the State House from the party led by Clymer, Fitzsimons, and Robert Morris. Polling some added votes from urban artisans and workers hoping for improved trade under the Constitution, federalists did even better in the November elections for deputies to the ratifying convention than in the Assembly elections.[101]

Pennsylvania federalists held a two-to-one majority in delegates going into their state convention on November 20 and voting patterns never changed. Deputies on both sides mostly shouted past each other such as when, with the final vote looming, antifederalist firebrand John Smilie threatened, "If this Constitution is adopted, I look upon the liberties of America as gone, until they shall be recovered by arms." Federalist deputy Benjamin Rush, a signer of the Declaration of Independence and friend of Washington, replied to Smilie by predicting "a millennium of virtue and happiness as the necessary consequences of the proposed Constitution."[102] On the evening of the twelfth, shortly after this exchange, deputies voted for ratification by the same margin that had marked most votes at the convention: 46 to 23.

"ALL RANKS OF PEOPLE here rejoice in the Event of this Evenings Deliberations, which was proclaimed thro' the City by repeated Shouts & Huzzas," Samuel Powel wrote to Washington from Philadelphia on the day that Pennsylvania ratified the Constitution.[103] Washington had followed the state's convention closely and regularly inquired about it in letters to Powel and other Philadelphia federalists. Now he rejoiced with them in the outcome and sent letters of congratulation.

Like Washington, none of Pennsylvania's Constitutional Convention delegates approved of everything in the final document, but all of them greatly preferred it to the Articles of Confederation. At the republican end of the constitutional spectrum, Franklin had favored a more representative Congress and a weaker presidency than the Constitution provided.[104] At the nationalist extreme, Gouverneur Morris wanted a more aristocratic senate and stronger presidency than it created. They knew, however, that the document left room for these institutions to develop over time. As Morris had reminded Washington shortly after the Convention broke up, "No Constitution is the same on Paper and in Life."[105]

With ratification achieved in Pennsylvania, both Franklin and Morris hoped that, with Washington as President, the new government would evolve in line with their ideals. In mid-1788, for example, Franklin confided in a friend, "General Washington is the man that all our eyes are fixed on for *president*, and what little influence I have, is devoted to him."[106] Expressing his sentiments directly to Washington, Morris earlier wrote of the presidency, "Of all Men you are best fitted to fill that Office. Your cool steady Temper is indispensably necessary to give a firm and manly tone to the new Government."[107]

Franklin had wanted Pennsylvania to ratify the Constitution first but its convention ran so long that Delaware slipped in ahead by five days. New Jersey followed six days after Pennsylvania. Somewhat isolated from other states and engaged in increasingly fierce battles with Native American peoples over land on the frontier, Georgia ratified on New Year's Eve. With its assent, four states had approved the Constitution by the end of 1787. Except for Pennsylvania, all acted quickly, unanimously, and without leaving much record of their public debates or convention deliberations.

Available evidence points toward the key role played by Washington's name in each state. Richard Henry Lee tried to stir up resistance to the Constitution in Delaware, for example, but one account from Wilmington stated that his opposition was effectively dismissed as mere "envy of the fame of General Washington and the dread he entertains of seeing that good man placed in the President's chair."[108] Before the convention in its state, the *New Jersey Journal* published an emphatic plea for ratification falsely attributed to Washington. "Should the states reject this excellent Constitution," he allegedly said upon signing it, "the probability is, an opportunity will never again offer to cancel another in peace—the next will be drawn in blood!" By year's end, the quote had appeared in more than three dozen newspapers, including two in Georgia.[109] Shortly before the Georgia ratifying convention in December, the leader of the state's Cincinnati advised convention president John Wereat that the popularity of framers like Washington was "so great that the public voices seem to be for adopting the Constitution in the lump on its first appearance as a perfect system."[110]

By this point if not before, the politics of ratification had all but consumed Washington. He followed developments in every state and was one of the first prominent federalists to predict the early and easy victory in Georgia. Time and again over the fall of 1787, his correspondents reported having heard nothing from that state. In early December, he commented to Madison that increasing hostilities on Georgia's frontier "will, or at least ought to shew the people of it, the propriety of a strict union, and the necessity there is for a general government."[111]

Washington's experiences with Native Americans in the Ohio River valley three years earlier had helped to convince him of the need for a true national government. He believed that the same would apply in Georgia. Indeed, he soon wrote in another letter that if Georgians "do not incline to embrace a strong *general* Government there must, I should think, be either wickedness, or insanity in their conduct."[112]

By the end of 1787, with final results having reached Mount Vernon from three states and favorable reports from many others, Washington exuded optimism about the Constitution. "New England (with the exception of Rhode Island, which seems itself, politically speaking, to be an exception from all that is good) it is believed will chearfully and fully accept it," Washington wrote to Lafayette in early January. "And there is little doubt but that the three Southern States will do the same. In Virginia and New York its fate is somewhat more questionable."[113]

Virginia particularly concerned Washington. In early December, his own state legislator had warned him about sentiments in the Virginia Assembly: "The Constitution has lost ground so considerably that it is doubtful wither it has any longer a majority in its favor."[114] Madison sent him similar reports. In a New Year's Day letter to Jefferson, Washington blamed the problems on Henry, Mason, Lee, and Randolph. Otherwise, Washington wrote, prospects for speedy ratification looked good and he personally expected Virginia and New York to come around. "The public attention is, at present, wholly engrossed by this important subject," he noted.[115]

As the Convention receded and ratification progressed, Washington's feelings toward the Constitution warmed and his sense of ownership increased. In his mind, the Constitution's defects, if any, had shrunk and the necessity of ratifying it had grown. "My decided opinion of the matter is that there is no alternative between the adoption of it and anarchy," he wrote privately about the Constitution in mid-December. "All the opposition to it, that I have yet seen, is I must confess addressed more to the passions than to the reason—and clear I am if another Federal Convention is attempted the sentiments of the members will be more discordant or less Conciliator than the last—in fine, that they will agree upon no gen[era]l plan."[116]

Although not conventionally religious, Washington had a profound personal sense of divine providence. Repeatedly, Washington believed, he had been saved from certain death in battle for a reason. At one point following the Revolutionary War, having secured American independence, he likely believed that purpose was behind him. Now, however, a new, grand role had emerged for him. "It appears to me," he wrote to Lafayette, early in 1788, "little short of a miracle, that the Delegates from so many different States . . . should unite in forming a system of national Government, so little liable to well founded objections."[117] Washington did not invoke miracles lightly.

Despite obstacles ahead, he entered the New Year at once hopeful that the states would ratify the Constitution and resigned to play his leading role in the new order. One of his autumn guests perceived it clearly. "I never saw him so keen for anything in my Life as he is for the adoption of this new form of Government," this visitor wrote to Jefferson about Washington late in 1787, and as for the presidency, "I am fully of opinion he may be induced to appear once more on the Publick Stage of life. I form my opinion from what passed between us in a very long & serious conversation as well as from what I could gather from mrs Washington on the same subject."[118] Only Virginia and New York appeared to stand in the way, though other states would pose greater problems than Washington expected.

BOOK III

————

From Mount Vernon to New York

1788–1789

REDEUNT SATURNIA REGNA.

☞It will rife.

STON, *Wednefday*, June 11.
EIGHTH PILLAR.

ve predicted in several preceeding pa-
has the fact been verified. Since our laft
afing intelligence of the acceffion of another
R in fupport of the *Grand Federal Super-
e*, has been received in this town by a vef-
3 days from Charleftown. On this event
gratulate the publick—as from her impor-

of celebrating the Ratification of the C
by that State, had been propofed—and v
ceed the day after the date of our accoun
the plan, it is to be fimilar to that *origin
ed in this town ; and befides SIXTY-C
ferent orders of FARMERS, MERCHA
MECHANICKS, would confift of the *Sc
ters* and *Scholars*—the *liberal profeffion*
State and city civil and political officers

Federalist cartoon from June 1788, portraying the states ratifying the Constitution as rising columns in the federal edifice.

CHAPTER 7

Ratifying Washington

THEN AS NOW, New Year's Day served for some as a time for taking stock of the past year and looking ahead to the next. In American political history, no New Year's offered a more pivotal occasion for this than January 1, 1788. With the states seemingly on a path toward disunion at the beginning of 1787 and many leaders, including Washington, fearing anarchy and civil war, an extraordinary convention had framed a strong new Constitution. By year's end, Congress had sent the document to the states for ratification and, acting in rapid succession, Delaware, Pennsylvania, New Jersey, and Georgia had ratified in December. Six additional states had called ratifying conventions for the new year, and at least two of the remaining three were expected to follow suit. Seventeen eighty-eight would decide the matter, and with it, America's future.

Prospects for ratification in some of those states appeared doubtful. Many Americans feared for their liberty and property under the new Constitution as much as Washington and other federalists feared for them without it. Fresh from the Convention, Elbridge

Gerry would fight ratification in Massachusetts. If the state's popular governor, John Hancock, joined him or insisted on amendments prior to ratification, then approval seemed unlikely. George Mason, Richard Henry Lee, and Patrick Henry had united to oppose the Constitution in Virginia, with the silver-tongued Henry seeking to rally the masses to their side. Edmund Randolph wavered on the issue, with Washington and Madison working to win his support or silence. North Carolina, many said, would follow Virginia. Despite his close ties to Washington, New York governor George Clinton had set his powerful political machine against ratification, and the majority of New Yorkers, who benefited from state imposts on goods passing through New York Harbor, typically followed his lead. With Rhode Island's legislative majority implacably opposed even to calling a convention, on New Year's Day 1788, no one could count on the necessary nine states approving the new government, much less all of the major ones. Without Virginia, Washington could not become President.

Depicting the Constitution as an assault on individual liberty and states' rights, all antifederalists harped on the absence of a bill of rights. Federalists invariably replied that none was needed because the government would possess only enumerated powers, not plenary ones. But those powers included exclusive jurisdiction over interstate commerce; control over armed forces, foreign affairs, and matters of war and peace; authority to tax and spend for the general welfare; and all powers "necessary and proper" to carry out the enumerated ones, which, antifederalists countered, would prove virtually limitless. Lee, Mason, and Henry homed in on the President's broad executive authority, including the power to make treaties and appoint judges with only the Senate's assent. Even if they trusted Washington with such power, they warned that, without term limits or a split executive, the government would end in despotism or aristocracy. Luther Martin foresaw further risks from empowering appointed judges to construe the Constitution as the supreme law of the land. Others carped on Congress's broad tax-ing powers. New Yorkers balked at constitutional limits placed on state imposts while Rhode Islanders objected to the ban on state-issued paper money. To rile Virginia and the South, Henry raised the specter of a Yankee-dominated Congress abolishing slavery and limiting westward expansion. And so it went as antifederalists pos-ited an elite conspiracy to subjugate America.

Washington closely studied the opposition's charges and found them not only baseless but vile and malicious. "To alarm the people, seems the ground work of his plan," he had said of Mason as early as the past October.[1] By the new year, Washington extended these charges to antifederalist leaders generally. "Every art that could inflame the passions and touch the interests of men has been essayed," Washington complained in early April 1788. "The ignorant have been told, that should the proposed Government obtain, their land would be taken from them and their property disposed of, and all ranks are informed that the prohibition of the Navigation of the Mississippi (their favorite object) will be a certain consequence of the adoption of the Constitution."[2] Their forte, Washington soon added about antifederalists, "seems to lie in misrepresentation . . . rather than to convince the understanding by some arguments or fair and impartial statements."[3] He dismissed most of them as "contemptible charac-ters" of "little importance."[4] He could not say that of Lee, Mason, Henry, Clinton, or Gerry, of course, but he still scorned their tactics and questioned their integrity.

Richard Henry Lee and the looming ratification battle in Virginia was a likely topic of discussion at Mount Vernon on New Year's Eve and New Year's Day, 1788, because Lee's cousin Charles came to din-ner and stayed the night. A staunch federalist, Charles Lee served as Washington's personal lawyer and was the brother of Revolutionary War cavalry hero Henry Lee. As fellow members of Virginia's del-egation in Congress, Henry Lee and Richard Henry Lee had already clashed over the Constitution when the document came before that body for transmittal to the states. Even though Charles soon married Richard Henry's daughter and named his son after his father-in-law, he sided with Henry Lee on the Constitution and served as a confidential conduit of information and informal vote counter for Washington on the prospects for ratification in Virginia. The Lees of Virginia were more a dynasty than a family, and often split on political issues—but never more so than over the Constitution. Although no record of the New Year's Day conversation between Washington and Charles Lee exists, their letters suggest that it included strategy and tactics for winning Virginia's assent to the Constitution.

After Charles Lee left Mount Vernon on the first, Washington wrote a long letter to Jefferson in Paris. The letter mentioned the opposition of Richard Henry Lee to the Constitution, as well as that of Henry and Mason, but assured Jefferson that the majority in Virginia would vote to ratify "notwithstanding their dissention," which was precisely the information that Charles Lee shared in a letter to Washington and likely had conveyed in person. Of course, the members of the state's ratifying convention had not been chosen yet, but Washington seemed certain of his "information." In wooing Jefferson to support ratification, it did not hurt that Jefferson loathed Patrick Henry for having pushed an official inquiry into Jefferson's wartime conduct as governor.

In his letter to Jefferson, Washington went on to ask about developments in France, where revolution loomed, and to express his sentiments on the coming changes. "The rights of Mankind, the privileges of the people, and the true principles of liberty," Washington wrote on that New Year's Day, "seem to have been more generally discussed & better understood throughout Europe since the American revolution than they were at any former period."[5] Washington saw America as a beacon for the Western world that would shine still brighter under the proposed new Constitution. Ratifying and implementing that Constitution, he believed, offered the best hope for Americans to preserve and expand their rights, privileges, and liberty.

On the same day that Washington wrote to Jefferson, another Parisian resident, Lafayette, penned a letter to Washington offering warm wishes for a new year—one that he felt certain would lead to Washington's selection as President. "I Read the New proposed Constitution with An unspeakable Eagerness and Attention," Lafayette declared, "and find it is a Bold, large, and solid frame for the Confederation." He objected only to the lack of a bill of rights and to the "great powers" and unlimited tenure of the President. By holding that executive office, Lafayette noted, Washington could correct these defects through his recommendations and precedents, "which cannot fail to insure a Greater perfection in the Constitution, and a New Crop of Glory to Yourself." The letter, which opened with Lafayette's depiction of himself as Washington's "adoptive son" and closed with a pledge of "filial love," spoke of his own hope for a constitution and bill of rights for France.[6]

TWO MORE STATES HELD ratifying conventions in January: Connecticut and Massachusetts. Washington would play only a minor role in the former, but when Massachusetts became the first real test for the Constitution's ratification, he showed his hand openly.

With its convention beginning on January 3, Connecticut came first. For months, his trusted confidant in the state, David Humphreys, had assured Washington that Connecticut would swiftly ratify. "All the different Classes in the liberal professions will be in favor of the proposed Constitution," Humphreys advised Washington. "The Clergy, Lawyers, Physicians & Merchants will have considerable influence on Society." Boasting of having "no inconsiderable agency" over several local newspapers, Humphreys added that the press would toe the line.[7] It did. During the fall, Connecticut newspapers repeatedly reminded readers of Washington's support for the Constitution while publishing a steady stream of federalist appeals and virtually nothing from the other side. In December, five of the state's papers featured a long essay written by Constitutional Convention delegate Oliver Ellsworth, under the pseudonym "A Landholder," that not only noted Washington's support for ratification but blamed the opposition of Richard Henry Lee on "his implacable hatred to General Washington."[8] Two of these papers also published Ellsworth's later charge, "Had the General not attended the Convention nor given his sentiments respecting the Constitution, the Lee party would undoubtedly have supported it, and Colonel Mason would have vented his rage to his own Negroes and the wind."[9] By month's end, Madison assured Washington that Connecticut "is pretty certain."[10]

Events played out as predicted in Connecticut. On January 9, six days after the state convened, Washington's former aide-de-camp Jonathan Trumbull Jr. wrote to the General from Hartford, "With great satisfaction I have the Honor to inform—that last Evening the Convention of this State, by a great majority, Voted to ratify & adopt the new proposed Constitution for the United States—Yeas 127— Nays 40." He added that, "in the list of Affirmants in this State, stand the names of all our principal Characters." As son of Connecticut's longest-serving governor and a future twelve-term governor himself, Trumbull knew these characters well.[11]

In his letter to Washington, Trumbull expressed his "hope" that the resounding vote in Connecticut would "have a happy influence on the Minds of our Brethren in Massachusetts."[12] He neglected to add that most of the dissent in his state came from delegates representing towns along the border with western Massachusetts, where Shays's Rebellion had centered. Towns across that border had already elected some former Shaysites to Massachusetts's convention, which began on January 9.

In his reply to Trumbull, Washington expressed a similar "wish" that Massachusetts would follow Connecticut, but sounded less optimistic. "The decision, it is even said, is problematical." He predicted that "the result of the deliberations in that state will have considerable influence on those which are to follow—especially in that of New York where I fancy the opposition to the form will be greatest."[13] Knowing the importance of ratification by Massachusetts, Washington was willing to lay his reputation on the line and step up his involvement.

OF COURSE, WASHINGTON ALREADY had been deeply involved in the ratification effort since returning home in September. He had personally endorsed the Constitution to public officials and influential people in Virginia and elsewhere. He had urged supporters with "literary abilities" to take up their pens on behalf of ratification, and then helped to distribute and republish their best efforts, including Wilson's defense of the Constitution and the *Federalist* essays written by Hamilton, Madison, and Jay under the pseudonym Publius.[14] He had never objected when federalists publicly invoked his name and had dispatched scores of letters of his own in support of ratification. "No subject is more interesting," Washington had remarked to Madison in early November.[15]

Indeed, although he stayed near home during the ratification process, Washington never took his attention off the unfolding state-by-state contest for the Constitution. "Nothing either interesting or entertaining in these quarters to communicate," he wrote of his life at Mount Vernon in one mid-January letter, "our faces being turned to the Eastward for news."[16] News from Massachusetts, he meant, where the Constitution hung in the balance.

To win in Massachusetts, Madison advised Washington in late December, more might be required of him. "I have good reason to believe that if you are in correspondence with any gentleman of that quarter, and a proper occasion offered for an explicit communication of your good wishes for the plan," Madison wrote, "that it would be attended with valuable effects." Then, as if he had crossed a boundary, Madison added, "I barely drop the idea. The circumstances on which the propriety of it depends, are best known to, as they will be best judged, by yourself."[17]

The boundaries here of Cincinnatus-type public service were hazy. Like many other Virginia lawmakers, Washington had openly campaigned for his seat in the House of Burgesses prior to the Revolutionary War, including throwing parties and providing food and drink for prospective voters. And in recent months he had urged Madison and other federalists to campaign actively for the Constitution. Yet he made a point of staying home during the entire ten-month ratification process and wanted desperately to appear above the fray. In letter after letter, he told correspondents that he had not traveled more than six or ten miles—the number kept changing—from Mount Vernon since his return from Philadelphia, which allowed him to reach Alexandria, but no farther.[18] He vowed that he would not lobby for ratification yet called on others to do so.[19]

This reticence arose less from objections to peddling the Constitution than from a desire to remain above reproach. Everyone so fully assumed that Washington would become President that his efforts on behalf of ratification might appear self-serving. Further, the Cincinnatus ideal demanded that he not seek power and taking sides now might limit his ability to serve as a unifying leader later. Thus, as he wrote to his wartime aide James McHenry about his life since the Convention, "I never go from home except when I am obliged by necessary avocations, and . . . meddle as little as possible with politics that my interference may not give occasion for impertinent imputations" of self-interest.[20]

In a mid-1788 letter that spoke of him becoming a target for "shafts of malice" from antifederalists who had "stigmatized the authors of the Constitution as Conspirators and Traitors," Washington repeated his oft-stated denial of interest in the presidency. "At my age, and in my circumstances, what sinister object, or personal emolument had I to seek after, in this life?" he asked about his part in forging a new government. For himself, Washington wrote, he only wished to live his remaining years as a private citizen at Mount Vernon.[21]

Responding to Madison's request for sending a letter of support to Massachusetts, Washington at first demurred. "I have no regular corrispondt in Massachusetts," he wrote to Madison in early January; "otherwise, as the occasional subject of a letter I should have had no objection to the communication of my sentiments on the proposed Government as they are unequivocal & decided."[22] Then Washington received a personal note from one of his former senior officers, Benjamin Lincoln, who recently had been elected to the Massachusetts ratifying convention. Seizing the opportunity, Washington promptly replied to Lincoln with a long letter endorsing the Constitution, stressing the importance of ratification by Massachusetts, and offering advice about how Bay State federalists should comport themselves.

Developments in Pennsylvania colored Washington's advice. Early in the new year, reports began circulating in newspapers that a mob of unreconstructed antifederalists had disrupted a federalist victory rally in Carlisle, Pennsylvania, and burned federalist leader James Wilson in effigy.[23] Soon it became apparent that this riot was not an isolated event. The problems went back to the previous year, when Pennsylvania federalists used high-handed means to force an early state convention and then rammed the Constitution through that body without listening to the opposition or letting it offer amendments. Dissenters then published their amendments, collected petitions signed by thousands asking the state assembly to rescind ratification, and worked with antifederalists in neighboring New York and Virginia to defeat the Constitution. Word of these developments reached Washington early in the new year and convinced him that victory alone was not enough. He would have to rule these people, and he knew from the Revolutionary Era that a disaffected minority could fatally disrupt public order. When the local militia from nearby counties freed the imprisoned rioters in Carlisle and prevented their prosecution, the lesson should have become clear to all, yet some federalists wanted the rioters punished as an example.

Washington knew better. For the new government to function,

he reasoned, antifederalists would need to accept the ratification process as fundamentally fair. After having initially hailed the results in Pennsylvania despite the strong-arm tactics, Washington now changed his emphasis. In his letter to Lincoln, Washington struck a note of conciliation. "The business of the Convention should be conducted with moderation, candor & fairness (which are not incompatible with firmness)," he wrote to Lincoln, "for altho' as you justly observe, the friends of the New system may bear down the opposition, yet they would never be able, by precipitate or violent measures, to sooth and reconcile their minds to the exercise of the Government." This reconciliation, Washington stressed, "is a matter that ought as much as possible to be kept in view."[24] Winning at all costs would not serve the public interest, he concluded. Whatever he thought of antifederalists, and various private letters betrayed his antipathy toward them, Washington knew better than to show it. He wanted to form an American nation by uniting its people, not dividing them.

ALTHOUGH WASHINGTON'S LETTER to Lincoln arrived too late to influence the convention in Massachusetts, confirmation of his position reached the members from another source. Washington often wrote private letters to influential friends, particularly in Virginia, discussing ratification along with other matters. Most of these messages remained strictly confidential. Key parts of one such letter to Virginia planter and former legislator Charles Carter, which endorsed the Constitution after a long discourse on crops, was published in a Virginia newspaper on December 27 and quickly spread. Within days, the extract surfaced in Maryland and Pennsylvania, and during the state's convention appeared in nine Massachusetts papers, beginning with the *Centinel* on January 23. "There is *no alternative* between the *adoption* of it and *anarchy*," Washington wrote of the Constitution, "and *clear I am*, if another federal Convention is attempted, that the sentiments of its members will be *more* discordant or *less* accommodating than the last. In fine, that they will agree upon no general plan."[25]

Federalists were hungry to hear such words from their icon. By March, some fifty papers published the letter. "I am fully persuaded it is the *best that can be obtained at this time*," the extract went on to say about the Constitution, "that it is free from many of the imperfections with which it is charged, and that *it* or *disunion* is before us to choose from."[26] In one sentence, Washington encapsulated the federalists' position.

Washington was furious about the disclosure. Although the letter accurately expressed his beliefs, he had never meant to speak so bluntly in public. He demanded an explanation from Carter, who apologized profusely, but neither man denied the extract's authenticity even though the published version was an inexact transcript of the original. Washington actually pointed to it, in his letter to Lincoln, as an expression of his "sentiments upon the Constitution."[27]

Having wasted a vast inheritance, Carter was down on his luck by this time and soon sold his plantation. Within a year, he was taking in boarders at a house in Fredericksburg and living off the income from the day labor of slaves who he had already sold. Washington could hardly hold him to account and quickly let the matter slide. Appearing as it did in Massachusetts during the state's ratifying convention, publication of the extract touched off a flurry of exchanges in the Boston press between opponents denouncing its arrogance and supporters hailing its insight.[28] Indeed, its rapid, widespread distribution gave federalists everywhere testimony directly from that "Great and Good Man"—as writers at the time often called Washington—on the imperative of ratification.[29]

THE MASSACHUSETTS CONVENTION played out as a pivotal act within the larger drama of federal ratification, complete with plot twists, intrigue, and a cliffhanger ending. From Mount Vernon, Washington followed the story closely in newspapers and private letters. At first, the prospects in Massachusetts looked rosy, with Washington receiving ever more upbeat reports over the course of the fall, especially after the federalist-minded majority in Cambridge, Massachusetts, excluded Gerry from its local delegation, which left the state's leading antifederalist without a seat at the 354-member convention.[30] The election of the other three Massachusetts delegates to the Constitutional Convention—Nathaniel Gorham, Rufus King, and Caleb Strong—to the state convention gave federalists an edge in expertise. Gerry was invited to attend as a resource strictly to answer questions about the federal convention, but that role proved so limiting to him that he soon stalked out of the chamber and never returned.

As the election returns from western Massachusetts and Maine came in during December, however, it became apparent the legacy of Shays's Rebellion was energizing the opposition: neither side would hold a clear majority in the assembly.[31] "Many of the insurgents are in Convention, even some of Shay's Officers," Lincoln warned Washington.[32] In a letter that reached Washington through Madison, Gorham put the number at "18 or 20 who were actually in Shay's army."[33] An article in the *Massachusetts Gazette* went so far as to observe, "the *Federalists* should be distinguished hereafter by the name of **WASHINGTONIANS**, and the *Antifederalists*, by the name of **SHAYITES**."[34] The sides were closely matched. With a foot in each camp and influence commensurate with his legendary ego, Governor Hancock—who would serve as the convention's president—might decide the outcome. That gave federalists both pause and hope.

When the convention opened on January 9, Hancock was bedridden with gout and antifederalists likely held a slender majority. Federalists opted to stall by agreeing to discuss the Constitution clause by clause before voting. With more practiced speakers on their side and ready answers to every charge, they hoped to win over some members and play for time.

They got the delay they wanted. The discussion of Article I

alone consumed two weeks as members wrangled over the authority of Congress, particularly its expansive taxing power. "In giving this power we give up everything," one antifederalist thundered. It is "as much power as was ever given to a despotic prince," another added. Federalists replied that since Congress would represent the people, any authority it held would serve the public. "Under the old Confederation, the delegates were our servants; now they are our masters," shot back a member who once led a militia that supported Shays's Rebellion; "they have all our money, a standing army, a Federal town."[35] Shaysites had objected to the concentration of power in the eastern, moneyed elite under the state's 1780 constitution and feared a similar result under the new federal one. Many demanded amendments prior to ratification. They would not be persuaded by words, but the federalists still hoped to gain a few wavering moderates with promises. By the last week of January, everyone knew the vote would be close.

Washington waited at Mount Vernon for news, which he received in letters dispatched almost daily. "No question ever clasped the people of this State in a more extraordinary manner, or with more apparent firmness," King wrote in a January 16 note that reached Washington through Madison. "But what will be [the Constitution's] fate, I confess I am unable to discern."[36] By the twenty-seventh, Lincoln wrote to Washington to say he now had "higher expectations" the Constitution would pass, but he added that "it is yet impossible to determine absolutely its fate."[37]

These higher expectations arose from a secret deal with Hancock, who, in exchange for support from federalists in the next governor's race, would rise from his sickbed, endorse ratification, and propose amendments to the Constitution. The amendments would not be added "as a condition of our assent & ratification," a subsequent letter from King explained, "but as the Opinion of the Convention subjoined to their ratification." In short, the delegates would simply recommend that the First Congress consider them. "This scheme may gain a few members," King added.[38] Federalists initially attached little importance to these "recommendatory" amendments, as Washington termed them, beyond their role in winning votes from moderates for the Constitution.[39] Letters to and from Washington referred to them only in the most dismissive terms (with Washington lamenting their adoption and Madison calling them a "blemish" on ratification) and never identified their content, much less analyzed their substance.[40] At the time, both viewed them as a mere sop to the opposition. Taken together, however, they offered the outlines for a bill of rights. Massachusetts's antifederalists—not its federalists—and Hancock's secret deal deserve credit for advancing this idea.

According to their later boasts, federalists also flattered Hancock, suggesting he would likely become Vice President under the new regime and, should Virginia not ratify, perhaps President. "If Mr Hancock does not disappoint our present expectations," King wrote on January 30 in another letter that reached Washington through Madison, "our wishes will be gratified."[41] He didn't, and they were. Hancock played his part to perfection by making a grand entrance at the convention swaddled in sick-clothes and borne on a daybed just in time to carry the Constitution with his compromise proposal for recommendatory amendments. Wealthy beyond the dreams of most Americans of his day, Hancock always had a flair for the dramatic.[42]

"Our convention this day ratified the constitution 187 affirmative 168 negative," King wrote to Washington on February 6. "The minority . . . publickly declare that the Discussion has been fair & candid, and that the majority having decided in favor of the constitution, they will devote their Lives & Fortunes to support the Government."[43] Washington welcomed this outcome. "Happy, I am, to see the favorable decision of your Convention," he wrote back to King. "It must be productive of good effects in other states, whose determination may have been problematical. The candid, and open behaviour of the minority, is noble and commendable. It will have its weight."[44]

Given the closeness of the final vote, Washington's endorsement likely played a critical role. The fact that the Constitution "comes authenticated" by Washington, one member had told the convention, "is a reason why we should examine it with care and caution, and that we ought not rashly and precipitately to reject it."[45] Just such careful examination led Massachusetts to become the crucial sixth state to ratify the Constitution, and the first one to do so over such a strong opposition.

WASHINGTON PARTICULARLY WELCOMED the vote in Massachusetts because the next three states holding conventions—New Hampshire, Maryland, and South Carolina—looked reliably federal.[46] Those three would bring the total to nine: the number needed for the new government to organize. Conventions in the key battleground states of Virginia and New York would then follow. "As nine states will have determined upon it," Washington commented in February on ratification, "it is expected that its opponents in those [two] States will not have sufficient influence to prevent its adoption there when it is found to be the general voice of the Union."[47] And once they, too, ratified, Washington predicted, North Carolina and Rhode Island surely would fall in line. "The force of this argument is hardly to be resisted," he added in early March. "Candor and prudence therefore, it is to be hoped, will prevail."[48] Simply put, Washington explained to Jay, "the favorable decision of the three which is likely to follow next, will . . . be too powerful, I conceive, for locallity and sophistry to combat."[49]

Maryland and South Carolina kept to the federalist script but New Hampshire surprised nearly everyone.[50] John Langdon, New Hampshire's former president and Constitutional Convention delegate, had assured Washington during the fall that New Hampshire would ratify. Reflecting this confidence, the state's federalist president, John Sullivan, had arranged for a convention to meet during February in federalist-friendly southeastern New Hampshire.[51] To Langdon and Sullivan, the stage seemed set for rapid ratification.

They did not anticipate that many central and western New Hampshire towns would instruct their convention delegates to vote against the Constitution—and that no amount of persuasion could get them to defy those orders. "Just at the moment of choice for members," Langdon explained in a letter to Washington, "a report was circulated by a few designing men who wished for confusion that . . . the liberties of the people were in danger, and that the great men (as they called them) were forming a plan for themselves together with a thousand other absurdities, which frightened the people almost out of what *little* senses they had." This, Langdon wrote, led to the limiting instructions.[52] Foreseeing certain defeat, federalists joined their sympathizers among the instructed members to adjourn the convention until June, by which time they hoped to get enough towns to lift their instructions for the Constitution to pass.

The postponement distressed Washington. A flurry of letters about it came and went from Mount Vernon. "The proceedings in New Hampshire, so directly opposite to what we had reason to hope for, from every account, has entirely baffled all calculation on the subject and will strengthen the opposition here," Washington wrote.[53] Virginia antifederalists were hailing the adjournment as a victory, he reported, by claiming that New Hampshire would now wait until Virginia voted on the Constitution. "If this state should reject it," they purportedly said, "all those which are to follow will do the same; & consequently, the Constitution cannot obtain, as there will be only eight States in favor."[54]

By giving Virginia antifederalists a reason for hope, Washington worried, this far-fetched scenario could influence elections to the state convention and the tenor of its proceedings. Virginia was back in play, he feared, even if New Hampshire ultimately voted to ratify as Langdon again assured him that it would.[55] The conventions in

Virginia, New Hampshire, and New York would now overlap in June, creating a bitter brew of possibilities. At least by then Maryland and South Carolina had approved the new union by wide majorities— but that, as antifederalists noted and Washington knew, still left the Constitution one critical state shy of ratification.

Maryland presented one brief scare that, after the setback in New Hampshire, caused Washington again to break his vow of not politicking for the Constitution. Facing defeat, Maryland's outnumbered antifederalists proposed postponing their state's convention ostensibly to give members time to work with their Virginia counterparts on amendments. Responding to pleas from Virginia federalists, Washington wrote to two top Maryland federalists, James McHenry and Thomas Johnson, asking that their state not delay lest it further embolden the opposition in Virginia.[56] "Postponement of the question would be tantamount to the final rejection of it," Washington advised McHenry, and "would have the worst tendency imaginable," he added to Johnson. In both letters, Washington alluded to his past reluctance to "meddle," as he called it, in "this political dispute," but he now confessed that, as "a man so thoroughly persuaded as I am of the evils and confusions which will result from the rejection of the proposed Constitution," he should have done more all along.[57]

"I have but one public wish remaining," Washington wrote to Governor Johnson. "It is, that in *peace* and *retirement*, I may see this Country rescued from the danger which is pending, & rise into respectability."[58]

With wealthy federalist planter-lawyers like John Rutledge and the Pinckneys managing events in their state, Washington had less need to intervene in South Carolina than in Maryland, but in both, his name propelled ratification. During the run-up to their states' conventions, federalist newspapers in Charleston and Baltimore trumpeted his role in drafting the Constitution and his support for ratification. One poem in the *State Gazette of South*

Carolina, for example, after referring to the call by "Washington the great" for "an indissolvable union of the states under one federal head," admonished readers:

> *Will you not hear your father's call,*
> *He loves his children one and all.*[59]

And Charleston's *Columbian Herald* declared, "God grant that there may be wisdom and goodness enough still found among the *majority* to adopt, without hesitation, what a WASHINGTON, a FRANKLIN, a MADDISON, &c. so warmly recommended."[60] In Maryland, the merchants of Baltimore recognized Washington's role in forging the new union by giving him the fifteen-foot miniature ship, *Federalist*, they had commissioned for the city's ratification celebrations. Accepting the model as a "specimen of American ingenuity," Washington moored it in the Potomac at Mount Vernon until a gale, which he called a "hurricane" and described as more "violent and severe . . . than has happened for many years," sank it in July.[61] By then, Virginia had taken center stage.

THE STORM THAT SANK the *Federalist* simply added to Washington's weather woes. The previous summer's record drought had forced him to buy corn to feed his slaves and livestock. "I raised nothing last summer for sale," he complained in January.[62] Then the rains came in similarly biblical proportions. Entry after entry in Washington's diary for spring 1788 spoke of all hands stopping work in the fields due to weather. "I am in a manner drowned," Washington wrote by June. The torrents had beaten down his oats and flax. "What will become of my Corn is not easy, at this moment, to decide; I am working it ancle deep in Water & mud," he lamented.[63] The hurricane followed in July. Trees crashed down and crops were leveled. "The tide," Washington noted, "rose near or quite 4 feet higher than it was ever known to do, driving Boats, &ca. into field where no tide had ever been heard of before." Fences washed away, livestock wandered loose, and the millrace breached its banks.[64] Yet in August, he wrote of agriculture being his "favorite amusement."[65] As much as he wished to deny it to others and perhaps himself, the steady stream of states ratifying the Constitution was unmooring him from his beloved Mount Vernon. Only Virginia now stood in the way, Washington believed, and he was doing everything in his power to secure its assent.

Wartime experiences had made Washington an American—arguably the first American—but he always remained a Virginian, too. For him, Virginia stood at the nation's heart.[66] It was America's largest, longest-settled, and most centrally located state as well as Washington's home. He could not image a United States without it and had been more than ankle deep in the mire of Virginia ratification politics since returning from the Constitutional Convention in September 1787. Within days of his arrival home, Washington began reaching out to Virginia's political elite, starting with a letter telling the states'-rights-minded former governor Benjamin Harrison that ratification "is in my opinion desirable."[67] Over the ensuing months, he regularly hosted Virginia federalists at Mount Vernon and continually corresponded with them about ratification.

In November 1787, Madison began sending Washington copies of the *Federalist* essays from New York, with a request that he pass them on to his "confidential correspondents at Richmond who would have them reprinted there."[68] Washington forwarded them to his most trusted contact in the state capital, David Stuart, with the request that it not be "known that they are sent by *me* to *you* for promulgation."[69] Washington directly lobbied Randolph and Jefferson in letters designed to bring or keep them on board, leading to rumors that he promised them posts in the first presidential administration.

"The plot thickens fast," Washington wrote as Virginia's ratifying convention neared.[70] To deal with the threat posed by Henry's spellbinding oratory, Washington all but ordered Madison to stand for election to the convention so that he could answer Henry point for point—a task that the mild-mannered Madison dreaded. When Madison's election looked doubtful without campaigning, Washington told him to return from Congress to stump for votes—another unpleasant task.

"The consciousness of having discharged that duty which we owe to our Country, is superior to all other considerations," Washington wrote to Madison in words that may have reflected his current thinking on his own duty to accept the presidency.[71] Washington, of course, maintained his public silence and declined nomination to the convention. To counter Henry, Mason, and their allies—most notably former congressmen William Grayson and James Monroe—federalists relied mainly on Madison, Madison's friend George Nicholas, Virginia's chief judge Edmund Pendleton, the rising young lawmaker John Marshall, and Henry Lee. Richard Henry Lee stayed away and Randolph moved toward the federalist camp.[72] "There will . . . be powerful and eloquent speeches on both sides of the question in the Virginia Convention," Washington predicted.[73] "The Northern, or upper Counties are *generally* friendly to the adoption of the Government, the lower *are said* to be generally unfriendly."[74]

SOME 170 MEMBERS STRONG, Virginia's ratifying convention opened on June 2 in Richmond, the first contested convention not held in a federalist-friendly coastal community. The state's capital only since the war, Richmond retained a frontier feel. The gallery here would not cheer on the federalists: many in it had come to hear Henry once again contend for liberty. Taking the floor early and holding it often, he did not disappoint his followers during the four-week-long convention.

After having tried to win him over early, Washington worried more about Henry's opposition than about that of any other Virginian, to the point of fearing that the former governor might seek to lead the state into a separate southern confederacy with himself at the helm.[75] While not a disciplined debater, Henry had a gift for stirring audiences with impassioned speeches that played more on emotion than reason, which was precisely how Washington depicted opposition arguments in Virginia generally.[76] Henry employed this approach at the convention to transform what was supposed to be a clause-by-clause consideration of the Constitution into a free-for-all in which federalists scrambled to refute his scattered charges.

Henry launched his assault on the first day of substantive debate. Representing the people as being "at perfect repose" and the country in "universal tranquility" prior to the Convention, Henry demanded to know why Virginia's delegates—which of course included Washington—had proposed replacing the confederation of states with a consolidated national government. "Who authorized them to speak the language of, *We, the People*, instead of *We, the States?*" he asked. "I would demand the cause of their conduct," he said. "Even from that illustrious man who saved us by his valor, I would have a reason for his conduct—that liberty which he has given us by his valor, tells me to ask this reason." That very liberty, Henry charged, was put at risk by the Constitution.

"This proposal of altering our Federal Government is of a most alarming nature," Henry declared, "for instead of securing your rights you may lose them forever."[77] He condemned the document wholly and suggested that Virginia could get along outside the union. Henry had Washington in his crosshairs.

The challenge to Washington drew gasps from federalists and brought Randolph to his feet for a two-hour-long oration. To this point, Henry still saw Randolph as an ally and expected his support.[78] Instead, the governor defended the Constitutional Convention and its delegates. "The gentleman," he said of Henry, "inquires, why we assumed the language of 'We, the people,' I ask why not? The Government is for the people; and the misfortune was, that the people had no agency in the Government before." With "the terror of impending anarchy" and no hope of saving the confederation, Randolph asked in defense of Washington, "Would it not have been treason to return without proposing some scheme to relieve their distressed country?" He had withheld his signature from the Constitution thinking that the states would insist on amendments prior to ratification, Randolph explained, but the actions of eight states now showed otherwise. "I will assent to the lopping of this limb," he declared in a mocking allusion to George Mason's earlier vow to cut off his hand rather than sign the Constitution, "before I assent to the dissolution of the Union."[79]

Eager to reply, Mason spoke next. Unlike Henry, Mason conceded that a new constitution was needed but, like Henry, argued that the proposed one went too far in consolidating power in a national government at the expense of individual liberty and states' rights, particularly by granting it power to tax people directly. "This power is calculated to annihilate totally the State Government," Mason claimed. He could not conceive of splitting sovereignty between the states and nation, as Madison argued that the Constitution would do, or that a remote central government would protect "the great essential rights of the people" without a bill of rights. "If such amendments be introduced as shall exclude danger, I shall most gladly put my hand to it," he said of the Constitution. Virginia federalists were moving to accommodate this concern by following the Massachusetts model of recommending amendments for the First Congress to adopt.

As he would throughout the convention, Madison promptly reported to Washington. "The Governor has declared the day of previous amendments past, and thrown himself fully into the federal scale," Madison wrote in a same-day letter to Mount Vernon. "Henry & Mason made a lame figure & appeared to take different and awkward ground. The federalists are a good deal elated by the existing prospect." Elated but cautious, Madison added, because the delegates from Virginia's western district of Kentucky seemed uniformly hostile—and given the close divide, even that small contingent could prove decisive. "Every piece of address is going on privately to work on the local interests & prejudices of that & other quarters," Madison assured Washington.[80]

Between letters and newspaper reports, Washington received virtually a blow-by-blow account of the convention. For two weeks, it did not proceed in a systematic fashion but instead followed Henry's lead as he discharged random "bolts," as Henry Lee called them, with federalists responding to each. It picked up speed after members began reviewing the document clause by clause and fairly raced through the final articles.[81] "Henry's confidence in the power and greatness of Virginia, which he said she might rest upon though dismembered from her sister States, was very well exposed," one member explained to Washington in a June 7 letter. "Madison followed, and with such force of reasoning, and a display of such irresistible truths, that opposition seemed to have quitted the field."[82] Yet Madison wrote Washington a week later, "Our progress is slow and every advantage is taken of the delay, to work on the local prejudices of particular setts of members."[83] Antifederalists repeatedly reminded Kentucky members that northern states had been willing to bargain away American rights to the Mississippi, for example, while federalists countered that a strong union could better protect those rights than a weak one. "Much appears to depend upon the final part which the Kentucke members will take," Washington concluded, particularly "respecting the navigation of the Mississippi."[84]

As the vote neared, Madison advised Washington, "We calculate on a majority, but a bare one."[85]

Though far away, Washington might as well have been in the assembly room at Richmond. "The truth was that not only at the Virginia convention but at all the state gatherings Washington was always present, a force more powerful for being insubstantial," biographer James Thomas Flexner observed.[86] Washington's role in drafting the Constitution and the prospect of him becoming the President made all the difference. Alluding to Washington near the end of Virginia's convention, for example, Grayson complained, "Were it not for one great character in America, so many men would not be for this Government. . . . We do not fear while he lives: But we can only expect his *fame* to be immortal. We wish to know, who besides him, can concentrate the confidence and affections of all America?"[87] And railing against the electoral system for selecting presidents, Mason charged that "so many persons would be voted for, that there seldom or never could be a majority in favor of one, except one great name."[88] When Henry had the gall to assert that Jefferson opposed ratification, Madison countered that Washington supported it: check and checkmate.[89] In making these arguments at the convention, Grayson, Mason, and Henry must have felt that they were shadowboxing with Washington, whose assumed role as President made what they saw as a fatally flawed system appear attractive to others.

ON JUNE 27, the evening stagecoach brought the news to Alexandria that Virginia had ratified the Constitution two days earlier. It had passed by a ten-vote margin out of 168 votes cast. The promise of recommendatory amendments won over more members than expected, including four from Kentucky.

With cannons booming in celebration, townspeople descended on Mount Vernon to invite Washington to local festivities scheduled for the next day. Before dawn, an express rider arrived with word that New Hampshire had ratified on the twenty-first by an eleven-vote margin, making it, not Virginia, the critical ninth state to approve the Constitution. "Thus the Citizens of Alexandria, when convened, constituted the first public company in America, which had the pleasure of pouring libation to the prosperity of the ten States that had actually adopted the general government," Washington wrote on June 28.[90] "This flood of good news, almost at the same moment, gave, as you can readily conceive, abundant cause for rejoicing in a place, the Inhabitants of which are *all* federal," he added a day later.[91]

Washington stood at the center of Alexandria's revelries. A mounted party met him near Mount Vernon and escorted him to town with light infantry saluting him along the way and a discharge of ten cannons marking his arrival at Wise's Tavern, Alexandria's finest public house. "As magnificent a dinner as Mr. Wise could provide," Washington wrote, "was displayed before the principal *Male* Inhabitants of the Town, whose Ears were saluted at every quaff with the melody of federal Guns."[92] Fiddling and dancing followed "for the amusement, & benefit of the Ladies," he added. Similar celebrations took place in countless cities and towns across the country as word spread that ten states had approved the new union.[93] Victors and vanquished alike recognized it as being as much a triumph for Washington as for the Constitution.

"Be assured," Monroe said of Washington shortly after Virginia's convention ended, "his influence carried this government."[94]

WITH VIRGINIA'S VOTE, Washington finally felt confident the Constitution would take effect, but he knew New York must also join for any federal government to operate successfully. That state—which was then the site of America's largest city, busiest port, and seat of government—was holding its convention when New Hampshire and Virginia ratified. It was, however, the only state other than renegade Rhode Island whose delegates had not endorsed the Constitution in Philadelphia. Prospects for ratification in New York never looked good.

"The determination of New York seems most problematical,"

Washington had written five months earlier, "and yet, I can hardly entertain an idea that She will be disposed to stand alone, or with one or two others."[95] That had become the federalists' best hope. New York was content with the current confederation, they knew, and would not budge so long as it lasted, but might choose the Constitution over disunion. "The decision of ten States cannot be without its operation," Washington wrote in June.[96]

As Washington knew from personal experience, in New York, partisan politics had split along national and state-minded lines for longer than in any other place. The divide stemmed from the early days of the Revolutionary War, when one part of New York's landed elite remained loyal to the king while another part supported independence as a means to protect its rights. The resulting upheaval allowed George Clinton, a middle-class lawyer-legislator who had distinguished himself as a military leader at the outbreak of war, to become the state's first elected governor in 1777.

A gifted politician with broad executive power, Clinton kept his state not only functioning but actively in the fight during the long, dark years that British troops occupied New York City. For this, he earned Washington's lasting respect. Clinton had supported strengthening the union during the war but afterward found that, by taxing goods passing through its booming harbor and issuing paper money that held its value, New York could flourish in a loose confederation even as other states floundered. New York's large landowners and merchant princes, however, foresaw still greater prosperity under a consolidated government that could expand interstate commerce and limit foreign competition through protective tariffs. Led by two of Washington's most trusted advisors, Hamilton and Jay, this faction embraced nationalism.

The split became apparent to all in 1787, when New York tapped two Clintonian antifederalists to serve with Hamilton at the Constitutional Convention. The proviso that the delegation could only vote if at least two of its members agreed showed which faction held the upper hand. "It is somewhat singular that a State which used to be foremost in all federal measures, should now turn her face against them in almost every instance," Washington wrote upon hearing about the arrangement, though he never criticized Clinton for it.[97]

Even after New York's two antifederalist delegates walked out of the Convention in July, leaving the state without a vote, Washington did not blame Clinton and reprimanded Hamilton for doing so. "It is with unfeigned concern that I perceive that a political dispute has arisen between Governor Clinton and yourself," Washington wrote to Hamilton about the matter. "For both of you I have the highest esteem and regard. . . . When the situation of this Country calls loudly for unanimity & vigor, it is to be lamented that Gentlemen of talents and character should disagree in their sentiments for promoting the public weal, but unfortunately, this ever has been, and more than probable, ever will be the case."[98] Washington never offered such a defense for Mason, Henry, Lee, Gerry, or any other antifederalist.

Elections to the state convention sharpened New York's already bitter partisan divide.[99] Through deft leadership and political patronage, Clinton had built a disciplined party that was based upstate and, in 1788, openly called itself antifederal. Under the federal banner, Clinton's traditional opponents closed ranks with downstate artisans and tradesmen to support ratification. "More than any other state," historian Pauline Maier noted, "the fight was between two organized parties."[100]

With friends on each side, Washington stayed out of this contest and, unlike his scathing private criticism of Mason and Henry, never questioned Clinton's motives. Some federalist writers cited Washington's support as one reason to ratify the Constitution,[101] but most left that argument unstated and none of the eighty-three *Federalist* essays written by Hamilton, Madison, and Jay to rally New Yorkers for the cause mentioned Washington's name. "This form of government is handed to you by the recommendations of a man who merits the confidence of the public," one early antifed-

eralist essay widely attributed to Clinton offered to counter federalist claims of Washington's support, "but . . . every man ought
to think for himself."[102] In these elections, however, most voters
followed their party. Antifederalists won every race upstate and on
Long Island while federalists swept New York City and its envi-
rons, giving Clinton's party a formidable 46–19 seat margin at the
ratifying convention.

Perhaps because of its partisan nature, the debate in New York
over the Constitution was particularly intense. Beyond the *Federalist*
essays, which Washington instantly hailed as lasting contributions to
the library of liberty and government,[103] it generated a flood of articles
and pamphlets on each side over a ten-month period. Antifederalists
harped on the threat to liberty poised by a distant, central government without a bill of rights or a sufficiently representative Congress.
Federalists at first defended the Constitution on its own terms but,
as a rising number of other states voted to ratify, later stressed the
consequences to New York and its commercial interests of being left
out of the union. Reminding New Yorkers of these costs in a pam-
phlet printed shortly before the elections, Jay wrote, "Consider then,
how weighty and how many considerations advise and persuade the
People of America to remain in the safe and easy path of Union [and]
to continue to move and act as they hitherto have done, as a *Band of
Brothers*."[104] The "good sense" of this argument, Washington commented to Jay upon reading it, "cannot fail, I should think, of making
a serious impression even upon the antifederal mind."[105]

Jay's argument, however, only became irresistible after Virginia
ratified the Constitution in late June. Until then, partisan antifederalists could hold out hope that the existing confederation might survive.
From the time that it began in antifederalist-friendly Poughkeepsie
on June 17, therefore, minority federalists sought to drag out the convention until word arrived from Richmond. They even arranged for
express riders to rush the news from Virginia when it came. In the
meantime, they talked and talked.

Accounts differ over why antifederalists let the deliberations run on when they had the votes to end them. Perhaps they, too, wanted to see what Virginia did before proceeding. "Some are sanguine enough to believe the Necessity of the Case will induce them to adopt the new Constitution," Postmaster General Ebenezer Hazard reported to Washington from New York one week after the convention began. "Much depends on the Conduct of Virginia, for whose Decision we wait with anxious Impatience."[106] No one doubted, though, that Clinton, as convention president and undisputed leader of his party, ultimately set the schedule. He must have wanted the proceedings to continue and later allowed them to conclude.[107]

"THE POINT IN DEBATE HAS, at least, shifted its ground from policy to expediency," Washington wrote about the New York convention as soon as he learned that Virginia and New Hampshire had ratified the Constitution.[108] "It is hardly to be conceived that New York will reject it [now]."[109] Perhaps thinking of Clinton, Washington soon added, "However great the opposition to it may be in that of New York, the leaders thereof will, I should conceive, consider the consequences of rejection well, before it is given."[110] He knew Clinton too well to believe that he would ever act contrary to his state's interests.

To ratchet up the pressure, Jay informed Washington, federalists spread the word that southern New York would secede from the north should the convention not ratify the Constitution.[111] Jay also reported to Washington that divisions had appeared among antifederalists, with some demanding amendments before ratification and others content with amendments after ratification, so long as New York had the right to rescind should those amendments fail. Although Jay and Hamilton told the convention that Congress would not accept either option as a valid form of ratification, Jay privately wrote to Washington on July 8 that at least they "afford Room for Hope." Importantly, he stressed, "The Ground of *Rejection* therefore seems to be entirely deserted."[112] The opposition now was seeking terms for conditional surrender.

While these wary adversaries negotiated in Poughkeepsie, federalists in New York City could not curb their enthusiasm for the proposed new federal union. Upon hearing in late June that nine states had ratified the Constitution, they organized a grand federal procession for Independence Day, but put it off in anticipation of a decision by New York. When that decision did not come, they held the procession on July 23. It was as much a celebration of Washington and Hamilton as of the Constitution. Five thousand federalists arrayed by trade or profession assembled in lower Manhattan and marched through the city to a temporary banqueting hall erected on the northern edge of town, where they raised a toast to Washington following a festive dinner with members of Congress and other dignitaries. At least nine of the trade groups carried banners or flags depicting Washington while printers, marching with a working press, handed out copies of odes hailing his "peerless worth" and crediting him with saving the country "again."[113] These federalists left no doubt about who they expected to become the first President.

On the very day that federalists paraded in New York City, antifederalists threw in the towel in Poughkeepsie. "The Convention proceeded to Day in debating on the Plan of *conditional* amendments," Jay wrote to Washington on July 23. "Some of the anti Party moved for striking out the words *on Condition* and substituting the words *in full confidence*—it was carried 31 to 29." By the barest majority, Jay was telling Washington, enough antifederalist members had voted with the federalists to pass a motion paving the way for New York to ratify the Constitution "in confidence" that certain amendments would be considered by Congress or a second federal convention rather than "on condition" that they be accepted. "So," Jay added, "if nothing new should occur this State will adopt unconditionally."[114] New York's convention then proposed more than fifty recommendatory or explanatory amendments—more than any other state—including the toughest ones yet to limit the government's taxing powers. "I can say," Washington soon wrote to Jefferson, "there are scarcely any of the amendments which have been suggested, to which I have *much* objection, except that which goes to the prevention of direct taxation."[115]

On these terms, New York ratified the Constitution on July 26. Clinton still voted no, but he released his partisans to vote in accord with the interests of their constituents in light of the changed circumstances.[116] Twelve antifederalists from Long Island and other parts of southern New York then voted for ratification.

Those who followed the proceedings in New York recognized that, close as it was, Washington had carried the day. "It is with the most sincere satisfaction that I congratulate *you* on the unconditional adoption of the constitution by the Convention of this state," Secretary of War Henry Knox wrote to Washington from New York.[117] In its next issue, the *Albany Journal* featured a song that began:

> *Behold Columbia's empire rise,*
> *On freedom's solid base to stand;*
> *Supported by propitious skies,*
> *And seal'd by her deliverer's hand.*[118]

In case any reader missed its meaning, newspapers reprinting this song added a footnote stating that the last line referred to Washington's signature on the Constitution.[119] Robert R. Livingston, New York's chancellor since 1777 and a federalist stalwart at the state convention, soon wrote Washington about the Constitution's adoption, "Never I believe was such a revolution effected in so short a time and in so tranquil a manner," he observed, "which I attribute (under heaven) not only to a sense of the imperfections of our old constitution, but to the general confidence which people of every rank reposed in the virtues & abilities of the man their common voice had designated to preside over the new one."[120] The people's delegates had ratified Washington as much as they had ratified a constitution.

TWO OF THE ORIGINAL thirteen states remained outside the new federal union. In March 1788, Rhode Island voters had rejected the Constitution in a referendum that was boycotted by federalists. The following August, North Carolina's state convention adjourned without taking a vote on ratification. Due to their size or location, these states were not needed to implement the Constitution, however, and Washington remained confident that both would eventually ratify it.[121] Once New York acted, the outgoing Congress began in earnest to arrange for the peaceful and orderly transfer of power to the new government.

This momentous event led Washington to reflect on all that Americans had achieved over the past year and a half. "We have the unequaled privilege of choosing our own political Institutions," he wrote in August, "and of improving upon the experiences of mankind in the formation of a confederated government, where due energy will not be incompatible with the unalienable rights of freemen." In a world hitherto ruled by hereditary monarchs, traditional dogmas, or military might, nothing like America's republican experiment had ever occurred. "We exhibit at present the novel & astonishing Spectacle of a whole People deliberating calmly on what form of government will be most conductive to their happiness; and deciding with an unexpected degree of unanimity in favor of a system which they conceive calculated to answer the purpose."[122] Washington rightly called this "a new phenomenon in the political & moral world; and an astonishing victory gained by enlightened reason over brutal force."[123]

Providence, too, Washington believed, played a part, and assured a bright future for the United States. "Should every thing proceed with harmony and consent according to our actual wishes and expectations," Washington wrote to Lafayette, "it will be so much beyond any thing we had a right to imagine or expect eighteen months ago, that it will demonstrate as visibly the finger of Providence, as any possible in the course of human affairs can ever designate it."[124]

Whereas at the beginning of 1787, Washington had despaired of the country's survival as a free, unified republic, now he exuded confidence. America's prospects appeared boundless, he believed, in part because of its new Constitution. "When the people shall find themselves secure under an energetic government," Washington told Lafayette, "when foreign Nations shall be disposed to give us equal advantages in commerce from dread of retaliation, . . . and when every one (under his own vine and fig-tree) shall begin to taste the fruits of freedom—then all of these blessings (for all these blessings will come) will be referred to the fostering influence of the new government."[125] Washington could scarcely refuse to play his ordained role in that grand experiment in human freedom.

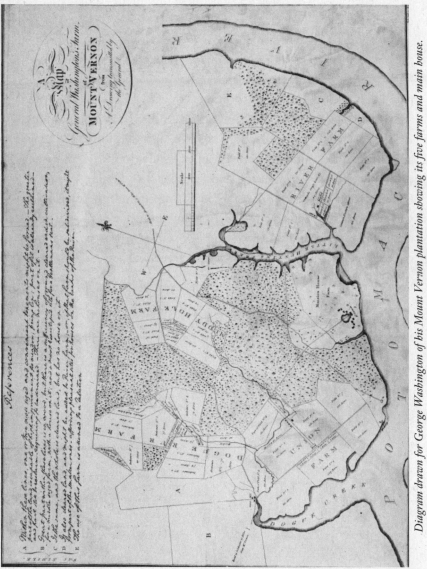

Diagram drawn for George Washington of his Mount Vernon plantation showing its five farms and main house.

CHAPTER 8

The First Federal Elections

‹⁂›

WASHINGTON STILL RODE THE CIRCUIT of his five Mount Vernon farms almost daily during the summer of 1788, conferring with his managers and observing the work of his slaves. But his mind was elsewhere. Since his return from Philadelphia in September 1787, more of his correspondence dealt with issues relating to ratification than with business, personal, or family matters. In January, for example, when the Constitution's fate hung in balance at the Massachusetts convention, he wrote to a friend of having nothing "either interesting or entertaining" to communicate from Mount Vernon because his full attention was concentrated on the news from Boston.[1] By July, when New York had replaced Massachusetts as the focus of federalists' fears, he commented to John Jay, "We are awaiting the results [from the New York convention] with the greatest anxiety."[2]

Even the news that New York had ratified the Constitution did not diminish Washington's obsession with federal politics. His concern merely shifted from ratifying to implementing the new government. The Constitutional Convention had asked Congress both to submit the Constitution to the states for ratification and, "as soon as" nine states had done so, to "fix the Day on which Electors should be appointed by the States which shall have ratified the same, and a Day on which the Electors should assemble to vote for the President, and the Time and place for commencing Proceedings under this Constitution."[3]

As the number of ratifying states approached nine, attendance at Congress in New York steadily increased. After months of inaction, it regained a quorum by late spring. In early July, after word spread that New Hampshire and Virginia had ratified, all thirteen states were represented for the first time since 1776. "Congress have deliberated in part on the arrangements for putting the new Machine into operation, but have concluded on nothing but the times for chusing electors," Madison reported to Washington from Congress on July 21.[4] Washington's response spoke to his single-mindedness. "We have nothing in these parts worth communicating," he wrote back. "Towards [Congress in] New York we look for whatever is interesting, until the States begin to act under the New form, which will be an important epocha in the annals of this Country."[5]

Washington actually began concentrating his attention on Congress as soon as Virginia ratified the Constitution in June. He asked Madison to stop at Mount Vernon on his way back to New York from the state convention. Madison had played a leading role at the ratifying convention and would do so as well in Congress. At both places, his words carried added weight due to his close ties to Washington. Fittingly, Madison arrived at Mount Vernon on July 4. He stayed for three days, with at least one of them spent almost entirely in conversation with Washington. Madison was a brilliant if compulsive political strategist—still single and childless at age thirty-seven—who eschewed idle chatter and social conversation. Any day spent planning or plotting with him would be as intense as it was rewarding. Based on their prior and subsequent correspondence, Washington and Madison likely discussed both congressional and state obstacles to launching the new federal government.

One ticklish task facing Congress upon Madison's return involved choosing a place for the new government to convene. Many states coveted the new federal seat, and while the government need not remain at the place first picked, that city might have an advantage in the final settlement. New York and Philadelphia stood out as the top contenders to serve as the government's temporary seat. Although not put forward as an immediate option, Washington and Madison already hoped that the government might end up on the banks of the Potomac River near Mount Vernon. They favored that site for its central location. It lay at the midpoint of the country's north-south axis and, if Washington's company could open the upper Potomac for commercial navigation, at the terminus of the main route west.

The tug-of-war in Congress went back and forth for two months with various cities considered but none able to win a majority, which delayed passage of legislation launching the new government. "The only chance the patowmac has is to get things in such a train that a coalition may take place between the Southern & Eastern States on the subject, and still more that the final seat may be undecided for two or three years, within which period the Western & S. Western population will enter more into the estimate," Madison advised Washington in August.[6] This led both men to hope that Congress would opt for an interim seat, with Washington favoring New York because it struck him as too far north to retain the prize.[7] He got his wish in September when, rather than name any specific city, and thereby give that place an edge in the contest for the permanent site, lawmakers simply agreed to have the new government convene at "the present seat of Congress."[8]

Despite the hoped-for outcome, the drawn-out debate vexed Washington. It not only set back the federal elections but, by exposing how local interests could stymie national action, raised worse fears in his mind. "The present Congress, by it great indecision in fixing on the place at which the new one is to meet, have hung the expectations & patience of the Union on Tenter hooks," Washington complained, "and thereby (if further evidence had been wanting) given a fresh instance of the unfitness of a government so constituted to regulate with precision and energy the Affairs of such an extensive Empire."[9] In short, he wrote to Madison in September, the impasse "might have given advantages to the Antifederalists,"[10] which by this point was Washington's greatest concern. It likely came up in his meeting with Madison; it certainly featured prominently in their letters. The antifederalists had lost the battle over ratification but vowed, as Patrick Henry put it at the end of Virginia's convention, to continue the war "in a constitutional way."[11] By this he meant both forcing a second federal convention by getting the requisite two-thirds of states to request one and seeking to elect antifederalists to the First Federal Congress.[12] Washington feared both prospects. Preventing them kept him fully engaged in the ongoing fight for a new union.

AT THE CONSTITUTIONAL CONVENTION, federalists had dismissed pleas by Randolph, Mason, and Gerry for a second convention, but the idea would not die. Antifederalists raised it at various state ratifying conventions and succeeded in getting New York's convention to endorse it in a circular letter to the states. Upon first reading the circular, Washington complained to Madison that it would "be attended with pernicious consequences."[13] He soon penned a long lament to Benjamin Lincoln, the Revolutionary War general who had led the militia that crushed Shays's Rebellion and who had just been elected Massachusetts's lieutenant governor. "My apprehension is," Washington wrote, "that the New York circular Letter is intended to bring on a general Convention at too early a period, and in short, by referring the subject to the Legislatures, to set everything afloat again."[14] By "everything" he meant the entire governmental structure and division of power between the states and center. The amendments proposed by New York's state convention included both structural ones shifting federal power back to the states and personal ones protecting individual rights within the federal system. Privately, Washington expressed his willingness to have the First Congress consider the latter but not the former.[15]

Even without a second convention, however, antifederalists could strangle the new government at birth by taking over the First Federal Congress.[16] Voicing this fear, Washington soon wrote to Madison about the antifederalists, "Their expedient will now probably be an attempt to procure the Election of so many of their own Junto under the New Government, as, by the introduction of local and embarrassing disputes, to impede or frustrate its operation."[17] Henry was already stumping Virginia to this end and Clinton's party would soon do the same in New York. Still smarting from their treatment at the state convention, Pennsylvania antifederalists met during September in Harrisburg to endorse a list of key constitutional amendments and slate of congressional candidates who supported them.

In his letter to Lincoln, Washington left no doubt about his determination to counter this strategy by pushing for a federalist Congress and administration. Declaring that nothing "on our part ought to be left undone," he wrote, "I conceive it to be of unspeakable importance, that whatever there be of wisdom, & prudence, & patriotism on the Continent, should be concentrated in the public Councils, at the first outset."[18] Given the consequences at stake, he could scarcely leave himself out of the federalists' phalanx. "To be shipwrecked in sight of the Port," Washington wrote to Madison in September, "would be the severest of all possible aggravations to our misery."[19]

Lincoln's reply deftly turned these expressed fears into compelling reasons why Washington *must* accept the presidency. "The information which your Excellency has received, respecting the machinations of the antifederal characters, appears from what circulates in this part of the country, but too well founded," Lincoln wrote from New England. "Every exertion will be made to introduce into the new government, in the first instance, characters unfriendly to those part of it, which in my opinion are its highest ornaments . . .

with a view to totally change the nature of the government." This, he asserted, would cost America its "honour" and Americans their "freedom and felicity." Federalists should counter by flooding "the executive and the legislative branches" with their best candidates, Lincoln argued, "for the first impressions made therein will probably give a tone to all future measures." You will receive a unanimous vote from the electors, Lincoln assured Washington, and antifederalists "must know that the influence of your Excellency will have in the organization of the new government and in enforcing the precepts of it, will embarrass their Scheames if not totally baffle them." Their only hope lies in you declining the presidency, Lincoln warned: "your election they cannot hinder." "Duty" calls, he told Washington; do not refuse it.[20]

Lincoln was not alone in appealing to Washington's sense of duty at this critical juncture. The flood of mail to Mount Vernon that followed ratification and preceded the naming of electors carried many such pleas. "In a matter so essential to the wellbeing of society as the prosperity of a newly instituted government a citizen of so much consequence as yourself to its success has no option but to lend his services," Hamilton advised Washington. "Permit me to say it would be inglorious in such a situation" to refuse.[21] "The World looks up to You Sir," the wealthy British reformer Samuel Vaughan implored Washington, "to put a finishing hand to a Constitution for settling the unalienable Rights of the People on a lasting foundation."[22] Chancellor Livingston, who had known Washington since the Revolutionary War, commented, "No motives of private ease, or personal convenience will weigh with you when the great interests of the community require your service."[23] Similar calls came from Madison, Lafayette, Gouverneur Morris, and others. They resonated with Washington's own core beliefs. "It behoves all the advocates of the Constitution," he wrote, "to combine their exertions for collecting the wisdom & virtue of the Continent to one centre; in order that the Republic may avail itself of the opportunity for escaping from Anarchy."[24] Washington had to count himself within this essential group.

BY ALL ACCOUNTS, HOWEVER, Washington did not want the presidency. On the same early autumn day that he wrote these stirring words about *all* the Constitution's advocates pulling together in one center to forge the new government, Washington made the rounds of his five Virginia farms. Seven plows broke the fields at one, he noted in his diary; most hands were drawing rails or making fodder at the others. Washington loved this life and knew it well. He was at home at Mount Vernon as nowhere else. Work continued on expanding his house and gardens. Washington always had new ideas for improving this or changing that on his plantation—and enough slaves at least to attempt their implementation. His letters spoke of domestic bliss and his impending end. "The great searcher of human hearts is my witness," Washington wrote in a typical assertion from this period. "I have no wish which aspires beyond the humble and happy lot of living and dying a private citizen on my own farm."[25] This, he pleaded in vain to Hamilton, "is my great and sole desire."[26]

Martha, too, wished to remain at Mount Vernon. She had two grandchildren, aged nine and seven, living with her there and doted on them excessively. Although comfortable in high society, Martha did not enjoy it as much as her husband did. She had more than enough visitors to satisfy her need for company. Having moved to Mount Vernon from an even grander plantation thirty years earlier, she had made it her home and a much finer estate. Slightly older than George, Martha wanted nothing more than to live out her life quietly with her husband. By all accounts, they were happily married.

Although Washington's friends knew of his reluctance to accept the presidency, the public did not. Not only had he never publicly declared that he would not serve but, by presiding over the Constitutional Convention, Washington led most Americans to think that he would.[27] Thus, as more states ratified the Constitution, more people wrote to him for jobs in the prospective new federal administration. Once ratification became assured, the trickle of supplications turned into a stream, particularly from persons holding state posts, like harbormaster and customs collector, that would pass to federal control. Many also came from down-on-their-luck war veterans looking to their former commander for relief.

Perhaps the most pathetic petition came from former Virginia governor Benjamin Harrison, a signer of the Declaration of Independence who had rebuffed Washington's pleas to support the Constitution and instead opposed it at the state ratifying convention. "It gives me great pain my dear sir, to make this application," Harrison wrote, "and I hope you will believe me when I say, that nothing but dire necessity, could have prevailed upon me to do it." Explaining that the postwar collapse in land prices had brought him "very deep distress," Harrison sought the post of customs collector at Norfolk.[28]

To every supplicant, high or low, Washington replied in a similar way. The new government did not yet exist, he observed, and he did not want to lead it.[29] "The impropriety of my anticipating events or hazarding opinions, would scarcely permit me to touch, however slightly, on these delicate topics," he explained to one job seeker in June 1788.[30] Further, Washington typically included words to the effect that, should he accept the presidency, he was "determined to go into it perfectly free from all engagements of every nature whatsoever."[31] He maintained this pose as late as March 1789, when his old friend Benjamin Lincoln, disappointed by the lack of income generated by the office of lieutenant governor and "embarrassed" by the depressed value of his investments, asked him for a job.[32] To Lincoln, though, Washington added, "You need not doubt my inclinations are very sincere & very strong to serve you."[33] By year's end, Lincoln had the customs post in Boston. Washington gave no such reassurance to Harrison but instead coldly noted that in all appointments "due regard shall be had . . . to political considerations."[34] Antifederalists like Harrison, Washington as much as said, need not apply. A member of Virginia's landed gentry with a pedigree far longer than Washington's, Harrison took offense at this rebuff. "I did not conceive the application improper," he wrote back. "The idea of being a placeman under any government is disagreeable."[35]

Written to senior leaders entitled to frank responses, these letters to Lincoln and Harrison tipped Washington's hand somewhat. Even though both letters still used a conditional construction— "if" or "should"—when speaking of him becoming President, they offered clues to Washington's plans for office.[36] He wanted the executive branch staffed by federalists, they suggested, just as he wanted Congress and even the states dominated by his faction. "There will be great reason," Washington had explained earlier to Maryland federalist James McHenry, "for those who are well-affected to the government, to use their utmost exertions that the worthiest Citizens may be appointed to the two houses of the first Congress and where State Elections take place previous to this choice that the same principle govern in these also."[37] Under the Constitution, the various state legislatures chose the federal senators and could pick the presidential electors, so state elections would directly impact the federal government. Washington wanted a clean sweep for the Constitution.

IN RETROSPECT, WASHINGTON'S ASCENT to the presidency seems so foreordained as to need no explanation. It appeared so at the time as well. Virtually everyone expected it, yet Washington's closest friends and advisors obviously felt a need to encourage him. The tenor of these appeals was different from those made prior to the Constitutional Convention, when Washington truly wavered on going. Then, he had asked his closest confidants—Madison, Jay, Knox, Humphreys, and others—whether he should attend and they differed in their responses. Everyone expressed pros and cons. Washington anguished over the choice. This time, he never asked anyone if he should serve—they simply offered their advice and uniformly stated that he *must* accept the presidency. "I am clearly of opinion that the crisis which brought you again into public view left you no alternative but to comply," Hamilton wrote in September 1788, "and I am equally clear in the opinion that by that act *pledged* to take part in the execution of the government." Washington's reputation and fame would suffer more by him *not* serving than it could by him serving, Hamilton maintained.[38]

Washington gave his own reasons for not committing himself on whether he would or would not accept the presidency. Beyond sincerely not wanting the job, he thought it both unfitting and counterproductive to take a public position. "I could hardly bring the question into the slightest discussion," he explained to Hamilton in October 1788, "without betraying, in my Judgment, some impropriety of conduct, or without feeling an apprehension that a premature display of anxiety, might be construed into a vainglorious desire of pushing myself into notice as a Candidate."[39] After all, he had pledged to retire following the war, and advancing himself could lead some to think that he supported the new government for selfish motives. Further, in several letters from this period he wrote about seeing "nothing but clouds and darkness before me" in the presidency.[40] Finally, to weaken the government, he cautioned, antifederalists might conspire to deprive him of the post.[41] So long as losing remained a risk, he observed, saying that he would not accept the presidency might make him sound like Aesop's fabled fox who disparaged the unreachable grapes.[42] "If after all, a kind of inevitable necessity should impel me" to become President, Washington wrote to Gouverneur Morris in late November, "it will be time enough to yield to its impulse."[43]

Any realistic worries that antifederalists might deny Washington the presidency should have disappeared by the time that he wrote to Morris. Reports reaching Mount Vernon pointed to a surge in federalist support and a willingness by all but hard-core antifederalists to give the Constitution a fair try. Although public opinion surveys did not then exist to gauge such sentiments, they were apparent from the results of various state elections conducted during 1788. With federalist support, for example, John Hancock crushed Elbridge Gerry for governor of Massachusetts and antifederalists lost ground in the state legislature. "In our last house of representatives the antifederalists could carry any vote they pleased," Lincoln wrote excitedly from Boston in early June. "In the present house [the Constitution] has . . . a great majority in its favor."[44]

Even better news came later in the same month from Connecticut, where federalist Jonathan Trumbull reported on his own election as Speaker of the state assembly and the defeat of nearly all "opposition" candidates.[45] Similar reports reached Washington from elsewhere. "Indeed," Madison wrote near the end of 1788, "Virginia is the only instance among the ratifying States in which the Politics of the Legislature are at variance with the" Constitution.[46] Even New York had a federalist senate and Clinton faced the toughest reelection fight of his career in 1789. "So far as I am able to learn, federal principles are gaining considerable ground," Washington concluded. "I hope the political Machine may be put into motion, without much effort or hazard of miscarrying."[47] Only Virginia backed New York's call for a second convention.

The federalist surge intensified the clamor for Washington to become President. The Constitution's least tested and potentially most significant innovation, the American presidency stood at the heart of federalists' hopes for the new union. "No other man can sufficiently unite public opinion or can give the requisite weight to the office in the commencement of the Government," Hamilton wrote to Washington in November.[48] "No other Man can *fill* that Office," Gouverneur Morris echoed a month later. "You alone can awe the Insolence of opposing Factions, & the greater Insolence of assuming Adherents."[49] Refusing to serve, Hamilton added, "would have the worst effect imaginable."[50]

By this point, Washington probably agreed.[51] In a January 1789 letter to Lafayette that again expressed his reluctance to become President, Washington conceded that he would serve if doing so "will insure permanent felicity to the Commonwealth" and declared, "I see a *path*, as clear and as direct as a ray of light, which leads to the attainment of that object."[52] After months of speaking about his future in terms of clouds and darkness, these words had a revelatory ring.

Over the course of 1788, Washington had articulated three main objectives for America under the Constitution: respect abroad, prosperity at home, and development westward.[53] Toward these ends, he envisioned a vigorous federal government encouraging trade, manufacturing, and agriculture through effective tariffs, sound money, secure property rights, and a nonaligned foreign policy. "America under an efficient government, will be the most favorable Country of any in the world for persons of industry and frugality," he asserted in mid-1788, and "not be less advantageous to the happiness of the lowest class of people because of . . . the great plenty of unoccupied land."[54]

By the beginning of 1789, Washington was writing to Lafayette and others about the clear path forward. Indeed, on the same January day that he wrote to Lafayette, Washington addressed Rochambeau: "We are on the point of seeing the completion of the Government, which, by giving motives to labour and security to property, cannot fail to augment beyond all former example . . . the aggregate amount of property in the Country."[55] And as he surveyed the alliance-induced wars engulfing the Old World and King George's insanity disrupting Britain, Washington closed his letter to Lafayette with the observation, "While you are quarrelling among yourselves in Europe—while one King is running mad—and others are acting as if they were already so, . . . we shall continue in tranquility here" and trade with all.[56]

Notwithstanding his continuing protests, by this time Washington had resigned himself to accept the presidency. Providence guided his destiny, he believed, and that of the country.[57] "You will become the Father to more than three Millions of Children,"

Gouverneur Morris assured the childless Washington in December.[58] For his part, Washington now wrote, "The prospect that a good general government will in all human probability be soon established in America, affords me more substantial satisfaction than I have ever before derived from any political event."[59] Under that government, he had predicted the dawn of "a new era, and perhaps . . . a more happy one than hath before appeared on this checquered scene of existence."[60] The thespian in him was prepared to play his part in what he already called "a greater Drama . . . than has heretofore been brought on the American Stage."[61] With new legislatures and governors in place in many states, it only remained for the states to choose their electors in January, those electors to cast their ballots in February, and Congress to count the votes. Elections to the first federal House of Representatives and appointments to the Senate would occur at roughly the same time on a schedule set by the individual states.

A COMPLEX, JURY-RIGGED COMPROMISE, the electoral vote system worked seamlessly for installing Washington as the first President. As originally contrived, however, it only worked well when he was a candidate. Two ensuing near-catastrophic elections led to its overhaul by the Twelfth Amendment in 1804. In 1789, however, it operated much as its framers at the Constitutional Convention hoped and produced a result that reflected the popular will.

Those framers devised the electoral vote system to meet objections raised to three more obvious means of picking the President. Mimicking the method then used by most states to select their governors, the original Virginia Plan called for Congress to appoint the President. Even Madison, the plan's chief architect, soon realized that this method could undermine executive independence in a system that relied on checks and balances to curb abuse. With Washington's concurrence, Virginia turned against it at the Convention. From the start, James Wilson and the Pennsylvania delegation wanted "the people" to elect the President directly, but merely counting individual votes from across the country would slash the influence of southern states, where disenfranchised black slaves made up about one-third of the population.[62] Again with Washington's apparent support, Virginia consistently voted against direct elections. Finally, some delegates urged that the states pick the President—one vote per state as under the Articles of Confederation—but Virginia and the other big states objected. For three months, the delegates failed to find a solution. "There are objections agst. every mode that has been, or perhaps can be proposed," Madison noted midway through the Convention.[63]

During the Convention's first week, Wilson offered the idea of indirect elections using electors as an alternative to direct elections. Wilson's proposal would have divided the states into electoral districts. Voters in each district would choose one elector. These electors would then meet at a central site to elect the President much as the College of Cardinals selects the pope. Variations offered by other delegates over the summer would have given states one, two, or three electors depending on population and had electors chosen by state legislatures rather than voters. None of these options gained sufficient support to win final approval, but they remained in the mix until the Convention's final days, when desperate delegates referred all such unresolved issues to a select committee that included such Washington intimates as Madison and Gouverneur Morris.

Combining elements from earlier proposals into a viable compromise, this so-called Committee on Postponed Parts devised the electoral vote system. Balancing state and individual interests, the system gave each state the same number of electors as senators and representatives, which meant more for big states, at least three for small ones, and a three-fifths factor for slaves. Each state would decide how to choose its own electors, which allowed the Convention to dodge the thorny issues of popular versus legislative selection and district versus statewide election.

However picked, electors would convene on the same day in their respective states and every elector would vote for two different candidates, not more than one of whom could reside in the elector's home state. By forcing electors to vote for at least one out-of-state candidate and barring them from meeting as a single multistate body, the framers hoped to encourage the emergence of national candidates and to discourage cabals. The candidate receiving the most votes from at least a majority of the electors would become President. The second-place finisher would become Vice President. If no one received votes from a majority of the electors or in case of a tie, Congress would select from among the top candidates.

Although not explicitly designed to lift Washington to the presidency, the electoral vote system served that purpose. Under it, Washington need not seek a party's nomination or campaign for votes. He was not even required to put himself forward for the office or comment in advance on whether he would take it. He could simply await his country's call at Mount Vernon, which by this point was the only way he would accept the presidency. From start to finish, the process became a long but predictable pageant suitable for America's Cincinnatus: more of a prelude to a coronation than a campaign before an election.

Virtually everyone predicted that Washington would sweep the election by receiving one vote from each elector. With Rhode Island and North Carolina not yet in the new union, federalists effectively controlled the government in every participating state except Virginia and New York, and Washington surely would win in those states, too. Even if he wanted to, Patrick Henry could not deny Washington in his home state and even if he could, George Clinton would not want to deny his old friend in New York.[64] Antifederalists focused instead on how to elect one of their own as Vice President while federalists struggled to coalesce around a shared second choice.

WITH FEWER THAN FOUR MONTHS between when Congress called the election in September and when electors were chosen in

January, and with no experience to guide them, states labored to devise and implement their electoral vote systems on time. Four methods for choosing electors emerged: legislative or gubernatorial selection and district or statewide election.

In each state, political traditions, partisan politics, and practical considerations influenced the decision of how to take part in this first grand experiment in a truly national election. Concerned that voters in some regions might choose antifederalists, the federalist-dominated legislatures in Pennsylvania, Maryland, Massachusetts, Delaware, and New Hampshire opted to have electors run statewide or, in the case of Massachusetts, to have the legislature choose between the two candidates receiving the most votes in each district.[65] In South Carolina, Connecticut, and Georgia, where local elites held sway, the legislature picked the electors. The politically divided state of New Jersey, whose government was recently captured by West Jersey commercial interests supportive of the Constitution, entrusted this power to the federalist-friendly governor and his handpicked privy council.[66] Antifederalist Virginia used a district election method that its proponents hailed as the most democratic way to pick electors under an inherently undemocratic Constitution and its opponents disparaged as designed to advance Patrick Henry's political interests. In New York, where federalists held the Senate but antifederalists dominated the lower house or "Assembly," lawmakers became embroiled in a bitter partisan struggle over choosing electors that had national implications.

The battle over electors in New York turned on vice presidential politics. Everyone conceded the presidency to Washington. Antifederalists in New York and elsewhere, however, remained committed to amending the Constitution both to reform the federal structure and to protect individual rights. As the central government's second officer, a supportive Vice President could aid this cause, especially since Washington talked about serving as President only long enough to get the government going—perhaps not even a full four-year term.[67] If he retired (or died) before the end of his term, the Vice President would succeed him. By parallel reasoning, to back up Washington, federalists wanted a vigorous supporter of both national authority and a strong executive, and not someone who favored early amendments to the Constitution. Further, although federalists foresaw no executive role for the Vice President, no one knew just how meaningless the task of presiding over the Senate would become. At least in the first federal election, political leaders took the office seriously.

For antifederalists, Clinton offered the obvious choice for Vice President. He had a strong base in New York and should do well in Virginia. Along with scattered votes from other states, this might give him enough support to place second if federalist electors spread their second votes among home-state favorites.[68] He did not need a majority—just more votes than anyone but Washington. In contrast, Henry could not get votes in Virginia because casting one vote for Washington would preclude its electors from voting for another Virginian. But Clinton needed both solid support from New York's electors and deep division in the federalist ranks for this strategy to work.[69] Seeing the risk, Hamilton and other federalists took steps to disrupt it.

Hamilton learned about Clinton's candidacy from Madison, who heard in November 1788 that Henry was pushing it in Virginia.[70] "The attempt merits attention and ought not to be neglected as chimerical," Hamilton warned at the time.[71] By this point, New York antifederalists had already formed a committee to promote Clinton's election and opened communications with like-minded politicians in Virginia and elsewhere.

To further his candidacy, Clinton held off calling the legislature into session to vote on how to conduct New York's federal elections until December. By this time it was too late to have the people choose electors. If New York was to have any, legislators would have to select them. By past practice, the legislature voted on such matters by joint ballot, with each member casting one vote. Due to their broad majority in the Assembly, this approach would allow antifederalists to name all eight New York electors despite the federalists' slim margin in the state senate. In contrast, federalist candidates surely would have won some district elections and, by proclaiming their support for Washington, might have swept a statewide contest. Putting party first, New York would become the one state where antifederalists wanted lawmakers to pick electors while federalists wanted to let the people choose.[72] Having the two houses vote separately rather than by joint ballot, however, would give federalists in the state senate a veto over the outcome.

A pugnacious politician with a penchant for brinksmanship, Hamilton decided to fight Clinton over electors in New York. Eschewing precedent, he urged federalist state senators to reject any arrangement that did not allow them to pick half of New York's eight electors. Privately, he did not care whether New York voted. If Clinton and his partisans in the Assembly caved, then Clinton would get only four votes from New York. If both sides held fast and New York did not vote, then Clinton would get none. Either way, he would lose the vice presidency. Washington would win the presidency with or without New York. "If matters are well managed we may procure a majority for some pretty equal compromise," Hamilton confided to Madison at the outset.[73] Soon Hamilton was writing newspaper essays blasting Clinton and was on the scene at the state capital orchestrating the opposition.

In the end, after a brutal state convention and weeks of legislative gridlock, two battle-scarred parties held their ground and New York sat out the election. "For the last circumstance I am not sorry as the most we could hope would be to balance accounts and do no harm," Hamilton gloated after the deadline for choosing electors passed. "The Antifederalists incline to an appointment notwithstanding, but I discourage it with the Federalists."[74] Clinton would have to wait sixteen years to become Vice President, when he succeeded his onetime protégé, Aaron Burr, after Burr killed Hamilton in a duel.

EVEN AS FEDERALISTS BATTLED antifederalists to a standstill over electors in New York, they reluctantly rallied behind John Adams for Vice President. Hamilton was among the first to realize that they needed to agree on a candidate for the office or risk losing it to the opposition.[75] Coupled with Washington, Adams represented something of a ticket balancer. Federalists generally agreed that, with Washington from the South, the Vice President should come from the Northeast. Some liked a candidate who, while supportive of federalist policies and opposed to early constitutional amendments, might appear more moderate and less elitist than the stereotypical federalist. Finally, to complement Washington's military background, they welcomed someone known for his work in government.[76]

Following his crucial role at the Massachusetts ratifying convention, many commentators predicted that Hancock would get the nod, but his continued support for constitutional amendments and his reputed ambitions for the presidency put off many leading federalists.[77] Knox and Jay—both mentioned by some—were destined for more substantial posts than Vice President: Knox as secretary of war and Jay as chief justice. These subtractions left Adams at the top of many federalists' short list for Vice President.[78]

In June 1788, after spending nearly ten years as a senior diplomat in Europe, Adams returned home to a hero's welcome in Massachusetts just four days before neighboring New Hampshire became the ninth state to ratify the Constitution. Son of a pious Puritan farmer, educated at Harvard, and trained in law, the hardworking and highly ambitious Adams was an early advocate of American independence. In the First and Second Continental Congresses, he had joined with Samuel Adams, Arthur Lee, and Richard Henry Lee to form the radical Adams-Lee faction in Revolutionary War politics that clashed with the conservative patriots like John Dickinson and Robert Morris who later led the drive for a new Constitution.

His time in Europe had tempered him, though.[79] From 1786 to 1788, Adams wrote a three-volume *Defense of the Constitutions of Governments of the United States*, which praised checks and balances in republican government, espoused an almost kinglike executive, and closed with a ringing endorsement of the new federal constitution. Splitting with R. H. Lee, who opposed ratification, and his cousin Samuel, who supported early amendments, Adams maintained that the new government should receive a fair trial before any amendments. These positions plus his experience, popularity in New England, and willingness to serve under Washington made Adams stand out as a viable vice presidential candidate for federalists.

Yet Adams had drawbacks, too. Vain, opinionated, and thin-skinned, as a diplomat in Europe Adams had clashed bitterly with his colleagues and irritated America's allies. He still hated Britain at a time when most federalists wanted to restore cordial ties with America's former imperial master. Even worse, as president of the Board of War during the American Revolution, Adams had often criticized Washington's leadership and his ideas on army organization.[80] These concerns led Hamilton to send Knox on a visit to Adams with instructions to sound him out on the vice presidency.[81] "The Lees and Adams' have been in the habit of uniting; and hence may spring up a Cabal very embarrassing to the Executive," Hamilton wrote about the prospect of Adams as Vice President.[82] Knox reported back that Adams wanted the job and promised to support Washington faithfully as President.

Massachusetts federalist Theodore Sedgwick also assured Hamilton that Adams could be trusted.[83] This brought Hamilton around. "On the whole I have concluded to support Adams; though not without apprehensions," he wrote in November. "If he is not Vice President, one of two worse things will be likely to happen. Either he must be nominated to some important office for which he is less proper, or will become a malcontent and possible expose and give additional weight to the opposition to the Government."[84] Newly returned from Europe, Adams had nothing to do other than tend his family farm and nurture a burning desire for the seemingly exalted position of Vice President.[85] He felt it his due.

Perhaps because he saw the vice presidency as a legislative office, Washington did not seem to care who held it so long as that person supported the Constitution. As early as September, Lincoln wrote to Washington expressing the "general" view that the Vice President should come from Massachusetts and named Hancock and Adams as the leading contenders.[86] "So little agency did I wish to have in electioneering," Washington wrote back, "that I have never entered into a single discussion with any person, nor expressed a single sentiment orally or in writing respecting the appointment of a Vice-President." Provided that the person was "a true Federalist," Washington declared, he would "acquiesce in the prevailing sentiments of the Electors without giving any unbecoming preference or incurring any unnecessary ill-will."[87]

Over the following months, Knox, Madison, and other party leaders wrote to Washington about Adams as Vice President, and Washington seemed agreeable to the choice. Indeed, alert to the risk of an antifederalist winning through a split vote by federalists, before electors voted in February, Washington let some of them know that he favored a unified vote for Adams. "I consider it to be the only certain way to prevent the election of an Antifederalist," Washington wrote in January.[88] This was the limit of his efforts for Adams or against Clinton.

Hamilton, however, began to have doubts about too strong a vote for Adams. Ostensibly he feared that Adams might come in ahead of Washington. Hamilton may have also wanted to humble Adams somewhat so that he would know his place in the federalist hierarchy. "You know the constitution has not provided the means of distinguishing [between votes for President and Vice President] & it would be disagreeable even to have a man treading close upon the heels of the person we wish as President," Hamilton wrote to Madison in November. "We must in our different circles take our measures accordingly."[89] For his part, Hamilton sent confidential letters or trusted messengers to several states urging federalist electors to scatter some second votes. "For God's sake, let not our zeal for a secondary object defeat or endanger a first," he wrote to James Wilson. "It is much to be desired that Adams may have the plurality of suffrages for Vice President; but if risk is to be run on one side or on the other can we hesitate where it ought to be preferred?"[90]

The secret plan worked so well that fewer than half of the electors voted for Adams. With the other federalist votes scattered and New York not voting, Adams still finished second, far ahead of Hancock or Clinton. Unaware of the scheme and humiliated by his total, Adams talked of refusing office.[91] After learning who caused it, he never forgave Hamilton.

WHILE WASHINGTON KEPT QUIET about the contest for President and Vice President, he could not refrain from commenting on the battle for Congress. He desperately wanted federalists to win, especially in his home state of Virginia, where they faced long odds.[92] The new Constitution was at stake, he believed, not only because Congress would enact the laws needed to implement it but also because Congress held the power to initiate amendments. Washington favored giving the Constitution a fair trial without amendment and felt that only federalists could be trusted with that responsibility. "It is my most earnest wish that none but the most disinterested, able and virtuous men may be appointed to either house of Congress: because, I think, the tranquility and happiness of this Country will depend upon that circumstance," he explained to a Georgia federalist.[93] In context, this read as a plea to elect *only* federalists. "As the period is now rapidly approaching which must decide the fate of the new Constitution as to the manner of its being carried into execution & probably as to its usefulness," he wrote to Lincoln in October about the upcoming elections for Congress, "we should all feel an unusual degree of anxiety."[94]

As soon as the old Congress passed the Election Ordinance in September 1788, states with legislatures in session began appointing their federal senators and organizing elections for their federal representatives and presidential electors. Others followed over the fall as their legislatures convened. Despite Washington's dream that disinterested nationalism would somehow prevail in federal politics, it did not take long for party spirit and local interests to exert themselves. In some states, division over the Constitution and federal authority allied itself with preexisting political parties; in other states, it incubated factions that evolved into parties.

Pennsylvania's unicameral Assembly acted first. Since the Revolutionary War, two organized parties had battled for control of this powerful body. One party embraced federalism; another included most of the state's antifederalists. With a small majority in the Assembly— yet facing an uncertain fate in the upcoming October elections—federalists rushed to select the state's two senators in late September, scarcely two weeks after Congress passed the Election Ordinance. In this vote, lawmakers split along party lines, 37 to 31, to select Washington's friend Robert Morris for one seat, but they unanimously settled on a little-known supporter of rural interests as their other senator. "You will have great Satisfaction in hearing that Mr. [William] Maclay, our Agricultural Senator, is a decided federalist," a Morris associate perhaps overoptimistically informed Madison after the vote. "I consider this election of Mr. Maclay by all the opposition as of great importance, as a sort of Acceptance of the government."[95]

Party spirit soon returned, however, as federalist legislators then voted to have candidates for the House of Representatives run statewide rather than in districts, which made a federalist sweep of all eight seats likely. The results encouraged Washington. "From the good beginning that has been made in Pensylvania, a State from which much was to be feared, I cannot help foreboding well of the others," he noted.[96]

Two states, Connecticut and Delaware, selected senators and adopted election laws in October. With federalists in complete control, lawmakers in each state lifted their two senators from the ranks of former delegates to the Constitutional Convention and opted for statewide races for the House of Representatives. Delaware had only one House seat, but in Connecticut this method assured the election of five federalists to Congress. District voting should have yielded at least one antifederalist. Washington followed these developments closely and hailed the outcome. "I was extremely happy to find that your state was going on so well as to federal affairs," he wrote to Connecticut's Trumbull. "In general the appointments to the Senate seem to have been very happy. . . . A few months will, however, shew what we are to expect."[97]

With Patrick Henry still railing against the Constitution, the Virginia legislature met in early November to elect federal senators and to call elections for Congress. Even though antifederalists controlled both houses, Washington hoped that, with Governor Randolph's support, Madison could win a Senate seat. Antifederalists Richard Henry Lee and William Grayson were the only other candidates and the dynamics of a three-way race for two seats should have helped Madison finish second as each of the two antifederalists sought to elbow past the other. Turning his legendary oratory against Madison in advance of the vote, however, Henry managed to keep his forces in line.[98] Madison finished third. Compounding the assault, the legislature opted for district elections for Congress and, at Henry's urging, put Madison's Orange County plantation in a district dominated by antifederalists and barred him from running in any other one. "In short," Randolph now wrote to Madison, "nothing is left undone, which can tend to the subversion of the new government."[99]

Washington was furious. "Our Assembly," he wrote on the fourteenth, "has proved itself to be . . . very much under the influence of Mr Henry. . . . Federalists in the Assembly, as I am given to understand, were exceeding mortified that Mr Madison should have lost his Election by 8 or 9 votes. It is now much dreaded by the same characters, that the State (which is to be divided into districts for the appointment of Representatives to Congress) will be so arranged as to place a large proportion of those who are called Antifederalists in that Station."[100] Washington urged Madison to return to Virginia from New York, where he served in the old Congress, and campaign for a seat in the new one.[101] Although Washington wanted Madison in the Senate, where he could consult on appointments and treaties, membership in "the other House," as Washington called it, would have to suffice.[102]

New Hampshire and Massachusetts came next. After pitched battles over ratification in both states, some saw them sending antifederalists to the Senate.[103] In early November, however, Madison privately assured Washington that supporters of the new government would win in both.[104] Madison was right, but barely. Voting separately, the lower house in each state selected one firm federalist and one candidate who either opposed the Constitution or wanted to amend it. In both, the upper houses confirmed the former but rejected the latter and offered federalist alternatives. The standoff went on for days in Massachusetts. It ended quicker in New Hampshire, but in both states the lower house ultimately relented. "In our General Assembly," one New Hampshire antifederalist complained, where for a "long time there was a decided majority against the new system, opposition has ceased—and the language [about the Constitution] is 'it is adopted, let us try it.' "[105] Turning to their election laws, New Hampshire legislators then approved federalist-friendly statewide voting for Congress while Massachusetts lawmakers crafted congressional districts favoring federalists. Reporting these developments to Washington, Knox rejoiced, "I can assert from personal observation that affection for the new system is increasing in those states and that it is dayly becoming highly popular."[106]

Driven in part by support for Washington, the federalist tide swept through Maryland in December. "It is hoped by every true Federalists, that GENERAL WASHINGTON will be called to fill the high and important office of President," one campaign publication declared, "but to induce him to accept that trust, there ought to be a certain prospect of his meeting men in both House of Congress, in whom he can place confidence, from their well known character and attachment to the New Constitution."[107] Such reasoning carried the day. Over the bitter resistance of Attorney General Luther Martin, who had stormed out of the Philadelphia Convention in opposition to the Constitution, the Maryland legislature named two federalists to the United States Senate and all but ensured the election of six federalists to Congress by having representatives run at-large even though they represented districts. With Maryland being the eighth state to choose its senators and enact its election law, 1788 ended with federalists already certain to control the new Senate and in a commanding position to take the House.

"The elections have been hitherto vastly more favorable than we could have expected," Washington noted in January. "Federal sentiment seems to be growing with uncommon rapidity."[108]

Georgia and South Carolina elected four more federalists to the United States Senate in January 1789, leaving only New York to act. There the process bogged down much as it had for naming electors. Led by Clinton, antifederalists in the state assembly demanded a joint vote on senators, which would allow them to pick both. Led by Hamilton, federalists in the state senate demanded a separate vote on senators, with each house getting the final say on one seat. "I assure you upon my honor that . . . the [Senate] majority will *in no event* accede to the unqualified idea of a joint ballot," Hamilton warned an antifederalist leader in late January. "Allow me to hope that you will dispassionately weigh all the consequences of an obstinate adherence to the ground taken in the assembly."[109]

As with the manner of choosing electors, both sides held fast, leaving New York without any federal senators until after state elections installed a new legislature in July.[110] At least in part because neither knew what approach would serve its interests, the two sides managed to settle on district elections for Congress. Meanwhile, fearing that antifederalists would sweep a statewide vote, South Carolina's federalist-led legislature also adopted district elections for its state, while the Georgia legislature prescribed at-large voting for the three representatives from its state.

THROUGHOUT THE FIRST FEDERAL ELECTIONS, which spread over the fall and winter of 1788–89, Washington stayed close to home. Indeed, reaching the age of fifty-eight in February, he acted as if his time at Mount Vernon would go on for years. Looking far ahead, for example, he assigned crops for each field through 1795, laid out an added field at one farm, and oversaw construction of a huge brick barn: "the largest and most convenient one in the country," he boasted.[111] Heavy spring and early summer rains had reduced his current crop, especially his root vegetables. "The same unfavorableness of the Season has rendered it unimportant to give a detail of my experiments this year in flax," he wrote in December to the editor of an English farm journal.[112]

A steady stream of visitors came to Mount Vernon, including Comte de Moustier, France's new arch-royalist minister to the United States, and his consort Madame de Bréhan, the married sister of his deceased wife. "It is not necessary to tell you, Sir, how much we have been pleased with his person and his settlement," the minister and his consort wrote to Jefferson about Washington and Mount Vernon. "Every thing there is enchanting."[113] The couple's open intimacy scandalized many Americans but apparently not the Washingtons, who sat for drawings by de Bréhan, a noted artist.[114]

Except when hosting important guests, confined by bad weather, or engaged in urgent business, Washington continued to ride the circuit of his five farms almost daily—often through mud and sometimes in snow—inspecting crops, livestock, and field work. His longest trips were to nearby Alexandria, where he cast his individual ballot for a presidential elector on January 7 and, four weeks later, joined the festivities as voters from across the community participated in the district's first congressional election. In both contests, he voted for federalists, and they won handily. Otherwise, Washington remained at Mount Vernon.

"I have endeavoured in a state of tranquil retirement to keep my self as much from the eye of the world as I possibly could," he explained in one letter from the period. "For I wish most devoutly to glide silently and unnoticed through the remainder of my life."[115] Other letters, however, reveal a fully engaged political leader more concerned with his country's future than his own retirement.

Though Washington voted in Virginia's Fourth Congressional District, he cared most about the outcome in the state's Fifth District, where Madison fought the race of his life for Congress. Antifederalists in the state legislature had not only drawn the district to make it as hard as possible for him to win, but also recruited his old friend and future political ally James Monroe to run against him. Both men were protégés of Jefferson and had served in Congress, but Monroe opposed the Constitution at the state convention and called for structural amendments as well as a bill of rights. Informed Americans already viewed Madison as one of the Constitution's principal architects. Defeating him would send a strong message to Congress and the country, Henry believed.[116]

To have any hope of winning, Madison would have to stump for votes in the dead of winter. "I am pressed much on several quarters to try," he wrote to Washington on December 2, "and am apprehensive that an omission of that expedient may expose me to blame. At the same time I have an extreme distaste to steps having an electioneering appearance."[117] Still, he would do his duty. Heading south from Congress in mid-December, Madison stayed with the Washingtons for a week at Christmas before reaching his district and the dreaded campaign.

If not on the advice of Washington then surely with his full knowledge, Madison launched his campaign for Congress by switching his position on amending the Constitution.[118] He had opposed a bill of rights at the Constitutional Convention and dismissed it as a meaningless "parchment" barrier in one of his *Federalist* essays, but the Convention's records remained secret and the *Federalist* essays appeared under a pseudonym.[119] Antifederalists, in contrast, typically demanded both a bill of rights and structural amendments restoring power to the states. In response to the outpouring of support for some alteration in the Constitution, both Madison and Washington had belatedly signaled a willingness to accept nonstructural amendments.[120] Now, to open his campaign, Madison dispatched a flurry of letters that not only embraced a bill of rights but disingenuously suggested that he "was an unsuccessful advocate" for one at the Convention.[121] With Monroe calling for structural amendments and a second federal convention, Madison seized the middle ground.[122] Further, voters were told, once in office, Madison would have more stature than Monroe to wring a bill of rights from a federalist Congress. This became the major issue of the campaign: who could better protect the people's rights under the new Constitution?

Madison relied mainly on letters and newspapers to get out his new message—"epistolary means," he called them in a mid-January letter to Washington—but he also made appearances in three key counties and debated Monroe.[123] Despite snow and freezing temperatures for one outdoor debate, Madison later recalled, voters "stood it out very patiently [and] seemed to consider it a sort of fight, of which they were required to be spectators."[124] Appealing to religious voters, Madison stressed his support for a constitutional amendment to secure "the rights of Conscience in the fullest latitude."[125] Lending their support, key Baptist ministers reminded voters of Madison's role in enacting Virginia's 1786 Statute for Religious Freedom, which ended state support for the Episcopal Church and guaranteed "that all men shall be free to profess, and by argument to maintain, their opinions in matters of Religion."[126] The district's many Baptists and Lutherans rallied to Madison, as did voters in his home county of Orange, which he carried nearly unanimously.

Madison won by 336 votes. Attributing his victory to his "appearance in the district" and ability to counter "the calumnies of antifederal partizans," he went to Congress committed to support a bill of rights.[127] Along with drafting the Virginia Plan, it would become his greatest contribution to American liberty.

Washington rejoiced in the outcome. "All the political maneuvres which were calculated to impede, if not prevent the operation of the new government, are now closed," Washington crowed three days after Virginians voted on February 2, "and although the issue of *all* the Elections are not yet known, they are sufficiently *displayed* to authorise a belief that the opposers of the government have been defeated."[128] Despite Henry's best efforts, federalists won six of Virginia's ten House seats. By that point, with only three states yet to elect representatives, friends of the Constitution had won all but a handful of contests, with their losses all coming in district rather than statewide races.

"Because so many of the elections of Senators and Representatives to Congress are already made," Washington wrote to Rochambeau in late January, "there is the best reason to believe, the wisdom, the patriotism, and the virtue of America will be conspicuously concentered in that Body."[129] While his name did not appear on ballots anywhere, Washington effectively headed the federalist ticket everywhere. In Baltimore, for example, the *Maryland Journal* reported, federalists "appeared at the Polls with a Figure representing the Goddess of Federalism and an excellent Painting of General Washington." When they then won all six of the state's seats in Congress, the newspaper added the couplet, "Now all our factions, all our wars shall cease / And FED'RALS *rule* our happy land in peace."[130]

The trend continued through the remaining contests, which concluded in March with federalists even winning four of six sharply defined House races in Clinton's New York, giving them an overall four-to-one margin in Congress. As President, Washington would have a supportive House as well as Senate. "I cannot help flattering myself the new Congress on account of the self-created respectability and various talents of its Members, will not be inferior to any Assembly in the world," he boasted to Lafayette.[131]

To complete the federalist triumph, it only remained for electors to cast their ballots for Washington on February 4 and Congress to open and count the votes after it convened at some point after March 4. When Madison visited Mount Vernon in February following the Virginia elections, even though Washington still publicly shunned the presidency, he asked Madison to review a seventy-three-page draft inaugural address.[132] Clearly Washington was thinking about the task ahead.

GEORGE WASHINGTON ENTERING TRENTON 1789.

Later print of George Washington's triumphant entrance into Trenton on his journey from Mount Vernon to New York for his inauguration as President.

CHAPTER 9

The Inaugural Parade

❧

CHRISTMAS AT MOUNT VERNON was typically a tranquil time for George and Martha Washington. Even though they surely suspected that it would be their last one there for some time, the 1788 holiday season followed the normal routine. They stayed home, as usual, and invited family and friends to visit. The weather, however, turned unusually cold and snowy before Christmas, keeping some guests away, before warming after the twenty-fifth, with sleet and rain replacing snow. Madison arrived on December 19, but headed home on Christmas morning for a month of campaigning for Congress in his district. Washington's faithful wartime aide, Connecticut's David Humphreys, stayed through the holidays and into the new year. Five years earlier, he had ridden with the General from Annapolis to Mount Vernon after Washington's resignation as commander in chief, arriving on Christmas Eve 1783, and had remained through those especially joyous holidays. Collecting notes for a book on Washington, Humphreys returned in 1787 for another Christmas at Mount Vernon and was back again in 1788. Other visitors came and went.

For the Washingtons and their guests, Christmas at Mount Vernon meant feasts and relaxation. They dined together but otherwise remained free to do as they pleased. The main house had more than a half dozen guest rooms and a separate family suite.[1] Visitors could enter and exit without bothering their hosts. Having British tastes, the Washingtons liked meat pies for dinner, and celebrated Christmas with truly enormous ones. One recipe for Christmas Pie from a cookbook used at Mount Vernon called for a bushel of flour to make the crust, which encased a Russian doll–like nesting of five successively larger birds—pigeon, partridge, duck, goose, and turkey—each skinned, boned, and inserted in the next, and then cooked for four hours in a very hot oven.[2] "I lament the effect . . . which has deprived us of your aid in the Attack on Christmas Pyes," Washington wrote to Humphreys on December 26, 1786. "We had one yesterday on which all the company (and pretty numerous it was) were hardly able to make an impression."[3]

Washington often took his male guests foxhunting one or more times over the holidays—twice in 1787—but the bad weather apparently curtailed this activity in 1788. Cards, board games, and dancing commonly occupied the evenings, but few lavish parties. Washington paid for a traveling exhibitor to bring a camel to Mount Vernon over the holidays in 1787, but nothing of that sort occurred in 1788.

For many eighteenth-century Americans, Christmas was mainly a religious holiday, but not for Washington. In the mid-1770s, he stopped going to church on Christmas, and never resumed the practice while at Mount Vernon. About the same time, he ceased taking Communion and stopped attending Sunday services regularly. Many contemporary observers and later historians attributed these widely noted but never explained changes to a loss of faith in the divinity of Christ.[4] Washington retained an intense personal belief in God and divine providence but perhaps not the Trinity. Episcopal prelate William White, who had the closest ties to Washington of any minister, later noted that he knew of no "fact which would prove

General Washington to have been a believer in the Christian revelation."[5] Respecting the religious origins of Christmas, however, and in line with English tradition, the Washingtons reserved family gift-giving for Twelfth Night, which fell on their wedding anniversary. For them, Christmas focused on family and friends.

Like most American businesses of the era, Mount Vernon operated on a six-day workweek with only Sundays free from the normal routine. Washington also allotted his workers four days off at Christmas, usually from December 25 to 29. Field work ceased and everyone—slave, indentured, or free—received extra food or pay. On Christmas 1788, for example, Washington gave twelve shillings to his secretary, Tobias Lear, and six shillings each to two of his favorite slaves, Peter and Giles. Nearly all of Washington's several hundred workers lived on the plantation and remained there over the holidays. As their only long break from work during the year, Christmas could become a riotous affair for some. Alcohol flowed freely, with even field slaves receiving whiskey. Washington's contract with his head gardener, for example, written in 1787 and in force for the holidays in 1788, provided that this free white employee would receive "four Dollars at Christmas, with which he may be drunk 4 days and 4 nights."[6] Of course, giving workers four days off meant that Washington did not need to ride the circuit of his plantation overseeing their work. He could stay home with his guests, which he did in 1788 from the time Madison arrived on the nineteenth until the workers returned to the fields on December 29. With the new government about to take over, Washington had much to discuss with Madison and Humphreys.

HUMPHREYS STYLED HIMSELF A WRITER, though little survives to justify that view. His projected book on Washington never got beyond a jumble of notes. His ponderous poetry, which won him entry into a home-state literary circle called the "Hartford Wits," quickly lost favor. His only lasting fame came from his service as an American diplomat in Europe and his close ties to Washington. "'Twas mine," Humphreys wrote in a 1786 poem about his relationship with Washington, "return'd from Europe's courts, / To share his thoughts, partake his sports, / And sooth his partial ear."[7]

Around the Christmas holidays in 1788, Washington asked Humphreys to draft an inaugural address. Much as Humphreys's 1786 poem suggested, what remains of the seventy-three-page speech, though never delivered, provides a window into Washington's thoughts as he approached the presidency. The General and his trusted aide likely worked closely together, with Humphreys serving as something between a scribe and ghostwriter for Washington's ideas. Washington then made Humphreys's draft his own by copying it in longhand, perhaps revising as he went, and sending a copy for comment to Madison, who deemed it too long, specific, and politically indiscreet for use. By laying out his vision for the new government, it showed how broadly Washington interpreted the Constitution. Three decades later, the first editor of Washington's papers, after deciding with Madison's approval to destroy the only copy, cut it in pieces for souvenir hunters seeking samples of the General's handwriting. Surviving parts of this magisterial address make up less than half of the whole. Historians treasure the remainder as authoritative: it articulated Washington's vision for America and outlined the future course of his administration.[8]

Washington's draft inaugural began by denouncing the Articles of Confederation for giving the central government too little direct power and by embracing the Constitution for greatly expanding central authority. "No other or greater powers appear to me to be delegated to this government than are essential to accomplish the objects for which it was instituted, to wit, the safety & happiness of the governed," the address declared in a direct refutation of antifederalist claims to the contrary. And in a world of self-justifying monarchies, the stated goal of serving the people's interests signaled a sea change for government. "I rejoice in the belief," the new President was to say, "that mankind will reverse the absurd position that *the many* were made for *the few;* and that they will not continue slaves in one part of the globe, when they can become freemen in another." Toward this end, the speech exclaimed, America would play a part, "the salutary consequences of which shall flow to another Hemisphere & extend throughout the interminable series of ages!"[9] Washington never made a clearer proclamation of what made the United States special.

Republican rule founded on secure institutions stood at the heart of Washington's vision for an American empire destined to grow through free immigration and western expansion rather than at the expense of other nations. "This Constitution is really in its formation a government of the people; that is to say, a government in which all power is derived from, and at stated periods reverts to them," his address declared, and "the balances, arising from the distribution of the Legislative, Executive, and Judicial powers are the best that have been instituted." Given its prospects for advancing republican ideals, Washington's address urged Congress and the states not to amend the Constitution until "a fair experiment of its effects," except perhaps to add a bill of rights. Instead, Congress should "take measures for promoting the general welfare" by utilizing its powers afforded under the Constitution to regulate coinage and currency, set just weights and measures, improve education and manners, boost arts and sciences, enhance postal services, provide patents for useful inventions, and cherish institutions favorable to humanity.[10] In these terms, the speech articulated the clear path to national felicity that Washington alluded to in his January letter to Lafayette.[11]

WASHINGTON FIRST ASKED MADISON to review the draft address in early January, but did not send a copy to him until mid-February. By then, the presidential electors had voted, though their votes remained uncounted. Whether selected by the people or the legislature, federal law required that each state choose its electors on

January 7 and that all electors cast their two ballots on February 4. Although both federalists and antifederalists sought these coveted new positions, they disagreed only on whom to vote for Vice President. "For President, not a name is even whispered in any part of the union but Washington," Georgia congressman Abraham Baldwin commented from New York.[12] "All parties and descriptions of men revere him," one self-proclaimed Republican wrote about Washington in a Boston newspaper; "there is hardly one but ardently wishes his election, whether Federalists or Antifederalist, Aristocratic or Republican."[13] Americans would not know many times like this.

In four of the ten participating states—Pennsylvania, Maryland, Virginia, and Delaware—voters chose the electors. These races generated most of the newspaper stories about the presidential contest. To turn out their own voters, for example, federalist papers in these states circulated rumors that antifederalists "*secretly*" sought to elect Patrick Henry as President. "Oh ye Gods, what a worthy competitor with a WASHINGTON!!" Philadelphia's bellwether *Federal Gazette* sarcastically sneered in a widely reprinted mid-December article. "It is highly necessary that the friends of the constitution, in every state, should be active in choosing federal electors only who will undoubtedly elect *the man of the people*."[14] Later in the month, the *Maryland Gazette* warned its readers against "sending any man, as an elector, whose federalism was even equivocal, lest he should vote for Mr. Patrick Henry as president . . . and against the great and good General Washington."[15] Antifederalist candidates tried to counter these accounts by pledging their support for Washington, with one going so far as to denounce any report to the contrary as an "illiberal, ungenerous Lie."[16] Only after the January elections did the *Federal Gazette* concede, "It seems the anties have relinquished Patrick Henry, esquire, and have resolved not to deprive general Washington of an unanimous vote."[17] By then, the people had voted.

Electors ran statewide in Maryland, Pennsylvania, and Delaware, with each side endorsing a formal slate of candidates and contesting every position in the two larger states. In Maryland, although several antifederalists polled well in some counties and might have prevailed in one or more contiguous districts, federalists won by a two-to-one margin statewide and carried every race.[18] They did even better in Pennsylvania. In a contest marked by low turnout apparently caused by disengaged antifederalists mostly staying home on a cold, damp election day, federalist candidates carried more than 90 percent of the statewide vote and all but swept Philadelphia and surrounding counties.[19] With no organized antifederalist opposition in Delaware, the contest for electors in that small state turned on local matters, with voters in each of its three counties unanimously choosing one of the state's three electors.[20]

The federalist tide even reached Virginia, where the antifederalist legislature had carved the state into electoral districts designed to serve its partisan purposes. To Washington's delight, the plan failed miserably. While "much pain has been taken and no art left unessayed to poison the mind, and alarm the fears of the people into opposition," he wrote to a close friend after the election, "in the list of Electors which has been published by the Executive authority of this State, there appears eight decided friends of the New Constitution."[21] Washington's in-law and close friend David Stuart won easily in the district incorporating Mount Vernon. Henry carried his home district and two antifederalists prevailed in southern Virginia, but this netted Clinton only three out of twelve possible electoral votes for Vice President in a state where he had hoped to rack up a sizable majority.[22] Even Henry and his partisans ultimately cast their other votes for Washington. After all, they were first and foremost Virginians.

With lawmakers doing the choosing in Connecticut, South Carolina, New Jersey, and Georgia, the process in those states quickly and quietly led to the selection of reliable federalist electors. Indeed, in a letter to Washington, the Speaker of Connecticut's Assembly attributed the decision to have lawmakers choose electors to the conviction that the heavily federalist state assembly would exercise more "judgment & discretion" than the people at large.[23] As it turned out, all of Connecticut's seven electors had served as delegates to the state ratifying convention and voted for the Constitution. The results were much the same in the other states that appointed electors, with South Carolina naming a particularly distinguished group that included former Continental Congress president Henry Laurens, signer of the Declaration of Independence Thomas Heyward, and former Constitutional Convention delegate Charles Cotesworth Pinckney. In fact, most of South Carolina's electors knew Washington personally and several of them had visited him at Mount Vernon.

The remaining two states, Massachusetts and New Hampshire, used a mixed approach to select electors. Adapting more than two centuries of New England democratic tradition to a radically new political situation, they convened town meetings in mid-December for citizens to nominate and vote for electors. The names of candidates receiving the most votes went forward to the state legislature, which made the final selection. Not many people turned out for these special meetings, and most of the attention focused on contests for Congress, which took place at the same time. Nevertheless, the procedure worked well for federalists.[24] "By the returns of Gentlemen for electors of President," Lieutenant Governor Benjamin Lincoln reported to Washington after this first round of the process ended in Massachusetts, "we cannot have a bad set indeed we must have a good one. What we call good here are Gentlemen who love the constitution & will vote for _____ President."[25] The blank line, of course, stood for Washington.

The only glitch in the process occurred in New Hampshire, when the two legislative houses split over whether to make the final decision by joint or separate ballot. Just minutes before midnight on January 7, the House gave way because its members, as one newspaper reported, did not want New Hampshire to miss the deadline *"and thereby be prevented from paying that tribute which her citizens owe to the great American Fabius,"* Washington.[26]

News of these developments trickled into Mount Vernon through newspapers and letters from across the country during January. While invariably welcome, the reports finally laid to rest Washington's peculiar notion that he might be spared the presidency through an antifederalist election triumph. "If the friends of the Constitution conceive that my administering the government will be a means of its acceleration and strength, is it not probable that the adversaries of it may entertain the same idea?" Washington had asked Hamilton in October 1788. "That many of this description will become Electors, I can have no Doubt."[27] On New Year's Day 1789, Washington could still write about the presidency, "the choice is as yet very far from being certain."[28] Perhaps he believed the rumors circulated by the federalist press about Henry; perhaps he just wanted to believe them. By the end of January, however, Washington realized that federalists had virtually swept the election.

"With all the electors yet chosen," the *Massachusetts Centinel* reported in a January 21 article that surely reached Washington, "the American Fabius and Mr. Adams, are the persons for President and Vice-President of the United States—and in this the people appear to say *Amen*."[29] By this point, Fabius was eclipsing Cincinnatus as the favored Roman name for Washington, reflecting Fabius's fame as a political and military savior.

By month's end, as if to acknowledge the massive federalist elector triumph, Washington began preparing for his inauguration by asking Henry Knox in New York to buy and send him cloth for a new suit. Washington appreciated fine clothes and, like most wealthy American gentlemen of his day, his finest ones came from Europe. Before this time, no American mill had looms capable of weaving suit-quality broadcloth. In January, Washington saw an advertisement in a New York newspaper for superfine textile from a new Connecticut woolen mill. He thought that wearing a suit cut from American cloth at his inauguration might make a statement about domestic manufacturing. He asked Knox to send enough material for a suit for himself and a riding habit for his wife. He left the choice of color for the suit to Knox, noting only that, "if the dye should not appear to be well fixed, & clear, or if the cloth should not really be very fine, then (in my Judgment) some colour mixed in grain might be preferable." Knox chose brown.[30]

Washington may have borrowed the idea. In early January, the *Federal Gazette*, which Washington often read, published two articles about new lines of domestic textiles suitable for formal dress. One of them expressly urged newly elected federal officials to wear "complete suits of American manufactured cloth" when sworn into office. Such a display, the article predicted, would do more good "than twenty laws to encourage American manufacturing, or to restrain undue or improper imports."[31] Washington explained his own motives in a letter to Lafayette. "I have been writing to our friend Genl Knox this day, to procure me homespun broad cloth," Washington wrote on January 29. "I hope it will not be a great while, before it will be unfashionable for a gentleman to appear in any other dress."[32]

GATHERING IN THEIR RESPECTIVE STATES, America's chosen electors voted on February 4. "The events of this day will be as important as ever occurred in the annals of America," the *Massachusetts Centinel* asserted. "It is the prayer of every friend to our dear country that no warring and contradictory spirit may prevail."[33] Unity, at least in this newspaper's view, meant all voting for Washington. While Congress would not open the sealed ballots from each state and count the votes for at least a month, more-or-less accurate reports seeped out about how the electors voted. Papers across America published these reports as they came in so that readers could follow the rising totals.

Relying as much on predictions as solid information, the tallies from early February overstated the sums for Adams and Clinton by discounting the extent of vote scattering, but they were right on

Washington: a clean sweep everywhere.[34] "By the accounts received last evening from Connecticut, we learn that their Electors have been unanimous for Mr. Washington, and five out of seven were for Mr. Adams," read a typical mid-month report. "In Pennsylvania the Electors were unanimous for Washington; and six out of the ten, for Mr. Adams."[35] These figures came close to correct, and by month's end many papers had them right except for returns from far-off Georgia, which remained a mystery across most of the country into March.

Washington followed these returns from Mount Vernon, where he received them in newspapers and personal letters. Fittingly, the final item came in a letter from Madison, who, on his way to Congress in early March, fell in with the bearer of Georgia's electoral votes. "They are all unanimous as to the President and are all thrown away on individuals of the State as to the Vice President," he reported to Washington.[36] Even this did not get the votes quite right, because one of Georgia's scattered second votes went to Washington's old friend Benjamin Lincoln of Massachusetts, but the main point was clear. Washington had swept the state, and with it the country. As it turned out, Georgia's electors had voted in an Augusta coffeehouse under the watchful eyes of former Continental Army officers. When the electors announced the vote, those officers discharged thirteen rounds from two cannons in honor of their former commander in chief.[37] Washington had devoted supporters in even the most remote states and, despite the large egos of the revolutionary generation, virtually no one begrudged him the presidency.

February also brought Washington's birthday. With enthusiasm mounting over his ascension to the presidency, the day took on popular significance. During the colonial era, Americans joined British subjects everywhere in celebrating the king's birthday. They no longer recognized the date, of course, except to mock their former monarch, but, hungry for holidays, they began to celebrate Washington's birthday instead. In 1789, for example, Philadelphians marked the day with church bells ringing, cannons firing, and a banquet opening with the toast, "May General Washington preside as President of the United States of America."[38] As for the temporarily deranged king in England, his delusions had become so grandiose that he now fancied himself George Washington! Gouverneur Morris reported this bizarre development in the madness of King George to Washington in a late February letter from Paris, which also noted that Washington's acceptance of the presidency would enhance America's standing in Europe.[39] For his part, Washington took these potentially head-turning reports in stride along with all his many tributes.

AMERICANS KNEW THE ELECTION'S OUTCOME by early March but the Constitution mandated that, to make it official, the Senate president must open the certified ballots before a joint session of Congress, and have the votes counted. This could not happen until Congress convened, which the law formally set for March 4, but it also required the presence of a majority of the members in each house. The old Congress had not had a quorum for five months and expired without adjourning on March 3, long after it ceased functioning. To mark the transition, cannons at the Battery in lower Manhattan fired thirteen rounds for the states of the old confederation at sunset on the third and eleven rounds for the states in the new union at sunrise on the fourth.[40] North Carolina and Rhode Island remained outside looking in as the new Constitution took effect.

The much-celebrated new Congress could no more convene on the fourth than the much maligned old Congress could adjourn on the third, however, because it, too, lacked a quorum. Only eight of twenty senators and thirteen of fifty-nine representatives arrived on time. Heavy, unstable ice in the rivers of the middle states slowed travel for members coming from the South.[41] Some from nearby states stayed home until a quorum mustered.

The resulting delay in counting the electoral votes left Washington waiting in the wings, as he had no desire to leave Mount

Vernon until formally called to office. He used the extended time at home to tie up loose ends. In late February, he made one last trip to inspect work on Potomac River navigation before resigning his position with the project.

Early March brought a final visit to his eighty-one-year-old mother in Fredericksburg, Virginia. Few visits to this demanding woman ever went well for Washington, and this trip may have been one of the worst. Since he had first sought to join the navy more than four decades earlier, she had always tried to stop him from taking posts that took him far from home. For her, none of his honors, none of his fame, could compensate for a perceived lack of filial piety. As she lay dying from untreatable cancer, he came one last time to take leave of her for a distant duty. At the time, Washington referred to this visit as "the last Act of *personal* duty, I may, (from her age) ever have it in my power to pay upon my Mother."[42] If nothing else, she had given him a strong will and now he left her to die without him.

Also in March, Washington sent a letter with detailed instructions to the nephew who would oversee Mount Vernon in his absence. "Frugality & economy are . . . all that is required," Washington wrote about managing the plantation that still supplied most of his income.[43] But frugality and economy, as he frankly added, were rarely practiced at Mount Vernon. Between his slaves, servants, and family, Washington had more than four hundred mouths to feed on the plantation. In addition, he entertained a steady stream of visitors, sometimes many at the same time. "Unless some one pops in unexpectedly," Washington wrote to his longtime secretary Tobias Lear in 1798, "Mrs Washington and myself will do what I believe has not been done within the last twenty years by us, that is to set down to dinner by ourselves."[44] This period covered his years at Mount Vernon following his retirement from the military in 1783.[45] These expenses combined with two years of poor crops caused by bad weather and an inability to lease or sell his frontier holdings at a profit because of instability in the Ohio Valley left Washington land-rich but cash-poor by the time he became President. "My means are not adequate to the expence at which I have lived since my retirement," he now admitted to his nephew. At least as President, Washington added, the government would cover his expenses. "If this had not happened," he noted, frugality and economy would have become his own lot, too.[46]

Before departing, Washington dealt with the immediate consequences of living beyond his means. So as not to leave Virginia with outstanding debts, he borrowed money at interest for the first time in his life. "Never 'till within these two yrs have I experienced the want of money," Washington explained to a local lender on March 4. "Short Crops, & other causes not entirely within my Controul, make me feel it now . . . and Land, which I have offered for Sale, will not command cash but at an under value."[47] He asked for five hundred pounds and agreed to what he later described as "rigid conditions" on the loan, which included paying the maximum legal interest rate of 6 percent.[48] Two days later, Washington asked for one hundred more pounds to cover "the expences of my Journey to New York."[49] He initially tried to borrow twice that total amount and later asked a wealthy friend for a loan, presumably to refinance the earlier one at a lower rate, but never obtained alternative credit and ultimately took nearly two years to repay the six-hundred-pound note. To raise more cash, Washington sent demand letters to his own debtors in March, some offering discounts for prompt payment, but got little in return.

THE HOUSE OF REPRESENTATIVES finally gained a quorum on April 1, but the Senate still remained one shy of half. "I feel for those Members of the New Congress, who, hitherto, have given an unavailing attendance," Washington wrote to Knox on that day. "For myself, the delay may be compared to a reprieve; for . . . my movements to the chair of Government will be accompanied with feelings not unlike those of a culprit who is going to the place of execution." He described himself as unequal to the task ahead, but promised to bring integrity and firmness to the job. "I am embarking the voice of my Countrymen and a good name of my own, on this voyage," he concluded, "but what returns will be made for them—heaven alone can foretell."[50]

Still not knowing when Congress would call him to New York, Washington sent Tobias Lear and a trusted house slave named Will ahead to prepare for his arrival. Martha Washington decided to remain behind until her husband settled into permanent quarters. Governor Clinton had offered his home as a temporary residence, but Washington did not want to accept favors from any individuals, even close friends. "Hired (private) lodging would not only be more agreeable to my own wishes," he wrote to Madison on March 30, "but, possibly, more consistent with the dictates of sound policy." Washington asked Madison to find something for him before he arrived, if only "rooms at the most decent Tavern."[51]

The delay in convening Congress also gave workers more time to complete renovations on the building that would house the new government. A rounded, colonial structure built in 1700 to serve as New York's City Hall and depicted by some as "a gothic heap," the new "Federal Hall" received a complete face-lift under the direction of French-born civil engineer Peter Charles L'Enfant, who had served on Washington's staff during the Revolutionary War and later devised the city plan for Washington, D.C.[52] Topped now with a towering cupola and fronted by a second-floor outer balcony or "gallery," the building remained sheathed in scaffolding even after Congress began meeting. The timbers finally came down in mid-April, revealing a new, upright façade with Doric columns capped by a classical pediment inset with an imposing American eagle. "The general appearance of this front is truly august," New York's *Gazette of the United States* reported on April 22.[53] It helped give birth to the new Federal style, which dominated American architecture for a generation.

The arrival of Richard Henry Lee from Virginia finally supplied the quorum needed for the Senate to organize and then meet in joint session with the House on April 6 for the counting of electoral votes. Elected to the Senate by antifederalists in Virginia with the hope that he would throw sand in the federal machinery, Lee visited Mount Vernon on his way to New York and cemented his peace with Washington in a letter sent on April 6. "On this day we went to business, and to my very great satisfaction I heard a unanimous vote of the electing States in favor of calling you to the honorable office President," Lee informed the General. "The public happiness, which I know you have so much at heart, will be very insecure without your acceptance."[54] Madison wrote on the same day to explain that Congress would send Charles Thomson to notify Washington officially of the election results.[55] An early patriot in the mold of John Dickinson, Thomson had served as Congress's hands-on secretary since 1774.

After a week on the road, Thomson arrived at Mount Vernon about noon on April 14 with the news that Washington both expected and dreaded. "I am honored with the commands of the Senate to wait upon your Excellency with the information of your being elected to the office of President," Thomson stated. "You are called not only by the unanimous votes of the Electors but by the voice of America."[56] Knowing that his words would reach a national audience, Washington spoke from a prepared text. "I have been long accustomed to entertain so great a respect for the opinion of my fellow citizens, that the knowledge of their unanimous suffrages having been given in my favour scarcely leaves me the alternative for an Option," he said. "While I realize the arduous nature of the task which is conferred on me and feel my inability to perform it, I wish there may not be reason for regretting the choice." To Thomson, then, Washington added, "I shall therefore be in readiness to set out the day after to morrow, and shall be happy in the pleasure of your company."[57] They would travel in Washington's closed carriage together with Humphreys and, perched outside, three or four liveried servants.[58] Thus began a

250-mile journey that had no American precedent and few parallels: a grand inaugural procession consummating America's love affair with George Washington.

"ABOUT TEN O'CLOCK I bade adieu to Mount Vernon, to private life, and to domestic felicity; and . . . set out for New York in the company of Mr. Thomson and colonel Humphreys," Washington wrote in his diary for April 16.[59] The party did not travel alone for long. A crowd of Virginians met Washington outside Mount Vernon and led him to Alexandria for a midday reception. "Again your country demands your care," the mayor proclaimed. "Go; and make a grateful people happy." Echoing the theme of national unity that resonated throughout his trip, Washington replied that, despite his "love" of retirement, "an ardent desire, on my own part, to be instrumental in conciliating the good will of my countrymen towards each other" had induced him to accept the presidency.

After an early dinner with those he called "my affectionate friends and kind neighbors," Washington left Virginia about 2 P.M. aboard the Potomac River ferry.[60] A sea of Marylanders hailing him as *their* President waited at the Georgetown landing to escort him as far as Spurrier's Tavern on the post road about halfway to Baltimore. There, he spent the night. With Washington assuming the office, the presidency was already serving as a source for American identity.

Crowds grew as Washington advanced deeper into the more densely populated middle states. "This great man was met some miles from Town, by a large body of respectable citizens on horseback, and conducted, under a discharge of cannon . . . through crowds of admiring spectators," a report from Baltimore noted.[61] A committee of merchants and former army officers had organized this rousing reception in what was then America's fifth-largest city. Calling on "citizens of the United States" to venerate their President, the committee's welcoming address declared, "We behold a new era springing out of our independence."[62] Then or the night before, Washington received a long poetic tribute that closed with the plea:

> *The Federal Union closer bind,*
>   *Firm public faith restore;*
> *Drive discord from the canker'd mind,*
>   *Each mutual blessing pour.*[63]

The scene in Maryland repeated itself in Delaware, where local citizens met Washington at the state line on the nineteenth, escorted him to Wilmington for the night, and accompanied him as far as Pennsylvania early on the twentieth.[64] There, with portraitist of the Revolution and Philadelphia impresario Charles Willson Peale orchestrating events, celebrations topped anything Washington's party had yet encountered.

State president Thomas Mifflin, who as president of the Confederation Congress had received the General's resignation six years earlier, greeted Washington at the Pennsylvania border and— with other officials, two cavalry units, a detachment of artillery, and a body of light infantry—escorted him to Philadelphia. After breakfast in Chester, Pennsylvania, Washington mounted a richly ornamented white horse to lead the procession, which grew as more troops and citizens joined it along the way. Cedar and laurel branches lined the bridge across the Schuylkill River, with evergreen arches covering each end. As Washington passed under the first triumphal arch, Peale's daughter Angelica, hidden in the branches, lowered a laurel wreath onto or just above his head.[65]

Philadelphia exploded upon Washington's arrival. Cannons fired and bells rang through the day; fireworks lit the night's sky. "The number of spectators who filled the doors, windows, and streets, which he passed, was greater than on any other occasion," a newspaper noted. "All classes and descriptions of citizens discovered . . .

the most undisguised attachment and unbounded zeal for their dear chief."[66] A banquet followed at City Tavern, beginning with a toast to "The United States" and ending with one to "Liberty without licentiousness."[67] After spending one night at Robert Morris's home, where he received more civic tributes in the morning, Washington left the city at 10 A.M. on the twenty-first.[68]

After traveling north along the Delaware River for thirty miles in Pennsylvania, Washington took a commercial ferry across to New Jersey. This passage occurred near to where Washington and his army had crossed in rowboats on that fateful Christmas Night in 1776, to surprise the Hessian troops at Trenton and reverse the course of the Revolutionary War. Now, however, a vast throng lined the far side to hail Washington's return with such loud "huzzas" that, according to one observer, "the shores reecho the cheerful sounds."[69]

Local units of the New Jersey militia then preceded Washington, again on horseback, to the old stone bridge over Assunpink Creek, south of Trenton, where his army had held off British troops on January 2, 1777. A floral arch now spanned the bridge, with laurel-entwined pillars and a banner reading "The Defender of the Mothers, will be the Protector of the Daughters."[70] Led by some of those mothers defended by his army in 1777, white-robed daughters to be protected by his presidency serenaded Washington at the arch:

Virgins fair, and Matron grave,
Those thy conquering Arms did save,
Build for thee triumphal Bowers.
Strew, ye Fair, his Way with Flowers.[71]

At the last line, the girls scattered petals along Washington's path. "The scene was truly grand," one newspaper observed, and the sentiments it evoked "bathed many cheeks with tears."[72]

From the Assunpink bridge, Washington rode into Trenton for dinner and a public reception, then to Princeton for another formal welcome. On April 22, he traveled with military escort to New Brunswick, New Jersey, for dinner and finally to Woodbridge for the night.

By 9 A.M. on the twenty-third, Washington had reached Elizabethtown, New Jersey, on the Hudson River's western bank, where a purpose-built barge waited to ferry him to New York. "She is 47 feet keel," one newspaper reported, "and rows with 13 oars on each side, to be manned by pilots of New-York, who are to be dressed in white frocks and black caps, trimmed and ornamented with fringe."[73] Fit for a king or perhaps a pharaoh—another paper likened it to "Cleopatra's silken-corded barge"—the craft had a canopied pavilion with festooned red curtains.[74]

Seven members of Congress and three New York officials joined Washington on the barge, which gathered a flotilla of boats in its wake, including two with choirs and one bearing Henry Knox, John Jay, and other federal officers. Ships in the harbor and batteries onshore fired their guns in salute as the barge rounded Manhattan Island heading for Murray's Landing on the East River at the foot of Wall Street. Pulling alongside, one of the floating choirs sang its version of "God Save the King":

These shores a HEAD shall own,
Unsully'd by a throne,
Our much lov'd WASHINGTON,
The Great, the Good![75]

"We now discovered the Shores crowded with thousands of people," one congressmen on board wrote about the barge's approach to Manhattan. "You could see little else along the Shores, in the Streets, and on Board every Vessel, but Heads standing as thick as Ears of Corn before Harvest."[76] Governor Clinton warmly greeted his old friend at the landing and walked with him, other officials, a military honor guard, and two bands through a crush of well-wishers to the residence rented by Congress for the President about a half mile away. They finally arrived there about 3 P.M. The near-universal response to the jubilation was, one newspaper reported, "Well, he deserves it all!"[77]

EVEN AS NEW YORKERS added to the prestige of the presidency by cheering Washington's entrance into their city, John Adams displayed a misunderstanding of the foundations for power under republican rule by futilely trying to impose authority on the office by fiat. Installed as Vice President and the Senate's presiding officer two days earlier, as Washington entered the city Adams was lecturing the Senate about the imperative of giving the President a proper title. He wanted something like "his Most Benign Highness" or "your Majesty," it turned out, and dismissed the mere designation of "President" as something suited to the chief officer of a cricket club or fire company. America's chief executive must have a title equal to that of European royalty or he will lose respect at home and abroad, Adams believed, and one superior to the "your Excellency" commonly afforded state governors, or else the relative place of the central government in the federal scheme will slip and anarchy result. Further, he claimed that titles would attract people to serve in government and sought a similar or the same one for his office, too.[78]

At the time, Congress still had not yet fixed when, where, and how to inaugurate the President. On a motion apparently made by Adams himself, the Senate named a committee on the twenty-third to consider both this pressing issue, as well as the question of what titles to confer on the President and Vice President.[79] The House appointed a parallel committee on the following day. Opposition quickly surfaced to the second matter. Privately calling it "truly ridiculous," Pennsylvania senator William Maclay tried to delete consideration of titles from the Senate committee's charge.[80] He later blamed "this Whole silly Business" mostly on Adams. No title could possibly "add to the respect entertained for General Washington," Maclay maintained.[81] Rather than gain respect by becoming President, Washington gave respect to the presidency by holding it. Later, with Madison taking the lead and Washington in full accord, the House formally refused to confer any supplementary title on the President. Aware that everything he did in office set precedent, Washington answered to "Mr. President."

DODGING THE CONTROVERSIAL ISSUE of executive titles, on April 25 the House and Senate agreed on the time, place, and manner for inaugurating the President. With Washington's assent, they set the date for April 30 and asked the highest available judicial officer, New York chancellor Robert Livingston, to administer the oath of office.[82] By then, sixty-seven of Congress's seventy-nine members had reached New York and taken their seats. Both houses initially agreed to stage the event inside Federal Hall's first-floor House chamber, which (while larger than the second-floor Senate chamber) would have limited the audience to invited guests.

Then the members had a brilliant idea. "To the end that the oath of office may be administered to the President in the most public matter, and that the greatest number of people of the United States, and *without distinction*, may be witnesses to solemnity," the *New-York Daily Gazette* reported, Congress switched the venue for the swearing-in ceremony to "the outer gallery adjoining to the senate-chamber."[83] This put the event outside, on a balcony overlooking the wide intersection of Wall and Broad Streets. At the urging of local clergy, Congress also added that, after the inauguration, the official party would go to the Episcopal Church's stately St. Paul's Chapel on Broadway for prayers led by one of the congressional chaplains.[84]

By moving the inauguration outside where thousands could watch and scheduling public prayers for the new President in a local church, Congress implicitly recognized the remarkable popular response to Washington becoming President. More than Congress, the presidency was becoming the publicly recognized symbol of the constitutional union, and, by reaching out to the public as he did during his journey to New York, Washington helped to forge a nation. Countless individual spectators to his journey spoke in almost breathless wonder about the moment when they seemed to catch his eye or he appeared to doff his hat or bow to them alone.[85] In Europe, all Americans knew, people bowed to kings. On his journey, Washington continually bowed to people as his way of acknowledging tributes and cheers. It endeared him to them.

Adams missed this point by wanting to separate the people from the President by interposing regal titles. "The glare of royalty and nobility, during his mission to England, had made him believe their fascination a necessary ingredient to government," Jefferson later wrote about Adams, but Washington knew better.[86] The American experience, he had noted in his undelivered inaugural address, reversed the presumption that "the many were made for the few" by establishing that government was made for the many.[87]

Washington would replicate his jubilant journey to New York with trips through New England and the South over the next two years, making it his goal as President to visit every state. Further, while in office, he regularly received the public at his residence.[88] Although not an informal man, his became an open presidency quite unlike the insulated monarchies of Europe.[89] Indeed, Madison soon observed that Washington was the only feature of the new government that captured the popular imagination.[90]

In his diary for the day of his triumphal entry into New York, Washington wrote that, while he found the pageantry pleasing, "considering the reverse of this scene, which may be the case after all my labors do no good," he also found it painful.[91] Expanding on this point in a letter written two weeks later to South Carolina's Edward Rutledge, Washington cautioned about the cheering crowds, "I fear if the issue of the public measures should not corrispond with their sanguine expectation, they will turn the extravagant (and I may say undue) praises which they are heaping upon me at this moment, into equally extravagant (though I will fondly hope unmerited) censures."[92]

Washington saw public opinion as a formidable but fickle foundation for political power and tried to cultivate it. His evident success led the less popular Adams, with a mixture of esteem and envy, to view Washington somewhat as an actor playing a part: a "Character of Convention," Adams called him, designedly made "popular and fashionable with all parties and in all places and with all persons as a center of union" first during the war and again as President.[93] Designed or not, it worked. Washington unquestionably was the most popular person in America.

With Congress scheduling his inauguration for the last day of April, Washington had a week to settle in before becoming President. Upon his arrival in New York, he dined at the governor's mansion but thereafter let people know that he would not accept any further dinner invitations, and so received none.[94] He took his meals at the presidential residence with Lear and Humphreys.[95] Having hired the innkeeper Samuel Fraunces to oversee the kitchen, Washington had come full circle from the emotional farewell dinner with his officers at Fraunces Tavern more than six years earlier. Now, however, it was members of Congress and other dignitaries, not military officers, who called on Washington. From "the time I had done breakfast, thence 'till dinner, & afterwards 'till bed time," he noted about these days between his arrival and inaugural, "I could not dispatch one ceremonius visit before I was called to another—so that in fact I had no leizure to read, or answer the dispatches which were pouring in from all quarters."[96]

Many accounts had Washington conferring often with Madison on matters of state and the inaugural address during this period.[97] Meanwhile, Congress worked mostly on raising revenue and establishing courts. By the thirtieth, if not before, Washington had a brief new inaugural address in hand and was ready to take office. With people streaming into New York to watch the ceremonies, local, state, and federal officials hurriedly organized the various events.

"WE HAVE HEARD MUCH of the BIRTH DAY of our COLUMBIA," New York's *Gazette of the United States* proclaimed in large type on April 29. "TO MORROW is the Day of her ESPOUSALS—when, in presence of the KING of KINGS, the solemn Compact will be ratified between her, and the darling object of her choice." Washington, the paper exclaimed, by "UNIVERSAL SUFFRAGES OF A GREAT AND VARIOUS PEOPLE" would become President![98] In lower Manhattan, that much-awaited day began with a cannon volley at sunrise followed by church bells ringing throughout the morning.

Crowds gathered in front of the President's house but Washington remained inside until a deputation from the Senate and House arrived shortly after noon to report that Congress was ready to receive him. The retired General wore a tailed suit of brown Connecticut broadcloth with American eagle buttons and tight, calf length pants; white, knee-high silk stockings; and silver-buckle shoes. A hat, powdered hair, and dress sword completed his inaugural costume.[99] Stepping outside, Washington bowed to the crowd before boarding a state coach. His own carriage with Humphreys and Lear on board waited behind the presidential coach as troops and dignitaries arrayed themselves in a preset order. At 12:30 P.M., the parade began moving slowly south on Cherry to Queen Street, then around to Broad Street before swinging north toward Federal Hall.

One company of cavalry and three of infantry, about five hundred soldiers in all, led the procession through cheering crowds from the presidential residence onward. The delegation from Congress followed the troops, then came Washington, his two aides, heads of the federal departments, Chancellor Livingston, and other invited dignitaries. Citizens fell in behind the official party as it passed, all winding their way toward Federal Hall. "About two hundred yards before reaching the hall," wrote the popular American author Washington Irving, who witnessed the event as a child, "Washington and his suite alighted from their carriages and passed through the troops, who were draw up on each side, into the hall and senate chamber, where the Vice-President, the Senate and House of Representatives were assembled."[100]

The senators had gathered in their chamber first and, at the Vice President's prodding, discussed whether they should stand or sit while the President spoke. The underlying issue, debated now on the fly, involved the weighty matter of whether members of Congress stood equal, superior, or inferior to the President. Adams, Lee, and South Carolina senator Ralph Izard related their personal observations of the king addressing Parliament, but others dismissed those comments as of "no consequence" in a republic. Before the Senate settled anything, however, House members filed in behind their Speaker and took seats to the senators' right. More than an hour more passed before Washington finally reached the chamber, passed between the now-standing members, bowed to each side, and took a seat on the dais between the Vice President and Speaker. Then the members sat. Lacking any clear instruction on protocol, the members tended to stand and sit along with the President, suggesting a rough sort of respectful equality between the branches.[101]

Soon after Washington sat down, Adams stood up to invite him onto the Senate's outer gallery for the oath of office. Thousands were waiting to watch.[102] "The windows and the roofs of the houses were crowded," Eliza Morton observed from atop one of those roofs, "and in the streets the throng was so dense that it seemed as if one might literally walk on the heads of the people."[103] Washington stepped outside first, followed by Adams, Livingston, and as many of the assembled dignitaries and members of Congress as would fit. The only known live drawing of the event, a sketch by Peter Lacour turned into a print in 1790, shows eighteen people crammed on the narrow porch with Washington. Decades later, Morton could still recall the "universal shouts of joy and welcome" that greeted Washington's appearance on the gallery.[104]

Placing his hand on the large, red Bible fetched for the occasion from Livingston's Masonic Lodge, Washington repeated the oath of office administered by the chancellor. Most spectators heard none of it, however, until the end, when Livingston proclaimed in a loud voice, *"Long live George Washington, President of the United States!"*[105] Then the audience erupted again, cannons fired, and church bells rang.

President Washington, after bowing to the people, went back into the Senate chamber to address Congress and invited guests—perhaps a hundred persons in all. The audience for this speech, however, was much larger than Congress. Newspapers across America printed it and foreign ministers in attendance reported on it to Europe. By substituting the short, general inaugural address crafted by Madison for the long, specific one prepared with Humphreys, Washington chose to reveal little about his policy objectives or incoming administration. Historian Joseph Ellis has described the speech as "deliberately elliptical."[106] It gave no hint of the nation-building efforts that Washington's administration would pursue, particularly after Hamilton replaced Madison as the President's closest advisor, even though that basic course of action flowed logically from much that Washington had expressed in private and in public since his circular letter of 1783. It did not even disclose much about Washington beyond his faith in divine providence.

While Washington had "the Gift of Silence," as Adams once put it, and could command an audience with a bow or stare, he was not a natural orator and never owned this speech.[107] Still, delivered in a low voice that people strained to hear, the address had a quiet dignity. The Spanish minister called it "eloquent and appropriate" even if the presentation struck some as "ungainly."[108]

Six paragraphs long, the speech began with the President noting his "incapacity as well as disinclination for the weighty and untried cares before me." Then, after expressing his trust in God and

Congress to carry the government forward, Washington reminded Americans of their national purpose. "The preservation of the sacred fire of liberty," he stated, "and the destiny of the republican model of Government, are justly considered as deeply, perhaps as finally, staked, on the experiment entrusted to the hands of the American people." Turning to the widely discussed issue of amending the Constitution, after urging Congress to "avoid every alternation which might endanger the benefits of untied government," Washington endorsed additions that might "more impregnably fortif[y]" the "rights of freemen." By this turn of phrase, he backed a bill of rights for some while artfully dodging both the already pressing subject of slavery and the then more far-off topic of women's rights. Looking heavenward, he closed his address by asking divine blessing for "the enlarged views, the temperate consultations, and the wise measures, on which the success of this Government must depend."[109]

Reading with some hesitation from pages that he shifted awkwardly from hand to hand, Washington took twenty minutes to deliver the fourteen-hundred-word address. From his entrance to his exit, the ceremony at Federal Hall ran under an hour. Thousands waited outside for the resumption of the inaugural parade, which the whole Congress now joined. Led by the same troops and assembled in a similar order as during the procession to Federal Hall, the augmented official party now walked several blocks up Broadway to St. Paul's Chapel, which it entered for divine services. More than five years earlier, Washington and his troops had paraded down this same wide avenue after liberating New York at the end of the American Revolution. With most of its war-ravaged buildings restored or replaced, the city now looked fresh and vibrant. Even though its population had increased dramatically since the war, many of the individuals now hailing Washington on this late April afternoon had done so in November 1783. Despite all that had happened to him and them in the intervening five years, Washington still embodied their hope for better times ahead.

The church service did not last long. Episcopal bishop Samuel Provoost, who also served as the Senate's chaplain, led prayers and sang praises but did not deliver a sermon. After the service, Washington rode by coach to his residence in time for a private dinner with Humphreys and Lear before going out at dusk to watch fireworks from Livingston's house overlooking the harbor.[110] These fireworks likely reminded Washington of those that he had watched from a similar viewpoint on the evening after liberating New York in 1783. Many of the same types were used—spirals, fire-trees, serpents, fountains, and flights of thirteen rockets—and the display again ran more than an hour.

So many people packed the streets of lower Manhattan during and after the fireworks that coaches could not pass. Washington walked home. That night, he had much to see. At the urging of civic leaders, New Yorkers celebrated the inauguration by illuminating the city with arrays of candles and lanterns in street-facing windows, front doors, open spaces, and public buildings. The most elaborate displays added transparencies that cast images fit for the occasion. In some, Washington could see himself, his victories, or his virtues; in others, he saw America's shape or symbols. By overlaying transparencies, a few of the images appeared to move or to re-create a recognizable scene in three dimensions.

After walking north for nearly a mile through thinning crowds and darkening neighborhoods, Washington reached the presidential residence on Cherry Street after 10 P.M. and retired for the night. "It was a day which will stand immutable and indelebale in the Annals of America," Lear wrote in a letter to Mount Vernon urging Martha Washington to come soon.[111] "Good government, the best of blessings, now commences under favorable auspices," the next day's newspaper announced. "We beg to congratulate our readers on the great event."[112] Those readers and all Americans arose that morning, May 1, 1789, to the first full day of the first federal administration. Neither they nor their President would ever be the same.

Image of George Washington from his private study at Mount Vernon.

Epilogue

WASHINGTON'S PRESIDENCY LIVED UP to the immense popular expectations. Paired with his service as commander in chief during the Revolutionary War, it became a second pinnacle in a career that has no parallel in American history. Each of these two periods covered roughly eight years of a remarkably rich life that would span nearly seven decades. Modern rankings of presidents, whether conducted by historians, political scientists, or a wider sample, generally place Washington and Abraham Lincoln at the top. For his part, among presidents, Lincoln esteemed Washington most. There was much to admire.

To head the various executive departments and to form a cabinet of advisors, Washington tapped prominent leaders from a broad spectrum of Americans who had supported the Constitution's ratification. For the critical domestic post of secretary of the Treasury, after first offering it to former superintendent of finance Robert Morris, Washington turned to the brilliant and energetic nationalist Alexander Hamilton, an enthusiast for all things British. State—the former office of Foreign Affairs—went to America's Francophile ambassador in Paris, Madison's close friend Thomas Jefferson, a fel-

low Virginian whose support for ratification had been more qualified than Washington suspected. Another Virginian, the on-and-off
supporter of the Constitution Edmund Randolph, became attorney
general. Washington named his loyal second in command during
the Revolutionary War and successor as army chief, Henry Knox, an
ardent federalist, as secretary of war.

In dealing with Congress, Washington at first relied most heavily
on Representative Madison but retained close ties with many others in the Senate and House, particularly Robert Morris. Half of the
twenty-two initial senators and eight of the new representatives had
served with Washington at the Constitutional Convention. Because
he viewed the vice presidency as a legislative position, Washington
excluded John Adams from his administration's inner counsels. He
probably could not have suffered that officious New Englander's
harangues, which he had more than enough of when Adams headed
Congress's Board of War during the American Revolution. To launch
the judicial branch, Washington nominated John Jay as chief justice and three friends from the Convention, James Wilson, John
Rutledge, and John Blair, as associate justices. The final open nomination to the five-member Supreme Court went to Massachusetts
chief justice William Cushing, who had worked to keep local courts
open during Shays's Rebellion and served as vice president of his
state's critical ratifying convention.

The results transformed America. Working almost as a team
under Washington, the executive, legislative, and judicial branches
began the process of forging a continental republic from an assortment
of states. The principal policies for doing so came from Hamilton,
who emerged as Washington's most influential advisor: a veritable
prime minister within the administration, much to the dismay of the
more states'-rights-minded Jefferson and the despair of antifederalists. Jefferson, though, made his contributions to the emerging order,
such as by devising a broad regime of federally protected intellectual
property rights. With Knox, he also backed Washington's efforts to

open the Ohio country for settlement, leading to prolonged warfare with the Western Confederacy of native tribes until its capitulation in 1795. And with surprisingly little dissent after all the opposition the idea had generated at the Convention, Congress authorized a network of lower federal courts that projected central authority into every state. True to his campaign promises, Madison took on the task of pushing a bill of rights through an indifferent, federalist-dominated Congress. Though the final amendments were less protective of states' rights than antifederalists wanted, they passed Congress by the end of its historic first session and Washington forwarded them to the states for ratification.

Hamilton's nationalizing policies were founded on funding the full debt run up by Congress and the states during the Revolutionary War. He viewed this as a means to align the interests of wealthy Americans with the central government, displace the states as independent economic actors, and enhance the country's credit. To pay for it, Hamilton pushed a tariff on imported goods, which would have the side effect of sheltering American industry, and an excise tax on some domestic items such as whiskey, which he saw as a means to exert authority over frontier distillers. Jefferson reluctantly endorsed Hamilton's idea of assuming state debts in return for northern support for moving the seat of government to the banks of the Potomac River near Mount Vernon, a dream of all Virginians, including Washington.

As a capstone for his economic program, Hamilton wanted a quasi-independent central bank for the United States, co-owned by private investors, which would in effect regulate fiscal policy and provide a stable national currency. Here Jefferson and Madison drew the line, claiming the Constitution did not authorize Congress to charter a bank. Madison even cited his notes from the Convention, which he had vowed to keep confidential for a generation, to argue that the delegates had rejected such an idea.

Invited by Washington to reply, Hamilton countered that the

Necessary and Proper Clause, already reviled by antifederalists, authorized Congress to do virtually anything that advanced its express powers to lay taxes and regulate interstate commerce. Washington sided with Hamilton, and the bank was chartered in 1791. By this point, North Carolina, Rhode Island, and Vermont had joined the union, with Kentucky coming in a year later—all fertile grounds for anti-national sentiment. Two distinct factions had emerged, with the leaders of each—Hamilton and Jefferson—in Washington's cabinet.

Endorsed by both camps and encouraged to run as the only one able to bridge the growing partisan divide, Washington was unanimously elected to a second four-year term in 1792. Under the façade of unity, however, two political parties were forming. It showed in the contest for Vice President, in which Clinton now finished a close second to Adams, and in a growing tendency for congressional candidates to identify with one of the factions. Jefferson's partisans began calling themselves Republicans while Hamilton's supporters increasingly formalized their designation as Federalists. On both sides, the outlines of party organizations emerged in the rise of partisan newspapers, the coordination of voting by factions in Congress, and party endorsements for political candidates. Members aligned with Jefferson even gained a slight edge in the House of Representatives following the elections of 1792, and held it through the remainder of Washington's tenure.

Events pushed partisanship during Washington's second term. Frustrated by Hamilton's domination over the administration, Jefferson left the cabinet in 1793. A year later, Republicans denounced the government for suppressing resistance to the whiskey tax in western Pennsylvania with a thirteen-thousand-soldier army personally led by Washington. Then convulsions caused by the French Revolution and ensuing war between republican France and aristocratic England engulfed domestic politics. Washington's decision to proclaim neutrality without consulting Congress outraged Republicans, who viewed the United States as bound to support its

Revolutionary War ally, France. When the British navy nevertheless seized hundreds of American merchant ships bound for French
ports in the West Indies, and impressed American sailors into service
to boot, many Republicans demanded a second war with England.
Instead, in 1794, Washington sent Jay to resolve differences between
the United States and its former colonial master. Bargaining from a
weak position, Jay's treaty did little more than accept British limits on
American trade with France in exchange for seemingly meaningless
concessions. For the first time, Washington's popularity sagged. He
was excoriated in the Republican press. The settlement with Britain,
however, paved the way for a widely applauded treaty with Spain
opening the Mississippi River for American navigation.

In 1796, at age sixty-four, Washington announced that he would
not accept a third term as President. He wanted to retire, again, to
Mount Vernon. His Farewell Address, printed in newspapers as a
letter to the people rather than delivered as a speech to Congress,
denounced partisanship, embraced economic nationalism, and discouraged permanent foreign alliances. Speaking to all Americans,
Washington wrote, "The unity of Government which constitutes
you one people, is also now dear to you. It is justly so; for it is a main
pillar in the edifice of your real independence, the support of your
tranquility at home, your peace abroad; of your safety; of your pros
perity; and of that very Liberty which you so highly prize."[1] This
address joined his circular letter of 1783 as one of Washington's two
most significant public writings: a legacy to the American people.

By this point, Washington's reputation as President was secure.
His initiatives and reforms had created lasting national institutions,
restored American credit, opened the Ohio country for settlement
and the Mississippi River for commerce, fostered economic expansion, and established the presidency as a powerful office of overarch-
ing significance. Perhaps most important of all, he had kept the United
States at peace with Europe during a period of widening transatlantic
war. In the election of 1796, Adams, Washington's preferred candi-

date, narrowly beat Jefferson in America's first contested balloting for President. By coming in second, however, Jefferson became Vice President, and the partisan split only deepened. Washington tried to stay out but inevitably was drawn in on the Federalist side, most notably in 1798 by accepting formal command of American forces during Adams's quasi-war with France.

Back at his beloved Mount Vernon beginning in March 1797, Washington threw himself into farming and even became a whiskey distiller. No product ever netted him a larger return on his investment than this potent, rye-based intoxicant that he sold without aging it. His distillery became the largest in the United States by 1799. On December 12 of that year, however, a heavy snow started falling during Washington's daily ride around his plantation's five farms. He returned home wet and cold. The accumulated snow and his physical condition kept him from riding on the thirteenth, a Friday. "He had taken cold (undoubtedly from being so much exposed the day before) and complained of having a sore throat," wrote Tobias Lear, Washington's secretary since 1784.[2]

The sore throat grew into something much worse by the next morning. Washington struggled for breath and could scarcely speak. To counter the inflammation that strangled him, he asked for a bleeding by the overseer who generally treated Mount Vernon's slaves. When they arrived, Washington's doctors repeated the procedure three more times and administered two laxatives. Nothing helped. In all likelihood Washington had contracted epiglottis, which no available medical treatment could cure. He accepted his fate. After reviewing his two wills, Washington confirmed the one that would free his slaves upon his wife's death and waited for his own to come. It did not take long. "Doctor, I die hard, but am not afraid to go," he said at dusk. The end came later that night. His final words were, " 'Tis well."[3]

News of the unexpected death touched off an outpouring of grief unprecedented in the country's history. "Every paper we received from towns which have heard of Washington's death, are enveloped in mourning," one journalist reported near the year's end. "Every city, town, village and hamlet has exhibited spontaneous tokens of poignant sorrow."[4]

Although Washington's body was entombed after four days at Mount Vernon, President Adams ordered all military stations to observe funeral honors for the fallen leader, which the army interpreted to mean military processions, gun salutes, solemn music, a riderless horse, spoken eulogies, and sometimes a flag-draped coffin on a horse-drawn caisson. Communities across America followed suit with funerary processions and public eulogies of their own, which allowed countless citizens to mourn Washington's passing in a collective manner. The largest ceremony occurred in Philadelphia, which then served as the seat of government pending its final move to the District of Columbia.

Congress designated Washington's friend, Representative Henry Lee of Virginia, to deliver the eulogy at Philadelphia. There Lee coined the three phrases that still characterize Washington: "First in war—first in peace—and first in the hearts of his countrymen."[5] Of these superlatives commonly ascribed to Washington, the first speaks to his role during the Revolutionary War and the second refers principally to his presidency. The third, the one that Washington would have most treasured, relates in large part to the trust and affection he earned between those two periods of official service, when he voluntarily relinquished power yet never stopped nurturing the new republic. Washington was as indispensable to America during these middle years as before or after them. During that pivotal phase of the country's development, he laid the foundation for the Constitution, the government, and the sacred union of states and people that has lasted for more than 225 years and promises to continue long into the future.

Notes

❧

List of Abbreviations for Frequently Cited Works

AFP: *Adams Family Papers*. Massachusetts Historical Society, Boston, 1954–59. Microfilm ed.

Annals of Congress: *The Debates and Proceedings in the Congress of the United States*. 42 vols. Washington, DC: Gales and Seaton, 1834.

DGW: Donald Jackson and Dorothy Twohig, eds. *The Diaries of George Washington*, 6 vols. Charlottesville: University Press of Virginia, 1976–79.

DHFFC: Linda Grant DePauw et al., eds. *The Documentary History of the First Federal Congress of the United States of America*. 15 vols. Baltimore: Johns Hopkins University Press, 1972–.

DHFFE: Merrill Jensen et al., eds. *The Documentary History of the First Federal Election*. 4 vols. Madison: University of Wisconsin Press, 1976–89.

DHRC: Merrill Jensen et al., eds. *The Documentary History of the Ratification of the Constitution*. 26 vols. Madison: State Historical Society of Wisconsin, 1976–.

Farrand: Max Farrand, ed. *The Record of the Federal Convention of 1787*. 4 vols. Rev. ed. New Haven, CT: Yale University Press, 1937.

GWD: John C. Fitzpatrick, ed. *The Diaries of George Washington, 1748–1799*. 4 vols. Boston: Houghton Mifflin, 1925.

JCC: Library of Congress. *Journals of the Continental Congress, 1774–1789*. 34 vols. Washington, DC: U.S. Government Printing Office, 1904–37.

PAH: Harold C. Syrett and Jacob Cooke, eds. *The Papers of Alexander Hamilton*. 27 vols. New York: Columbia University Press, 1961–87.

PGM: Robert A. Rutland, ed. *The Papers of George Mason, 1725–1792.* 3 vols. Chapel Hill: University of North Carolina Press, 1970.

PGW, CS: W. W. Abbot et al., eds. *The Papers of George Washington: Confederation Series.* 6 vols. Charlottesville: University Press of Virginia, 1992–97.

PGW, PS: W. W. Abbot et al., eds. *The Papers of George Washington: Presidential Series.* 16 vols. Charlottesville: University Press of Virginia, 1987–.

PGW, RS: Dorothy Twohig et al., eds. *The Papers of George Washington: Retirement Series.* 4 vols. Charlottesville: University Press of Virginia, 1998–99.

PGW, RWS: W. W. Abbot et al., eds. *The Papers of George Washington: Revolutionary War Series.* 22 vols. Charlottesville: University Press of Virginia, 1985–.

PJM: Robert A. Rutland et al., eds. *The Papers of James Madison.* 17 vols. Chicago and Charlottesville: University of Chicago Press and University Press of Virginia, 1962–.

PTJ: Julian P. Boyd et al., eds. *The Papers of Thomas Jefferson.* 39 vols. Princeton, NJ: Princeton University Press, 1950–.

WBF: Jared Sparks, ed. *The Works of Benjamin Franklin.* 10 vols. Philadelphia: Childs & Peterson, 1840.

WGW: John Clement Fitzpatrick et al., eds. *The Writings of George Washington from the Original Manuscript Sources, 1745–1799.* 39 vols. Washington, DC: U.S. Government Printing Office, 1931–44.

WTJ: A. A. Lipscomb and A. E. Bergh, eds. *The Writings of Thomas Jefferson.* 20 vols. Washington, DC: Thomas Jefferson Memorial Association, 1900–1904.

Preface

1. George Washington to James Madison, Sept. 23, 1788, *PGW*, CS 6: 534.
2. George Washington to Lafayette, April 5, 1783, *WGW*, 26: 298.
3. George Washington to James Warren, Oct. 7, 1785, *PGW*, CS 3: 300.
4. George Washington to William Grayson, Aug. 22, 1785, *PGW*, CS 3: 194.
5. George Washington to David Humphreys, Dec. 26, 1786, *PGW*, CS 4: 480.

Chapter 1: Retiring Becomes Him

1. "Report of a Committee of Arrangements for the Public Audience," Dec. 22, 1783, *PTJ*, 6: 410 n. 1.
2. Dec. 23, 1783, *JCC*, 25: 837–38.
3. James McHenry to Margaret Caldwell, Dec. 23, 1783, *PTJ*, 6: 406.
4. Dec. 23, 1783, *JCC*, 25: 838.
5. Ibid., p. 839.
6. Thomas Fleming, *The Perils of Peace* (New York: Collins, 2007), 321.
7. Benjamin West, quoted in Garry Wills, *Cincinnatus: George Washington and the Enlightenment* (Garden City, NY: Doubleday, 1984), 13.
8. Jonathan Trumbull Jr., quoted in ibid.
9. E.g., "Extract of a Letter from a Gentleman in Annapolis," *New Jersey Gazette*, Jan. 6, 1784, p. 3.

10. McHenry to Caldwell, Dec. 23, 1783, *PTJ*, 6: 406.

11. "New York," *Independent Gazette* (New York), Jan. 15, 1784, p. 2.

12. Thomas Jefferson to George Washington, April 16, 1784, *PTJ*, 7: 106–7.

13. George Washington, *WGW*, 3: 305.

14. George Washington to Lafayette, Feb. 1, 1784, *PGW, CS* 1: 88.

15. April 29, 1783, *JCC*, 24: 291.

16. For example, at the time, Madison wrote that officers' petitions would "furnish new topics in favor the Impost." James Madison to Edmund Randolph, Dec. 30, 1782, *PJM*, 5: 473.

17. George Washington to Joseph Jones, March 12, 1783, *WGW*, 26: 214.

18. Along with Gates, Washington at first blamed Robert Morris but then shifted his accusation to Gouverneur Morris, who then served as Robert Morris's assistant. Compare George Washington to Alexander Hamilton, April 4, 1783, *WGW*, 26: 293, with George Washington to Alexander Hamilton, April 16, 1783, *WGW*, 26: 324. Stewart carried letters from Robert and Gouverneur Morris. See generally, Charles Rappleye, *Robert Morris: Financier of the Revolution* (New York: Simon & Schuster, 2010), 331–51; and Richard H. Kohn, "The Inside History of the Newburgh Conspiracy," *William and Mary Quarterly*, 3rd Ser., 27 (1970): 205–6.

19. James Madison, "Notes of Debates," Feb. 20, 1783, *JCC*, 25: 906. See generally, John Ferling, *The Ascent of George Washington* (New York: Bloomsbury Press, 2009), 231–33.

20. March 10, 1783, *JCC*, 24: 295–97.

21. "General Orders," March 11, 783, *WGW*, 26: 208.

22. March 12, 1783, *JCC*, 24: 299.

23. George Washington, "To the Officers of the Army," March 15, 1783, *WGW*, 26: 226–27.

24. Ibid., 222 n. 38.

25. Horatio Gates, [Minutes of Meeting of Officers], March 15, 1783, *JCC*, 24: 311.

26. George Washington to Theodorick Bland, April 4, 1783 (first letter), *WGW*, 26: 288.

27. Washington to Hamilton, April 4, 1783, *WGW*, 26: 293.

28. Ibid.

29. Washington to Hamilton, April 16, 1783, *WGW*, 26: 324.

30. Washington to Bland, April 4, 1783 (first letter), *WGW*, 26: 289. See also, Washington to Bland, April 4, 1783 (second letter), *WGW*, 26: 294.

31. Alexander Hamilton to George Washington, April 8, 1783, *PAH*, 3: 317–19. See also Alexander Hamilton to George Washington, March 25, 1783, *PAH*, 3: 306.

32. Compare Washington to Hamilton, April 16, 1783, *WGW*, 26: 324 with Hamilton to Washington, April 8, 1783, *PAH*, 3: 319.

33. In his sympathetic biography of Hamilton, Ron Chernow depicted this incident as showing "Hamilton at his most devious." Ron Chernow, *Alexander Hamilton* (New York: Penguin, 2004), 177. That Washington saw it this way, see Ferling, *Ascent of George Washington*, 239 ("Whatever Washington had thought of

Hamilton before this, he now knew the frightening and menacing lengths to which his former aide would go"); and Chernow, *Hamilton*, 177 ("Washington must have seen that Hamilton, for all his brains and daring, sometimes lacked judgment and had to be supervised carefully").

34. Washington to Hamilton, April 4, 1783, *WGW*, 26: 293.

35. Washington to Hamilton, April 16, 1783, *WGW*, 26: 324.

36. George Washington to Alexander Hamilton, March 31, 1783, *WGW*, 26: 276–77.

37. George Washington, "Sentiments on a Peace Establishment," [May 1783], *WGW*, 26: 374–98.

38. George Washington, "Circular to the States," June 8, 1783, *WGW*, 26: 483–96.

39. Ibid.

40. James Thomas Flexner, *George Washington in the American Revolution* (Boston: Little, Brown, 1967), 514.

41. George Washington, "General Orders," April 18, 1783, *WGW*, 26: 336.

42. George Washington to Marquis de Lafayette, April 5, 1783, *WGW*, 26: 298.

43. George Washington to Nathanael Greene, March 31, 1783, *WGW*, 26: 275.

44. George Washington to John Augustine Washington, June 15, 1783, *WGW*, 27: 12.

45. E.g., George Washington to William Gordon, July 8, 1783, *WGW*, 27: 49.

46. George Washington, "Farewell to the Armies of the United States," Nov. 2, 1783, *WGW*, 27: 222–27.

47. The officers' response was widely reprinted in newspapers throughout the country, including in "To His Excellency George Washington," *South-Carolina Weekly Gazette*, Dec. 19, 1783, p. 2.

48. "From Rivington's New-York Gazette," *Connecticut Journal*, Dec. 3, 1783, p. 2.

49. "New-York, December 6," *Connecticut Journal*, Dec. 17, 1783, p. 2. For a description of the display, see "New-York, Dec. 3," *Political Intelligencer*, Dec. 9, 1783, p. 2.

50. "December 10," *Massachusetts Spy*, Dec. 18, 1783, p. 3 (text of Washington's toast).

51. "New-York, December 6," *Independent New-York Gazette*, Dec. 6, 1783, p. 3; Douglas Southall Freeman, *George Washington: A Biography*, vol. 6 (New York: Scribner's, 1952), 468.

52. Chernow, *Hamilton*, 185.

53. George Washington, "To the Citizens of New Brunswick," Dec. 6, 1783, *WGW*, 26: 260.

54. George Washington, "To the Burgesses and Common Council of the Borough of Wilmington," Dec. 16, 1783, *WGW*, 26: 277.

55. "Address from a Committee of Merchants," *Freeman's Journal*, Dec. 10, 1783, p. 3.

56. John Adams to Benjamin Rush, 1790, quoted in Joseph Ellis, *Founding Brothers: The Revolutionary Generation* (New York: Knopf, 2000), 167.

57. "Annapolis," *Pennsylvania Packet*, Jan. 1, 1784, p. 3.

58. Ibid.

59. "Extract of a Letter from Annapolis," *Providence Gazette*, Jan. 17, 1784, p. 3.

60. Dec. 23, 1783, *JCC*, 25: 838.

Chapter 2: Reeling in the West

1. George Washington to Thomas Jefferson, March 3, 1784, *PGW*, CS 1: 169.

2. George Washington to Lauzun, Feb. 1, 1784, *PGW*, CS 1: 91. See also George Washington to Robert Morris, Jan. 4, 1784, *PGW*, CS 1: 11 ("this retreat from my public cares").

3. George Washington to Tankerville, Jan. 20, 1784, *PGW*, CS 1: 65.

4. For an extended discussion with references, see Edmund S. Morgan, "George Washington: The Aloof American," in Don Higginbotham, ed., *George Washington Reconsidered* (Charlottesville: University of Virginia Press, 2001), 290–91.

5. For an extended discussion with references, see Henry Wiencek, *An Imperfect God: George Washington, His Slaves, and the Creation of America* (New York: Farrar, Straus & Giroux, 2003), 92–96.

6. George Washington to Fielding Lewis Jr., Feb. 27, 1784, *PGW*, CS 1: 161.

7. George Washington to Henry Knox, Feb. 20, 1784, *PGW*, CS 1: 137–38.

8. George Washington to Chastellux, Feb. 1, 1784, *PGW*, CS 1: 85–86.

9. George Washington to Lafayette, Feb. 1, 1784, *PGW*, CS 1: 87–89.

10. George Washington to Jonathan Trumbull Jr., Jan. 5, 1784, *PGW*, CS 1: 12.

11. George Washington to Benjamin Harrison, Jan. 18, 1784, *PGW*, CS 1: 57.

12. For an extended discussion with references, see Dorothy Twohig, "'That Species of Property': Washington's Role in the Controversy over Slavery," in Higginbotham, ed., *Washington Reconsidered*, 121–25.

13. Wiencek, *Imperfect God*, 354–58. According to this account, Martha did not even free her own half sister, Ann, who served as a house slave on the plantation, but her granddaughter did so as soon as Ann passed to her and her husband after Martha died. Ibid., 84–86, 282–83. Martha's father, John Dandridge, allegedly sired Ann near the end of his life. She was about the same age as Martha's children by her first husband, Daniel Parke Custis, one of whom, the rakish John Parke "Jacky" Custis, possibly fathered a son, William Costin, with Ann (his aunt). Although born of a slave and thus part of Martha's dower property, William was never enslaved. He would have been Martha's grandson by Jacky and half nephew by Ann. Wiencek posits that Martha kept him out of bondage. Ibid., 289.

14. John Ferling, *The Ascent of George Washington* (New York: Bloomsbury, 2009), 245.

15. George Washington to Thomas Jefferson, March 29, 1784, *PGW*, CS 1: 239.

16. George Washington to Lafayette, Dec. 8, 1784, *PGW*, CS 2: 175.

17. Thomas Jefferson to Madame de Tesse, Dec. 8, 1813, *WTJ*, 10: 450.

18. For an extended discussion with references, see James Thomas Flexner, *George Washington and the New Nation (1783–1793)* (Boston: Little, Brown, 1969), 7.

19. Washington to Trumbull, *PGW*, CS 1: 413.

20. George Washington to Chastellux, June 2, 1784, *PGW*, CS 1: 413.

21. Washington to Lafayette, *PGW*, CS 2: 175.

22. George Washington to John Augustine Washington, June 30, 1784, *PGW*, CS 1: 278.

23. *GWD*, April 4, 1748, 1: 9–10.

24. George Washington, Certificate to James Rumsey, Sept. 7, 1784, *WGW*, 27: 468; George Washington to Benjamin Harrison, Oct. 10, 1784, *WGW*, 27: 480.

25. *GWD*, 2: 288.

26. George Washington to Lund Washington, Aug. 20, 1775, *PGW*, RWS 1: 335.

27. George Washington to Gilbert Simpson, Feb. 13, 1784, *PGW*, CS 1: 117.

28 *GWD*, Sept. 13, 1784, 2: 291.

29. Joel Achenbach, *The Grand Idea: George Washington's Potomac and the Race West* (New York: Simon & Schuster, 2004), 84.

30. George Washington to Thomas Freeman, Oct. 16, 1785, *PGW*, CS 3: 308.

31. *GWD*, Sept. 14, 1784, 2: 291–92.

32. George Washington to Thomas Smith, Dec. 7, 1785, *PGW*, CS 3: 438–39.

33. *GWD*, Sept. 22, 1784, 2: 297.

34. George Washington to Charles Simms, Sept. 22, 1786, *WGW*, 29: 8.

35. *GWD*, Sept. 22, 1784, 2: 298.

36. Boyd Crumrine, ed., *History of Washington County, Pennsylvania* (Philadelphia: L. H. Everts, 1882), 859.

37. George Washington to John Witherspoon, March 10, 1784, *PGW*, CS 1: 197.

38. George Washington to Jacob Read, Nov. 3, 1784, *PGW*, CS 2: 118–19.

39. *GWD*, Sept. 12, 1784, 2: 290.

40. George Washington to William Irvine, Aug. 6, 1782, *WGW*, 24: 474.

41. George Washington to Henry Knox, Dec. 5, 1784, *PGW*, CS 2: 171.

42. Thomas Freeman to George Washington, June 19, 1785, *PGW*, CS 3: 45.

43. George Washington to Benjamin Harrison, Oct. 10, 1784, *PGW*, CS 2: 92.

44. George Washington to Richard Henry Lee, June 18, 1786, *PGW*, CS 4: 118.

45. Washington to Read, *PGW*, CS 2: 121.

46. George Washington to Richard Henry Lee, March 15, 1785, *PGW*, CS 2: 437.

47. Washington to Read, *PGW*, CS 2: 119–21.

48. Ibid., 120.

49. George Washington to Hugh Williamson, March 15, 1785, *PGW*, CS 2: 400.

50. Washington to Lee, *PGW*, CS 4: 118. Washington observed that closing the river was against Spain's best interests in Washington to Lee, *PGW*, CS 2: 438.

51. Thomas Jefferson to George Washington, *PTJ*, 7: 26–27.

52. George Washington to Thomas Jefferson, *PGW*, CS 1: 237–39.

53. *GWD*, Sept. 25, 1784, 2: 307.

54. Ibid., 306.

55. Ibid., 306–7.

56. *GWD*, Oct. 2, 1784, 2: 316.

57. *GWD*, Oct. 4, 1784, 2: 317–18, 325.

58. "Editorial Note," *PGW*, CS 2: 86.

59. Washington to Harrison, *PGW*, CS 2: 92.

60. Washington to Jefferson, *PGW*, CS 1: 239.

61. Washington to Harrison, *PGW*, CS 2: 95.

62. George Washington to George Plater, Oct. 24, 1784, *PGW*, CS 2: 109; Washington to Read, *PGW*, CS 2: 122.

63. "Alexandria, Nov. 2, 1784," *Virginia Journal*, Nov. 4, 1784, p. 2.

64. "Alexandria, Nov. 25," *Virginia Journal*, Nov. 25, 1784, p. 2.

65. George Washington to James Madison, Dec. 3, 1784, *PGW*, CS 2: 166. For an insightful analysis of Washington's view of self-interest as a key motivating force, see Morgan, "George Washington," 289–91, 294–302. Along with other evidence, Morgan quotes Washington's observation about his troops during the American Revolution: "To expect, among such People, as compose the bulk of an Army, that they are influenced by any other principles than those of Interest, is to look for what never did, and I fear never will happen." Ibid., 296.

66. Ibid.

67. George Washington to Lafayette, Feb. 15, 1785, *PGW*, CS 2: 366.

68 George Washington to Robert Morris, Feb. 1, 1785, *PGW*, CS 2: 315.

69. George Washington to Lafayette, July 25, 1785, *PGW*, CS 3: 152.

70. George Washington to Benjamin Franklin, Sept. 26, 1785, *PGW*, CS 3: 275.

71. George Pointer, "Petition of Captain George Pointer to President and Director of the Chesapeake and Ohio Canal," Sept. 5, 1829, quoted in Robert J. Kapsch, *The Potomac Canal: George Washington and the Waterway West* (Morgantown: University of West Virginia Press, 2007), 224.

72. *GWD*, Sept. 22, 1785, 2: 415.

73. Robert Hunter Jr., *Quebec to Carolina in 1785–1786: Being a Travel Diary and Observations of a Young Merchant of London* (San Marino, CA: Huntington Library, 1943), 193.

74. George Mason and Alexander Henderson to Speaker of the House of Delegates, March 28, 1785, *PGM*, 2: 815.

75. Achenbach, *The Grand Idea*, 152.

76. George Washington to James Madison, Nov. 30, 1785, *PGW*, CS 3: 420.

77. Annapolis Convention, "Address of the Annapolis Convention," Sept. 14, 1786, *PAH*, 3: 687.

78. James Madison to Thomas Jefferson, Aug. 12, 1786, *PTJ*, 10: 233.

79. Alexander Hamilton to James Duane, Sept. 3, 1780, *PAH*, 2: 401–6.

80. "Address," *PAH*, 3: 689.

Chapter 3: To Go or Not to Go

1. Thomas Jefferson to John Adams, June 27, 1813, in Thomas Jefferson Randolph, ed., *Memoir of Thomas Jefferson* (Charlottesville: Carr, 1829), 4: 209.

2. John Jay to Thomas Jefferson, Oct. 27, 1786, *PTJ*, 10: 489.

3. John Jay to George Washington, March 16, 1786, *PGW*, CS 3: 601–2.

4. See George Washington to Lafayette, Nov. 8, 1785, *PGW*, CS 3: 345; George Washington to Rochambeau, Dec. 1, 1785, *PGW*, CS 3: 428.

5. George Washington to John Jay, May 18, 1786, *PGW*, CS 4: 55–56.

6. John Jay to George Washington, June 27, 1786, *PGW*, CS 4: 131.

7. Ibid.

8. George Washington to John Jay, Aug. 15, 1786, *PGW*, CS 4: 213.

9. Ray Raphael, *Constitutional Myths: What We Get Wrong and How to Get It Right* (New York: New Press, 2013), 21.

10. For an analysis of the value of Continentals, see E. James Ferguson, *The Power of the Purse* (Chapel Hill: University of North Carolina Press, 1961), 51–52.

11. Benjamin Franklin to M. Le Roy, Nov. 13, 1789, *WBF*, 10: 410.

12. Jay to Washington, June 27, 1786, *PGW*, CS 4: 131–32.

13. Washington to Jay, Aug. 15, 1786, *PGW*, CS 4: 213.

14. George Washington to George William Fairfax, June 30, 1786, *PGW*, CS 4: 137.

15. James Madison, "Notes for Speech Opposing Paper Money," Nov. 1, 1786, *PJM*, 9: 159.

16. James Madison to Thomas Jefferson, Aug. 12, 1786, *PJM*, 9: 94–95.

17. Ibid., 95.

18. George Washington to Theodorick Bland, Aug. 15, 1786, *PGW*, CS 4: 211.

19. Washington to Jay, Aug. 15, 1786, *PGW*, CS 4: 213.

20. James Madison to James Monroe, April 9, 1786, *PJM*, 9: 25.

21. Washington to Jay, Aug. 15, 1786, *PGW*, CS 4: 212–13.

22. "America," *Pennsylvania Packet*, Sept. 23, 1786, p. 2.

23. Woody Holton, *Unruly Americans and the Origins of the Constitution* (New York: Hill & Wang, 2007), 145–46.

24. George Washington to David Humphreys, Oct. 22, 1786, *PGW*, CS 4: 297.

25. James Madison to James Monroe, May 29, 1785, *PJM*, 8: 285.

26. Henry Lee Jr. to George Washington, Oct. 17, 1786, *PGW*, CS 4: 295.

27. George Washington to Henry Lee Jr., Oct. 31, 1786, *PGW*, CS 4: 319.

28. Henry Knox to George Washington, Oct. 23, 1786, *PGW*, CS 4: 300–301.

29. Henry Knox to George Washington, Dec. 17, 1786, *PGW*, CS 4: 460.

30. George Washington to Henry Knox, Dec. 26, 1786, *PGW*, CS 4: 481–82.

31. Washington to Lee, Oct. 31, 1786, *PGW*, CS 4: 318–19.

32. George Washington to David Humphreys, Dec. 26, 1786, *PGW*, CS 4: 478.

33. Washington to Knox, Dec. 26, 1786, *PGW*, CS 4: 481.

34. George Washington to James Madison, Nov. 5, 1786, *PGW*, CS 4: 331.

35. George Washington to Lafayette, March 25, 1787, *PGW*, CS 5: 106.

36. "Bill Providing for Delegates to the Convention of 1787," Nov. 6, 1786, *PJM*, 9: 163.

37. James Madison to George Washington, Nov. 8, 1786, *PJM*, 9: 166.

38. George Washington to James Madison, Nov. 18, 1786, *PGW*, CS 4: 382–83.

39. Edmund Randolph to George Washington, Dec. 6, 1786, *PGW*, CS 4: 445.

40. James Madison to George Washington, Dec. 7, 1786, *PJM*, 9: 199.

41. George Washington to Edmund Randolph, Dec. 21, 1786, *PGW*, CS 4: 471–72.

42. George Washington to James Madison, Dec. 16, 1786, *PGW*, CS 4: 458.

43. Edmund Randolph to George Washington, Jan. 4, 1787, *PGW*, CS 4: 501.

44. James Madison to George Washington, Dec. 24, 1786, *PJM*, 9: 224.

45. "Philadelphia, December 27," *Connecticut Courant*, Jan. 8, 1787, p. 3 (reprint from Dec. 27, 1786, *Philadelphia Herald*).

46. John Jay to George Washington, Jan. 7, 1787, *PGW*, CS 4: 503–4.

47. Resolution, Feb. 21, 1787, *JCC*, 32: 74.

48. David Humphreys to George Washington, Jan. 20, 1787, *PGW*, CS 4: 528–29; Henry Knox to George Washington, Jan. 14, 1787, *PGW*, CS 4: 520; Jay to Washington, Jan. 7, 1787, *PGW*, CS 4: 503.

49. Jay to Washington, Jan. 7, 1787, *PGW*, CS 4: 502; Knox to Washington, Jan. 14, 1787, *PGW*, CS 4: 520; Humphreys to Washington, Jan. 20, 1787, *PGW*, CS 4: 527.

50. Jay to Washington, Jan. 7, 1787, *PGW*, CS 4: 503; Knox to Washington, Jan. 14, 1787, *PGW*, CS 4: 522; Humphreys to Washington, Jan. 20, 1787, *PGW*, CS 4: 527.

51. Humphreys to Washington, Jan. 20, 1787, *PGW*, CS 4: 527.

52. George Washington to Henry Knox, Feb. 3, 1787, *PGW*, CS 5: 8 (emphasis added); George Washington to John Jay, March 10, 1787, *PGW*, CS 5: 80; George Washington to David Humphreys, March 8, 1787, *PGW*, CS 5: 72–73.

53. Washington to Jay, March 10, 1787, *PGW*, CS 5: 79–80; Washington to Knox, Feb. 3, 1787, *PGW*, CS 5: 9.

54. Henry Knox to George Washington, April 19, 1787, *PGW*, CS 5: 96.

55. George Washington to Edmund Randolph, March 28, 1787, *PGW*, CS 5: 113.

56. George Washington to Henry Knox, Jan. 5, 1785, *PGW*, CS 2: 253. Speaking generally about the subject, near the end of his life and perhaps reflecting on a lifetime of ailments, Washington observed that good health was "among (if not the most) precious gift of Heaven," and added that without it "we are but little capable of business." George Washington to James Anderson, Sept. 16, 1799, *PGW*, RS 4: 305.

57. See *GWD*, Dec. 22, 1786, 3: 149; *GWD*, Dec. 26, 1786, 3: 150; *GWD*, Feb. 9, 1787, 3: 166. For further discussion of Washington's use of transplanted teeth, see Mary V. Thompson, "They Work Only from Sun to Sun: Slavery at George Washington's Mount Vernon," publication pending; Henry Wiencek, *An Imperfect God: George Washington, His Slaves, and the Creation of America* (New York: Farrar, Straus & Giroux, 2003), 112–13.

58. George Washington to Henry Knox, April 2, 1787, *PGW*, CS 5: 119.

59. By this point, Washington's concerns about the meeting of the Society of the Cincinnati had abated. In his letter to Knox, who was a founder and leader of the organization, Washington added that he would even try to meet with some of his friends among the Cincinnati while in Philadelphia and promote the cause of a new national government. Ibid.

60. George Washington to James Madison, March 31, 1787, *PGW*, CS 5: 115–16.

61. George Washington, "Notes on the Sentiments on the Government of John Jay, Henry Knox, and James Madison," April 1787, *PGW*, CS 5: 163–66.

62. James Madison to George Washington, April 16, 1787, *PJM*, 9: 383.

63. Ibid., 383–84.

64. James Madison, "Vices of the Political Systems of the United States," April 1787, *PJM*, 9: 355–57.

65. Madison to Washington, April 16, 1787, *PJM*, 9: 384.

66. George Washington to Edmund Randolph, April 9, 1787, *PGW*, CS 5: 137.

67. Benjamin Franklin to George Washington, April 3, 1787, *PGW*, CS 5: 122.

68. Henry Knox to George Washington, April 9, 1787, *PGW*, CS 5: 134.

69. George Washington to Mary Ball Washington, Feb. 15, 1787, *PGW*, CS 5: 36.

70. George Washington to Robert Morris, May 5, 1787, *PGW*, CS 5: 171.

Chapter 4: The Center Holds

1. George Washington to Robert Morris, May 5, 1787, *PGW*, CS 5: 171.

2. George Washington to Lund Washington, Aug. 15, 1778, *WGW*, 12: 327.

3. Ibid.

4. E.g., George Washington to Henry Knox, April 2, 1787, *PGW*, CS 5: 119; George Washington to James Madison, March 31, 1787, *PGW*, CS 5: 116.

5. "Richmond, April 11," *Connecticut Journal*, May 2, 1787, p. 3.

6. "On the Coming of the American Fabius to the Federal Convention," *Providence Gazette*, May 5, 1787, p. 3.

7. "Portsmouth, May 19," *New Hampshire Gazette*, May 19, 1897, p. 3.

8. "Philadelphia, May 11," *Maryland Chronicle*, May 30, 1787, p. 2.

9. Z, "For the Freeman's Journal," *Freeman's Journal*, May 16, 1787, p. 3.

10. E.g., Rustick, "Mr. Oswald," *Independent Gazetteer*, May 31, 1787, p. 3. This essay also urged "that the Congress, as the supreme head, be empowered to nominate and appoint the governor in each respective state, which governors being subject to the control of Congress, no law can be enacted in any state but by the governor's approbation and signature, and if any law should be proposed by any state contrary to the general interest of the union, the governor of course will put his negative upon it."

11. Harrington, "For the Independent Gazetteer," *Independent Gazetteer*, May 30, 1787, p. 2.

12. Patrick Henry, in Hugh Blair Grigsby, *History of the Virginia Federal Convention of 1788* (Richmond: Virginia Historical Society, 1890), 1: 32 n. 36. This is the earliest documented source for this widely quoted but possibly apocryphal comment.

13. "A View of the Federal Government," *American Museum* 1 (1787): 295, 299.

14. Jackson had written Washington earlier about the post. William Jackson to George Washington, April 20, 1787, *PGW*, CS 5: 150–51.

15. "Philadelphia, May 16," *Philadelphia Herald*, May 16, 1787, p. 3.

16. "Philadelphia, May 12," *Philadelphia Herald*, May 12, 1787, p. 3.

17. "On the Meeting of the Grand Convention," *Independent Gazette*, May 19, 1787, p. 3.

18. Richard Beeman, *Plain, Honest Men: The Making of the Constitution* (New York: Random House, 2009), 35–36.

19. Although this story has been widely told for nearly two centuries, Morris's best biographer, James J. Kirschke, argues that it is apocryphal. James J. Kirschke, *Gouverneur Morris: Author, Statesman, and Man of the World* (New York: St. Martin's Press, 2005), 185–86.

20. L. H. Butterfield et al., eds., *Diary and Autobiography of John Adams*, vol. 4 (Cambridge, MA: Belknap Press, 1961), 81 (April 29, 1778).

21. "Rules and Regulations of the Society for Political Enquiries," *Pennsylvania Packet*, April 4, 1787, pp. 2–3.

22. *GWD*, May 14, 1787, 3: 216.

23. George Washington to George Augustine Washington, May 17, 1787, *PGW*, CS 5: 189.

24. Benjamin Franklin to Thomas Jordan, May 18, 1787, *WBF*, 10: 304.

25. George Washington, "Notes on the Sentiments on the Government of John Jay, Henry Knox, and James Madison," April 1787, *PGW*, CS 5: 163–66.

26. George Mason to George Mason Jr., May 20, 1787, *PGM*, 3: 880. At one point in this letter when discussing a different matter, Mason noted when Washington did not participate with the other Virginia delegates. Ibid., 881.

27. Beeman, *Plain, Honest Men*, 54.

28. Mason to Mason, *PGM*, 3: 880.

29. Ibid., 880–81; George Mason to Richard Henry Lee, May 15, 1787, *PGM*, 3: 878–79.

30. Virginia Plan, paragraph 5, Farrand, May 29, 1787, 1: 20.

31. George Mason to Arthur Lee, May 21, 1787, *PGM*, 3: 882.

32. George Washington to Arthur Lee, May 20, 1787, *PGW*, CS 5: 191.

33. George Washington to George Augustine Washington, May 17, 1787, *PGW*, CS 5: 189.

34. Mason to Mason, *PGM*, 3: 881.

35. "Philadelphia, May 30," *Pennsylvania Herald*, May 31, 1787, p. 3.

36. *GWD*, May 27, 1787, 3: 219. Washington regularly attended William White's church in Philadelphia during both his service in the Continental Congress from 1774 to 1775 and as President after the seat of government moved to Philadelphia. Of these periods, White wrote, "General Washington never received the communion, in the churches at which I am parochial minister. Mrs. Washington was a habitual communicant." William White to Bird Wilson, Aug. 15, 1835, in Wilson, *Memoir of Wright*, 197.

37. George Washington to Lafayette, Aug. 15, 1787, *PGW*, CS 5: 295.

38. Farrand, May 25, 1787, 1: 3–6.

39. See Farrand, May 25, 1787, 1: 4 (Madison's Notes), 6 (Yates's Notes), and 3: 173 (Luther Martin's "Genuine Information").

40. George Mason to George Mason Jr., May 27, 1787, *PGM*, 3. 001.

41. William Pierce, "Character Sketches of Delegates to the Federal Convention," Farrand, 3: 91.

42. Franklin to Jordan, May 18, 1787, *WBF*, 10: 304.

43. Farrand, May 28, 1787, 1: 9.

44. Ibid., 15.

45. Jared Sparks, *Journal*, April 19, 1830, Farrand, 3: 479 (Sparks's notes on visit to 46 Madison).

46. *GWD*, May 28, 1787, 3: 220.

47. William Pierce, "Anecdote," in Farrand, 3: 86–87.

48. Among the other delegates taking notes, Robert Yates kept the most detailed ones. Luther Martin also compiled his own account of key events. Some of these notes and accounts, most notably those by Yates and Martin, became public after the Convention ended.

49. John Adams to James Warren, July 15, 1776, *Warren-Adams Letters* (Boston: Massachusetts Historical Society, 1917), 1: 260.

50. Farrand, May 29, 1787, 1: 18.

51. Ibid., 18–27 (notes of Madison, Yates, and Paterson).

52. Ibid., 23.

53. George Washington to Thomas Jefferson, May 30, 1787, *PGW*, CS 5: 208.

54. Christopher Collier, *Roger Sherman's Connecticut: Yankee Politics and the American Revolution* (Middletown, CT: Wesleyan University Press, 1971), 129 (first Adams quote); John Adams to Abigail Adams, March 16, 1777, in Charles Francis Adams, ed., *Familiar Letters of John Adams and His Wife Abigail Adams During the Revolution* (Boston: Riverside Press, 1876), 251; Pierce, "Character Sketches," Farrand, 3: 89.

55. Jeremiah Wadsworth to Rufus King, June 3, 1787, Farrand, 3: 34.

56. Farrand, May 30, 1787, 1: 30–41 (extracted from journals or notes of Madison, Yates, and McHenry, with emphasis from Madison's notes).

57. Farrand, May 30, 1787, 1: 33–34, 42–43 (notes of Madison and McHenry).

58. Ibid., 34, 43 (notes of Madison and McHenry).

59. George Washington to David Stuart, July 1, 1787, *PGW*, CS 5: 240. Stuart was the second husband of Washington's stepson's widow and a member of the Virginia House of Delegates.

60. Farrand, May 30, 1787, 1: 34–35, 42–44 (notes of Madison and McHenry).

61. Ibid., 35.

62. Farrand, May 29, 1787, 1: 21 (Virginia Plan); Farrand, May 31, 1787, 1: 54 (Madison); Farrand, July 18, 1787, 2: 46 (Gorham).

63. Farrand, May 29, 1787, 1: 21 (Madison's text of Virginia Plan).

64. Farrand, May 31, 1787, 1: 53.

65. George Washington to Alexander Hamilton, July 10, 1787, *PGW*, CS 5: 257.

66. Farrand, June 18–19, 1787, 1: 287–88, 323.

67. Farrand, June 20, 1787, 1: 334.

68.   Randolph's original draft language and subsequent committee revisions as preserved among Wilson's papers are reprinted in Farrand, 2: 129–75.

69.   James Madison to Thomas Jefferson, Sept. 6, 1787, *PJM*, 10: 163–64 (writing about the Constitution generally).

70.   James Madison, "Number 39," in Alexander Hamilton, James Madison, and John Jay, *The Federalist* (Indianapolis: Liberty Fund, 2002), p. 197.

71.   George Washington to Lafayette, Aug. 15, 1787, *PGW*, CS 5: 296.

Chapter 5: In His Image

1.   E.g., Richard Beeman, *Plain, Honest Men: The Making of the Constitution* (New York: Random House, 2009), 92. Beeman here commented, "As one of America's most effective spokesmen for the continuing sovereignty of the states, Henry would have been James Madison's worst nightmare."

2.   "Federal Convention," *Massachusetts Centinel*, June 20, 1787, vol. 7, p. 107.

3.   "Philadelphia, June 16," *Middlesex (Conn.) Gazette*, June 25, 1787, p. 2.

4.   E.g., on Rhode Island, see "Philadelphia, June 9," *New Hampshire Gazette*, June 23, 1787, p. 3; on George III's son, see "From the Virginia Independent Chronicle," *Independent Gazette*, Aug. 1, 1787, p. 3; and "Philadelphia, August 4," *Connecticut Journal*, Aug. 29, 1787, p. 1.

5.   "Philadelphia, June 2," *Philadelphia Evening Herald*, June 2, 1787, p. 3.

6.   Thomas Jefferson to John Adams, Aug. 30, 1787, *PTJ*, 12: 69.

7.   Votes at the Convention were recorded by state rather than by delegate, so it is not usually possible to determine how or if individual delegates voted on various motions and resolutions. In his detailed analysis of Washington's role at the Convention, political scientist Glenn A. Phelps concluded that Washington "very likely voted on every substantive issue before the convention." Glenn A. Phelps, *George Washington and American Constitutionalism* (Lawrence: University Press of Kansas, 1993), 102.

8.   For example, beyond his public advocacy of it prior to the Convention, Washington's support for giving broad taxing authority to the general government appeared in his vote at the Convention against a ban on taxing exports. Over the objections of Madison and other big-state nationalists, the ban passed with Virginia joining other export-rich planation states in supporting it. Within the five-member Virginia delegation, however, Washington joined Madison in voting against it. Farrand, Aug. 21, 1787, 2: 364.

9.   For a discussion of these salons focused on the 1790s, see Susan Branson, *These Fiery Frenchified Dames: Women and Political Culture in Early National Philadelphia* (Philadelphia: University of Pennsylvania Press, 2001), 125–42. About Elizabeth Powel, Anne Bingham, and Washington's host Mary Morris during the Convention, Branson writes, "Morris, Powell, and Bingham had already established themselves as intimates of Washington and many prominent Federalists during the Convention in the summer of 1787" (p. 133).

10.   E.g., *GWD*, June 28, 1787, 3: 225; *GWD*, Aug. 14, 1787, 3: 232.

11.   *GWD*, May 23, 1787, 3: 218.

12. David W. Maxey, *A Portrait of Elizabeth Willing Powel* (Philadelphia. American Philosophical Society, 2006), 26–30 (including quoted material).

13. *GWD*, May 21, 1787, 3: 218.

14. See Beeman, *Plain, Honest Men*, xx.

15. Maxey, *Portrait of Powel*, 30 (Franklin quote to Powel). For Franklin's preference for a less aristocratic senate (or no senate at all) and less monarchical president than many other delegates, see Edmund S. Morgan, *Benjamin Franklin* (New Haven, CT: Yale University Press, 2002), 310–12.

16. Jack N. Rakove, *Original Meanings: Politics and Ideas in the Making of the Constitution* (New York: Knopf, 1997), 14.

17. Pierce Butler to Weedon Butler, May 5, 1788, Farrand, 3: 302.

18. Virginia Plan, Resolutions 7 and 8, Farrand, May 29 and June 1–2, 1787, 1: 21, 63, 94.

19. See Max Farrand, *The Fathers of the Constitution: A Chronicle of the Establishment of the Union* (New Haven, CT: Yale University Press, 1921), 111 ("Washington was the great man of this day and the members not only respected and admired him; some of them were actually afraid of him").

20. Farrand, June 1, 1787, 1: 65.

21. Farrand, June 4, 1787, 1: 103.

22. The Declaration of Independence, para. 2 (U.S. 1776).

23. George Washington to Lafayette, Nov. 8, 1785, *PGW*, CS 3: 345. In this letter, Washington accepted that Franklin acted with "the best designs . . . to reconcile the jarring interests of the State," but doubted if it would be "to the satisfaction of both parties."

24. Farrand, June 1, 1787, 1: 66; Farrand, June 2, 1787, 1: 88.

25. Farrand, June 4, 1787, 1: 113. Randolph agreed that the three members of the Executive should represent different sections of the country. Farrand, June 2, 1787, 1: 65–66.

26. Farrand, June 2, 1787, 1: 90. Echoing this argument, Wilson stated about a triumvirate executive, "Among three equal members, he foresaw nothing but uncontrouled, continued, & violent animosities; which would not only interrupt the public administration; but diffuse their poison thro' the other branches of Govt." Farrand, June 4, 1787, 1: 96.

27. Farrand, June 1, 1787, 1: 65–66, 70, 73. Making a similar comment, Rutledge at this point added, "A single man would feel the greatest responsibility and administer the public affairs best." Ibid., 65.

28. Farrand, June 4, 1787, 1: 97.

29. Farrand, June 2, 1787, 1: 83, 86. On this day, Randolph again warned of a single President as being "the fetus of a Monarchy." Ibid., 92.

30. Butler to Butler, Farrand, 3: 302.

31. Farrand, June 4, 1787, 1: 97.

32. It was Madison who moved and Wilson who seconded replacing the Virginia Plan's broad language that the future presidency "ought to enjoy the Executive rights vested in Congress by the Confederation" with language naming

certain specific executive powers in a form suggesting that the delegates would later revisit the list to add other powers. The motion passed without dissent. Farrand, June 1, 1787, 1: 67. The Virginia Plan would have lodged an absolute power to veto legislation in a council of revision composed of the executive and members of the national judiciary. After considerable debate on the proper nature and extent of the veto, the delegates approved by a margin of eight to two (with Virginia voting yes) a much-amended motion giving "the Executive alone without the Judiciary the revisionary control on the laws unless overruled by 2/3 of each branch" or house of Congress. Farrand, June 4, 1787, 1: 104. At the urging of the big-state national-ists who favored a strong executive, the Convention at one point raised the frac-tion of both houses needed to override a presidential veto to three-fourths. During its final week, however, the Convention restored the two-thirds requirement. At that point, a divided Virginia delegation was one of four states voting to retain the three-fourths fraction. Skeptical of a powerful presidency, Mason and Randolph supported the two-thirds fraction; Washington, Madison, and Blair voted to retain the three-fourths fraction and carried Virginia (but not the Convention) with them. Farrand, Sept. 12, 1787, 2: 587. It was one of the few clear defeats for Washington on a core matter relating to the executive.

33.   Farrand, June 1, 1787, 1: 65–66. At this point in the debate, Wilson depicted powers of "war and peace" as legislative. Speaking about these and other possible executive powers, Madison here reportedly added, "Executive powers ex vi termini, do not include the Rights of war & peace &c. but the powers sh[oul]d be confined and defined—if large we shall have the Evils of elective Monarchy." Ibid., at 70. Under British and Continental legal theory, however, John Locke, Montesquieu, and William Blackstone presented powers of war and peace as effectively a royal prerogative.

34.   Farrand, June 13, 1787, 1: 226.

35.   Farrand, July 26, 1787, 2: 119.

36.   Ibid., 121. Washington and Madison cast their no votes against the whole resolution on the executive as it then stood. The dispute likely focused on the part of that resolution relating to the executive being chosen by Congress because only minutes earlier Virginia had voted in favor of Mason's motion "that the Executive be appointed for seven years, & be ineligible a 2d. time" without an indication in Madison's notes that Washington objected. Farrand, July 26, 1787, 2: 220. Logically, given his age and attachment to Mount Vernon, Washington could be happy with a single seven-year term as President while still wanting the independence of not hav-ing been chosen by Congress. By this point, Madison seemed more concerned with legislative selection than the term limit. In his analysis of the episode, however, Phelps argues that Washington here was voting against a one-term limit but Phelps reaches that conclusion on the erroneous premise that the Convention had *already* approved having an electoral college rather than Congress choosing the executive. Phelps, *Washington and Constitutionalism*, 105–6. As discussed below, most delegates opposed the term limit after the Convention in September approved having inde-pendent electors choose the President.

37. Farrand, June 1, 1787, 1; 65. The following day, Sherman added, "The National Legislature should have power to remove the Executive at pleasure." Farrand, June 2, 1787, 1: 85.

38. Farrand, Sept. 4, 1787, 2: 501.

39. *GWD*, June 10, 1787, 3: 222.

40. George Washington to George Augustine Washington, June 15, 1787, *PGW*, CS 5: 224.

41. George Washington to George Augustine Washington, June 3, 1787, *PGW*, CS 5: 217.

42. Farrand, June 9, 1787, 1: 179.

43. Ibid.

44. Farrand, June 30, 1781, 1: 483.

45. Ibid., 502.

46. Ibid., 490.

47. Ibid., 488.

48. Ibid., 482, 494.

49. Ibid., 492.

50. Ibid., 499.

51. Jared Sparks, *Life of Gouverneur Morris* (Boston: Gray & Bowie, 1832), 1: 283.

52. Alexander Hamilton to George Washington, July 3, 1787, *PAH*, 4: 224.

53. George Washington to Alexander Hamilton, July 10, 1787, *PGW*, CS 5: 257.

54. Farrand, July 2, 1787, 1: 510–16, 519.

55. George Washington to David Stuart, July 1, 1787, *PGW*, CS 5: 240. Stuart was the second husband of Washington's stepson's widow and a member of the Virginia House of Delegates.

56. "Philadelphia, July 4," *Pennsylvania Evening Herald*, July 4, 1787, p. 3; "The Twelfth Anniversary," *Independent Gazette*, July 6, 1787, p. 3; "Philadelphia, July 6," *Pennsylvania Packet*, July 6, 1787, p. 3; "Philadelphia, July 7," *Pennsylvania Evening Herald*, July 7, 1787, p. 3; and see generally Beeman, *Plain, Honest Men*, 190–93.

57. "Trenton, July 10," *Independent Gazetteer*, July 14, 2787, p. 2; "New York, July 12," *Pennsylvania Packet*, July 19, 2787, p. 2; "Extract from a Letter from Lancaster," *Independent Gazetteer*, July 17, 2787, p. 3; "Extract from a Letter from Boston," *Independent Gazetteer*, July 6, 1787, p. 3.

58. C. W. Peale, "The Subscriber," *Pennsylvania Packet*, Aug. 20, 1787, p. 3; "A Messotinto Print," *Pennsylvania Packet*, Sept. 18, 1787, p. 3.

59. Farrand, July 5, 1787, 1: 525–27.

60. Farrand, Aug. 8, 1787, 2: 224–25; Farrand, Aug. 13, 1787, 2: 274, 280.

61. Farrand, Sept. 10, 1787, 2: 568.

62. Farrand, June 11, 1787, 1: 192.

63. Ibid., 201.

64. Ibid., 193. They borrowed this formula from a 1783 proposal passed by Congress but never ratified by the states for equitably allocating requisitions among the states.

65. Ibid., 208.

66. For a clear expression of this distinction by Morris, see his comments at Farrand, July 13, 1787, 1: 604.

67. Farrand, July 9, 1787, 1: 561.

68. Farrand, July 11, 1787, 1: 587.

69. Farrand, July 13, 1787, 1: 605.

70. Farrand, July 9, 1787, 1: 560.

71. Beeman, *Plain, Honest Men*, 207 ("General Washington—recognizing that the report from Morris's committee had managed to stir up more unease among the delegates—used his authority as presiding officer to appoint another committee"). In explaining what he meant in this sentence by "appoint," Richard Beeman said that the better word might be "create"—by which he meant, Washington created the committee, he did not necessarily name its members. That was likely done by ballot of the delegates.

72. Farrand, Sept. 17, 1787, 2: 644. In his analysis of Washington's decision to speak on this relatively minor point after he had refrained from speaking substantively on other matters, Glenn Phelps agrees that it "reveals the pragmatic side of [Washington's] constitutional thinking." Phelps paints the amendment as a minor concession to small-scale republicans calculated to help secure ratification. Phelps, *Washington and Constitutionalism*, 101.

73. George Washington to Henry Knox, Aug. 19, 1787, *PGW*, CS 5: 297.

74. Farrand, Aug. 21–22, 1787, 2: 364, 371, 373.

75. Paul Finkelman, "Slavery and the Constitutional Convention: Making a Covenant with Death," in Richard Beeman et al., *Beyond Confederation: Origins of the Constitution and American National Identity* (Chapel Hill: University of North Carolina Press, 1987), 221.

76. The northeastern states, which went along with this restriction, participated in the slave trade by being home to many of the shippers and merchants transporting enslaved Africans to the South. Virginia, which by that point could profit from the sale of slaves born on plantations in the state, resisted it. For a succinct analysis of this aspect of Convention politics, see Ray Raphael, *Constitutional Myths: What We Get Wrong and How to Get It Right* (New York: New Press, 2013), 48–49.

77. Historian of the Convention Richard Beeman makes this supposition in Beeman, *Plain, Honest Men*, 333.

78. Fritz Hirschfeld, *George Washington and Slavery: A Documentary History* (Columbia: University of Missouri Press, 1997), 173.

79. On this point, Hirschfeld concluded, "Whatever Washington may have thought of the slavery issue being debated and decided at the federal convention, it is interesting to note that the proslavery views that found their way into the Constitution were (coincidentally or not) those most compatible with Washington's own values and beliefs." Ibid., 177. Accord, Henry Wiencek, *An Imperfect God: George Washington, His Slaves, and the Creation of America* (New York: Farrar, Straus & Giroux, 2003), 269–70.

80. Farrand, July 23, 1787, 2: 94.

81. Farrand, Aug. 13, 1787, 2: 274, 278.

82. Farrand, June 18–19, 1787, 1: 288–89.

83. Farrand, July 23, 1787, 2: 94–95. Mirroring this debate, on August 14 the delegates considered whether senators should receive their pay from their state governments (as under the Articles of Confederation) or from the general government. Predictably, Martin maintained that "as the Senate is to represent the States, the members of it ought to be paid by the States." Butler agreed that, given their long terms, senators "will lose sight of their Constituents unless dependent on them for their support." Madison countered, however, that making senators "constantly dependent on the [State] Legislatures" would prevent them from being "really independ[en]t for six years," which was the purpose of giving them long terms. Others agreed. "The States can now say," Carroll now noted, "if you do not comply with our wishes, we will starve you: if you do we will reward you. The new Gov[ernmen]t in this form was nothing more than a second edition of the [Confederation] Congress." The delegations voted nine to two for paying Congress from the national treasury. Farrand, Aug. 14, 1787, 290–92.

84. George Washington to John Jay, Sept. 2, 1787, *PGW*, CS 5: 307.

85. *GWD*, July 31, 1787, 3: 230.

86. George Washington to Elizabeth Powel, July 30, 1787, *PGW*, CS 5: 280.

87. Farrand, Aug. 13, 1787, 2: 278.

88. Farrand, Aug. 6, 1787, 2: 185.

89. From the Convention's outset, there was a clear sense that Congress should hold power over war and peace. See Farrand, June 1, 1787, 1: 66–70. The Committee of Detail's draft constitution assigned Congress the power to make war and the Senate the power to draft treaties, including peace treaties. On August 17, with little debate, the Convention changed the wording of this congressional power: "To make war" became "To declare war." Apparently the delegates saw this as a clarifying amendment. Madison and Gerry proposed it in response to Charles Pinckney's concern that vesting the power of making war in Congress might cause too much delay. Madison and Gerry stated that their change would leave "to the Executive the power to repel sudden attacks," which apparently addressed Pinckney's concern. Sherman immediately added, "The Executive should be able to repel and not to commence war." In support of the change, Mason said that he "was against giving the power of war to the Executive, because [he was] not safely to be trusted with it." In a similar vein, King noted "that '*make*' war might be understood to 'conduct' it which was an Executive function." Farrand, Aug. 17, 1787, 2: 318–19.

90. In addition to the shift of duties from the Senate to the presidency, which are discussed below, during the final deliberations the power to adjudicate disputes between states passed from the Senate to the Supreme Court while the duty to try impeachments passed from the Supreme Court to the Senate. See Farrand, Aug. 24, 1787, 2: 401; Farrand, Aug. 27, 1787, 2: 427; Farrand, Sept. 4, 1787, 2: 493; and Farrand, Sept. 8, 1787, 2: 554.

91. Farrand, Aug. 8, 1787, 2: 224.

92. Farrand, Aug. 13, 1787, 2: 278.

93. On June 30, for example, Madison complained, "The plan in its present shape makes the Senate absolutely dependent on the States. The Senate there-

fore is only another edition of [the Confederation] Cong[res]s. He knew the faults of that Body & had used a bold language ag[ain]st it." Farrand, June 30, 1787, 1: 491.

94. Farrand, Aug. 23, 1787, 2: 392.

95. Ibid., 389.

96. Farrand, Sept. 4, 1787, 2: 493–95. For early advocacy of this approach, see Farrand, July 18, 1787, 2: 41–44.

97. Farrand, Sept. 7, 1787, 2: 539.

98. Farrand, Sept. 4, 1787, 2: 493. With the added language Congress arguably gained the power to tax for the general welfare; without it, Congress arguably could only tax to further purposes otherwise authorized under the Constitution. A further example of the nationalists' principled commitment to a broad taxing power involved a late August dispute over exports. The Committee of Detail's draft constitution included a clause barring Congress from taxing exports. The clause was supported by the export-rich plantation states of the South. When the full Convention debated this clause, Madison, Wilson, and Gouverneur Morris spoke against it even though Virginia and perhaps Pennsylvania would benefit from it. "These local considerations ought not to impede the general interest," Morris declared. Arguing that "we ought to be governed by national and permanent views," Madison proposed limiting the "evil" by allowing Congress to tax exports if two-thirds of its members agreed. Madison's proposal lost five votes to six with a divided Virginia delegation voting no. The Convention then approved the bar on taxing exports with a divided Virginia voting yes. In both cases, against the interest of their state but in support of nationalist principle, Washington and Madison voted in the minority. Farrand, Aug. 21, 1787, 2: 360–64.

99. The committee's recommendations authorizing the President to make treaties and appoint officers with the advice and consent of the Senate passed the Convention without dissent. Farrand, Sept. 7, 1787, 2: 538–39. The key vote "for Appointing the President by electors" passed by a margin of nine to two. Farrand, Sept. 6, 1787, 2: 525. Most of the discussion over using electors to choose the President involved what would happen if no candidate received votes from a majority of the electors. The committee recommended that the Senate then choose the President from the five candidates receiving the most votes from electors. Addressing objections from many delegates that this gave too much power to the Senate, the Convention resolved that the House of Representatives would make this choice with "the members from each state having one vote." Farrand, Sept. 6, 1787, 2: 527. The expanded language in the taxing clause passed without dissent. Farrand, Sept. 4, 1787, 2: 499.

100. For example, at one point, Hamilton painted the single-term president as a "Monster" who would "consider his 7 years as 7 years of lawful plunder." Farrand, Sept. 6, 1787, 2: 524, 530.

101. Farrand, Sept. 6, 1787, 2: 499.

102. George Washington to George Augustine Washington, Sept. 9, 1787, *PGW*, CS 5: 321.

Chapter 6: "Little Short of a Miracle"

1. Farrand, Sept. 17, 1787, 2: 651.

2. Morris later claimed credit and Madison confirmed it. See Gouverneur Morris to Timothy Pickering, Dec. 22, 1814, Farrand, 3: 420 ("That instrument was written by the fingers that write this letter"); James Madison to Jared Sparks, April 8, 1831, Farrand, 3: 449 ("The *finish* given to the style and arrangement of the Constitution fairly belongs to the pen of Mr. Morris").

3. The Convention adopted the new preamble as part of the Constitution without comment or objection. Less than a year later, however, at the Virginia ratifying convention, anti-nationalist Patrick Henry made it one focus of his objections. "Who authorized them to speak the language of, We, the People, instead of We, the States?" he asked, pointing the finger directly at Washington, or "that Illustrious man," as he called him. "If the State be not the agents of this compact, it must be one great consolidated National Government of the people of all the States." Patrick Henry, June 4, 1788, *DHRC*, 9: 930–31.

4. The Declaration of Independence also uses the phrase "the united States of America," and the first article in the Articles of Confederation states, "The Stile of this Confederacy shall be 'The United States of America.'"

5. Farrand, Aug. 6, 1787, 2: 177 (Committee of Detail's Preamble); Farrand, Aug. 7, 1787, 2: 196 (vote). In describing his principles for writing the Preamble for the Committee of Detail, Randolph observed, "A preamble seems proper not for the purpose of designating the ends of government and human polities—This business . . . howsoever proper in the first formation of state governments, (seems) *is* unfit here; since we are not working on the natural rights of men not yet gathered into society, but upon those rights, modified by society." Farrand, Committee of Detail IV, 2: 137.

6. In fact, Vermont joined the union in 1791, less than a year after Rhode Island. Newspaper articles published during the Convention speculated that the delegates would admit Vermont to the new union. E.g., "New York, August 16," *Cumberland Gazette*, Aug. 30, 1787, p. 3. Some historians have suggested that Morris deleted the listing of states simply to address the concern that the Constitution might take effect prior to its ratification by some of the listed states, but others see it as a statement of his nationalism. E.g., see Richard Brookhiser, *Gentleman Revolutionary: Gouverneur Morris—The Rake Who Wrote the Constitution* (New York: Free Press, 2003), 91; and Max M. Mintz, *Gouverneur Morris and the American Revolution* (Norman: University of Oklahoma Press, 1970), 200.

7. Jonathan Dayton to Ellas Dayton, Sept. 9, 1787, Farrand, 3: 80.

8. Madison later credited Morris with the initial work of reorganizing the articles into their finished form, adding that subsequent alterations by the full committee "were not such, as to impair the merit of the composition." Madison to Sparks, Farrand, 3: 499.

9. Farrand, Committee of Detail IV, 2: 137.

10. Hamilton's attendance at the Convention had been erratic after the delegates rejected a purely nationalist approach to the Constitution. On June 18, he countered the anti-nationalists' New Jersey Plan with one of his own that would

effectively abolish the states as sovereign entities and consolidate power in a British-style national government headed by a monarchical executive with life tenure and largely dominated by an aristocratic senate composed of members with life tenure. Farrand, June 18, 1787, 1: 291–93. After his plan received no support from any other delegates, he soon left Philadelphia, returned briefly in August, and then again by September 6, just in time to be added to the Committee of Style. Hamilton was haunted throughout his political life for having advocated such an anti-republican plan, with opponents pointing to it as exposing the "real" Hamilton. Ron Chernow, *Alexander Hamilton* (New York: Penguin Press, 2004), 234–39.

11. On the ideological makeup of this committee and some of the puzzles involved, see Richard Beeman, *Plain, Honest Men: The Making of the Constitution* (New York: Random House, 2009), 345–46; and Christopher Collier and James Lincoln Collier, *Decision In Philadelphia: The Constitutional Convention of 1787* (New York: Ballantine Books, 1986), 337–38.

12. Farrand, June 20, 1787, 1: 335.

13. Compare Farrand, May 29, 1787, 1: 20 (Resolution 1) with Farrand, Committee of Detail I, 2: 129–33.

14. Morris reportedly tried to expand the nationalistic implications of the reference to "general welfare" in the Taxing Power Clause by substituting a semicolon for a comma prior to the reference, and thus making it a separate grant of power, but Sherman supposedly detected and reversed it. Compare Farrand, Committee of Style, 2: 594 (Art. I, sec. 8 [a]) with Farrand, The Constitution, 2: 655 (Art. I, sec. 8). The Democratic-Republican Party leader Albert Gallatin made this charge on the floor of the House of Representatives in 1798. Albert Gallatin, June 19, 1798, Farrand, 3: 378. Historians have debated its merits ever since. E.g., see Brookhiser, *Gentleman Revolutionary*, 90. With respect to interpreting the Constitution, Morris later observed, "This must be done by comparing the plain import of the words, with the general tenor and object of the instrument." Morris to Pickering, Farrand, 3: 420.

15. Compare George Washington to Alexander Hamilton, July 10, 1787, *PGW*, CS 5: 257, with George Washington to Benjamin Harrison, Sept. 24, 1787, *PGW*, CS 5: 339. Washington made similar comments in late August. George Washington to Henry Knox, Aug. 19, 1787, *PGW*, CS 5: 297,

16. Letter to Congress, Sept. 17, 1787, Farrand, 2: 666–67 (Morris's draft at Farrand, Sept. 12, 1787, 2: 583–84) (emphasis added); Resolutions of the Convention, Sept. 17, 1787, Farrand, 2: 665–66 (committee draft at Farrand, Sept. 13, 1787, 2: 604–5) (emphasis added).

17. Farrand, Sept. 12, 1787, 2: 588.

18. Ibid. For a fuller discussion of this issue, including Wilson and Madison stressing the enumerated powers and rights argument, see Beeman, *Plain, Honest Men*, 343.

19. George Washington to James Madison, March 31, 1787, *PGW*, CS 5: 115–16.

20. Beeman, *Plain, Honest Men*, 354.

21. Farrand, Aug. 31, 1787, 2: 479.

22. Although previously drafted, both the transmittal letter and final resolutions to Congress now added the tagline "By the Unanimous Order of the Convention." See Farrand, Sept. 17, 1787, 2: 666–67.

23. Farrand, Sept. 17, 1787, 2: 648. By order of the Convention, miscellaneous papers from its proceedings not delivered to Washington were burnt. *GWD*, Sept. 17, 1787, 3: 237.

24. Edmund S. Morgan, *Benjamin Franklin* (New Haven, CT: Yale University Press, 2002), 310–12 (noting that "the government created by the Constitution contained none of the provisions that he would particularly have favored").

25. Farrand, Sept. 17, 1787, 2: 642–43. According to Madison, Gouverneur Morris drew up "this ambiguous form" for signing the Constitution and put it "into the hands of Docr. Franklin that it might have a better chance of success." Farrand, Sept. 17, 1787, 2: 643.

26. Farrand, Sept. 15, 1787, 631–32. Ironically, the dissenters held up the vice presidency for scorn—an office that Gerry would hold under two presidents. Farrand, Sept. 15, 1787, 639.

27. James Thomas Flexner, *George Washington and the New Nation (1783–1793)* (Boston: Little, Brown, 1969), 135. Washington later attributed Mason's continued opposition to the Constitution to "pride, on the one hand, and want of manly candor on the other." George Washington to James Craik, Sept. 8, 1789, *WGW*, 30: 396.

28. Farrand, Sept. 17, 1787, 2: 645–46.

29. Ibid. The three most vocal anti-nationalists at the Convention, Luther Martin, Robert Yates, and John Lansing, surely would have also refused to sign the Constitution. They had already left the Convention, however, and did not participate in the final vote or signing ceremony.

30. Ibid., 644. As described above in Chapter 5, this amendment lowered the minimum allowable ratio of representation in the House of Representatives from not to exceed one for every forty thousand persons to up to one for every thirty thousand persons. In his notes, Madison stated that this amendment "in some degree lessened" one of Mason's objections. Farrand, Sept. 15, 1787, 2: 638. Political scientist Richard Ellis cites Washington's vote as "an example of the general's making concessions to political opponents in order to build greater support for the final product." Richard J. Ellis, *Founding the American Presidency* (London: Rowman & Littlefield, 1999), 8. In a contemporary comment on Washington's intervention, one newspaper reported, "Such was the magic of this patriot's opinion! And it adds to the lustre of his virtues, that this critical interference . . . tended to promote the interests and dignity of THE PEOPLE." "Anecdote," *Pennsylvania Herald*, Nov. 7, 1787, p. 2.

31. Mason, Randolph, and Gerry appear with the thirty-nine signers and the Convention's secretary in Louis S. Glanzman's painting *Signing to the Constitution*, which hangs in Independence Hall and is less-well known than Christy's *Scene at the Signing of the Constitution of the United States*. Both present Washington and Franklin as the most prominent figures in the group portrait. Glanzman avoided

the issue of open or shuttered windows by only showing the Assembly Room's windowless back wall.

32.   Farrand, Sept. 17, 1787, 2: 648.

33.   Ibid., 649.

34.   *GWD*, Sept. 17, 1787, 3: 237.

35.   George Washington to Lafayette, Sept. 18, 1787, *PGW*, CS 5: 334. See also George Washington to Thomas Jefferson, Sept. 18, 1787, *PGW*, CS 5: 333.

36.   William Pierce, "Character Sketches of the Delegates to the Federal Convention," Farrand, 3: 95.

37.   "Philadelphia, October 10," *Connecticut Journal*, Oct. 17, 1787, p. 2. The article was reprinted in twenty-five newspapers from New Hampshire to Georgia by mid-November. *DHRC*, 13: 243 n. 2.

38.   George Washington to Henry Knox, Oct. 15, 1788, *PGW*, CS 5: 375 ("I arrived home . . . [to find] the fruits of the Earth almost entirely destroyed by one of the severest droughts (in this neighborhood) that ever was experienced").

39.   Washington to Lafayette, Sept. 18, 1787, *PGW*, CS 5: 334.

40.   Quoted from Washington to Harrison, Sept. 24, 1787, *PGW*, CS 5: 339. In this letter, Washington wrote that "the political concerns of this Country are, in a manner, suspended by a thread" and that if the Convention had not agreed on the Constitution, "anarchy would soon have ensued." Ibid. Washington sent the same letter to former governors Benjamin Harrison, Patrick Henry, and Thomas Nelson. Ibid., 240.

41.   In October, Washington wrote, "It is highly probable that the refusal of our Governor and Colo. Mason to subscribe to the proceedings of the Convention will have a bad effect in this state." Washington to Knox, Oct. 15, 1788, *PGW*, CS 5: 376.

42.   "To the Freemen of Pennsylvania," *Pennsylvania Gazette*, Oct. 10, 1787, p. 2; reprinted in "To the Freemen of Pennsylvania," *Independent Gazetteer*, Oct. 15, 1787, p. 2.

43.   "The Grand Constitution," *Columbian Herald*, Nov. 8, 1787, p. 4 (the same song appeared in newspapers from New Hampshire to South Carolina during October and November 1787).

44.   "For the Centinel," *Massachusetts Centinel*, Oct. 6, 1787, p. 34.

45.   In a private paper on the prospects for ratification probably dating from late September, Hamilton wrote at the outset, "The new constitution has in favour of its success . . . a very great weight of influence of the person who framed it, particularly in the universal popularity of General Washington." Alexander Hamilton, "Conjectures About the Constitution," Sept. 1787, *DHRC*, 13: 277.

46.   Gouverneur Morris to George Washington, Oct. 30, 1787, *PGW*, CS 5: 400.

47.   An example of such charges and their refutation appear in the essays signed "Centinel" and the responses to them that appeared in Philadelphia newspapers in October 1787, which are discussed more fully later in this chapter. E.g., Centinel, "To the Freemen of Pennsylvania," *Independent Gazetteer*, Oct. 5, 1787, p. 2; *Independent Gazetteer*, Oct. 13, 1787, p. 2. Underscoring the weakness of such

attacks, see "A few Observations," *Middlesex Gazette*, Nov. 26, 1787, p. 2 ("to suppose that any act of [Washington], could be intended, in the most distant degree, to injure a people whose freedom he has already established, at the risque of his life and fortune, would be a piece of base ingratitude, that no *honest* American can possibly be guilty of").

48. Hamilton, "Conjectures," *DHRC*, 13:277.

49. "Pennsylvania Gazette, 26 September," *DHRC*, 13: 253 (notes indicate that this observation was reprinted in thirty-eight newspapers within three weeks).

50. E.g., the principal French diplomat in the United States reported to his government in October that Americans "already speak of Gnl. Washington as the only man capable of filling the important position of President." Lois Guillaume Otto to Comte de Montmorin, Oct. 20, 1787, *DHRC*, 13:423.

51. David Humphreys to George Washington, Sept. 28, 1787, *PGW*, CS 5: 343.

52. Morris to Washington, Oct. 30, 1787, *PGW*, CS 5: 400.

53. The eleven delegates to the Constitutional Convention then serving in Congress were Nicholas Gilman and John Langdon of New Hampshire, Nathaniel Gorman and Rufus King of Massachusetts, William Samuel Johnson of Connecticut, Robert Yates of New York, James Madison of Virginia, William Blount of North Carolina, Pierce Butler of South Carolina, and William Few and William Pierce of Georgia. Nine of these eleven members of Congress had signed the Constitution.

54. For Washington's take on Lee, see George Washington to James Madison, Oct. 10, 1787, *PGW*, CS 5: 366.

55. Articles of Confederation, Article XIII.

56. Constitution, Article VII.

57. Farrand, Aug. 31, 1787, 2: 482. Madison and Wilson also favored seven states so long as they made up a majority of the population, which may have been Washington's position. Farrand, Aug. 31, 1787, 2: 471, 477.

58. Farrand, Sept. 17, 1787, 2: 665.

59. Congress met in secret and its official journal did not include minutes. The debate over the Constitution is reconstructed from surviving notes and letters of members in "The Confederation Congress and the Constitution," Sept. 26–28, 1787, *DHRC*, 13: 229–41. All quotes come from these pages. An excellent summary of the debates appears in Pauline Maier, *Ratification: The People Debate the Constitution, 1787–1788* (New York: Simon & Schuster, 2010), 52–59.

60. "Congress and the Constitution," *DHRC*, 13: 238–40.

61. *JCC*, Sept. 28, 1787, 33: 549.

62. "New York, Sept. 26," *Daily Advertiser*, Sept. 26, 1787, p. 2.

63. Lee's resolution and the vote on postponing it, with strike marks through them, appears at *JCC*, Sept. 27, 1787, 33: 540–42. This material was stricken from the published journal after Congressman Abraham Clark commented, "The motion by Mr. Lee for amendments, will do injury by coming on the Journal." "Congress and the Constitution," *DHRC*, 13: 241.

64. Washington to Madison, Oct. 10, 1787, *PGW*, CS 5: 366.

65. Maier, *Ratification*, p. 39.

66. Humphreys to Washington, *PGW*, CS 5: 343.

67. Henry Knox to George Washington, Oct. 3, 1787, *PGW*, CS 5: 352.

68. Alexander Hamilton to George Washington, Oct. 11, 1787, *PGW*, CS 5: 369.

69. James Madison to George Washington, Oct. 14, 1787, *PGW*, CS 5: 373 (emphasis added).

70. See *GWD*, Oct. 12–13, 1787, 3: 244.

71. David Humphreys to George Washington to Alexander Hamilton, Oct. 18, 1787, *PGW*, CS 5: 381. See also George Washington to David Humphreys, Oct. 10, 1787, *PGW*, CS 5: 366 ("In these parts of [Virginia], it is advocated beyond my expectation").

72. Committee of Voters in Fairfax County to George Mason and David Stuart, Oct. 2, 1787, *PGM*, 3: 1000.

73. Washington to Madison, Oct. 10, 1787, *PGW*, CS 5: 366–67 (by "latter," Washington meant Mason).

74. Richard Henry Lee to George Washington, Oct. 11, 1787, *PGW*, CS 5: 370 (speaking of his opposition to Washington over the Constitution, Lee writes, "I feel it among the first distresses that have happened to me in my life"); George Mason to George Washington, Oct. 7, 1787, *PGW*, CS 5: 356 (without expressly expressing regret, Mason goes out of his way to endorse at least holding a state ratifying convention). In what must have been cold encounters, Lee also visited Washington at Mount Vernon in early November and Mason's son, George Jr., visited Washington in October. *GWD*, Oct. 28–29, 1787, 3: 261–62; *GWD*, Nov. 11–12, 1787, 3: 266.

75. Patrick Henry to George Washington, Oct. 19, 1787, *PGW*, CS 5: 384 (expressing lament for differing "with the opinion of those personages for whom I have the highest Reverence," which presumably included Washington).

76. Richard Henry Lee to George Mason, Oct. 1, 1787, *PGM*, 3: 996.

77. Farrand, Sept. 15, 1787, 2: 632.

78. "Congress and the Constitution," *DHRC*, 13: 238. For the complete first quote, see "Melancton Smith's Notes, 27 September," *DHRC*, 1: 336. Smith took the most complete notes of the debate. They are presented along with other available notes in the original shorthand form in *DHRC*, vol. 13, and in revised form in *DHRC*, vol. 1.

79. "Assembly Proceedings," Sept. 17, 1787, *DHRC*, 2: 58.

80. About Pennsylvania's representation at the Convention, minority members of the Assembly wrote, "We lamented at the time that a majority of our legislature appointed men to represent this state who were all citizens of Philadelphia, none of them calculated to represent the landed [or rural] interests of Pennsylvania, and almost all of them of one political party, men who have been uniformly opposed to [the state] constitution. . . ." "The Address of the Seceding Assemblymen," Oct. 2, 1787, *DHRC*, 2: 112.

81. "Assembly Debates, A.M.," Sept. 28, 1787, *DHRC*, 2: 71. See also "Address of Seceding Assemblymen," *DHRC*, 2: 113.

82. "Assembly Debates, A.M.," *DHRC*, 2: 76.

83. "Address of Seceding Assemblymen," *DHRC*, 2: 116. Washington had read the broadside within a week of its publication. On October 10, he wrote to Madison that Mason's objections "are detailed in the address of the seceding members of the Assembly of Pennsylvania; which no doubt you have seen." Washington to Madison, Oct. 10, 1787, *PGW,* CS 5: 367. A group depicted by some as a "mob" assisted the sergeant at arms in capturing the two seceders, James M'Calmont and Jacob Miley. At M'Calmont's request, the attorney general attempted to prosecute the only identified member of this group, John Barry. "James M'Calmont's Appeal," Oct. 2, 1787–Feb. 16, 1788, *DHRC*, 2: 111. Barry worked for Robert Morris, which led historian Ray Raphael to suggest that Morris orchestrated the capture. See Ray Raphael, *Founders: The People Who Brought You a Nation* (New York: New Press, 2009), 464.

84. Washington to Madison, Oct. 10, 1787, *PGW,* CS 5: 367.

85. Morris to Washington, Oct. 30, 1787, *PGW,* CS 5: 399.

86. George Washington to Bushrod Washington, Nov. 9, 1787, *PGW,* CS 5: 421. In other letters from this period, Washington (like Morris) attributed much of the opposition to the Constitution to "sinister and self-important considerations" of opponents who would be adversely "affected by the change" in government. Washington to Humphreys, Oct. 10, 1787, *PGW,* CS 5: 365; Washington to Knox, Oct. 15, 1787, *PGW,* CS 5: 375.

87. Washington to Humphreys, Oct. 10, 1787, *PGW,* CS 5: 366.

88. George Washington to David Stuart, Oct. 17, 1787, *PGW,* CS 5: 379.

89. E.g., "The arguments, if they be arguments, most insisted upon, in favor of the proposed constitution, are; that if the plan is not a good one, it is impossible that either General Washington or Dr. Franklin would have recommended it." A Confederationalist, "To the Editor," *Pennsylvania Evening Herald*, Oct. 27, 1787, p. 2. See also Centinel, "To the Freemen of Pennsylvania," *Independent Gazetteer*, Oct. 5, 1787, p. 2 (Pennsylvania federalists "flatter themselves that they have lulled all distrust and jealousy of their new plan by gaining the concurrence of the two men in whom America has the highest confidence"). For examples of such federalist arguments, see "My Fellow Citizens," *Independent Gazetteer,* Nov. 17, 1787, p. 3 ("Remember, a WASHINGTON, a FRANKLIN, a MORRIS, with other illustrious enlighten patriots composed it"); "From a Correspondent," *Pennsylvania Packet*, Sept. 22, 1787, p. 3 ("with what solicitude the great council of America, headed by a *Franklin* and a *Washington*, the fathers of their country, have . . . laboured to frame a system of laws and constitutions that shall perpetuate the blessings of that independence, which you obtained by your swords!"); "Northumberland, October 1787," *Pennsylvania Gazette*, Oct. 17, 1787, *DHRC*, 2: 179 (denying "that a WASHINGTON and his colleagues, whose interests and political salvation are inseparable from ours, would tender a constitution to their brethren fraught with such evils as is by that diabolical junto [the anti-federalists] set forth"); "Poet's Corner," *Carlisle Gazette*, Dec. 5, 1787, p. 4 ("For who so buried in the ocean / Of ignorance to credit notion, / That Washington could have design, / Our government to undermine").

90. Centinel, "To the Freemen," p. 2. The special interests that Centinel referred to in his essay were "the wealthy and the ambitious." Centinel, it is now known, was Samuel Bryan, who lost his post as Assembly clerk when the supporters of the old constitution lost control of that body in 1786. For a similar comment, see B. Russell, "Mr. Oswald," *Independent Gazetteer,* Dec. 4, 1787, p. 2 ("Their honest unsuspecting hearts have made them the dupes of a cunning, aristocratic majority").

91. Confederationist, "To the Editor," p. 2.

92. "A Correspondent," *Independent Gazetteer,* Oct. 13, 1787, p. 2.

93. E.g., "A Federalist," *Independent Gazetteer,* Oct. 10, 1787, p. 3 ("Not even the *immortal* WASHINGTON, nor the *venerable* FRANKLIN escapes [Centinel's] satire."); "Mr. Printer," *Independent Gazetteer,* Oct. 10, 1787, p. 3 (condemning Centinel for depicting "*Doctor* Franklin as a *fool* from age, and *General* Washington as a *fool* from nature").

94. Centinel, "CENTINEL, No. II," *Freeman's Journal,* Oct. 24, 1787, p. 1. Centinel made similar claims about Washington in later essays. E.g., Centinel, "CENTINEL, No. IX," *Independent Gazetteer,* Jan. 8, 1788, p. 3 (accusing federalists of prostituting the "august name of a *Washington*"); and Centinel, "CENTINEL, No. XII," *Independent Gazetteer,* Jan. 23, 1788, p. 2 (accusing federalists of "endeavouring to screed their criminality by interposing the shield of the virtues of a Washington").

95. E.g., as reprinted in a Massachusetts newspaper, one commentator in the *Pennsylvania Gazette* answered Centinel's question with one of his own about Washington, "Can the subject of government be new to a man of his reflection, his reading, and his opportunities?" "Philadelphia, October 30," *Massachusetts Gazette,* Nov. 13, 1787, p. 3. See also "A Few Observations," *Middlesex Gazette,* Nov. 26, 1787, p. 2. In response to the charge that Washington signed the Constitution only as a witness, a federalist wrote, "I know this to be groundless in point of fact, though I do not wish from delicacy to produce the proof." Honor and Honesty, "To the Editor," *Pennsylvania Herald,* Nov. 10, 1787, p. 2.

96. A Plain Citizen, "To the Honorable the Convention of the State of Pennsylvania," *Independent Gazette,* Nov. 22, 1787, p. 2.

97. E.g., *Independent Gazetteer,* Sept. 21, 1787, p. 3 (supposedly quoting a common worker at a beer house, the writer states, "We are in no danger, *Washington* is still *at the helm*").

98. An American Citizen, "On the Federal Government, No. 1," *Independent Gazetteer,* Sept. 26, 1787, pp. 2–3. Coxe supported Washington's election as President, and held various major posts in the Washington administration.

99. While he supported ratification, South Carolina Convention delegate Pierce Butler expressed similar concerns when he privately confided about the powers of the President that he did not "believe they would have been so great had not many of the Members cast their eyes toward General Washington as President; and Shaped their Ideas of the Powers to be given to the President, by their opinions of His Virtue." Pierce Butler to Weeden Butler, May 5, 1788, *DHFEE,* 4: 35 (this reproduction includes Pierce Butler's spelling of Weedon Butler's first name).

100. An Old Whig, "Mr. Printer," *Independent Gazetteer*, Nov. 1, 1787, p. 2. Although the authorship of this essay remains disputed, it is often attributed to "Centinel's" father, Pennsylvania Supreme Court justice George Bryan.

101. For an analysis of this election, see Beeman, *Plain, Honest Men*, 378–79.

102. "The Pennsylvania Convention," Dec. 12, 1787, *DHRC*, 2: 592–93.

103. Samuel Powel to George Washington, Dec. 12, 1787, *PGW*, CS 5: 488. As part of "the public rejoicing for the ratification," one newspaper reported, "a number of ship carpenters and sailors conducted a boat, on a wagon drawn by five horses, through the city, to the great amusement of many thousand spectators." In reference to the vote on ratification, the carpenters and sailors would throw out a sounding line and shouted, "Three and twenty fathom—*foul* bottom" or "Six and forty fathom—sound bottom—safe anchorage." John Bach McMaster and Fredrick D. Stone, eds., *Pennsylvania and the Federal Convention, 1787–88* (Indianapolis: Liberty Fund, 2011), 454 (quoting newspaper report).

104. For an insightful discussion of Franklin's position, see Morgan, *Franklin*, 310–12.

105. Morris to Washington, Oct. 30, 1787, *PGW*, CS 5: 400.

106. Benjamin Franklin to Louis-Guillaume LeVeillard, June 8, 1788, *DHFEE*, 4: 37.

107. Morris to Washington, Oct. 30, 1787, *PGW*, CS 5: 400.

108. "Extract of a Letter from Wilmington," *Pennsylvania Gazette*, Nov. 21, 1787, *DHRC*, 3: 94.

109. "Elisabeth-Town, November 7," *New Jersey Journal*, Nov. 7, 1787, p. 2. The quote came from an earlier long essay that did not attribute it to Washington by name. After appearing in the *New Jersey Journal* as the feature of a short squib that named Washington as the speaker, the quote was reprinted in thirty-nine other newspapers, including the two in Georgia, by the end of the year. For this publishing history, see *DHRC*, 3: 151 n. 1 and 13: 567 n. 1. Prior to the Convention, the *New Jersey Journal* also published an ode to ratification that included the lines "The great, the immortal Washington attends, / To save the falling States, and help his friends." "The Final Decision," *New Jersey Journal*, Oct. 31, 1787, p. 1. The same issue included an advertisement for a grammar school text by Noah Webster featuring advice from Mirabeau, "Begin with the Infant in his cradle: Let the first word he lisps be Washington." *New Jersey Journal*, Oct. 31, 1787, p. 3.

110. Lashlan McIntosh to John Wereat, Dec. 17, 1787, *DHRC*, 3: 256. Prior to the ratifying conventions in their states, newspapers in both New Jersey and Georgia had published the squib from the *Pennsylvania Gazette* stating that Washington was "destined, by a thousand voices, to fill the place of the first President." *DHRC*, 13: 254 n. 7.

111. George Washington to James Madison, Dec. 7, 1787, *PGW*, CS 5: 478.

112. George Washington to Samuel Powel, Jan. 18, 1788, *PGW*, CS 6: 46.

113. George Washington to Lafayette, Jan. 10, 1788, *PGW*, CS 6: 31.

114. David Stuart to George Washington, Dec. 4, 1787, *PGW*, CS 5: 479 (quoted in extract by Washington).

115.   George Washington to Thomas Jefferson, Jan. 1, 1788, *PGW*, CS 6: 3. He expressed optimism about ratification in Virginia in both his letter to Jefferson and his January 10 letter to Lafayette; Washington wrote about New York only in his letter to Lafayette.

116.   George Washington to Charles Carter, Dec. 14, 1787, *PGW*, CS 5: 492.

117.   George Washington to Lafayette, Feb. 7, 1788, *PGW*, CS 6: 95.·

118.   Alexander Donald to Thomas Jefferson, Nov. 12, 1787, *DHFEE*, 4: 21–22.

Chapter 7: Ratifying Washington

1.   George Washington to James Madison, Oct. 10, 1787, *PGW*, CS 5: 367. Regarding his close study of opposition arguments, see George Washington to Alexander Hamilton, Aug. 28, 1788, *PGW*, CS 6: 481.

2.   George Washington to Benjamin Lincoln, April 2, 1788, *PGW*, CS 6: 188. Washington believed that most people acted out of self-interest most of the time. See Edmund S. Morgan, "George Washington: The Aloof American," in Don Higginbotham, ed., *George Washington Reconsidered* (Charlottesville: University Press of Virginia, 2001), 289–91, 294–302.

3.   George Washington to John Armstrong, April 25, 1788, *PGW*, CS 6: 226.

4.   George Washington to Richard Butler, April 3, 1788, *PGW*, CS 6: 189.

5.   George Washington to Thomas Jefferson, Jan. 1, 1788, *PGW*, CS 6: 3.

6.   Lafayette to George Washington, Jan. 1, 1788, *PGW*, CS 6: 5–6.

7.   David Humphreys to George Washington, Sept. 28, 1787, *PGW*, CS 5: 343.

8.   A Landowner, "To the Landowners and Farmers. Number VI," *Connecticut Courant*, Dec. 10, 1787, p. 1. A subsequent front-page article in the *Connecticut Courant* repeated the charge against Lee by attributing his opposition to the Constitution to "a low envy of the brilliant virtues and unbounded popularity" of Washington. New England, "To the Hon. Richard Henry Lee, Esq.," *Connecticut Courant*, Dec. 24, 1787, p. 1.

9.   A Landowner, "The Landowner, No. 8," *Connecticut Courant*, Dec. 24, 1787, p. 2.

10.   James Madison to George Washington, Dec. 20, 1787, *PGW*, CS 5: 500.

11.   Jonathan Trumbull Jr. to George Washington, Jan. 9, 1788, *PGW*, CS 6: 25.

12.   Ibid.

13.   George Washington to Jonathan Trumbull Jr., Feb. 5, 1788, *PGW*, CS 6: 93.

14.   George Washington to David Humphreys, Oct. 10, 1787, *PGW*, CS 5: 366 (quote); George Washington to David Stuart, Oct. 17, 1787, *PGW*, CS 5: 379 (Wilson's speech); George Washington to David Stuart, Nov. 30, 1787, *PGW*, CS 5: 467 (the Federalist).

15.   George Washington to James Madison, Nov. 5, 1787, *PGW*, CS 5: 409.

16.   George Washington to Samuel Powel, Jan. 18, 1788, *PGW*, CS 6: 45.

17.   Madison to Washington, Dec. 20, 1787, *PGW*, CS 5: 499.

18.   E.g., George Washington to Henry Knox, Feb. 5, 1788, *PGW*, CS 6: 88 (ten miles); George Washington to Rufus King, Feb. 29, 1788, *PGW*, CS 6: 133 (six miles).

19. Compare George Washington to Lafayette, Sept. 18, 1787, *PGW*, CS 5: 334 with Washington to Humphreys, Oct. 10, 1787, *PGW*, CS 5: 366.

20. George Washington to James McHenry, June 31, 1788, *PGW*, CS 6: 409.

21. George Washington to Charles Pettit, Aug. 16, 1788, *PGW*, CS 6: 448.

22. George Washington to James Madison, Jan. 10, 1788, *PGW*, CS 6: 33.

23. The report first appeared in "Carlisle, January 2," *Carlisle Gazette*, Jan. 2, 1788, p. 3; was reprinted eight days later in a newspaper that Washington generally read, the *Pennsylvania Packet;* and subsequently appeared in more than three dozen newspapers from New Hampshire to Georgia.

24. George Washington to Benjamin Lincoln, Jan. 31, 1788, *PGW*, CS 6: 74.

25. "Extract of a Letter," *Massachusetts Gazette*, Jan. 25, 1788, p. 3. For the original letter, see George Washington to Charles Carter, Dec. 14, 1787, *PGW*, CS 5: 489–92.

26. "Extract of a Letter," p. 3.

27. Washington to Lincoln, Jan. 31, 1788, *PGW*, CS 6: 74.

28. This exchange is captured with excerpts from various newspapers in "George Washington and the Constitution," *DHRC*, 5: 788–96.

29. See John P. Kaminski and Jill Adair McCaughan, eds., *A Great and Good Man: Washington in the Eyes of His Contemporaries* (Lanham, MD: Rowman & Littlefield, 1989), 2 and passim.

30. E.g., James Madison to George Washington, Dec. 26, 1787, *PGW*, CS 5: 510 ("It appears that Cambridge the residence of Mr Gerry has left him out of the choice for the Convention, and put in Mr Dana formerly a Minister of the U. States in Europe, and another Gentleman, both of them firmly opposed to Mr Gerry's Politics").

31. E.g., Nathan Dane to Henry Knox, Dec. 27, 1787, *DHRC*, 5: 527 ("since I arrived here [Boston] yesterday I find the elections of the province of Main and in the three Western Counties have not been so much in favor of the Constitution as supposed"); Edward Bangs to George Thatcher, Jan. 1, 1788, *DHRC*, 5: 571.

32. Benjamin Lincoln to George Washington, Feb. 3, 1788, *PGW*, CS 6: 82.

33. James Madison to George Washington, Feb. 3, 1788, *PGW*, CS 6: 83 (including transcription of Gorham's letter).

34. "By Last Night's Mail," *Massachusetts Gazette*, Oct. 19, 1787, p. 2.

35. "The Massachusetts Convention, Tuesday, 21 January 1788," *DHRC*, 6: 1287 (Abraham White), 1296 (Amos Singletary), 1297 (Martin Kingsley).

36. James Madison to George Washington, Jan. 25, 1788, *PGW*, CS 6: 61 (including transcription of King's letter).

37. Benjamin Lincoln to George Washington, Jan. 27, 1788, *PGW*, CS 6: 68.

38. James Madison to George Washington, Feb. 1, 1788, *PGW*, CS 6: 77 (including transcription of King's letter).

39. George Washington to John Jay, March 3, 1788, *PGW*, CS 6: 139.

40. Ibid.; George Washington to Henry Knox, March 3, 1788, *PGW*, CS 6: 140; James Madison to George Washington, Feb. 15, 1788, *PGW*, CS 6: 115.

41. James Madison to George Washington, Feb. 8, 1788, *PGW*, CS 6: 101 (including transcription of King's letter).

42. For a classic portrayal of Hancock, including his dramatic wearing of regal purple during his service as the first president of the Continental Congress following independence, see Herbert S. Allan, *John Hancock: Patriot in Purple* (New York: Macmillan, 1948).

43. Rufus King to George Washington, Feb. 6, 1788, *PGW*, CS 6: 93–94. Lincoln sent Washington a similar letter on the same day. Benjamin Lincoln to George Washington, Feb. 6, 1788, *PGW*, CS 6: 94.

44. George Washington to Rufus King, Feb. 29, 1788, *PGW*, CS 6: 133.

45. "The Massachusetts Convention, Monday, 4 February 1788," *DHRC*, 6: 1417 (Thomas Thatcher).

46. E.g., writing about the Constitution on March 3, Washington observed, "Of the two [states] which are next to Convene, (New Hampshire and Maryland) there can be no doubt of its adoption and So. Carolina but little." George Washington to Henry Knox, March 3, 1788, *PGW*, CS 6: 140.

47. George Washington to Edward Newenham, Feb. 24, 1788, *PGW*, CS 6: 131; George Washington to Rufus King, Feb. 29, 1788, *PGW*, CS 6: 133. Writing to Madison three days later, Washington described the Massachusetts vote as "a severe stoke to the opponents of the proposed Constitution of this State; and with the favorable determinations of the States which have gone before, and such as are likely to follow after, will have a powerful operation on the minds of Men." George Washington to James Madison, March 2, 1788, *PGW*, CS 6: 136–37.

48. Washington to Knox, March 3, 1788, *PGW*, CS 6: 140.

49. Washington to Jay, March 3, 1788, *PGW*, CS 6: 139.

50. Washington himself called it "a matter of general suprize." George Washington to John Langdon, April 2, 1788, *PGW*, CS 6: 186.

51. E.g., John Langdon to George Washington, Nov. 6, 1787, *PGW*, CS 5: 471. In December, Washington received a similarly rosy report about New Hampshire from Henry Knox and James Madison in New York. Henry Knox to George Washington, Dec. 11, 1787, *PGW*, CS 5: 485; Madison to Washington, Dec. 20, 1787, *PGW*, CS 5: 500. Madison repeated his prediction to Washington in mid-January. James Madison to George Washington, Jan. 14, 1788, *PGW*, CS 6: 41. For Sullivan's role, see "President John Sullivan on the Constitution," *DHRC*, 14: 408–10.

52. John Langdon to George Washington, Feb. 28, 1788, *PGW*, CS 6: 132.

53. George Washington to Benjamin Lincoln, April 2, 1788, *PGW*, CS 6: 187.

54. George Washington to Henry Knox, March 30, 1788, *PGW*, CS 6: 183.

55. John Langdon to George Washington, Feb. 28, 1788, *PGW*, CS 6: 133 ("this State must and will receive it, I have but very little doubt, notwithstanding their late Conduct"). For Washington's views on Virginia, see George Washington to John Langdon, April 2, 1788, *PGW*, CS 6: 187; George Washington to Thomas Jefferson, April 20, 1788, *PGW*, CS 6: 218 (here Washington added about the impact of New Hampshire on Virginia, "a similar event in Maryland, would have the worst tendency imaginable").

56. For the requests by Virginia federalists James Madison, George Nicholas, and David Stuart, and Washington's response, see "George Washington and the Maryland Convention," *DHRC*, 17: 187–88.

57. George Washington to Thomas Johnson, April 20, 1788, *PGW*, CS 6: 218; George Washington to James McHenry, April 27, 1788, *PGW*, CS 6: 234. Responding to Washington's intervention, Virginia antifederalists claimed that Johnson considered it inappropriate, but Johnson denied the charge when asked about it by Washington. "George Washington and the Maryland Convention," *DHRC*, 17: 188–89.

58. Washington to Johnson, April 20, 1788, *PGW*, CS 6: 218.

59. "Poetry," *State Gazette of South-Carolina*, Dec. 3, 1787, p. 3. Other poems published in Charleston newspapers at or around this time hailed Washington as "Columbia's glory" and "the noblest Hero." "Poetry," *City Gazette*, Jan. 14, 1788, p. 4; "Poetry," *City Gazette*, April 26, 1788, p. 3.

60. "Extract of a Letter from Rhode-Island," *Columbian Herald*, Dec. 6, 1787, p. 2.

61. George Washington to William Smith, June 8, 1788, *PGW*, CS 6: 322; *GWD*, July 24, 1788, 3: 393.

62. George Washington to John Francis Mercer, Jan. 11, 1788, *PGW*, CS 6: 36.

63. George Washington to David Stuart, June 23, 1788, *PGW*, CS 6: 353.

64. *GWD*, July 24–28, 1788, 3: 393–95.

65. George Washington to John Beale Bordley, Aug. 17, 1788, *PGW*, CS 6: 450.

66. In a letter from this period, Washington observed that in terms of population and wealth, Virginia "certainly stands first in the Union," but added that "Virginians entertain *too* high an opinion of the importance of their" state. George Washington to Bushrod Washington, Nov. 9, 1787, *PGW*, CS 5: 422.

67. E.g., George Washington to Benjamin Harrison, Sept. 24, 1787, *PGW*, CS 5: 339.

68. James Madison to George Washington, Nov. 18, 1787, *PGW*, CS 5: 444.

69. George Washington to David Stuart, Nov. 30, 1787, *PGW*, CS 5: 467.

70. George Washington to Lafayette, May 28, 1788, *PGW*, CS 6: 297.

71. George Washington to James Madison, March 2, 1788, *PGW*, CS 6: 137.

72. At the time, Washington attributed Richard Henry Lee's decision "to withdraw his opposition" to having found "himself in bad Company," and noted that Lee's brother, "Francis H. Lee on whose judgment the family place much reliance, is decidedly in favor of the new form." George Washington to James Madison, Jan. 10, 1788, *PGW*, CS 6: 32. Regarding Randolph, Washington predicted in April, "if he opposes it at all [he] will do it feebly." George Washington to Lafayette, April 28, 1788, *PGW*, CS 6: 244.

73. George Washington to Lafayette, April 28, 1788, *PGW*, CS 6: 243.

74. George Washington to Benjamin Lincoln, April 2, 1788, *PGW*, CS 6: 188.

75. As early as December 1787, Washington's personal secretary, Tobias Lear, expressed this concern in a letter from Mount Vernon to Washington's old friend, New Hampshire federalist John Langdon. "If I may be allowed to form an opinion," Lear wrote of Henry in a message that likely reflected Washington's thinking as well, "of

what would be his wish, it is to divide the Southern States from the others. Should this take place, Virginia would hold the first place among them, & he the first place in Virginia." Tobias Lear to John Langdon, Dec. 3, 1787, *DHRC*, 8: 197. Madison regularly expressed this concern in letters to Washington and others and it was often raised in Virginia newspapers. E.g., James Madison to Edmund Randolph, Jan. 10, 1787, *PJM*, 10: 355; A Freeholder, *Virginia Independent Chronicle*, April 9, 1788, *DHRC*, 9: 728.

76.   See, e.g., ibid.; Washington to Lincoln, April 2, 1788, *PGW*, CS 6: 187; George Washington to John Armstrong, April 25, 1788, *PGW*, CS 6: 226.

77.   "The Virginia Convention, Wednesday, 4 June 1788," *DHRC*, 9: 929–31 (Patrick Henry).

78.   Harlow Giles Unger, *Lion of Liberty: Patrick Henry and the Call to a New Nation* (Cambridge, MA: Da Capo Press, 2010), 212.

79.   "The Virginia Convention, Wednesday, 4 June 1788," *DHRC*, 9: 931–35 (Edmund Randolph).

80.   James Madison to George Washington, June 4, 1788, *PGW*, CS 6: 313–14. In April, Washington had reported not knowing the sentiments of the Kentucky members. Washington to Lincoln, April 2, 1788, *PGW*, CS 6: 188.

81.   Complaining about "the desultory manner in which [Henry] has treated the subject," at this point Lee noted that Henry "seems to have discarded in a great measure, solid argument and strong reasoning, and has established a new system of throwing those bolts, which he has so peculiar a dexterity at discharging." "The Virginia Convention, Monday, 9 June 1788," *DHRC*, 9: 1072 (Henry Lee). Bushrod Washington made a similar comment in a June 7 letter to George Washington. Bushrod Washington to George Washington, June 7, 1788, *PGW*, CS 6: 316 (calling the debates "general and desultory" or random).

82.   Washington to Washington, June 7, 1788, *PGW*, CS 6: 316.

83.   James Madison to George Washington, June 13, 1788, *PGW*, CS 6: 326.

84.   George Washington to Henry Knox, June 17, 1788, *PGW*, CS 6: 333.

85.   James Madison to George Washington, June 23, 1788, *PGW*, CS 6: 351–52.

86.   James Thomas Flexner, *George Washington and the New Nation* (Boston: Little, Brown, 1969), 150.

87.   "The Virginia Convention, Thursday, 24 June 1788," *DHRC*, 10: 1498 (William Grayson).

88.   "The Virginia Convention, Wednesday, 18 June 1788," *DHRC*, 10: 1375 (George Mason).

89.   "The Virginia Convention, Monday, 9 June 1788," *DHRC*, 9: 1051 (Patrick Henry); "The Virginia Convention, Thursday, 12 June 1788," *DHRC*, 10: 1223 (James Madison).

90.   George Washington to Charles Cotesworth Pinckney, June 28, 1788, *PGW*, CS 6: 361.

91.   George Washington to Tobias Lear, June 29, 1788, *PGW*, CS 6: 364.

92.   Ibid.

93.   E.g., "The Tenth Pillar," *Maryland Journal*, July 1, 1788, *DHRC*, 10: 1719 (reports on the celebration in Baltimore, where "the illustrious George Washington"

received the third toast, after only the Constitution and the two last states to ratify, Virginia and New Hampshire).

94. James Monroe to Thomas Jefferson, July 12, 1788, *DHRC*, 10: 1705.

95. George Washington to Henry Knox, Jan. 10, 1788, *PGW*, CS 6: 28.

96. Washington to Pinckney, June 28, 1788, *PGW*, CS 6: 362.

97. George Washington to James Madison, March 31, 1787, *PGW*, CS 5: 116.

98. George Washington to Alexander Hamilton, Oct. 18, 1787, *PGW*, CS 5: 380–81. The esteem between Washington and Clinton was mutual. Clinton named one of his sons George Washington Clinton and one of his daughters Martha Washington Clinton. Washington frequently stayed with Clinton in New York and they invested together in real estate on the New York frontier, which proved to be Washington's most profitable land investment.

99. One week prior to the elections, Jay wrote to Washington, "The Constitution still continues to cause great party Zeal and Ferment." John Jay to George Washington, April 20, 1788, *PGW*, CS 6: 217.

100. Pauline Maier, *Ratification: The People Debate the Constitution, 1787–1788* (New York: Simon & Schuster, 2010), 328.

101. E.g., "A Citizen," *Hudson Weekly Gazette*, Jan. 31, 1788, *DHRC*, 20: 679 (writing about Washington, "Can you, O ye ungrateful people, doubt the constitution you received from his hands?").

102. Cato, "To the Citizens of the State of New York," *New York Journal*, Sept. 27, 1787, p. 3. At the time, many New Yorkers thought that Clinton wrote this article but later historians disagree on its authorship. See "Cato I," *DHRC*, 19: 58–59. An essay generally attributed to Hamilton replied to Cato, in an apparent reference to the anarchy that would result without the Constitution, that Americans would be better off accepting Washington as President under a new government "than that he should be solicited again to accept of the command of an army." Caesar, "For the Daily Advertiser," *New York Daily Advertiser*, Oct. 1, 1787, p. 2.

103. George Washington to Alexander Hamilton, Aug. 28, 1788, *PGW*, CS 6: 481. "I shall certainly consider them as claiming a most distinguished place in my library," he noted. Ibid., 480–81.

104. A Citizen of New-York, "An Address to the People of the State of New York," April 15, 1788, *DHRC*, 20: 941. Although the piece was published under a pseudonym, Jay acknowledged his authorship.

105. George Washington to Henry Knox, May 15, 1788, *PGW*, CS 6: 275.

106. Ebenezer Hazard to George Washington, June 24, 1788, *PGW*, CS 6: 354.

107. In his superb biography of Clinton, John Kaminski explores Clinton's role at the convention and concludes that he released members of his antifederalist party to vote for ratification, thereby allowing it to pass. John P. Kaminski, *George Clinton: Yeoman Politician of the New Republic* (Madison, WI: Madison House, 1993), 163–64.

108. Washington to Pinckney, June 28, 1788, *PGW*, CS 6: 362.

109. Washington to Lear, June 29, 1788, *PGW*, CS 6: 364.

110. George Washington to Benjamin Lincoln, June 29, 1788, *PGW*, CS 6: 366.

111.   John Jay to George Washington, May 29, 1788, *PGW,* CS 6: 303; John Jay to George Washington, July 4, 1788, *PGW,* CS 6: 371.

112.   John Jay to George Washington, July 8, 1788, *PGW,* CS 6: 371.

113.   Samuel Low, "Ode for the Federal Procession," and William Pitt Smith, "Ode on the Adoption of the Constitution," *DHRC,* 21: 1608, 1614.

114.   John Jay to George Washington, July 23, 1788, *PGW,* CS 6: 394.

115.   George Washington to Thomas Jefferson, Aug. 31, 1788, *PGW,* CS 6: 493.

116.   Kaminski, *George Clinton,* 163–64.

117.   Henry Knox to George Washington, July 28, 1788, *PGW,* CS 6: 405 (emphasis added).

118.   "A Federal Song," *Albany Journal,* Aug. 4, 1788, p. 3.

119.   E.g., "A Federal Song," *New York Daily Advertiser,* Aug. 15, 1788, p. 2.

120.   Robert R. Livingston to George Washington, Oct. 21, 1788, *PGW,* PS 1: 56.

121.   Washington to Pinckney, June 28, 1788, *PGW,* CS 6: 361–62. With respect to Rhode Island, however, Washington added a day later that "he must be a hardy man, indeed, who will undertake to declare what *will be* the choice of the majority of *that* State, lest he should be suspected of having participated in *their phrensy.*" Washington to Lear, June 29, 1788, *PGW,* CS 6: 364.

122.   George Washington to Edward Newenham, Aug. 29, 1788, *PGW,* CS 6: 387–88.

123.   George Washington to John Lathrop, June 22, 1788, *PGW,* CS 6: 349.

124.   George Washington to Lafayette, May 28, 1788, *PGW,* CS 6: 299.

125.   George Washington to Lafayette, June 18, 1788, *PGW,* CS 6: 338.

Chapter 8: The First Federal Elections

1.   George Washington to Samuel Powel, Jan. 18, 1788, *PGW,* CS 6: 45.

2.   George Washington to John Jay, July 385, 1788, *PGW,* CS 6: 385. See also, George Washington to Jonathan Trumbull Jr., July 20, 1788, *PGW,* CS 6: 389 ("We shall impatiently wait the result from New York & North Carolina").

3.   "Resolutions of the Convention," Sept. 17, 1787, Farrand, 2: 665.

4.   James Madison to George Washington, July 21, 1788, *PGW,* CS 6: 392.

5.   George Washington to James Madison, Aug. 3, 1788, *PGW,* CS 6: 420.

6.   James Madison to George Washington, Aug. 11, 1788, *PGW,* CS 6: 438.

7.   George Washington to James Madison, Aug. 18, 1788, *PGW,* CS 6: 455. According to the French minister, Washington's ally Henry Lee made this argument in Congress, stating, "It is in Virginia's interest to attract this assembly to the shores of the Potomac, and that it would be much easier to fix it there in the event that it remained in New York, than if it found itself wrapped in the net of the Philadelphians." *Journal of Comte de Mousier,* July 31, 1788, *DHFFE,* 1: 55. Madison favored Philadelphia.

8.   Sept. 13, 1788, *JCC,* 34: 523. In October, Madison wrote to Washington, "It gives me great pleasure to find that . . . the vote fixing N. York for the first meeting of the new Congress has your approbation." James Madison to George Washington, Oct. 21, 1788, *PGW,* PS 1: 58.

9. George Washington to Samuel Powel, Sept. 15, 1788, *PGW*, CS 6: 516. Washington wrote this lament in response to Powel's letter complaining about the impasse: "Is not this a matter of Proceeding destitute of all Dignity. I confess that as an American I feel mortified at this trifling with the Sensibilities of the Union, which I believe were never more alive than on the present Occasion." Samuel Powel to George Washington, Aug. 9, 1788, *PGW*, CS 6: 435–36.

10. George Washington to James Madison, Sept. 23, 1788, *PGW*, CS 6: 534.

11. "The Virginia Convention, Wednesday, 25 June 1788," *DHRC*, 10: 1537 (Patrick Henry).

12. Washington to Madison, Sept. 23, 1788, *PGW*, CS 6: 534.

13. George Washington to James Madison, Aug. 17, 1788, *PGW*, CS 6: 454.

14. George Washington to Benjamin Lincoln, Aug. 28, 1788, *PGW*, CS 6: 483.

15. See, e.g., George Washington to Thomas Jefferson, Aug. 31, 1788, *PGW*, CS 6: 493.

16. In a late June letter to Washington, written after the Virginia convention, Madison depicted the antifederalists' new strategy as getting "a Congress appointed in the first instance that will commit suicide on their own Authority." James Madison to George Washington, June 27, 1788, *PGW*, CS 6: 356.

17. Washington to Madison, Sept. 23, 1788, *PGW*, CS 6: 534.

18. Washington to Lincoln, Aug. 28, 1788, *PGW*, CS 6: 483. For similar comments by Washington, see George Washington to James McHenry, July 31, 1788, *PGW*, CS 6: 409–10 and Washington to Madison, Sept. 23, 1788, *PGW*, CS 6: 534.

19. Washington to Madison, Sept. 23, 1788, *PGW*, CS 6: 534.

20. Benjamin Lincoln to George Washington, Sept. 24, 1788, *PGW*, PS 1: 6, 8.

21. Alexander Hamilton to George Washington, Sept. 1788, *PGW*, PS 1: 24. A month earlier, Hamilton had written to Washington about the new government, "It is indispensable you should lend yourself to its first operations—It is to little purpose to have *introduced* a system, if the weightiest influence is not given to its firm *establishment*, in the outset." Alexander Hamilton to George Washington, Aug. 13, 1788, *PGW*, CS 6: 444.

22. Samuel Vaughan to George Washington, Nov. 4, 1788, *PGW*, PS 1: 92.

23. Robert R. Livingston to George Washington, Oct. 21, 1788, *PGW*, PS 1: 56.

24. Washington to Madison, Sept. 23, 1788, *PGW*, CS 6: 534.

25. George Washington to Charles Pettit, Aug. 16, 1788, *PGW*, CS 6: 448.

26. George Washington to Alexander Hamilton, Aug. 28, 1788, *PGW*, CS 6: 481.

27. Hamilton used this as one of many arguments why Washington must accept the presidency. Hamilton to Washington, Sept. 1788, *PGW*, PS 1: 23.

28. Benjamin Harrison to George Washington, Feb. 26, 1789, *PGW*, PS 1: 345–46.

29. Explaining his procedure, Washington wrote to one job-seeking former army officer, "It would take up more time than I could well spare, to notice the applications which have been made to me in consequence of the new government. In answer to as many, as I have been at leisure to acknowledge, I have invariably represented the delicacy of my situation, the impropriety of bringing such things

before me, the decided resolution I had formerly made, and the ardent wishes I still entertain, of remaining in private life." George Washington to Henry Emanuel Lutterloh, Jan. 1, 1789, *PGW*, PS 1: 226–27.

30. George Washington to Samuel Hanson, June 8, 1788, *PGW*, CS 6: 317.

31. George Washington to Samuel Meredith, March 5, 1789, *PGW*, PS 1: 367. A well-connected Philadelphia merchant, Meredith was a former member of Congress and brother-in-law of Constitutional Convention delegate George Clymer. Washington appointed him treasurer of the United States. Expanding on this point in a letter to one particularly persistent applicant, Washington wrote that, if he did accept the presidency, "It is my fixed determination to enter there not only unfettered by promises but even unchargeable with creating or feeding the expectations of *any man living* for my assistance to Office." George Washington to Samuel Hanson, Jan. 10, 1789, *PGW*, PS 1: 241.

32. Benjamin Lincoln to George Washington, Feb. 20, 1789, *PGW*, PS 1: 331.

33. George Washington to Benjamin Lincoln, March 11, 1789, *PGW*, PS 1: 383.

34. George Washington to Benjamin Harrison, March 9, 1789, *PGW*, PS 1: 376–77.

35. Benjamin Lincoln to George Washington, April 3, 1789, *PGW*, PS 2: 14. Harrison's grandfather and father, also named Benjamin, were members of the Virginia House of Burgesses; his son and great-grandson (the latter also named Benjamin) became Presidents of the United States.

36. In both of these letters dating from early March 1789, Washington used a conditional construction—"if" or "should"—when speaking of becoming President. Washington to Harrison, March 9, 1789, *PGW*, PS 1: 376; Washington to Lincoln, March 11, 1789, *PGW*, PS 1: 383.

37. George Washington to James McIIenry, July 31, 1788, *PGW*, CS 6: 410.

38. Hamilton to Washington, Sept. 1788, *PGW*, PS 1: 23.

39. George Washington to Alexander Hamilton, Oct. 3, 1788, *PGW*, PS 1: 32.

40. George Washington to Jonathan Trumbull Jr., Dec. 4, 1788, *PGW*, PS 1: 159. See also George Washington to Benjamin Fishbourn, Dec. 23, 1788, *PGW*, PS 1: 198 ("The future is all a scene of darkness and uncertainty to me").

41. E.g., Washington to Hamilton, Oct. 3, 1788, *PGW*, PS 1: 33.

42. George Washington to Henry Lee Jr. Sept. 22, 1788, *PGW*, CS 6: 531.

43. George Washington to Gouverneur Morris, Nov. 28, 1788, *PGW*, PS 1: 136.

44. Benjamin Lincoln to George Washington, June 3, 1788, *PGW*, CS 6: 310.

45. Jonathan Trumbull Jr. to George Washington, June 20, 1788, *PGW*, CS 6: 345.

46. James Madison to George Washington, Nov. 5, 1788, *PGW*, PS 1: 95.

47. Washington to Lincoln, Aug. 28, 1788, *PGW*, CS 6: 483; Washington to Hamilton, Aug. 28, 1788, *PGW*, CS 6: 481.

48. Alexander Hamilton to George Washington, Nov. 18, 1788, *PGW*, PS 1: 119.

49. Gouverneur Morris to George Washington, Dec. 6, 1788, *PGW*, PS 1: 165.

50. Hamilton to Washington, Nov. 18, 1788, *PGW*, PS 1: 119.

51. E.g., Washington to Fishbourn, Dec. 23, 1788, *PGW*, PS 1: 199.

52. George Washington to Lafayette, Jan. 29, 1789, *PGW*, PS 1: 263.

53. E.g., reporting to Lincoln on Virginia's ratification of the Constitution, Washington wrote of his joy at every step taken by Americans "to render the Nation happy at home & respected abroad." George Washington to Benjamin Lincoln, June 29, 1788, *PGW*, CS 6: 365.

54. George Washington to Richard Henderson, June 19, 1788, *PGW*, CS 6: 340.

55. George Washington to Rochambeau, Jan. 29, 1789, *PGW*, PS 1: 266.

56. Washington to Lafayette, Jan. 29, 1789, *PGW*, PS 1: 264.

57. E.g., George Washington to Annis Boudinot Stockton, Aug. 31, 1788, *PGW*, CS 6: 497 ("I can never trace the concatenation of causes, which led to these events, without acknowledging the mystery and admiring the goodness of Providence").

58. Morris to Washington, Dec. 6, 1788, *PGW*, PS 1: 166.

59. George Washington to William Gordon, Dec. 23, 1788, *PGW*, PS 1: 201.

60. George Washington to John Langdon, July 20, 1788, *PGW*, CS 6: 388.

61. George Washington to Edward Newenham, Aug. 29, 1788, *PGW*, CS 6: 488.

62. For the first of many times when Wilson spoke at the Constitutional Convention in favor of "an election by the people," see Farrand, June 1, 1787, 1: 68.

63. Farrand, July 25, 1787, 2: 109.

64. Commenting on his state's electors, Virginia federalist Henry Lee reassured a doubtful Washington, who thought that antifederalists might oppose his election to weaken the new government, "Among the electors will be many antifederal characters, but not one of them will act on the principles you suggest in their choice of president." Henry Lee to George Washington, Jan. 17, 1789, *PGW*, PS 1: 247–48. See also "Philadelphia, 6th January," *Federal Gazette*, Jan. 6, 1789, p. 3 ("We hear from Virginia, that the anti-federalists intend to vote for General Washington, as president, but that Governor Clinton will have all their votes for vice-president of the United States"). For Clinton's support for Washington's election as President, see George Clinton to George Washington, March 10, 1789, *PGW*, PS 1: 378, and John P. Kaminski, *George Clinton: Yeoman Politician of the New Republic* (Madison, WI: Madison House, 1993), 172.

65. In Massachusetts, electors ran in the congressional districts, which left out two of the state's electors. Those two added electors were chosen directly by the state legislature. In New Hampshire, every voter had only one vote. Since the state had five electors, any candidate that received at least 10 percent of the vote was elected. In the event that fewer than five candidates received 10 percent of the vote, the legislature would chose the other electors from among the candidates receiving the most popular voters.

66. E.g., the Speaker of the Connecticut House explained in a letter to Washington that the federalist-dominated legislature retained the power to appoint electors because its members thought that this power would "more likely to be exercised with Judgment & discretion by the legislature, than it would probably be, was [it] to be entrusted to the people at large." Jonathan Trumbull Jr. to George Washington, Oct. 28, 1788, *PGW*, PS 1: 345.

67. E.g., Washington to Hamilton, Oct. 3, 1788, *PGW*, PS 1: 79.

68. For contemporaneous public discussion of this issue, see, e.g., "Federal Hints," *Federal Gazette*, Jan. 3, 1789 ("Should different federalists be put in nomination for vice-president, the federal interest will be divided and Clinton of New-York may *creep* in. If the federalists act with unanimity, Clinton's chance of being appointed vice-president, will be as bad as Paddy Henry's prospect of being chosen president").

69. For Madison's assessment of Clinton's prospects, see James Madison to Thomas Jefferson, Dec. 8, 1788, *PJM*, 11: 382 ("The enemies to the Government, at the head & the most inveterate, of whom, is Mr. Henry, are laying a train for the election of Governor Clinton, but it cannot succeed unless the federal votes are more dispersed than can well happen").

70. Edward Carrington to James Madison, Nov. 9, 1788, *PJM*, 11: 337 ("Mr. H. is putting in agitation the name of Clinton for vice Presidt. Which takes well with the Anti's—indeed it is more than probable he will receive a Majority among the Electors to be chosen").

71. Alexander Hamilton to James Madison, Nov. 23, 1788, *PAH*, 5: 235.

72. In its response to the governor's formal address to the legislature, the federalist-controlled Senate criticized Clinton for not calling the legislature into session soon enough to hold elections for the state's electors. "We should on our part, have referred it to the suffrages of the People at large, with the utmost satisfaction," the Senate response declared. "Assembly and Senate Proceedings, Wednesday, A.M.," Dec. 24, 1788, *DHFFE*, 3: 245.

73. Hamilton to Madison, Nov. 23, 1788, *PAH*, 5: 235.

74. Alexander Hamilton to Theodore Sedgwick, Jan. 29, 1789, *PAH*, 5: 251.

75. Among the first federalist newspapers to report this threat, the *Pennsylvania Gazette* noted on December 31, 1788, "Nothing but a union in the choice of Mr. Adams can exclude Governor Clinton from the Vice-President's chair." *Pennsylvania Gazette* (Philadelphia), December 31, 1788, *DHFFE*, 4: 122.

76. E.g., Crito, "Mr. Russell," *Massachusetts Centinel*, Nov. 29, 1788, p. 3 ("WASHINGTON's services in the field, have been only equaled by ADAM's [sic] exertions in the cabinet and the council").

77. E.g., Theodore Sedgwick to Alexander Hamilton, Nov. 2, 1788, *PAH*, 5: 228 ("Mr. Hancock has been very explicit in patronizing the doctrine of amendment"); Madison to Washington, Nov. 5, 1788, *PGW*, PS 1: 96 (Hancock "*it is said* rejects the idea of any secondary station").

78. For two representative letters from Madison discussing the four candidates and settling on Adams, see James Madison to George Washington, Nov. 5, 1788, *PJM*, 11: 335 (characterizing the vice presidency as "an unprofitable dignity"); James Madison to Thomas Jefferson, Oct. 8, 1788, *PJM*, 11: 276 ("For the vice Presidency, are talked of principally Mr. Hancock & Mr. Adams. Mr. Jay or Genl. Knox would I believe be preferred to either, but both of them will probably chuse to remain where they are"). For two representative letters by federalist leaders expressing a preference for Adams over Hancock, see Theodore Sedgwick to Alexander Hamilton, Oct. 9, 1788, *PAH*, 5: 225; Samuel A. Otis to Theodore Sedgwick, Oct. 13, 1788, *DHFFE*, 4: 77.

79. E.g., Theodore Sedgwick to Alexander Hamilton, Oct. 16, 1788, *PAH*, 5: 226 (noting as a positive development to Hamilton that "Mr. Adams was formerly infinitely more democratical than at present").

80. Madison raised these objections in a letter to Jefferson, concluding with the observation that Adams "would not be a very cordial second to the general." James Madison to Thomas Jefferson, Oct. 17, 1788, *PJM*, 11: 296.

81. Page Smith, *John Adams* (Garden City, NY: Doubleday, 1962), 2: 739.

82. Alexander Hamilton to Theodore Sedgwick, Oct. 9, 1788, *PAH*, 5: 225. In this letter, Hamilton also expressed concern that Adams "is unfriendly in his sentiments to General Washington." Ibid.

83. Sedgwick explained to Hamilton that Adams formerly questioned authority more than at present and noted "that any suggestion that he is unfriendly to general Washington is entirely unfounded." Sedgwick to Hamilton, Oct. 16, 1788, *PAH*, 5: 226; Theodore Sedgwick to Alexander Hamilton, Nov. 2, 1788, *PAH*, 5: 228 (quote). Madison soon wrote to Jefferson that Adams had pledged to support Washington. James Madison to Thomas Jefferson, Dec. 8, 1788, *PJM*, 11: 381.

84. Alexander Hamilton to James Madison, Nov. 23, 1788, *PAH*, 5: 236. See also Alexander Hamilton to Theodore Sedgwick, Nov. 9, 1789, *PAH*, 5: 231 ("I have upon the whole concluded that [Adams] ought to be supported").

85. John Adams to Abigail Adams Smith, July 16, 1788, *DHFFE*, 4: 43; John Ferling, *John Adams: A Life* (Newtown, CT: American Political Biography Press, 1992), 298.

86. Benjamin Lincoln to George Washington, Sept. 24, 1788, *PGW*, PS 1: 6.

87. George Washington to Benjamin Lincoln, Oct. 26, 1788, *PGW*, PS 1: 72.

88. George Washington to Benjamin Lincoln, Jan. 31, 1789, *PGW*, PS 1: 267.

89. Alexander Hamilton to James Madison, Nov. 23, 1788, *PAH*, 5: 236.

90. E.g., Alexander Hamilton to James Wilson, Jan. 25, 1788, *PAH*, 5: 249.

91. Adams soon wrote to his close friend Benjamin Rush about the matter, "Nothing but the apprehension of great Mischief, and the final failure of the Government by my Refusal and assigning my reasons for it, prevented me from Spurning" the vice presidency. John Adams to Benjamin Rush, May 17, 1789, *AFP*, reel 115.

92. E.g., writing to his Virginia state legislator, Washington asked, "We are anxious to know who are to be our Senators—How the districts are formed—and whether the electors of the *representative* Branch of the Assembly are to vote for the whole number (ten) which are allowed them—or for one *only*, in the district where they reside?" George Washington to David Stuart, Nov. 10, 1788, *PGW*, PS 1: 102.

93. George Washington to Benjamin Fishbourn, Dec. 23, 1788, *PGW*, PS 1: 199. Washington expressed similar sentiments to Madison in September by urging "all the advocates of the Constitution" to combine their efforts to send their best candidates to Congress. Washington to Madison, Sept. 23, 1788, *PGW*, CS 6: 534.

94. Washington to Lincoln, Oct. 26, 1788, *PGW*, PS 1: 70. This letter goes on to discuss and urge the election of federalists.

95. Tench Coxe to James Madison, Oct. 12, 1788, *PJM*, 11: 312–13. If Maclay was a federalist when elected, he did not remain one for long.

96. Washington to Lincoln, Oct. 26, 1788, *PGW*, PS 1: 70.

97. George Washington to Jonathan Trumbull Jr., Dec. 4, 1788, *PGW*, PS 1: 158–59.

98. Henry reportedly declared that Madison's "election would terminate in producing rivulets of blood throughout the land." Henry Lee to James Madison, Nov. 19, 1788, *PJM*, 11: 356.

99. Edmund Randolph to James Madison, Nov. 10, 1788, *PJM*, 11: 339.

100. George Washington to Benjamin Lincoln, Nov. 14, 1788, *PGW*, PS 1: 108. Since this partisan "gerrymandering" occurred long before Massachusetts governor Elbridge Gerry orchestrated similar districting, perhaps we should call the activity "Henrymandering."

101. See George Washington to James Madison, Dec. 1, 1788, *PGW*, PS 1: 144 (alluding to advice in a lost letter); James Madison to George Washington, Dec. 2, 1788, *PGW*, PS 1: 146–47 (discussing his return to campaign).

102. Prior to the vote for Senate in Virginia, federalist Edward Carrington passed along Washington's advice to Madison, "Your services in the Senate will be of more importance than in the other House, as there will be much depending on that branch unconnected with the other." Edward Carrington to James Madison, Oct. 11, 1788, *PJM*, 11: 306.

103. E.g., A Marylander, "To the Inhabitants of Baltimore-Town," *Maryland Gazette*, Sept. 12, 1788, in *DHFFE*, 2: 145.

104. James Madison to George Washington, Nov. 5, 1788, *PJM*, 11: 335.

105. Joshua Atherton to John Lamb, Feb. 23, 1789, *DHFFE*, 1: 839.

106. Henry Knox to George Washington, Dec. 21, 1788, *PGW*, PS 1: 195 (Knox's comments refer to Connecticut as well as New Hampshire and his home state of Massachusetts). Writing to Washington about the election in Massachusetts, Lincoln boasted, "Our Senators are federal indeed." Benjamin Lincoln to George Washington, Dec. 20, 1788, *PGW*, PS 1: 194.

107. H. D. Gough et al., "Baltimore, December 29, 1788," *Maryland Journal*, Dec. 30, 1788, *DHFFE*, 2: 169.

108. George Washington to Lafayette, Jan. 29, 1789, *PGW*, PS 1: 262.

109. Alexander Hamilton to Samuel Jones, Jan. 21, 1788, *PAH*, 5: 245.

110. In March, Jay wrote to Washington from New York, "It is still doubtful whether Senators will be appointed for this State." John Jay to George Washington, March 1, 1789, *PGW*, PS 1: 349.

111. George Washington to Arthur Young, Dec. 4, 1788, *PGW*, PS 1: 161. Washington wrote about laying out the field at Mount Vernon's Muddy Hole farm in his diary. *GWD*, Jan. 1, 1789, 4: 3.

112. Washington to Young, Dec. 4, 1788, *PGW*, PS 1: 162.

113. Madame de Bréhan and Moustier to Jefferson, Dec. 29, 1788, *PTJ*, 14: 399.

114. On the reaction to Comte de Moustier and de Bréhan, see James Madison to Thomas Jefferson, Dec. 8, 1788, *PJM*, 11: 383.

115. Washington to Young, Dec. 4, 1788, *PGW*, PS 1: 162.

116. At the time, during private deliberations on the state election law, Henry was reported to have asked about Madison and the new congressional districts,

"How shall we managed to lay them off oo, as to keep *him* altogether out of congress?" A Marylander, "Mr. Hayes," *Maryland Gazette*, Jan. 2, 1789, *DHFFE*, 2: 182.

117. James Madison to George Washington, Dec. 2, 1788, *PJM*, 11: 377.

118. No record exists of Madison's conversations with Washington in December other than Washington's diary entries suggesting that they spent considerable time together at Mount Vernon. In a mid-January letter to Washington, Madison freely discussed his efforts to convince voters that he supported amending the Constitution. James Madison to George Washington, Jan. 14, 1789, *PJM*, 11: 418.

119. At the Constitutional Convention, Virginia voted against Mason's motion for adding a bill of rights. Since Randolph supported the motion, Madison, Washington, and Blair must have voted against it. Farrand, Sept. 12, 1787, 2: 588. Madison dismissed bills of rights as "parchment barriers" in *Federalist* No. 48. Publius, "The Federalist, No. 47," *New-York Packet*, Feb. 1, 1788, p. 2 (later renumbered as 48).

120. See George Washington to Thomas Jefferson, Aug. 31, 1788, *PGW*, CS 6: 493 ("there are scarcely any of the amendments which have been suggested, to which I have *much* objection, except that which goes to the prevention of direct taxation"); Madison to Jefferson, Oct. 17, 1788, *PJM*, 11: 297 ("I have never thought the omission [of a bill of rights] a material defect, nor been anxious to supply it even by *subsequent* amendment, for any other reason than that it is anxiously desired by others"); James Madison to Thomas Jefferson, Dec. 8, 1788, *PJM*, 11: 382 ("The friends of the Constitution, some from an approbation of particular amendments, others from a spirit of conciliation, are generally agreed that the System should be revised. But they wish the revisal to be carried no farther than to supply additional guards for liberty, without abridging the sum of power transferred from the states to the general government or altering previous to trial, the particular structure of the latter"). In his October letter to Jefferson, Madison observed that, even though parchment barriers, bills of rights may "acquire by degrees the character of fundamental maxims of free Governments, and as they become incorporated with the national sentiment, counteract the impulses of interest and passion." Ibid: 298–99.

121. James Madison to Thomas Mann Randolph, Jan. 13, 1789, *PJM*, 11: 416. Various campaign letters from Madison, some published in local newspapers and all making the same argument, appear in *DHFFE*, 2: 330–41.

122. For Monroe's position, see "An Appeal for the Election of James Monroe," *DHFFE*, 2: 329–30.

123. Madison to Washington, Jan. 14, 1789, *PJM*, 11: 418.

124. "Observations by Mr. Madison," in Henry S. Randall, *The Life of Thomas Jefferson* (Philadelphia: Lippincott, 1871), 3: 255 n. 2.

125. James Madison to George Eve, Jan. 2, 1789, *PJM*, 11: 405. Eve was an Orange County Baptist minister.

126. See Benjamin Johnson to James Madison, Jan. 19, 1789, *PJM*, 11: 384 (discussing Eve's public endorsement of Madison on these grounds); John Leland to James Madison, Feb. 15, 1789, *PJM*, 11: 442. A leading Virginia Baptist, Leland lived in Madison's district.

127. James Madison to Edmund Randolph, March 1, 1789, *PJM*, 11: 453.

128. George Washington to Samuel Powel, Feb. 5, 1789, *PGW*, PS 1: 281.

129. George Washington to Rochambeau, Jan. 29, 1789, *PGW*, PS 1: 266.

130. *Maryland Journal*, Jan. 13, 1789, *DHFFE*, 2: 199–200.

131. Washington to Lafayette, Jan. 29, 1789, *PGW*, PS 1: 262.

132. On Washington's expressed dismay, see, e.g., George Washington to Benjamin Harrison, March 9, 1789, *PGW*, PS 1: 376 ("If it should be my inevitable fate to administer the government [for Heaven knows that no event can be less desired by me] . . ."). On Madison reviewing the inaugural address, see George Washington to James Madison, Feb. 16, 1789, *PGW*, PS 1: 316.

Chapter 9: The Inaugural Parade

1. The main house, or simply "Mount Vernon" or "Home House," had six guest bedrooms on the second floor separated by a wall from the family suite, with each grouping having a separate staircase. The house also had two guest bedrooms on the first floor and two or three on the third floor.

2. The cookbook was the sixth edition of Hannah Glasse's *"First Catch Your Hare . . .": The Art of Cookery Made Plain and Simple*, originally published in 1763. According to financial records, Washington acquired the book in 1771.

3. George Washington to David Humphreys, Dec. 26, 1786, *PGW*, CS 4: 480.

4. See, e.g., John Fea, *Was America Founded as a Christian Nation?* (Louisville, KY: Westminster, 2011), 171–90 (an extended analysis of Washington's religious beliefs based on original sources by a leading evangelical Christian scholar); Ron Chernow, *Washington: A Life* (New York: Penguin, 2010), 130–35 (a prize-winning biography).

5. William White to Bird Wilson, Dec. 21, 1832, in Bird Wilson, *Memoir of the Life of the Right Reverend William White, D.D.S.* (Philadelphia: Kay & Brother, 1839), 193. The brother-in-law of Robert Morris, White served as chaplain to the Continental Congress and became one of the initial bishops of the American Episcopal Church. Washington attended his church both as a member of the Continental Congress and when serving as President in Philadelphia. White also noted, "General Washington never received the communion at churches of which I am parochial minister." Ibid., 197 (White added, "Mrs Washington was a habitual communicant").

6. "Agreement with Philip Bater," April 23, 1787, *WGW*, 29: 207.

7. David Humphreys, "Mount-Vernon: An Ode," in *The Miscellaneous Works of David Humphreys* (New York: Swords, 1804), 224. The best-known members of the Hartford Wits were poet Joel Barlow, Yale president Timothy Dwight, and former Washington aide John Trumbull Jr., who served in Congress and as Connecticut's governor.

8. See, e.g., Kenneth R. Bowling, "George Washington's Vision for the United States," in Peter Onuf and Robert McDonald, eds., *The Vision of the Founders* (Charlottesville: University of Virginia Press, forthcoming) ("it belongs with the 1783 Address to the States and the 1796 Farewell Address as the most extensive and detailed statements of Washington's political views"); James Thomas Flexner, *George*

Washington and the New Nation (Boston: Little, Brown, 1967), 162–64 ("even in its mutilated form, the discarded inaugural is an extremely important document").

9. "Fragments of a Draft of the First Inaugural Address," January 1789, in John Rhodehamel, ed., *George Washington: Writings* (New York: Library of America, 1997), 706–9.

10. Ibid., 707–9, 712, 715–16.

11. George Washington to Lafayette, Jan. 29, 1789, *PGW*, PS 1: 263.

12. Abraham Baldwin to Joel Barlow, Jan. 10, 1789, *DHFFE*, 4: 135.

13. A Republican, "For the Boston Gazette," *Boston Gazette*, Feb. 23, 1789, p. 2.

14. "Philadelphia, December 13," *Federal Gazette*, Dec. 13, 1788, p. 3. This article was reprinted in at least three Maryland newspapers and two Virginia newspapers prior to the election, as well as in at least four newspapers in other states. Ten days later, the same newspaper warned, "The contest will be between the FIRST BENEFACTOR of the United States, and an ambitious demagogue in Virginia, who has placed himself at the head of the debtors and speculators of that state, and who sees that the establishment of the federal government must forever make him a contemptible state bawler." "Philadelphia, December 20," *Federal Gazette*, Dec. 20, 1788, p. 3. See also "Philadelphia, 26th January," *Federal Gazette*, Dec. 26, 1788, p. 3 ("The Antifederalists are active, and it is said have formed a plan for bringing in Henry . . . instead of our beloved Washington").

15. A Marylander, "Mr. Hayes," *Maryland Gazette*, Dec. 30, 1788, *DHFFE*, 2: 166. See also A Marylander, "Mr. Hayes," *Maryland Gazette*, Jan. 2, 1789, *DHFFE*, 2: 181–82 (accusing specific antifederalist candidates of secretly preferring Henry over Washington).

16. Samuel Sterett, "To the PUBLIC," Dec. 13, 1788, *DHFFE*, 2:170 (Sterett was an antifederalist candidate for elector in Maryland).

17. "Philadelphia, 14th January," *Federal Gazette*, Jan. 14, 1789, p. 3.

18. For the vote totals in Maryland by county, see *DHFFE*, 2: 204–5.

19. E.g., Carlisle antifederalists explained to state party leader John Nicholson, "There was an election held yesterday for Electors but our party left it to the others and did not vote. We are sorry that last election day proved such a wet day which was much to the advantage of the opposite party." Alexander McKeehan and George Logue to John Nicholson, Jan. 8, 1789, *DHFFE*, 1: 282. For the vote totals in Pennsylvania by county, see *DHFFE*, 1: 390–91.

20. For the vote totals in Delaware by county, see *DHFFE*, 2: 83.

21. George Washington to Samuel Powel, Feb. 5, 1789, *PGW*, PS 1: 281 (parenthetical phrase deleted).

22. For the vote totals in Virginia by district, see *DHFFE*, 2: 306–8. No winner was certified in one of Virginia's twelve electoral districts.

23. Jonathan Trumbull Jr. to George Washington, Oct. 28, 1788, *PGW*, PS 1: 79.

24. The process was somewhat different in the two states. In Massachusetts, town-meeting votes were combined at the district level, with the names of the top two candidates from each district going forward to the legislature. In New Hampshire, which had five electors, town-meeting votes were combined statewide,

with the names of the top ten candidates going forward to the legislature. Any candidate receiving more than 10 percent of the total town-meeting vote, or effectively a majority for a five-person field, was automatically elected. None did.

25. Benjamin Lincoln to George Washington, Jan. 4, 1789, *PGW*, PS 1: 233.

26. "Proceedings of the Legislature of this State," *New Hampshire Spy*, Jan. 13, 1789, p. 94.

27. George Washington to Alexander Hamilton, Oct. 3, 1788, *PGW*, PS 1: 33.

28. George Washington to William Pierce, Jan. 1, 1789, *PGW*, PS 1: 281.

29. If Washington did not see the article in its original Massachusetts source, he should have seen it reprinted in the *Federal Gazette* or *Virginia Centinel*. "BOSTON January 21," *Federal Gazette*, Feb. 2, 1789, p. 2. For an example of the letters reaching Washington during this period, see John Edger Howard to George Washington, Jan. 23, 1789, *PGW*, PS 1: 252, in which a Maryland correspondent reported that the federalist ticket had not only swept his state but "that in the county which bears your name out of 1164 taken there was not one for the antifederal ticket."

30. George Washington to Henry Knox, Jan. 29, 1789, *PGW*, PS 1: 260. The ad appeared in New York's *Daily Advertiser* and mentioned two colors, London Smoke and Hartford Gray, but clearly there were more. "American Woolens," *Daily Advertiser*, Jan. 21, 1789, p. 3. In his letter to Knox, Washington wrote that for her riding habit, his wife wanted the color London Smoke.

31. A Philadelphia Mechanic, "To the Editor," *Federal Gazette*, Jan. 7, 1789, p. 3. The other article, which appeared two days later and used similar phrases, reported on "a meeting of a number of the principal citizens in and about the borough of Wilmington," Delaware, at which everyone, by prior agreement, was "clad in complete suits of American manufacture." The writer urged all patriotic Americans to emulate their example. "From the Wilmington Gazette," *Federal Gazette*, Jan. 9, 1789, p. 3.

32. George Washington to Lafayette, Jan. 29, 1789, *PGW*, PS 1: 264. Washington added that he used only American-made porter and cheese. "Both those articles may now be purchased of an excellent quality," he noted.

33. "This Day," *Massachusetts Centinel*, Feb. 4, 1789, *DHFFE* 4: 166.

34. E.g., one widely reprinted tally first published just before the vote gave 76 votes to Washington, 53 to Adams, and 26 to Clinton. "Springfield, Jan. 24," *New-Hampshire Spy*, Feb. 3, 1789, p. 119. Just after the balloting, another tally put the vote for the seven northern states at 49 for Washington, 45 for Adams, and 4 for Clinton. "It Is Said, *Massachusetts Centinel*, Feb. 7, 1789, *DHFFE*, 4: 169.

35. "Extract of Another Letter," *Cumberland Gazette*, Nov. 19, 1789, p. 3.

36. James Madison to George Washington, March 5, 1789, *PGW*, PS 1: 366.

37. "Augusta, February 7," *Columbia Herald*, Feb. 26, 1789, p. 2.

38. "Philadelphia, February 14," *Pennsylvania Mercury*, Feb. 14, 1789, p. 4.

39. Gouverneur Morris to George Washington, Feb. 23, 1789, *PGW*, PS 1: 338–39.

40. "Portland," *Cumberland Gazette*, March 19, 1789, p. 3.

41. "From New York," *New-Hampshire Spy*, March 24, 1789, p. 175.

42. George Washington to Richard Conway, March 6, 1789, *PGW*, PS 1: 368.

43. George Washington to George Augustine Washington, March 31, 1789, *PGW*, PS 1: 475.

44. George Washington to Tobias Lear, July 31, 1797, *PGW*, RS 4: 157.

45. In the only know exception to this rule, Washington remarked in his diary on June 30, 1785, that he had "dined with only Mrs. Washington, which I believe is the first instance of it since my retirement from public life." *GWD*, June 30, 1785, 2: 386.

46. Washington to Washington, March 31, 1789, *PGW*, PS 1: 475. In this letter, Washington noted that "the event that I dreaded" (that is, becoming President) would save him from a necessity that he also dreaded (that is, living frugally).

47. George Washington to Richard Conway, March 4, 1789, *PGW*, PS 1: 361. Washington added, "Under this statement, I am inclined to do what I never expected to be reduced to the necessity of doing—that is, to borrow money at interest."

48. George Washington to Charles Carter, Sept. 14, 1790, *PGW*, PS 6: 432.

49. Washington to Conway, March 6, 1789, *PGW*, PS 1: 368. This letter also mentioned the 6 percent interest rate, which it depicted as the "Maryland" rate. At the time, states typically capped interest rates on loans and Maryland allowed a higher rate than Virginia. In the letter, Washington offered to make the loan in Maryland rather than in Virginia, presumably to allow the higher interest rate.

50. George Washington to Henry Knox, April 1, 1789, *PGW*, PS 2: 2.

51. George Washington to James Madison, March 30, 1789, *PGW*, PS 1: 464.

52. Born Pierre Charles L'Enfant, the architect and engineer consistently used the name "Peter" after arriving in America from France in 1777. For all practical purposes, that served as his legal American name. For an exhaustive analysis of this name controversy, see Kenneth R. Bowling, *Peter Charles L'Enfant: Vision, Honor, and Male Friendship in the Early American Republic* (Washington, DC: George Washington University, 2002), 1, 64–66. For a reference to the old New York City Hall as a Gothic heap, see "On the Federal Building," *Daily Advertiser*, March 19, 1789, p. 2 (praising the building's new look).

53. "Arrangement," *Gazette of the United States*, April 18, 1789, p. 11.

54. Richard Henry Lee to George Washington, April 6, 1789, *PGW*, PS 2: 29.

55. James Madison to George Washington, April 6, 1789, *PGW*, PS 2: 30.

56. "Address by Charles Thomson," April 14, 1789, *PGW*, PS 2: 54–55. Thomson also delivered a formal letter from Senate President Pro Tem John Langdon informing Washington of the vote and expressing Langdon's hope "that so auspicious a mark of public confidence will meet your approbation." John Langdon to George Washington, April 6, 1789, *PGW*, PS 2: 29.

57. "Address to Charles Thomson," April 14, 1789, *PGW*, PS 2: 56. Washington also gave Thomson a formal letter for Senate President Pro Tem John Langdon declaring his decision "to obey the important & flattering call of my Country." George Washington to John Langdon, April 14, 1789, *PGW*, PS 2: 54.

58. With Washington's diary for the trip lost, no record exists of the servants that accompanied this trip other than a letter from Tobias Lear noting that Washington's longtime valet William Lee went along as far as Philadelphia, where

he reinjured his knee and was forced to remain for medical treatment. Lear's letter also suggests that Mount Vernon coachman Jacob Jacobus, an indentured servant, served as a driver. Tobias Lear to George Augustine Washington, May 3, 1789, *DHFFC* Project (copies supplied by *DHFFC* co-editor Kenneth R. Bowling). Typically, Washington would travel on such a journey with a rider on the front horse, a driver on an outside front seat, and a valet on an outside rear seat.

59.   *DGW*, April 16, 1789, 5: 445.

60.   "To George Washington, Esquire" and "His Excellency's Answer," *Gazette of the United States*, April 29, 1789, p. 24.

61.   "Baltimore, April 21," *Pennsylvania Packet*, April 28, 1789, p. 2.

62.   "Address of the Citizens of Baltimore," *Federal Gazette*, April 27, 1789, p. 2.

63.   The ode carries the date and place of April 16, 1789, Bladensburg, Maryland, which was the nearest town to Spurrier's Tavern, but it was first published in a Baltimore newspaper. "From the Maryland Journal," *Pennsylvania Packet*, May 1, 1789, p. 3.

64.   "Wilmington, April 25," *Pennsylvania Packet*, April 28, 1789, p. 3.

65.   Accounts differ on whether the wreath landed on Washington's head or was suspended above it, though one contemporary article clearly states that the wreath fell "within a short distance of the Excellency's head as he passed under it." "Philadelphia, April 21," *Independent Gazetteer*, April 21, 1789, p. 3. Peale family accounts have Washington brushing off the wreath but kissing Angelica. Flexner, *George Washington*, 175 (also states that that wreath "landed on his head").

66.   "Philadelphia, 20 April," *Federal Gazette*, April 20, 1789, p. 2; "Philadelphia, April 29," *Freemans's Journal*, April 29, 1789, p. 3; "Philadelphia, 22 April," *New-York Daily Gazette*, April 27, 1789, p. 410; William Spohn Baker, *Washington After the Revolution* (Philadelphia: Lippincott, 1898), 124 (text of article from *Pennsylvania Gazette*).

67.   "Philadelphia, 21 April," *Federal Gazette*, April 21, 1789, p. 3. Morris was not at home for Washington's 1789 visit because he had already taken his seat in the federal senate.

68.   "Philadelphia, 22 April," *Federal Gazette*, April 22, 1789, p. 3.

69.   "Trenton, April 21, 1789," *Gazette of the United States*, April 25, 1789, p. 19.

70.   "Trenton," *New-York Daily Gazette*, May 1, 1789, p. 426.

71.   "A Sonata," *Federal Gazette*, April 25, 1789, p. 3.

72.   "Philadelphia, May 1," *Philadelphia Packet*, May 1, 1789, p. 2. Following the serenade, Washington wrote a note of appreciation to the singers stating (in the third person) that the event "made such impressions on his remembrance, as, he assures them, will never be effaced." George Washington to the Ladies of Trenton, April 21, 1789, *PGW*, PS 2: 108.

73.   "New-Brunswick, April 7," *Pennsylvania Packet*, April 13, 1789, p. 3.

74.   "In our account," *New-York Packet*, May 1, 1789, p. 3.

75.   "Ode to be Sung on the Arrival of the President of the United States," *New-York Daily Gazette*, April 23, 1789, p. 398. Several sources note that this song was sung by a mixed chorus on the boat.

76.　Elias Boudinot to Hannah Boudinot, April 24, 1789, Clarence Winthrop Bowen, ed., *The History of the Centennial Celebration of the Inauguration of George Washington* (New York: Appleton, 1892), 29.

77.　"New York, April 25," *Gazette of the United States*, April 25, 1789, p. 15.

78.　"Diary of William Maclay," April 24, 1789, and May 8, 1789, *DHFFC*, 9: 4–5, 28–29; James H. Hutson, "John Adams' Title Campaign," *New England Quarterly* 41 (1968): 31–34. The text of Adams's speech was not recorded. His proposed titles appear in private letters but at least one senator noted that Adams also suggested titles in the Senate. "Diary of Maclay," May 8, 1789, p. 28. At the time, the Vice President, as presiding officer of the Senate, could both speak and propose motions in the Senate. The Senate revoked these privileges in part due to Adams's extensive use of them. In a letter to Washington, Adams wrote about the presidency, "Neither Dignity, nor Authority, can be Supported in human Minds collection into nations or any great numbers without a Splendor and Majisty, in Some degree, proportioned to them." John Adams to George Washington, May 17, 1789, *PGW*, PS 2: 314.

79.　*Annals of Congress*, April 23, 1789, 1: 24 (Senate).

80.　"Diary of Maclay," April 24, 1789, p. 4.

81.　"Diary of Maclay," May 8, 1789, pp. 28–29.

82.　*Annals of Congress*, April 25, 1789, 1: 25 (Senate).

83.　"New-York, May 1," *New-York Daily Gazette*, May 1, 1789, p. 426 (emphasis added). For the shift in venue, see *Annals of Congress*, April 27, 1789, 1: 25 (Senate).

84.　*Annals of Congress*, April 29, 1789, 1: 241 (House).

85.　E.g., R--- R--- to S---, May 1, 1789, "Notes and Queries," *Historical Magazine* 3 (1859): 184 ("I caught his eye, and had the honor of a very gracious bow from him: this, from so great a man in so high a station, I thought myself highly honored"). This example comes from Washington's time in New York.

86.　Thomas Jefferson, *The Anas, WTJ*, 1: 279–80.

87.　"Fragments," 707. At this point, the address went on to observe, "Whenever a government is to be instituted or changed by Consent of the people, confidence in the person placed at the head of it, is, perhaps, more peculiarly necessary."

88.　Discussing the arrangement, see George Washington to David Stuart, July 26, 1789, *PGW*, PS 3: 322.

89.　At the outset, New York chancellor Robert Livingston advised as much when Washington asked for his views on the etiquette proper for the President. That titles, formality, and restricted access are "not essentially necessary I infer from the unlimited respect which every rank of Citizen feels for our Excellency tho in your public life you indulged them in an easy access," Livingston wrote to Washington. "Hereditary Monarchs must in the common course of things be frequently men of little abilities & often have great defects it is therefore necessary to surround them with guards & to dazel beholders with a false glare. Elective Magistrates are known before they are elected, their virtues are the cause of their elevation, the exposing these to [the] public can not tend to diminish the respect which they originally created." Robert R. Livingston to George Washington, May 2, 1789, *PGW*, PS 2: 193–94.

90.　James Madison referenced in Flexner, *George Washington*, 193.

91. *DGW*, April 23, 1789, 5: 447.

92. George Washington to Edward Rutledge, May 5, 1789, *PGW*, PS 2: 217.

93. John Adams to Benjamin Rush, March 19, 1812, in John A. Schultz and Douglas Adair, eds., *The Spur of Fame: Dialogues of John Adams and Benjamin Rush, 1805–1813* (San Marino, CA: Huntington, 1966), 211–12. In a similar vein, Adams also commented on Washington's popular style, "Virginian Geese are all Swans," and appraised it as worth "five Talents." John Adams to Benjamin Rush, Nov. 11, 1807, in Alexander Biddle, ed., *Old Family Letters* (Philadelphia: Lippincott, 1892), 169.

94. Washington to Stuart, *PGW*, PS 3: 323.

95. About this dining arrangement, Lear wrote at the time, "We have engaged Black Sam Frances [*sic*] as Steward & superintendent of the Kitchen, and a very excellent fellow he is in that latter department—he tosses up such a number of fine dishes that we are distracted in our choice when we set down to table, and obliged to hold a long consultation upon the subject before we can determine what to attack." Lear to Washington, May 3, 1789, *DHFFE* Project. Probably of mixed French and African descent, Samuel Fraunces, known as "Black Sam," was born in the Caribbean and had moved to New York by 1755. He opened what became known as Fraunces Tavern in 1762. Washington held the farewell dinner with his officers at the tavern on December 4, 1783. Along with hiring Fraunces, during his first week in New York, Washington added two liveried footmen, a porter, and a maid to the staff he brought from Mount Vernon. Ultimately, Washington's household staff in New York numbered about twenty and included a mix of paid workers, slaves, and indentured servants.

96. Ibid., 322. Lear also discussed this crush of midday visitors in Lear to Washington, May 3, 1789, *DHFFE* Project ("We have no company to eat or drink with us—but hitherto there has been the greatest abundance from 9 a.m. to 3 p.m. to pay their *etiquettical congee*").

97. The best direct evidence that Madison either drafted or assisted in drafting Washington's first inaugural address appears in a May 4 letter from Washington asking Madison "to finish the good work" he had started by writing the President's reply to the House response to the inaugural address. George Washington to James Madison, May 5, 1789, *PGW*, PS 2: 216. Madison had also written the House response, so he would be replying to his own response to his own address. Due to his dual role as House leader and key presidential advisor, the editors of the Madison Papers depict Madison as "in effect the 'prime minister'" during this period and attribute Washington's inaugural address to Madison. "Editorial Note," *PJM*, 12: 120–21.

98. "Of To-Morrow," *Gazette of the United States*, April 29, 1789, p. 19.

99. The description of Washington's dress is compiled from contemporary newspaper articles and private letters. Experts believe that Washington wore a black, beaverskin, bicorned hat, not a tricorne, and carried the dress sword now at Mount Vernon. In the end, Washington was dressed as elaborately as a Cossack riding into battle.

100. Washington Irving, *Life of George Washington* (New York: Putnam's Sons, 1882), 581. Born in 1783 and then living on Pearl Street near Federal Hall, Irving was named for George Washington. When told that, Washington reportedly pat-

ted the youngster's head. Contemporary accounts vary somewhat on the order of the procession, with some, for example, putting the heads of the departments in front of Washington and some noting that the diplomatic corps rode among the invited dignitaries. The order presented in the text appeared in many newspapers.

101. "Diary of Maclay," April 30, 1789, pp. 11–12.

102. No precise estimate of the number of spectators survives. Some accounts refer to thousands; several local newspapers simply call it "an immense concourse of citizens." E.g. "New-York, May 7," *New-York Journal*, May 7, 1789, p. 3.

103. *Memoir of the Life of Eliza S. M. Quincy* (Boston: Wilson & Son, 1861), 51.

104. Ibid., 51–52.

105. *Annals of Congress*, April 30, 1789, 1: 27 (Senate). Many later accounts have Washington adding the words "so help me God" to the end of the oath, but no contemporary accounts do so. According to many contemporary accounts, however, he did kiss the Bible after saying the oath.

106. Joseph J. Ellis, *His Excellency: George Washington* (New York: Knopf, 2004), 186.

107. John Adams to Benjamin Rush, Nov. 11, 1807, in Alexander Biddle, ed., *Old Family Letters* (Philadelphia: Lippincott, 1892), 170.

108. Diego de Gardoqui to Florida Blanca, May 1, 1789, in Bowen, ed., *History of Inauguration*, 49. Maclay used the word "ungainly" in his account, but others made similar observations. "Diary of Maclay," April 30, 1789, p. 13.

109. *Annals of Congress*, April 30, 1789, 1: 27–29 (Senate). Characteristically, in speaking about "God" in this formal address, Washington never actually used that term. Instead, he referred to "the Great Author of every public and private good" at one point and "the benign Parent of the human race" at another.

110. Although many accounts only mention the presidential party visiting Livingston's house to view the fireworks, Lear noted that it also stopped at the nearby house of Henry Knox, "where we had a full view of the works." Lear to Washington, May 3, 1789, *DHFFE* Project.

111. Ibid.

112. "New-York, May 1," *Daily Advertiser*, May 1, 1789, p. 2.

Epilogue

1. George Washington, "To the PEOPLE of the United States," *Claypoole's American Daily Advertiser*, Sept. 19, 1796, p. 2.

2. Tobias Lear, "Narrative Accounts of the Death of George Washington: Diary Account," Dec. 14–15, 1799, *PGW*, RS 4: 546.

3. Ibid., 4: 549. Fearing that they might kill her to gain their freedom, Martha Washington freed her husband's slaves one year after his death.

4. "Boston, December 28, 1799," *Columbian Centinel*, Dec. 28, 1799, p. 2.

5. Henry Lee, *A Funeral Oration in Honor of the Memory of George Washington* (New Haven, CT: Read & Morse, 1800), 19.

Illustration Credits

Chapter-Opening Illustrations

His Excell: George Washington, Esqr. General and Commander in Chief of the Allied Armies, engraved by John Norman after Benjamin Blythe, 1782. Courtesy of Mount Vernon Ladies' Association.

Detail from "Carte De La Partie Nord Des Etats Unis," in G. T. Raynal, *Atlas de Toutes les Parties Connues du Globe Terrestre* (Geneva: Jean-Leonard Pellet, 1780). Provided to Wikimedia Commons by Geographicus Rare Antique Maps.

Presentation Drawing of Mount Vernon, by Samuel Vaughan, 1787. Courtesy of Mount Vernon Ladies' Association.

Detail from *The State-House in Philadelphia 1776*, by John Serz, 1873. Courtesy of Library of Congress.

His Excel: G: Washington Esq.: L.L.D. Late, by Charles Willson Peale, 1787. Courtesy of Mount Vernon Ladies' Association.

Detail from *Scene at the Signing of the Constitution of the United States*, by Howard Chandler Christy, 1940. Courtesy of Architect of the Capitol.

"Eighth Pillar," *Massachusetts Centinel*, June 11, 1788. Courtesy of Ashbrook Center at Ashland University.

"A Map of General Washington's Farm of Mount Vernon from a Drawing transmitted by the General," in *Letters from His Excellency General Washington to Arthur Young* (London: B. McMillan, 1801). Courtesy of Mount Vernon Ladies' Association.

Detail from *George Washington Entering Trenton 1789*, by Kurz & Allison, 1907. Courtesy of Library of Congress.

Profile Portrait of George Washington, by Joseph Wright, 1783–1785, Courtesy of Mount Vernon Ladies' Association.

Insert Illustrations

Washington Taking Leave of the Officers of His Army, at Fraunces Tavern, Broad Street, New York, Dec 4th 1783, by Nathaniel Currier, 1848. Courtesy of Mount Vernon Ladies' Association.

General George Washington Resigning His Commission, by John Trumbull, 1824. Courtesy of Architect of the Capitol.

Martha Washington, by Charles Willson Peale, 1772. Courtesy of Mount Vernon Ladies' Association.

George Washington, by Robert Edge Pine, 1785. Courtesy of National Portrait Gallery, Smithsonian Institution.

West Front of Mount Vernon, attributed to Edward Savage, c. 1787–1791. Courtesy of Mount Vernon Ladies' Association.

The Washington Family, by Edward Savage, 1798. Courtesy of Mount Vernon Ladies' Association.

Robert Morris, by Robert Edge Pine, c. 1785. Courtesy of National Portrait Gallery, Smithsonian Institution.

Mrs. Samuel Powel, by Matthew Pratt, c. 1793. Courtesy of the Pennsylvania Academy of the Fine Arts, Philadelphia, Henry D. Gilpin Fund.

His Excellency B. Franklin L.L.D. F.R.S. President of Pennsylvania & Late Minister of the United States of America at the Court of France, by Charles Willson Peale, 1787. Courtesy of Mount Vernon Ladies' Association.

Gouverneur Morris Esq'r., published by R. Wilkinson after a drawing by Pierre Eugène Du Simitière, 1783. Courtesy of Library of Congress.

Major-General Henry Knox, published by Detroit Publishing Co. after a portrait by Gilbert Stuart, between 1900 and 1912. Courtesy of Library of Congress.

George Clinton, engraved by John Jester Buttre from portrait by Ezra Ames, between 1845 and 1890. Courtesy of Library of Congress.

James Wilson, by James Barton Longacre, copy after Jean Pierre Henri Elouis, c. 1825. Courtesy of National Portrait Gallery, Smithsonian Institution.

Alexander Hamilton, Detroit Publishing Co. after portrait by John Trumbull, between 1900 and 1912. Courtesy of Library of Congress.

Scene at the Signing of the Constitution of the United States, by Howard Chandler Christy, 1940. Courtesy of Architect of the Capitol.

[United States Constitution], *Pennsylvania Packet*, September 19, 1787. Courtesy of Library of Congress.

John Jay, 1745–1829, photographic print of painting by Gilbert Stuart, c. 1905. Courtesy of Library of Congress.

James Madison, Pendleton's Lithography after portrait by Gilbert Stuart, c. 1828. Courtesy of Library of Congress.

The looking glass for 1787, by Amos Doolittle, 1787. Courtesy of Library of Congress.

Richard Henry Lee, engraved from a drawing by James Barton Longacre from an original miniature, c. 1820. Courtesy of Library of Congress.

Patrick Henry, by George Bagby Matthews after Thomas Sully, c. 1891. Courtesy of United States Senate.

An East View of Gray's Ferry, Near Philadelphia, engraved by James Trechard from drawing by Charles Willson Peale, 1789. Courtesy of Library of Congress.

First in Peace. "*Representing the Arrival of General George Washington at the Battery, New York, April 23, 1789*," engraved by John C. McRae, 1867. Courtesy of Mount Vernon Ladies' Association.

Federal Hall, reengraved by Sidney L. Smith after print by Amos Doolittle of drawing by Peter Lecour, 1789. Courtesy of Library of Congress.

George Washington, Jean-Antoine Houdon, bust made from clay in Mount Vernon, Virginia, 1785. Courtesy of Mount Vernon Ladies' Association.

Index

abolitionism, 103
Achenbach, Joel, 62
Adams, John, 109, 126, 148; ambitions of, 35, 255; on constitutional government, 80, 114; as President, 301–3; in Revolutionary War, 4, 12, 68, 123, 298; vice presidency of, 253–56, 275–77, 287–93, 298, 300; and Washington's death, 303
Adams, Samuel, 11, 34–35, 253–54
advice and consent, 164
Aesop's fables, 244
Albany Journal, 231
Alexandria (Virginia), 40, 57, 62, 208, 224–25, 262, 283
Allegheny Mountains, 40–41, 45
American Museum, 106
American Philosophical Society, 29
Annapolis (Maryland), 3–7, 28–30
Annapolis Convention, 63–65, 69, 84, 87–88
antifederalists, 171; arguments of, 191–94, 202–3, 208, 213, 216, 221–23, 228; in first federal election, 237–41, 244, 247, 250–65, 272–75, 340*n16*; call for second constitutional convention, 238–39; during Washington administration, 298–301. *See also* Republican Party
Appalachian Mountains, xiii, 40–56
Army, American, 23–25, 137, 303; payment of, 10, 13–17, 22–27; structure of, 8–9, 20–22; unrest in, 9, 12–18, 23
Articles of Confederation, 9, 61–62, 160–70;

need for reform of, 19, 64–65, 70, 76–77, 114–15, 131, 195, 270; revision of, 88–89, 93, 127–29, 182–83, 248. *See also* Constitutional Convention
Assunpick Creek, 285
Atlantic Ocean, 51–52

balanced government, 69, 77–78, 80, 89–96, 271
Baldwin, Abraham, 176, 272
Baltimore (Maryland), 58, 217, 264; Washington in, 28, 101, 105, 283–84
Bank of the United States, 139, 172, 199
Baptists, 164
Bartram, John, 147–48
Bartram, John, Jr., 147–48
Bartram, William, 147–48
Bartram's Garden, 147–48
Bath (Virginia), 41
Battery, 26, 278
Bedford, Gunning, Jr., 151–52, 167
Beeman, Richard, 109, 112
Biddle, Charles, 172
Biddle, Nicholas, 172
Bill of Rights, 171–72, 183–88, 202–5, 213, 222, 228, 238–39, 262–64, 271, 294, 299, 346*nn119–20*
Bingham, Anne and William, 138–39
Birmingham (England), 50
Blair, John, 85, 177–78, 298
Blue Ridge, 54

Boston (Massachusetts), 79, 211, 235, 242, 245, 277; during Revolutionary War, 11
Bowdoin, James, 81–83
Braddock, Edward, 41–42, 51
Braddock's Road, 40–41, 53
Brandywine, Battle of, 12, 28, 107
Bréhan, Madame de, 261
Briery Mountains, 53
Britain, 50, 102, 131, 246, 277; American relations with, 83, 297, 300; in Ohio country, 48, 68–69; peace treaty with, 9, 14, 17, 20, 22–28, 47, 108; in Revolutionary War, 8–12, 20, 68, 139, 285
Burr, Aaron, 253
Butler, Pierce, 122, 141, 144–45, 158–59, 182

cabinet, Washington's, 297–300
Caesar, Julius, 6, 15, 18, 149, 194
Calvinism, 43, 67, 69, 102
Camden, Battle of, 12
Canada, 12, 21, 83
canals, 50, 56, 59–61
Capitol, U.S., 5, 30, 173
Caribbean, 68, 102
Carlisle (Pennsylvania), 209
Carolinas, 102, 130. See also North Carolina; South Carolina
Carrington, Edward, 183
Carroll, Daniel, 117, 161
Carter, Charles, 210–11
Catholic, Roman, 116–18, 120. 137
Charlestown (South Carolina), 12, 102, 217
Chastellux, François-Jean de, 35, 38, 138–39
Cheat River, 55
Chernow, Ron, xii, 28
Chesapeake Bay, 102
Chester (Pennsylania), 107, 284
Chew, Benjamin and Elizabeth, 138
Christ Church, 107, 118
Christmas, 6, 11, 29, 263, 267–69, 285
Christy, Howard Chandler, 173–76
church and state, separation of, 166–67, 171
Cincinnati: Society of, 25, 85–88, 96, 107, 110, 153, 183, 196; Washington as, 7, 18, 149, 178, 208, 244, 275
circular letter to the states, 21, 123, 293, 301
City Tavern, 126, 144–45, 172, 177, 285
Civil War, 159
Cleopatra, 286
Clinton, George: and first federal election, 239, 249–53, 260, 265; as governor, 68–69, 245, 281, 286; on ratification, 202–3, 226–31, 338n107; vice presidential candidacy of, 251–53, 255–56, 273, 276, 300, 343nn68–70; and Washington, 23, 26–28, 226–27, 249, 338n98
Clymer, Daniel, 189
Clymer, George, 87, 172, 188–90, 194
Columbian Centinel, 180, 218

Committee of Detail, 132, 161 63, 167, 109
Committee on Postponed Parts, 164–65, 248
Committee of Style and Arrangement, 168–172
Concord (Massachusetts), 79
Concord, Battle of, 11, 71
Confederation Congress: actions by, 49, 81, 183, 232–38; factions in, 13, 18, 139; funding for, 10, 13–15; and Newburgh Conspiracy, 13–16; receipt of Constitution by, 170–71, 181–84, 187; receives Washington, 3–6, 23; seat of, 3, 23, 25, 29; weaknesses of, 8–10, 15–16, 19, 31, 35, 46–48, 63, 68–78, 87–92, 164, 278
Congress, U.S.: first, 213, 222, 238, 256–65, 278–82, 287–95; structure of, 90–94, 140–41, 149–52, 155–65, 249. See also House of Representatives, U.S.; Senate, U.S.
Connecticut, 6, 36, 63, 102, 267, 275; delegates to Constitutional Convention from, 90, 121, 132, 169; elections in, 245, 250, 257, 273–74, 277; ratification of Constitution by, 205–6; votes at Constitutional Convention by, 129, 150–52
Connecticut Compromise, 150–52
Connecticut Journal, 104
Constitution, U.S., 24, 271, 278, 303; amendments to, 183, 186, 209, 217, 222, 229, 238–39, 247, 250, 254, 256, 262–64, 271, 294; interpretation of, 270, 299–300; preamble of, 167–70, 221–22, 324n3; recommendatory amendments to, 213–14, 222–24, 229–31; signing of, 166, 173–77; structure of, 168–70; transmittal to Congress of, 170–71, 181–84, 236; Twelfth Amendment to, 247. See also Constitutional Convention; ratification
Constitutional Convention: call for, 24, 65–66, 84–88; delegates to, 85–88, 121, 298; meeting of, 119–77; proposed second, 230, 238–39, 245, 263; rules for, 122–23; secrecy at, 122–23, 135–37, 174, 263, 297; Washington's role at, xii–xiii, 84, 119–77
Continental Congress, 10–12, 68, 123, 182, 253
Corbin, Francis, 107
corporations, 56
Cornwallis, Lord, 12
Coxe, Tench, 193
Craik, James, 39, 53
Crawford, William, 46–47
Cromwell, Oliver, 6
Cumberland (Maryland), 40, 51–53
Cushing, William, 298

Dailey, Mary, 144
Dayton, Jonathan, 150
debts, 56, 280; of Congress, 10, 22, 35, 71–78, 299; of states, 8, 72–78, 81, 299
Declaration of Independence, 5, 29, 35, 74, 108,

113, 133, 143; signers of, 46, 58, 103, 153, 194, 242, 274
Defense of the Constitutions (Adams), 254
deflation, 75
deism, 44
DeLancey family, 27
Delaware, 284; and Annapolis Convention, 63; delegates to Constitutional Convention of, 88, 110, 128–29; first federal election in, 250, 258, 272–73; ratification of Constitution by, 191, 195–97, 201; as small state, 112, 119, 121; vote at Constitutional Convention of, 129, 149–52
Delaware River, 11, 63, 102, 162, 285
democracy, perceived excesses of, 70–72, 74, 77–80, 88, 114
Dickinson, John, 63, 68, 162, 254; as delegate to Constitutional Convention, 88, 119, 142; positions at Constitutional Convention of, 123–34, 128–31, 145, 165
Dutch, 67

East River, 286
economic development, limits to, 61, 74–76
electors, presidential, 164–65, 170, 236, 247–48; choice of, 247–53, 271–75; counting votes of, 265, 282; voting by, 265, 276–78
Elizabethtown (New Jersey), 286
Elk River, 178
Ellis, Joseph, 293
Ellsworth, Oliver, 132, 150, 158
enumerated powers, 131–32
Episcopal Church, 44, 69, 107, 117, 264, 268, 288, 295
Epple's Tavern, 153
Erie Canal, 52, 61
Europe, xiv, 6–7, 50
Evening Herald, 136
executive power, 81, 142–47, 178, 202; proposals for stronger, 65, 91–94, 106, 115, 247–48; unitary, 143–45, 175, 202, 318n26. *See also* presidency, U.S.

Fabius Maximus, Washington as, 104, 274–75
faction, 114; perceived danger from, 69, 87, 94–95, 301; rise of, 171, 298–302
Federal Gazette, 272, 276
Federal Hall, 281, 288, 291–94
federalists, 94, 171; and first federal election, 224–47, 250–65, 272–75; as formal political party, 300–2; and ratification, 191–94, 210–11, 221–23, 226, 228. *See also* nationalism
Federalist (ship), 218
Federalist, The (essays), 207, 219, 227–28, 263
Ferling, John, 37
Finkelman, Paul, 159
fireworks, 26, 153, 284, 295
Fisher, David Hackett, xiii
Fitzsimons, Thomas, 117–18, 187, 190, 194

Fleming, Thomas, 6
Flexner, James Thomas, xii, xiii, 79, 224
Fort Necessity, 41
Fort Pitt, 24, 46
France, 27, 41, 51, 67, 69, 92, 117–18, 140, 204–5; relations with America, 297, 300–2; during Revolutionary War, 8, 12, 108, 118, 153, 281
Franklin, Benjamin: on constitutional reform, 108–9, 188; as delegate to Constitutional Convention, 87, 121; influence of, 105–6, 180, 218, 330n89; observations of, 75, 122, 126, 140, 142–45, 174; as president of Pennsylvania, 34, 70, 107, 119, 187; during Revolutionary War, 12, 153–54; and slavery, 103; and Washington, 60, 70, 95, 108–9, 172, 195
Fraunces, Samuel, 27, 290, 353n95
Fraunces Tavern, 27–28, 290
Freeman, Douglas Southall, xii
French and Indian War, 11, 39–42, 44, 46, 51
frontier, western: settlers of, 40–45, 48, 52–55; Washington's view of, 39–55, 298–99
Fugitive Slave Clause, 159–60

Gates, Horatio, 6, 12, 14, 30
Gazette of the United States, 281, 291
George III, King of England, 6, 136, 143, 246, 278
Georgetown (Maryland), 40, 283
Georgia, 12, 102; at Constitutional Convention, 121, 123, 130, 159–60, 176; first federal election in, 250, 256, 260–61, 273–74, 277; ratification of Constitution by, 195–97, 201
Germantown, Battle of, 12, 28
Gerry, Elbridge, 171, 212, 245; at Constitutional Convention, 123–24, 127–29, 142–44, 152–58, 238; opposes Constitution, 175–76, 202–3, 227
Giles (slave), 101, 269
Gorham, Nathaniel, 125, 132, 182–83, 212–13
Grand Committee, 152, 155–57
Grayson, William, 220–24, 258
Gray's Ferry, 107, 177
Great Barrington (Massachusetts), 79
Great Falls of the Potomac, 40, 57
Great Kanawha River, 46–47, 53, 55
Great Lakes, 21, 47–48
Great Meadows, 41
Greene, Nathanael, 12, 24
Gulf of Mexico, 52

Hamilton, Alexander, 18–19, 161, 230, 309n33; in Congress, 13–18, 23; correspondence with Washington of, 17–20, 185, 243–45, 275; as delegate to Constitutional Convention, 88, 90, 121, 151; and first federal election, 251–56, 260; as nationalist,

Hamilton, Alexander (*continued*): 63–65, 109, 131–32, 297–301; policies at Constitutional Convention of, 151, 161, 169, 175–76; on ratification, 180, 191, 207, 226–30; as Treasury Secretary, 297–300; as Washington's aide, 19, 28, 31, 252–54, 293

Hamlet, 84

Hancock, John: as governor, 35, 81–83, 245; and ratification, 180, 202, 212–14; and vice presidency, 253, 255

Harrison, Benjamin, V, 36, 55, 57, 219, 243–45

Hartford Wits, 269

Harvard College, 151, 253

Harve de Grace (Maryland), 101

Hazard, Ebenezer, 229

Henry, Patrick: and Constitutional Convention, 85, 106, 135; and first federal election, 238–39, 247, 250–53, 258–64, 272–75, 345n100, 348n14; on ratification, 185–87, 197, 202–4, 219–24, 227, 336n75, 337n81

Hessian soldiers, 20, 285

Heyward, Thomas, 274

Hirschfeld, Fritz, 160

Holton, Woody, 80

House, Mary, 108, 144

House of Burgesses, 182, 208

House of Lords, 131, 140, 161

House of Representatives, U.S., 140, 155–59, 176, 300; first federal, 247, 257–65, 278, 280, 282–88, 291–92

Hudson River, 28, 286–87

Hudson valley, 9, 12, 19, 26, 67, 102

Humphreys, David, 3, 30, 107, 267–71, 282–83, 290–91, 295; correspondence with Washington of, 80, 83, 88–92, 181, 184, 191, 205

imposts, 13, 16, 19, 72, 202–3

Independence Day, 152–55, 230

Independent Gazetteer, 154, 191–92

Indian Queen, 144

inflation, 74–78

interstate commerce, 62–65, 106, 132, 137, 300

Irish, 102, 106, 117

Irving, Washington, 292

Izard, Ralph, 292

Jackson, William, 120, 181

James River, 54–55, 58

Jay, John, 67–68, 117, 161, 253, 301; correspondence with Washington of, 69–72, 76, 78, 87–94, 112, 127, 215, 229–30, 235, 243; as Foreign Secretary, 64, 68–69, 206; as nationalist, 69, 90, 226; on ratification, 207, 227–29

Jefferson, Thomas, 4–7, 26, 30, 198, 224, 261; correspondence with Washington of, 33, 37–38, 51–52, 56, 197, 204, 291, 231; on

government, 68, 114, 137, 780; as Secretary of State, 297–300; as vice presidency, 302

Johnson, Thomas, 51, 217

Johnson, William Samuel, 169, 182, 186

judiciary, national, 94, 106, 130, 202, 291, 298–99, 322n90

Kentucky, 223–24, 300

King, Rufus, 112, 126, 129, 160, 164, 169, 174, 182–83, 186, 212–14

King's College, 18, 67

Knox, Henry, 107, 254; correspondence with Washington of, 34, 47, 82, 88–96, 112, 159, 184–85, 231, 243, 255, 259–60, 275–76, 280; as Secretary of War, 81, 253, 286, 298

Lacour, Peter, 292

Lafayette, Marquis de, 106–7, 118; letters from Washington to, 8, 24, 35, 38, 84, 133, 177–79, 197–98, 232–33, 245–46, 265, 271, 276; letters to Washington from, 205, 240

Langdon, John, 176, 215–16

Lansing, John, Jr., 90, 129, 135–36, 173, 186

Laurens, Henry, 274

Lear, Tobias, 269, 281, 290–91, 295, 302

Lee, Arthur, 115–16, 253

Lee, Charles, 203–4

Lee, Henry, III, 81, 83, 203–4, 220–23, 303

Lee, Richard Henry, 113, 220, 253–54; correspondence with Washington of, 49, 51; on ratification, 182–87, 196–97, 202–6, 227; as senator, 258, 281–82, 292

Lee, William, 101, 351n58

Le Moyer, Jean Pierre, 92

L'Enfant, Peter Charles, 281, 350n52

Lexington, Battle of, 11, 71

Lincoln, Benjamin, 82–83, 209–13, 238–45, 255–57, 274, 277

Little Falls of the Potomac, 40, 51

Livingston, Robert R., 231, 240, 288, 291–95

London (England), 8, 108, 110

Long Island, Battle of, 11

Loyalists, 18, 26, 27, 68, 80, 96, 139

Lutheran, 264

Lynchburg (Virginia), 54

Maclay, William, 257, 287–88

Madison, James, 26, 51, 81, 137, 102; on amendments to Constitution, 186, 263, 294, 299; at Annapolis Convention, 62–65; in Congress, 5, 23, 30, 182–83, 259, 263; Constitutional Convention notes of, 123–24, 137, 142, 177, 299; as delegate to Constitutional Convention, 85, 108–12, 121, 178; in first federal election, 251, 256–59, 262–65; in House of Representatives, 288, 299; letters from Washington to, xii, 58, 86, 93, 172, 184–85, 196, 107–9, 236–39; letters to Washington from,

83–86, 93–95, 184–85, 197, 206–8, 212–14, 223–24, 236–37, 240, 243, 245, 255, 262, 277, 281–82; on paper money, 76–78; political theories of, 93–95, 114–15, 247; positions at Constitutional Convention of, 103–33, 146–47, 152, 156–60, 165, 247–48; role in Washington administration of, 267–71, 289–90, 297–98, 353*n95*

Maine, 212, 334*n31*

Maier, Pauline, vi, 184, 227

Manchester (England), 50

Martin, Luther, 129–30, 161, 186, 202, 260

Marshall, John, 220

Maryland, 3, 7, 51–65, 75–77, 116–17; delegates to Constitutional Convention from, 101, 110, 119, 129; first federal election in, 250–52, 260, 272–73; positions at Constitutional Convention of, 147, 150, 161; ratification of Constitution by, 186, 215–17; Washington in, 28, 40, 101, 283–84

Maryland Chronicle, 105

Maryland Journal, 264

Maryland Gazette, 272

Mason, George: on Bill of Rights, 171, 186, 222, 259; as delegate to Constitutional Convention, 85, 112–22, 156, 160, 165, 238; on Constitution, 172–76, 179, 182, 185–91, 197, 202–6, 220–24, 227; on presidency, 144, 175

Mason, George, Jr., 113–17

Massachusetts, 116–17, 245; debtor insurrection in, 78–84, 124; delegates to Constitutional Convention from, 90, 121, 125; first federal election in, 250, 259–60, 274, 342*n65*; state constitution of, 143, 164, 257; ratification of Constitution by, 180, 187, 205–15, 222, 235, 298

Massachusetts Centinel, 180, 210, 275–76

Massachusetts Gazette, 212

McClurg, James, 178

McHenry, James, 7, 30, 101, 208, 217, 243

McKean, Thomas, 46

Meredith, Samuel, 172

Mifflin, Thomas, 4–6, 30, 87, 107, 187, 284

Miles, Samuel, 107

militias, state, 9, 20–21, 79–81, 94

Miller's Run (Pennsylvania), 43–47

Mississippi River, 21, 47–49, 51, 63–64, 68, 223, 301

monarchism, 68–69, 76, 114–15, 131, 136, 143–46, 163, 174, 193–94

Monmouth, Battle of, 12, 28

Monroe, James, 5, 30, 78, 220–25, 262–64

Morris, Gouverneur: as Assistant Superintendent of Finance, 13–14, 17, 115; as delegate to Constitutional Convention, 87, 121; positions at Constitutional Convention of, 127–28, 146, 151–52, 156–60, 164–70, 175–76; on ratification,

180–81, 190–91; and Washington, 109–11, 161–62, 177, 180–81, 195, 240, 244–47

Morris, Mary, 126, 138–39

Morris, Robert, 56, 254; as delegate to Constitutional Convention, 87, 119–21, 151; and Pennsylvania politics, 114–15, 194, 257; as Superintendent of Finance, 13–14, 17, 287–88; and Washington, 29, 102, 108, 125, 162, 173, 177, 196, 285

Morton, Eliza, 292–93

Mount Vernon, 50, 102–4, 160, 148–49, 237, 273, 299; images of, 65, 234; meetings at, 62, 93; Washington at, 30–38, 55, 92, 96–97, 177–79, 184–85, 190–91, 203–25, 235–36, 240–41, 248–49, 261–62, 266–69, 274–83, 301–3; Washington's view of, xi–xv, 6–8, 35, 116

Mount Vernon Compact, 62–65

Moustier, Comte de, 261

nationalism: at Annapolis Convention, 64–65; in Confederation Congress, 13–15, 17–19, 72; and Constitutional Convention, 69, 78, 88–92, 105–6, 226, 124–33, 149–52, 167–70, 325*n14*; and Washington, 62, 124–28, 270–71, 283–95. *See also* Washington, George, as nationalist

"necessary and proper" clause, 132, 169, 175, 202, 300

New Brunswick (New Jersey), 29, 286

Newburgh (New York), 9, 23–24, 92

Newburgh conspiracy, 9, 12–20, 28, 122

New England, 11, 22, 83, 88, 102–3, 113, 126, 197, 239, 254, 289, 298. *See also specific states*

New Hampshire, 75, 106; delegates to Constitutional Convention from, 129, 176; first federal election in, 250, 259, 274, 342*n65*; ratification of Constitution by, 215–17, 224–25, 229, 236, 257

New Hampshire Gazette, 105

New Jersey, 11, 153–54; at Constitutional Convention, of, 147, 150, 161; first federal election in, 250, 273–74; politics in, 68, 75, 78, 80, 103; ratification of Constitution by, 185, 191, 195–97; as small state, 124; Washington in, 28–29, 162, 285–86

New Jersey Journal, 196

New Jersey Plan, 131–32

newspapers: partisan, 191–92, 205, 300–1; predictions of electoral vote count in, 275–77; ratification discussed in, 179–81, 184, 187, 190–94, 205–6, 210; reports in, 15–16, 22, 136, 276–77, 283–88, 293; Washington hailed in, 86, 104–8, 154, 178, 193, 217–18, 272, 291, 302–3. *See also specific newspapers*

New York, 7, 52, 63, 71, 80, 83, 275; delegates to Constitutional Convention from, 88, 90, 112, 135, 173; first federal election in, 239, 249–53, 260–61, 265; politics in, 18–19,

New York (continued): 67–69, 75, 103, 117,
143, 226 28, 215–53, ratification of
Constitution by, 184–85, 187, 197–98,
201–3, 206, 209, 215–17, 225–32, 235, 238;
during Revolutionary War, 11–17, 22–28;
state legislative election in, 90, 94–109,
116, 124–25, 132, 164, 185, 201; votes at
Constitutional Convention of, 129, 147,
149–51, 161; Washington in, 11–28, 286–95
New York City, 67, 103, 117, 161; British
evacuation of, 9, 20, 22–27; and
Constitution, 185, 230; occupation of, 8–9,
11, 25–27, 226, 294; as seat of government,
181, 236–37, 280–83, 291–95
New-York Daily Gazette, 288
Nichols, George, 220
Norfolk (Virginia), 242
North Carolina, 77: and Constitutional
Convention, 110, 119, 159–60; ratification of
Constitution by, 202, 215, 232, 249, 278, 300
Northampton (Massachusetts), 79
Northwest Ordinance of 1785, 49
Northwest Territory, 21, 46–51
Notes of the Federal Convention, 177

officers, American army, 10–17, 21, 27, 153,
162, 277; pensions for, 10, 16, 25, 81. See also
Cincinnatus, Society of
O'Flynn, Patrick, 107
Ohio country, 46–51, 299, 301
Ohio River, 21, 46–57, 197, 279

paper money: congressional issuance of, 74,
95, 114; state issuance of, 72–82, 95, 113,
124, 171
Paris (France), 8, 12, 77–78, 137–40, 204–5,
278, 297
Paris (slave), 101
Parliament, British, 8, 114–15, 131, 292
Patterson, William, 124, 129, 149–52, 158, 167
Peale, Angelica, 284
Peale, Charles Willson, 134, 154–55, 284
Pendleton, Edmund, 220
Pennsylvania, 11–12, 63; delegates to
Constitutional Convention from, 87, 109–
12; first federal election in, 239, 250, 257–58,
272–73; politics in, 70, 74–77, 108, 114–17,
143, 174, 185–95, 329n80, 330n83; positions
at Constitutional Convention of, 112–13,
130, 247; ratification of Constitution by,
179, 187–95, 201, 209–10; State House,
100, 108–10, 116, 155, 187; Washington in,
28–29, 36–46, 161–62, 284–85
Pennsylvania Gazette, 179, 190
Pennsylvania Herald, 86–87, 107
Pennsylvania Packet, 79, 190
Peter (slave), 269
Petersham (Massachusetts), 82
Philadelphia, 11–13, 16, 56, 103, 273, 277; as

seat of government, 3, 23, 237, 203, as site
for Constitutional Convention, 65, 84–85,
90, 96–97, 101, 119, 121, 151, 161; as site for
ratifying convention, 190–91, 195; social
life in, 115–16, 126, 137–40, 144–45, 152–
55; Washington in, 29, 104–9, 126, 137–40,
147–49, 153–55, 172–77, 235, 284–85
Pierce, William, 121, 123
Pine, Robert Edge, 172
Pinckney, Charles, 217; at Constitutional
Convention, 119, 127, 146; on slavery, 103,
157–59
Pinckney, Charles Cotesworth, 185, 217, 275;
at Constitutional Convention, 122, 127; on
slavery, 103
Pointer, George, 60
political parties, 188, 227–28, 300–1. See
also antifederalists; faction; federalists;
Republican Party
Polish, 118, 141
pope, 137, 141, 248
Potomac Company, 59–61, 279
Potomac River, 40, 54–57, 218, 237, 283;
navigation of, xiii, 50–61, 237, 279;
Washington's view of, xi, 21, 36
Poughkeepsie (New York), 26, 68, 228, 230
Powel, Elizabeth and Samuel, 138–40, 154,
162, 172, 195
Presbyterian, 117
presidency, U.S., 302; conception of,
140–47, 162–65, 170, 193–94, 245, 319n36;
impeachment process for, 146; regal title
for, 287–88, 352n89; selection process for,
142, 146–47, 161, 163–65, 247–50, 323n99;
as unifying institution, 283–95, 302; veto
power for, 146
Preston's Tavern, 154
Princeton (New Jersey), 23, 285
Princeton, Battle of, 11
Proclamation of 1763, 47
Progressive Seating, 48
property rights, 44, 69, 76–78, 81–84, 95,
171, 201
proportional representation, 112, 149–52
Provoost, Samuel, 295
Publius, 207
Pulaski, Casimir, 118

quasi-war, 302

Rakove, Jack, 140–41
Randolph, Edmund: as Constitutional
Convention delegate, 85–86, 108–11, 238;
correspondence with Washington of, 85–86,
95; opposes Constitution, 173–76, 179, 197,
202; positions at Constitutional Convention
of, 93, 124–27, 132–33, 144, 158–60, 163;
supports Constitution, 185, 219–22, 298; as
Virginia governor, 63, 93, 258

Ratification, of Constitution, 170–71, 177, 179–232, 297. See also individual states
Read, George, 119, 121, 129
Reformed Calvinist Church, 153
religion, 95, 116–18, 263–64
Republican Party, 300–2
requisitions, 72–73, 81
Revolutionary War, 10–12, 35, 68–72, 80, 298; Washington's role in, xii, 3, 7, 9–17, 285, 294
Rhode Island, 112, 136; and Constitutional Convention, 95, 168, 173, 225; paper money in, 77–79; ratification by, 197, 202–3, 215, 232, 249, 278, 300
Richmond (Virginia), 54–55, 219–20, 228
Rochambeau, Comte de, 246, 264
Rome, 20, 104, 141, 144
Royal Navy, 25, 279, 301
Rumsey, James, 41
Rush, Benjamin, 195
Rutledge, John, 119–20, 132, 217, 289, 298

St. Lawrence River, 48
St. Mary's Chapel, 118
St. Paul's Chapel, 288, 294
Saratoga, Battle of, 12
Savannah (Georgia), 12, 102
School for Scandal, 162
Schuylkill River, 56, 107, 147, 177, 284
Scotch-Irish, 43
Scottish, 111
seceders: in Pennsylvania politics, 189–90; religious sect of, 43–46
Sedgwick, Theodore, 254
Senate, U.S., 140–41, 155–56, 160–65, 170, 322n83; first federal, 247, 257–61, 278–82, 287–88, 291–93
"Sentiments on a Peace Establishment," 20–21
separation of powers, 89–91, 93–95, 115, 127–28, 140–41, 162–65, 222, 247. See also balanced government
Shays, Daniel, 81, 83
Shays's Rebellion, 78–84, 88, 124, 206, 212–13, 238, 298
Shenandoah Valley, 54
Sherman, Roger, 35, 126–31, 142, 167, 171
Simpson, George, 42–44
slavery: as issue at Constitutional Convention, 103, 156–60, 203, 248, 321n76; Washington's view of, 37, 103, 160, 294, 321n79
slaves, 67, 103; at Mount Vernon, 33–34, 36–37, 39, 103, 160, 269, 302, 309n13, 354n3; use of, 60, 97, 101, 211, 281–82; Washington's treatment of, 60, 92, 269
Smilie, John, 194
South, American, 22, 48, 103, 197, 289. See also specific states
South Carolina, 103, 292; delegates to

Constitutional Convention from, 112, 158; first federal election in, 250, 260–61, 273–74; positions at Constitutional Convention of, 159–60; ratification of Constitution by, 180, 185, 215–17
sovereignty: national, 89–90, 94, 105, 112, 125–28; state, 89–90, 222
Spaight, Richard Dobbs, 122
Spain, 48, 68, 73, 293; treaty with, 49, 63–64, 68–69, 189, 223, 301
Sparks, Jared, 151
specie, 73
speculation, in land, 45, 48
Springfield (Massachusetts), 82
Springsbury Manor, 144, 151
Spurrier's Tavern, 283
states, 49, 243–50; under Articles of Confederation, 8–11, 61, 127; large versus small, 112–13, 119, 121, 149–52, 155–56, 171, 245; north versus south, 156–60, 248
States' rights, 26, 90, 128, 238–39; limiting, 89–94, 105–6, 112–15, 127–28
State Gazette of South Carolina, 217
Strong, Caleb, 212
Stuart, David, 191, 219, 273
Sullivan, John, 215–16
supremacy clause, 130, 202–3
Susquehanna River, 56, 58, 101
Swiss cantons, 20–21, 114

Taunton (Massachusetts), 79
tax power, 19, 73–78, 137, 165, 169, 202–3, 213, 222, 231, 299, 300, 317n8, 323n98
Thomson, Charles, 282–83
Tilghman, Tench, 3
Travels (Bartram), 148
Trenton (New Jersey), 162, 266
Trenton, Battle of, 11, 28, 285
Trumbull, John, 6–7, 30
Trumbull, Jonathan, 36, 38
Trumbull, Jonathan, Jr., 206, 245, 257
Twelfth Amendment, 247

unicameral legislature, 74
union: of states, 21–22, 55, 58, 303; threats to, 64, 83–84, 174, 221–23, 228, 301
United States, 47–50, 64; as nation, 149, 167, 283–96, 300–1. See also states; Confederation Congress, Congress, U.S.

Valley Forge, 12, 153, 162
Vaughan, Samuel, 240
Venice, Doge of, 141
Vermont, 80, 82–83, 168, 300, 324n6
veto: executive, 146, 163, 319n32; of state laws, 94, 113, 124, 130
vice presidency, 249–56, 272–77, 287–88, 292, 298, 302, 326n26, 352n78

Virginia, 12, 47, 62–63, 112; delegates to Constitutional Convention from, 85–86, 110–16; first federal election in, 239, 249–51, 256–59, 262–65, 272–73; politics in, 30, 71, 80, 203–4, 208, 220, 245; and Potomac River navigation, 51–65; ratification of Constitution by, 187, 197–98, 202–4, 209, 215–25, 228–29, 236; slavery in, 103, 203; votes at Constitutional Convention by, 130–33, 137, 145, 147, 152, 159–60, 173–75, 247–48; western regions of, 21, 36–55. *See also* Kentucky

Virginia Plan, 111–16, 119, 124–35, 141–42, 146, 149, 169, 247, 264

Virginians, 45, 51, 102, 109, 273, 283, 298–99, 336n66

voting, property qualification for, 74, 81

war powers, 142–43, 146, 163, 193, 319n33, 322n89

Washington, Bushrod, 39, 53, 55, 111, 191

Washington, D.C., 237, 281, 299, 303, 339n6

Washington, George: as actor, 15, 120, 148, 247, 290; administration of, 297–301; on antifederalists, 203–4, 243–44, 262–64, 270, 330n86; on Articles of Confederation, 35, 70–71, 91–95, 181, 271; as consensus builder, 151–52, 156–59, 210, 321n72, 326n30; on attending Constitutional Convention, 84–97, 172; at Constitutional Convention, 109–77, 248; as Constitutional Convention president, 119–22, 133–34, 136–37, 151, 158, 170–77, 241; and constitutional amendments, 238–39, 256, 263, 271, 294, 299; death of, 302–3; diary of, 39, 43, 60, 109, 177; election as president of, 243, 249, 271–80; Farewell Address of, 301; as farmer, 33–38, 116, 147–49, 162, 178, 218–19, 235, 241, 261–62, 279–80, 302; finances of, 34, 36, 47, 279–80, 302, 350nn46–47; and first federal election, 135–47, 252–63; fishing by, 28, 161–62; health of, 84–85, 92, 97, 101, 302–3, 313n56; on human nature, 58, 70–71, 83, 91, 114, 232, 289–90, 311n65, 333n2; inaugural address of, 265, 269–71, 289, 291, 293–94, 353n97; inauguration of, 275–76, 283–95, 287–95; as indispensable, xii–xiv, 244, 303; to job seekers, 241–43, 341n31; as model for presidency, 141, 145, 163, 288; and his mother, 96, 279; as nationalist, 16, 19–24, 30, 55, 62, 70–71, 78, 93, 104, 120, 124–33, 152, 210, 233, 270–71, 283–301; and Newburgh Conspiracy, 9, 12–17; and Potomac Company, 50–62; as first president, 181, 184, 192–93, 195, 198, 202, 205, 224, 232, 239–46, 250–51, 265, 288–95, 303; portraits of, 2, 134, 154–55, 172, 261, 264, 295–96; and ratification, 177, 79, 193, 205, 207–9, 215, 217–25, 231–32, 235, 285, 332n109; and religion, 44, 102, 116–18, 120, 198, 232, 246, 268–69, 288, 293–94, 315n36, 342n57, 347n5; resignation as Commander in Chief of, 3–9, 23, 28–31; reputation of, 11, 16, 29, 69, 104–5, 179–81, 192, 230, 244, 283–90, 295, 297, 301–3, 330n89; retirement of, 33–38, 55, 70, 84, 104, 244, 262, 301; in Revolutionary War, 8, 10–12, 22–28, 297, 303; on Rhode Island, 78, 197, 232, 339n121; on Shays's Rebellion, 78–84; as slaveholder, 33–39, 103, 160, 269, 279. *See also* slaves; and Society of Cincinnatus, 25, 85–88, 96, 119, 153, 183, 196; travels by, 28–31, 38–47, 53–55, 101–7, 177–78, 280–89; on vice presidency, 255; vision for America of, 233, 246–47, 270–71, 293–95; western holdings of, 39–47, 189, 279–80

Washington, George Augustine, 116, 165, 279–80

Washington, John, 24

Washington, Martha: grandchildren of, 38, 101–2; and inauguration, 276, 281, 295; at Mount Vernon, 6, 102, 241, 279; slaves of, 37, 103, 309n13; travels by, 5, 22–23

Washington, Mary Ball, 95–97, 279

Washington's Bottom (Pennsylvania), 42–43, 47, 51

weather: at Mount Vernon, 33, 178, 218–19, 261, 267–69, 279, 302; in Philadelphia, 137, 148, 161; during Washington's travels, 53–54, 97, 101–4, 107

Wereat, John, 196

West, Benjamin, 6

West Indies, 18, 102, 301

West Virginia, 46

western frontier, 21, 39–55. *See also* frontier

whiskey, 299, 300, 302

White, William, 268–69, 347n5

Will (slave), 281

Willing, Thomas, 139

Wilmington (Delaware), 29, 107, 196, 284

Wilson, John, 209, 298; as Constitutional Convention delegate, 87, 111–12, 122, 174; positions at Constitutional Convention of, 131–32, 144–47, 150–52, 156–58, 162, 247–48; on ratification, 190–9, 207

Wise's Tavern, 225

Witherspoon, John, 35

Woodbridge (New Jersey), 286

Wythe, George, 35, 85, 120, 122, 178

Yates, Robert, 90, 125, 129, 135, 173, 186

York and Albany, Duke of, 136

Yorktown, Battle of, 8–9, 12, 28, 31, 107

Ron Hall

About the Author

EDWARD J. LARSON is University Professor of history and holds the Hugh & Hazel Darling Chair in Law at Pepperdine University. He received the Pulitzer Prize in History for *Summer for the Gods: The Scopes Trial and America's Continuing Debate over Science and Religion*. His other books include *An Empire of Ice: Scott, Shackleton, and the Heroic Age of Antarctic Science; A Magnificent Catastrophe: The Tumultuous Election of 1800, America's First Presidential Campaign; The Constitutional Convention: A Narrative History from the Notes of James Madison* (with Michael P. Winship); *Evolution: The Remarkable History of a Scientific Theory; Trial and Error: The American Controversy over Creation and Evolution; Evolution's Workshop: God and Science on the Galapagos Islands;* and *Sex, Race, and Science: Eugenics in the Deep South*. From 2013 to 2014, Larson was an inaugural Library Fellow at the Fred W. Smith National Library for the Study of George Washington located on the grounds of Mount Vernon. He lives in Georgia and California.